SOVIET FOREIGN POLICY, 1928-1934

VOLUME II

HOOVER INSTITUTION PUBLICATIONS

a publication of THE HOOVER INSTITUTION
ON WAR, REVOLUTION AND PEACE

SOVIET FOREIGN POLICY, 1928-1934

DOCUMENTS & MATERIALS

VOLUME II

by XENIA JOUKOFF EUDIN
and ROBERT M. SLUSSER

THE PENNSYLVANIA STATE UNIVERSITY PRESS
UNIVERSITY PARK AND LONDON

The Hoover Institution on War, Revolution and Peace, founded at Stanford University in 1919 by the late President Herbert Hoover, is a center for advanced study and research on public and international affairs in the twentieth century. The views expressed in its publications are entirely those of the authors and do not necessarily reflect the views of the Hoover Institution.

CONTENTS

DOCUMENTS

PART ONE

NARRATIVE SUMMARY

5

The Search for Security, 1932–1933

The situation confronting the Soviet Union grew even more serious in 1932 and 1933. Two problems overshadowed all others: the growth of the Nazi movement in Germany, made more ominous by Hitler's statements in *Mein Kampf* on Germany's need to expand eastward at the expense of Russia, and Japan's aggression against China, which might well develop into a full-scale attack on the Soviet Union. Internally the Soviet leaders faced a number of major difficulties: a man-made famine resulting from the forcible collectivization of agriculture, a catastrophe which the Soviet government was nearly successful in concealing from the outside world but which took a terrible toll in human lives and farm animals; unforeseen difficulties and shortcomings in the execution of the Five-Year Plan; and renewed signs of clandestine political opposition.

In this increasingly tense situation it was the task of the Commissariat of Foreign Affairs to attempt by means of diplomacy to improve relations with other countries, and thereby to strengthen the Soviet international position and provide security for the continuation of the economic transformation. Litvinov and other foreign-policy spokesmen intensified their pleas for peace, stressing the growing danger of war and seeking security through nonaggression pacts and other measures of diplomacy.

In this respect, the years 1932 and 1933 were particularly fruitful for Soviet diplomacy. Negotiations were resumed in 1932 with France on a nonaggression pact, leading to its signature by the end of the year. Preliminary contacts were established with the United States, looking toward eventual diplomatic recognition, which followed in late 1933. In addition, nonaggression pacts were concluded with most of the neighboring countries and with Italy; diplomatic relations were resumed with Nationalist China and were established with the Spanish Republic; and the strain on Anglo-Soviet relations was significantly reduced.

Efforts to effect a rapprochement with the capitalist countries meant no reduction in Soviet distrust or criticism of these countries. "Two worlds, two systems face each other," said *Revoliutsionnyi Vostok* (No. 1–2) in an editorial in January 1932, "the world of socialism, which is being successfully established, and the dying world, which continues its fierce resistance and launches attacks." Speaking at the Seventeenth Party Conference on January 30, Molotov expressed serious concern over the world situation. "Provocations designed to disrupt peace," he said, "continue without interruption" (Document 72). Eugene Varga, a leading Soviet economist, maintained that a new era of wars and revolutions was beginning, that a war for the redistribution of the world had already started in Manchuria. "The Versailles system threatens to crash at any moment." (Document 94.)

Relations with Germany

The growth of the Nazi movement in Germany was carefully watched by the Soviet leaders. Nevertheless the totalitarian nature of the Nazi movement, so similar in some respects to Soviet communism, seems to have escaped the notice of the Soviet leaders. In Max Beloff's concise phrase, "Communist theory made no allowance for a movement which was at once revolutionary and non-proletarian."[1] Intent as they were on the struggle against the social-democrats, the Soviet policy makers considered Nazism to be just another manifestation of bourgeois ideology, one primarily concerned with preventing the proletarian revolution. "The bourgeoisie is increasing its efforts to halt the development of the prerequisites for the revolutionary crisis," stated a *Pravda* editorial on March 17, 1932, commenting on the German presidential election:

> The bourgeoisie is intensifying its offensive against the working people and is turning more and more to open fascist dictatorship. . . . In addition to their chief candidate, Hindenburg,

who must be elected, the bourgeoisie found it necessary to advance Adolf Hitler, an openly fascist candidate, as a direct threat to the revolutionary workers, and for the purpose of gaining the support of nationalist elements who are dissatisfied with the existing order.

Hindenburg's victory *Pravda* saw as being due to the support given him by the social-democrats who were opposed to Hitler. Yet, the editorial added, "Hindenburg and Hitler are, in the last analysis, identical." It noted the "great success" of the communist candidate, Ernst Thälmann, who obtained the support of five million voters who were "ready, under any conditions, to oppose categorically the bourgeois front, since they know that unless social-democracy, the main social buttress of the bourgeois order, is shattered, there can be no successful proletarian revolution."

Nevertheless the Soviet leaders were determined to maintain normal diplomatic and economic relations with Germany, continuing the policy established at Rapallo ten years earlier. On the tenth anniversary of the signing of the Treaty of Rapallo, *Izvestiia* hailed it as "an event of outstanding significance, not merely in the foreign policy of the Land of Soviets, not only in the postwar policy of Germany, but in the history of postwar international relations in general" (Document 78).

The communist failure to grasp the dynamic nature of Nazism led V. G. Knorin, head of the Central European Secretariat of the Comintern, to write in *Pravda* on July 22 that "Von Papen effected a fascist *coup* in Prussia with the assistance of the Reichswehr; to all intents and purposes, a fascist dictatorship has already been declared in Germany." The Weimar Republic, said Knorin, was bankrupt, and the next few days would show whether "Germany would take a straight road toward the revolution, or whether the bourgeoisie, by consolidating a fascist dictatorship by means of violence and terror, will succeed in retarding for a time the growth of the prerequisites of the revolutionary crisis." However, Knorin believed that "in a country in which the proletariat constitutes an absolute majority of the population and possesses considerable Marxist traditions and the tradition of the revolutionary struggle, in such a country it would be impossible to have recourse to terror for any length of time."

When Hitler became chancellor on January 30, 1933, there was no immediate reaction in the Soviet press. At first Soviet newspapers simply published short communiqués concerning the changes that were taking place in Germany. Soviet criticism of the Nazi regime became more pronounced, however, after the Reichstag fire on February 28, for which the Nazis blamed German communists. On March 7, 1933, Radek discussed in *Izvestiia* the German press's assumption of a great victory for the Nazis because of the seventeen million votes cast in their favor in the recent elections. Actually, said Radek, this was no victory, since the Nazis had failed to crush the communists. Furthermore, the Nazis were incapable of improving the economic situation: "Events in Germany may move rapidly, or they may be protracted. But there is not the slightest doubt that it will prove impossible to rule a great country against the will of its toiling masses; it will be equally impossible to rule without any program, and in addition, to rule by adventurist methods."[2] On March 23 Hitler made a somewhat conciliatory gesture in a speech to the Reichstag: The Reich government intends to cultivate friendly relations, with the Soviet Union, he declared. "It is precisely the government of the national revolution that finds itself in a position to pursue such a positive policy toward Soviet Russia. The fight against communism in Germany is our internal affair, in which we shall never tolerate interference from the outside. Positive relations with other powers with which we are linked by important interests in common are not affected thereby." The Soviet press responded with caution. An editorial in *Izvestiia* on March 28 stated:

> If German policy actually aims at the establishment and consolidation of neighborly relations with the U.S.S.R., we shall only welcome it, both in the interests of our two powers, and also of the world in general. So far, the Reich Chancellor's declaration did not make clear what he meant by the important mutual interests of the new government or the policy toward the U.S.S.R. In view of the fact that this government's plans are little known, a more concrete statement would have clarified the situation.

In the following days the Soviet press referred more than once to police raids on Soviet premises in Germany and to the difficulties created for DEROP,[3] and gave detailed accounts of the molestation of Soviet citizens in Germany by the police. On April 3, Litvinov presented an official protest to the German ambassador, Dirksen. During the next few months the state of Soviet-German relations fluctuated, both sides aiming, at least officially, at the continuation of the former good relations. On April 28, Hitler gave an audience to the Soviet ambassador, L. M. Khinchuk, and in early May the protocol of June 1931 extending the 1926 treaty was ratified by Germany. On this occasion an *Izvestiia* editorial proclaimed the Soviet people's desire to live in peace with Germany, "in spite of their attitude toward fascism": Public opinion in the Soviet Union, the editorial stated, had never favored any plans against the integrity of German territory, and required no changes or revisions in policy toward Germany (Document 96).

In spite of this attitude, relations between the two countries became markedly cooler, and even the Soviet attitude to the Versailles Treaty, the special target of Soviet spokesmen in the past, underwent a significant modification. On March 16, 1933, a pact of understanding and cooperation was proposed by Mussolini, to include France, Great Britain, Italy, and Germany, allegedly to do away with the "injustices" of the Versailles Treaty. Although the Soviet attitude to the proposed pact was highly critical, Soviet spokesmen were also critical of the new attitude to the Versailles settlement that was taking shape in Germany and Italy. Radek, writing in *Pravda* on May 10, said that the proposed changes in the treaty would mean a gain for fascism. The Versailles peace could only be changed through war. Attempts to represent revision merely as a peaceful resettlement of old treaties could not deceive anyone. *"The word 'revision' is simply another name for a new world war"* (Document 97). A new realism in the Soviet evaluation of Nazism also found expression here and there. For example, Eugene Varga, although he claimed that Nazism was rapidly losing its attractiveness among the broad masses, admitted that Germany had a great war potential and was a "genuinely formidable threat."[4]

But both sides sought to give the appearance of seeking the continuation of the former friendly relations. On May 16, Dirksen, the German ambassador in Moscow, reported to his government a conversation with Litvinov who had protested the treatment of Soviet citizens in Germany and anti-Soviet pronouncements by Alfred Rosenberg:

M. Litvinov closed his remarks with the words that the basic attitude of the Soviet government toward Germany had remained entirely the same: that the Soviet government was convinced that it could have just as friendly relations with a National Socialist Germany as with a fascist Italy. The same was true of other basic questions of German-Soviety policy: the relations with Poland and the fight against the Versailles

Treaty. These were simply fluctuations now in public opinion in the Soviet Union which are evident, for example, in Radek's article, too; these fluctuations were to be attributed to the uncertainty which still existed about German policy.[5]

In spite of such efforts, however, relations between the two countries continued to deteriorate. Germany was particularly suspicious of the Soviet rapprochement with France. In a conversation with the German ambassador in Moscow on August 4, Molotov denied categorically that there had been any change in the Soviet attitude to Germany, and maintained that the Soviet Union's closer relations with France would not affect in any way its relations with Germany: "The treaties now concluded by the Soviet government were not directed against other countries but were dictated by a general peace policy. If Germany's policy toward the Soviet Union remained unchanged, the latter would also not change her policy toward Germany."[6]

The most significant change in Soviet-German relations was the ending of the military cooperation between the two countries which had been carried on clandestinely since the early twenties. In the second half of 1933 the Soviet government closed down German military training stations for aviation, tanks, and gas warfare at Lipetsk, Kazan, and Saratov. Regret over the end of military cooperation was voiced by M. N. Tukhachevsky, Deputy Commissar of the Army and Navy, at the banquet given to the departing German officers.[7] Voroshilov, Commissar for War, conveyed to the German ambassador, Nadolny, the Red Army's great satisfaction over its cooperation with the Reichswehr, and expressed the hope that "the old good relationship should be restored again."[8]

Soviet Policy in the Sino-Japanese Crisis

Japan's conquest of Manchuria began on the night of September 18/19, 1931. After rapidly occupying the whole of South Manchuria, the Japanese army swung northward. Within a short time, Harbin, a major center on the Chinese Eastern Railway, was in Japanese hands. On January 29, 1932, the Japanese ambassador in Moscow, Hirota, informed Soviet Deputy Commissar of Foreign Affairs Karakhan that Harbin had been occupied only after the mutiny of the Chinese troops in that city, and that the occupation was merely an attempt to safeguard the lives and property of Japanese subjects. The interests of the Chinese Eastern Railway,

Hirota said, would not be violated. True, Japan would be obliged to use the railway for the transportation of troops, but the Japanese government was prepared to pay the cost of transportation. Karakhan replied that the transportation of troops through the Harbin region required the consent of the Chinese authorities as well as that of the Soviet government. This exchange of views was the beginning of protracted negotiations and mutual recriminations as Japan's war against China developed.[9]

The Soviet leaders were determined to avoid at any price involvement in the Manchurian conflict. They could not fail, however, to be aware of the danger that threatened the Soviet Union as Japanese troops moved closer to its boundaries. On December 31, 1931, the Soviet government proposed a nonaggression pact to Japan, but weeks passed and no reply was forthcoming. "No impartial politician," wrote *Izvestiia* on March 4, 1932, "can ignore the symptomatic meaning of the fact that, during the past two months, the Japanese government has not deemed it necessary to reply to the Soviet proposal for a nonaggression pact" (Document 77). Seeking to avoid war, Soviet spokesmen repeatedly warned would-be aggressors. On February 22, celebrated as the anniversary of the founding of the Red Army, General V. K. Blücher, commander of the Special Far Eastern Army, said that his troops were "always ready to take up the struggle in defense of the country which is building socialism. We shall not permit either White Guardist or imperialist rabble to set foot on our socialist territory, our kolkhoz fields . . . We shall fight for every ton of coal, every square foot of timber, every tractor, and every catch of fish which belongs to us."[10] Commissar of War Voroshilov made similar remarks to marchers in the May Day parade in 1932 (Document 79).

Soviet fear of involvement in war with Japan was intensified by the conviction that other imperialist powers were supporting Japan in its war against China. According to Mif, in an article published in 1932:

> Japanese imperialism receives its main support from France. The French bourgeoisie aids the Japanese imperialists in the hope that future events will turn the latter against the U.S.S.R. England, likewise, actively abets the anti-Soviet efforts and is ready to come to an agreement with the Japanese imperialists, attempting at the same time to assure itself the most substantial portion of China when the redivision of the latter takes place.

The U.S.A.'s position depends primarily on the extent to which the occupation of Manchuria is actually directed against the U.S.S.R. It encourages Japan in every possible way to adopt this course. However, in claiming a particularly large portion of China for itself, the United States does not wish Japan to grow stronger. Consequently, the possibility exists of a sharp intensification of contradictions, and in particular between Japan and the United States.[11]

The Soviet suspicion of other governments' intentions in Manchuria led to a similar attitude toward the Lytton Commission set up by the League of Nations to investigate the situation in Manchuria: "By setting up this commission, by dragging out its work, and by delaying the examination of the commission's report," an unsigned article in *Pravda* stated on October 7, "the League of Nations has rendered valuable service to Japan, and Japan was enabled thereby to carry out its plan in Manchuria and China without being disturbed by interference by other imperialist powers."

On December 13, 1932, the Japanese Ministry of Foreign Affairs finally delivered a note to the Soviet diplomatic representative in Tokyo, A. A. Troianovsky, rejecting the proposal for a non-aggression pact. In its reply the Japanese government stated that the time for such a pact was not appropriate: "For the present the Japanese government would prefer an exchange of views concerning methods of averting the difficulties which may arise from the contiguity of the troops of both parties, and of settling locally such difficulties by peaceful means." The Soviet reply was conciliatory and regretful, stating that the Soviet government's original proposal "was not dictated by passing considerations, but was the outcome of its entire pacific policy, and it will therefore hold good in the future."[12]

In an effort to eliminate a possible source of friction the Soviet government offered to sell the Chinese Eastern Railway to the newly formed puppet government of "Manchukuo." Negotiations began in mid-1933, when Litvinov proposed the sale as a means of strengthening peace in the Far East. According to the Soviet estimate, the total expenditure on the railway from the time it was built through 1932 amounted to approximately 411,700,000 rubles, plus nearly 178,530,000 gold rubles loaned by the Tsarist government to the C.E.R. to cover the deficit and running costs in the early years of the railway.[13]

The first conference to discuss the sale took place in Tokyo on June 26, 1933, with Japan acting as intermediary between the Soviet government and Manchukuo (Document 100). The asking price for the railroad was 250 million gold rubles (i.e., 625 million yen). To facilitate payment, the Soviet Union indicated that it was prepared to accept half the sum in goods, to be paid in four semiannual installments. As for the remaining 125 million rubles, one quarter was to be paid in cash when the agreement was consummated, the rest in bonds bearing four per cent interest and redeemable within three years. In a counterproposal the Manchukuoan delegation offered 50 million yen (20 million gold rubles), and refused to budge in further negotiations after the Soviet delegation reduced the asking price to 200 million gold rubles. Meanwhile difficulties continued to pile up between the Soviet officials on the C.E.R. and the Manchukuoan authorities. The Soviet government protested to Tokyo, laying the responsibility for violation of the existing status of the railway on the Japanese government.[14]

A significant change in the diplomatic situation in the Far East had occurred on December 12, 1932, when Nationalist China resumed diplomatic relations with the Soviet Union. The Chinese government and press were naturally highly critical of the Soviet plan to sell the C.E.R. Radek, however, writing in *Izvestiia* on May 10, 1933, argued that Chinese criticism was prompted by the imperialist powers.

Negotiations on the sale of the railroad were resumed after six months' interval, each party gradually making concessions, particularly the Soviet government. Finally agreement was reached on September 19, 1934, for the sale of the C.E.R. for 67.5 million gold rubles (160 million yen), with half of the sum to be paid in Japanese goods. On March 23, 1935, agreements on additional points were signed.

Soviet Peace Efforts

In order to protect its frontiers, the Soviet government at this time concluded a number of nonaggression pacts, especially with its immediate neighbors. Nonaggression pacts had already been concluded with Germany and Turkey in 1925, Afghanistan and Lithuania in 1926, and Persia in 1927. In a TASS interview

January 25, 1932, before his departure for the Disarmament Conference in Geneva, Litvinov stated that the pacts were very simple, merely obligations to undertake no aggressive action and to eliminate so far as possible causes which might disturb peaceful relations between the governments concluding the treaties.[15]

Commenting on Litvinov's statement, an *Izvestiia* editorial on January 28 claimed that "the Soviet struggle for peace, which has been made particularly clear in the negotiation of nonaggression pacts, is now beginning to attract the attention of world public opinion more and more." Unfortunately, *Izvestiia* added, the peaceful principles that guided Soviet policy met with constant obstruction from other countries. Therefore the Soviet Union, "engaged in the building of socialism in an epoch when the entire capitalist world is suffocating in the clutches of an unprecedented economic crisis, must pay particular attention to the danger of an imperialist attack."

The first in the new series of nonaggression treaties was concluded with Finland on January 21, 1932, at Helsinki and was followed by one with Latvia on February 5. (For *Izvestiia's* editorial comment, see Documents 71 and 73.) On May 4 a similar treaty was signed with Estonia. Potentially the most significant of these treaties was the Soviet-Polish nonaggression pact initialed in Moscow in January 1932 and signed on July 25 of the same year. Negotiations on the pact had begun in 1926, on the initiative of the Soviet Union, but had dragged on. Soviet leaders feared that Poland was attempting to form under its leadership a Polish-Baltic bloc directed against the Soviet Union. According to *Pravda* of July 30, 1932,

> This time, the negotiations between the Soviet Union and Poland began in a completely different international climate and a completely changed domestic situation in Poland. In 1931–32, the world economic crisis has shaken the Polish economy to its very foundation. . . . The direct result is deep unrest among the worker and peasant masses. . . . Sympathy with the Soviet Union, the fatherland of the toilers of all countries, with the country which has successfully concluded the Five-Year Plan, is increasing among the broadest masses of the workers and peasants.

The ratification of the nonaggression pact and a conciliation convention was announced simultaneously in Moscow and Warsaw on November 27, and the next day *Izvestiia* stated that

In this act the long years of struggle carried on by the Soviet government to strengthen the guarantees of peace between the U.S.S.R. and the strongest of its neighbors in the West have come to successful fruition.

The policy of peace with regard to Poland, the policy of creating the strongest possible guarantees of good neighborly relations between the U.S.S.R. and Poland, is a part of the policy of peace which the Soviet government has carried on from the first days of its existence.

Closer relations with France were felt to be particularly important by the Soviet leaders. On January 4, 1932, an agreement on conciliation procedure was signed between the two countries, followed by a nonaggression pact on November 29. These agreements marked a sharp change in the relations between the two countries, since only recently Soviet spokesmen had accused France of planning intervention against Soviet Russia and aiding and encouraging Japanese aggression in Manchuria. In its editorial commentary, *Izvestiia* placed special emphasis on the fifth article of the pact, by which the signatories pledged themselves not to interfere in each other's internal affairs, nor to permit propaganda or preparations for intervention (Document 92).

When the nonaggression pact was ratified by the French government on February 15, 1933, *Pravda* (18th) analyzed it as the consequence partly of France's worsening international position and partly of the rapidly growing sympathy of the French proletariat for the Soviet Union, the growing interest of the French intellectuals, and the "increasingly obvious disinclination of the French petty bourgeoisie to participate in a new anti-Soviet war."[16] After the ratification relations began to improve between the two countries. Litvinov visited France in July 1933, was received by Premier Daladier, and met with Paul-Boncour, the foreign minister. In October, the former French Premier Edouard Herriot visited the U.S.S.R. Soon afterward, the French Minister of Aviation, Pierre Cot, also paid a visit.

Of lesser importance, but still significant, was the Soviet-Italian trade and credit agreement of May 6, 1933, which strengthened the mutually satisfactory relations between Soviet Russia and Fascist Italy. According to *Izvestiia* (May 9), the agreement "served as a new proof that the Soviet Union sincerely desires to establish peaceful relations with the capitalist countries and will gladly meet any of them halfway if they seriously wish to establish normal and close relations." Good relations were also maintained with Turkey. On the occasion of Turkish Foreign Minister Ismet Pasha's visit to Moscow, *Izvestiia* of April 28, 1932, declared that "in spite of differences in social structure," the two countries had "correctly outlined and firmly followed the line of cooperation in their foreign policies."

Relations with Great Britain deteriorated, however, when the Soviet secret police claimed to have uncovered acts of sabotage involving British citizens. On March 14, 1933, the GPU issued the following statement:

> As a result of an examination by officials of the GPU in connection with a number of unexpected and continually occurring acts of damage to the big power works recently (in Moscow, Cheliabinsk, Zuevo, Zlatoust, etc.), it was ascertained that this damage was the result of the sabotage activity of a group of criminal elements among the state employees of the People's Commissariat for Heavy Industry, who made it their aim to destroy the power works of the Soviet Union and cause a stoppage of the state factories supplied with power by these stations.
>
> As a result of the investigation, it was found that the activity of this group of wreckers had also been participated in by some employees of the English firm of Metropolitan Vickers, Ltd., who under an agreement with this firm were employed as technical experts in the electric undertakings of the Soviet Union.
>
> In all, thirty-one persons were arrested in connection with this affair, among them being some English citizens.
>
> After being examined and having given written guarantees that they would not attempt to leave the country, a number of the accused were released. The investigation is still proceeding.[17]

Even before this event, difficulties had been evident in Anglo-Soviet relations. On October 17, 1932, a trade agreement with the Soviet Union was terminated by Great Britain, but in March 1933, negotiations were undertaken for its resumption. However, following the arrest of two British subjects, MacDonald and Thornton, engineers employed by Metropolitan Vickers, the British government on April 19 introduced an embargo on eighty per cent of Great Britain's imports from the Soviet Union. Retaliatory restrictive measures were promptly taken by the Soviet government, and the

Soviet trade representative in London, Aleksandr Ozersky, was recalled to Moscow on April 21.[18]

In July the Presidium of the Central Executive Committee commuted the prison sentence of MacDonald and Thornton and deported them; the British government lifted the embargo the same day, and the Soviet government revoked its retaliatory measures on October 20. Following this action, the British government proposed that negotiations for the conclusion of a new trade agreement between the two countries be resumed. In a speech to the Central Executive Committee on December 29, Litvinov referred to the unsatisfactory state of relations with Great Britain: "Certain elements," he said, "still cherish the fond dream of a general capitalist fight against the land of socialism . . . However, since they can neither destroy nor upset this land of socialism, it is rather astonishing that notwithstanding the renowned practical common-sense of the British, there should still remain among them such quixotic snipers and partisans. As far as we are concerned, we are ready and desirous of maintaining the same good relations with Great Britain as with other countries."[19]

The new Soviet-British provisional trade agreement was, in fact, signed in London on February 16, 1934, and entered into force March 21 on exchange of acts of ratification in Moscow. Despite its provisional character, it continued to serve as the basis for Soviet-British trade relations through at least the end of 1961, although the two states reached an agreement in principle on May 24, 1959, to conclude a trade and navigation treaty to replace it.[20]

The most important diplomatic achievement of the Soviet government in 1933 was recognition by the United States and the establishment of diplomatic relations between the two countries. American recognition had long been desired by the Soviet leaders, notwithstanding their criticism of the United States and its system of government. *Pravda,* for example, commenting on the election of Franklin D. Roosevelt in 1932, expressed the opinion that "the two parties of big capital—the Republicans and the Democrats— actually do not differ in their policies. Both attempt to find a capitalist way out of the crisis by means of wage cuts, casting the burden of the crisis on the shoulders of the toiling masses, and direct subventions to the huge banks and trusts." In referring to the policies to be expected from the new president, *Pravda* added:

> Roosevelt cannot overcome the crisis. The Democratic administration will pursue the same line of economic and political

attacks on the working class. This repressive domestic policy will be followed by an active foreign policy of the United States capitalists. As Hoover's defeat was partly an expression of discontent on the part of the United States bourgeoisie in the face of the growing aggressiveness of Japan, Roosevelt's policy will be characterized by greater aggressiveness, the quest for new allies, and attempts to form new blocs and alliances.[21]

On October 10, 1933, President Roosevelt sent to M. I. Kalinin, the Chairman of the Central Executive Committee, a letter proposing "friendly, frank conversations" in order to discuss "all questions outstanding between our two countries," as a preparation for full diplomatic recognition.[22] Kalinin replied a week later, designating Litvinov as the Soviet negotiator. The negotiations, which took place in Washington from November 8 to 16, led to the conclusion of a series of agreements constituting diplomatic recognition and providing for the exchange of ambassadors.[23] *Izvestiia* (November 20) stated on this occasion:

> The Soviet government and Soviet public opinion have aimed in every way for a rapprochement with the United States. They based these efforts on their peace policy and their daily struggle for peace. Cooperation between the United States and the U.S.S.R. would have undoubtedly been one of the most practical means for the safeguarding of peace. From this viewpoint diplomatic relations between the U.S.S.R. and the United States must be considered as the greatest victory of our policy of peace. [See also Documents 104 and 112.]

Litvinov's visit to the United States also served to advance Soviet pleas for peace and disarmament. Speaking at a reception in New York, he referred to the Disarmament Conference at Geneva as a "corpse which no efforts can bring to life." He called for complete disarmament and joint efforts by the two countries to preserve peace. "Who can doubt," he concluded, "that the combined voices of these two giants will make themselves heard and that their joint efforts will weight the scales in favor of peace?"[24]

The Problem of Disarmament

After several years of preliminary work by the Preparatory Commission, the Disarmament Conference finally met on February 2, 1932. An editorial in *Izvestiia* on February 10 recalled past efforts by

Soviet representatives and the rejection of Soviet proposals on the grounds that they were "unrealistic." "Today, when the sound of gunfire in the Far East serves as the strongest argument for denouncing the imperialists' unspeakable lies about their peace policy, the bourgeois press tries to downgrade the significance of the conference in order to absolve the bourgeois politicians from the responsibility for complete failure and intentional sabotage [of disarmament] during thirteen years of the postwar period." Radek, in the same spirit, wrote, "On the fields of Manchuria, the last hope of the last blockheads that the League of Nations could prevent and wanted to prevent war has perished" (Document 74).

On February 5, André Tardieu, the French representative and initial speaker at the conference, proposed that civilian and military aircraft and certain land and naval forces be placed at the disposal of the League of Nations. He also suggested that an international force be created, together with a permanent international police, for preventive and defensive actions. These proposals were particularly objectionable to Germany, and Litvinov also rejected them. "I feel bound," Litvinov said, "to state frankly that, as far as security against war, and, therefore, security of states are concerned, the French proposals arouse grave doubts in our mind. The Soviet delegation is thereby strengthened in its conviction that the only infallible way to solve the problem of averting war and assuring security to all nations is through . . . general disarmament." He added, however, that it would be wrong to infer that the Soviet delegation denied the importance and efficacy of other ways of consolidating peace short of total disarmament. Returning to the principle of total disarmament, and praising the Soviet political system, Litvinov concluded:

> The Soviet delegation knows that the triumph of socialist principles, which removes the causes that give rise to armed conflicts, is the only absolute guarantee of peace. However, as long as these principles prevail in only one-sixth of the world, there is but one way to secure peace, and that is total and general disarmament. Proof of its practicability is the fact that it is proposed by a state with a population of over 100 million. This idea is by no means utopian in itself, but it can be made utopian if rejected by other states represented here.[25]

On February 20 Litvinov outlined Soviet policy on disarmament in an address to an American group in Geneva, devoting special attention to the relation between security and disarmament.

The address, which marks a significant shift in Litvinov's thinking toward collective security, concluded with a broad hint of the desirability of the establishment of diplomatic relations between the Soviet Union and the United States (Document 76).

As the discussions at the Disarmament Conference developed, a new principle for disarmament was advanced by Sir John Simon, the British delegate—that of "qualitative" disarmament as contrasted with "quantitative" disarmament. Various subcommittees and technical commissions were formed to determine the feasibility of the British proposal. Commenting on the situation, *Izvestiia* maintained that the points of view of the capitalist powers represented at the conference had "nothing in common with the task of the limitation of armaments" (Document 75). On June 22 President Hoover proposed that all states reduce their military forces by one-third. He also recommended that all tanks, all means of chemical warfare, and all large mobile guns be abolished, as actions which "would reduce the offensive character of all forces as distinguished from the defensive character."[26] This proposal, a landmark of the conference, met with Litvinov's approval: "I welcome [these] proposals . . . because they proceed along the same lines, though not so far, as the Soviet proposals which were made here and were not supported . . . namely, the principle of the objective method of proportional reduction [of armaments]." Litvinov used the occasion to make a general assessment of the state of affairs at the conference, remarking that nearly five months had passed "without our having made the least progress or achieving the slightest result."[27]

"Hoover's proposal," wrote a Soviet correspondent from Geneva, "is a document unprecedented in the history of the foreign policy of the capitalist states. Such a massive limitation of armament has so far never been proposed by any capitalist state." The American plan, however, according to the Soviet reporter, was "a kind of shield for the problem of debts." He was doubtful, moreover, that the proposal would have any effect on the work of the conference or the Lausanne Conference on reparations, and added: "There is no doubt that the German-Lausanne game of imperialist contradictions has entered a new stage of its most dramatic moments."[28] When discussion of Hoover's proposal was postponed, *Pravda* wrote that it had been "shelved," and maintained that the real purpose of the conference was to serve as *"a means for preparing a new imperialist war, anti-Soviet intervention, and deceiving the toiling masses"* (Document 82).

On July 20, before the conference adjourned, Eduard Beneš, the Czechoslovak representative, introduced a draft resolution which included among other things a recommendation that an armament truce be concluded by all governments until March 1933. The Soviet delegation was quite critical of Beneš's proposal and declined to sign it. Litvinov remarked that the resolution was actually a step backward, bringing no new proposals and simply summarizing agreements on the humanization and regulation of war which had already been reached some years ago. In his concluding remarks, Litvinov stated, however, that he wished to believe that even limited disarmament would bring the time nearer "when, to use the happy reference to grammar made by the President of the Council of the French Republic, M. Herriot, the nations will never use the verb 'arm' in the present, or in the future, but only in the past tense, and then only with confusion and shame."[29]

Summing up the results of the conference, *Izvestiia* stated: "After five years of preparation and six months of work, the labors of the Disarmament Conference have come to an end, having accomplished nothing." It found in the failure of the conference the clearest indication that all the capitalist powers were preparing for war: ". . . all of them are getting ready for a new division of the world with weapons in their hands." (Document 83.)

The General Commission of the Disarmament Conference did not meet again until early 1933, by which time much had happened in the international arena. Germany was now strongly pressing for the right to rearm on the basis of equality with the other powers. As early as April 1932, at a conference in Geneva between the British Prime Minister, French Prime Minister Tardieu, the United States Secretary of State, and Reichschancellor Brüning, a decision was made that "as a result of the Conference on Disarmament, Part V of the Versailles Treaty could be replaced by a general convention." It was provided, however, that no considerable increase in German armament should follow.[30] On August 29, 1932, a German memorandum was presented to the French government in which confidential negotiations were proposed between the two countries on equality of armament. France declined the proposal, but a little later, at a conference of the United States, Britain, France, Italy, and Germany, "equality [for Germany] within the limits of the security system similar to all countries" was resolved upon.[31]

When the Bureau of the Conference for the Reduction and Limitation of Armaments met again on September 21, 1932, Litvinov supported the principle of quantitative limitation of disarmament rather than qualitative, and again urged the necessity of actual discussion of the limitation of armament to one-third as outlined in the American proposals and supported by the Soviet delegation. As to the problem of control of armaments, which some delegates wished to discuss, he believed it to be premature. There was no point in returning to this problem now, Litvinov said, since the degree of control which the governments would assume depended on the degree of disarmament. "To discuss control now is equivalent to the discussion of the frame of the picture before the picture is made," he said.[32] Commenting on this point, a Soviet reporter in Geneva wrote:

> The U.S.S.R. has never expressed itself against control over armaments. On the contrary, in its projects on disarmament it insisted on the necessity of the strictest control, both general and local. With this in view, it advanced the principle of workers' control as the most effective, efficient, and reliable verification. At the same time, the Soviet delegation has always insisted that it was necessary first to come to an agreement on *what* was to be controlled (i.e. the degree of the limitation of armaments), and only then to discuss *how* it was to be controlled. This clear and unambiguous position of the U.S.S.R. has been interpreted as being against control. Paul-Boncour and Madariaga have hastened to declare that unless there should be a preliminary discussion of the problem of the form and degree of control, they were not willing to assume any obligations in regard to the question of the limitation of armaments.[33]

When the General Commission of the Disarmament Conference met again in February 1933, it had before it a new plan, the "constructive plan" of Paul-Boncour, which dealt with proposals to increase the power of the defense through decreasing the power of attack. The plan again advocated the internationalization of armed forces for preventive and defensive duties. Litvinov commented on this plan in a speech on February 6. The Soviet delegation, he said, had studied "with deepest interest the French proposals now under discussion," but he added: "While far from desiring to minimize their importance, I am nevertheless bound to remark that we are unable to find among them any new proposals for the reduction of armaments, or, if any are to be found therein, they are made to depend strictly on the acceptance by the Conference of the French scheme of security."

Litvinov then emphasized the Soviet delegation's consistent position on the question of security: the best if not the only guarantee of security for all nations would be total disarmament, or at least the greatest possible reduction of armaments in the shortest possible period. However, Litvinov added, since so great and powerful a state as France insisted on security, "We shall have to consider with all seriousness the French proposals, and make up our mind whether there is any possibility of reaching an international agreement based upon these and other proposals which may be made on security by other delegations."[34]

As a positive contribution to the discussion, Litvinov presented a draft on the definition of "aggression."[35] The proposal was favorably received and was referred to a special committee for study. Litvinov was not satisfied, however, with the delay in the acceptance of his definition of aggression. He therefore opened negotiations with the states which were parties to the Litvinov Protocol of 1929, taking advantage of the opportunity provided by the World Monetary and Economic Conference in London from June 12 to July 27, 1933. Litvinov proposed that, without waiting for the conclusion of the Disarmament Conference, a convention defining aggression be signed. The proposal met with general acceptance, and the first convention was signed on July 3 between Afghanistan, Estonia, Latvia, Persia, Poland, Rumania, Turkey, and the U.S.S.R. On the following day Litvinov signed a similar convention with Turkey and the countries of the Little Entente, and on July 5 a separate but virtually identical agreement with Lithuania. The negotiations were completed with the adherence of Finland on January 31, 1934.

Speaking at the World Monetary and Economic Conference, Litvinov claimed that the Soviet Union's economic structure precluded economic crises such as the capitalist countries were experiencing. Nonetheless, he said, the world economic crisis reacted unfavorably on the development of Soviet foreign trade, and he reiterated a proposal he had made previously at the Commission of Inquiry into European Union for "economic disarmament." "Unfortunately," he said, "this proposal was taken prisoner and thrown into a dungeon—one of the League of Nations commissions." He added, "I am sure that you all realize that economic peace is only possible against the background of peace in all phases of international life."[36] Following up his suggestion, Litvinov presented to the conference a draft for an economic nonaggression pact (Document 99).

Germany withdrew from the League of Nations on October 14, 1933, and indicated it would refuse to continue to participate in the Conference for the Reduction and Limitation of Armaments. Commenting on this ominous event, *Izvestiia* stated that German fascism had "decided to take the path of preparation for war," an action which was "threatening international peace with exceptionally dangerous adventures." Yet *Izvestiia* interpreted Germany's action as an indication of weakness and of isolation in international relations. (Document 103.)

At the end of the year, a session of the Central Executive Committee was held at which Litvinov delivered a lengthy and important speech summing up Soviet foreign relations. The "era of bourgeois pacifism," he said, had come to an end. "But," he added, "you would get a wrong idea of the international situation if you concluded from what I have said that all capitalist states are now anxious for war and are preparing for it." A number of them were, for the time being, interested in maintaining peace and were prepared to follow a policy defending peace. "I shall not enter into an explanation of the reasons for this policy, but merely state the fact, which is of the utmost value to us."[37]

Molotov also spoke on Soviet foreign relations. He stated that the "greatest success" of Soviet foreign policy was the "resumption" of diplomatic relations between the Soviet Union and the United States. In regard to Germany, he spoke of the long-standing friendly relations between the two countries which "rested on their common desire for peace and for the development of economic relations." "We still adhere fully to those principles," he added. But since the policy of militant national socialist ideologues was "steeped through and through with reactionary desires and aggressive imperialist plans," it was "incompatible with a strengthening of friendly relations with the U.S.S.R."[38]

Radek's estimation of the situation was much gloomier. He stated that "the preparations for war to secure a redivision of the world" had "put an end to the disarmament comedy, whose aim it was to persuade the masses of the people everywhere that there was no danger of war."

The disarmament conference has gone bankrupt because all the imperialist powers realized *the rapid approach of a new war for the redivision of the world*. Some of them regard the prospect with horror, feeling that the redivision will take place to their disadvantage, whilst others look forward to it with joy in the belief that it will improve their situation. But both parties are unanimous in the conclusion which they draw from the obvious intensification of imperialist contradictions, namely, increased armament.[39]

L. I. Magyar (Madiar), a prominent Communist writer on foreign affairs, particularly on China, commented on Soviet policy in these circumstances (Document 114).

NOTES

1. Max Beloff, *The Foreign Policy of Soviet Russia, 1929–1941* (London, 1947–49), I, 61.
2. See also an article "Whither Germany?" in which Radek analyzed *Mein Kampf* (*Izvestiia*, March 22, 1933).
3. DEROP (*Deutsche Vertragsgesellschaft für russische Ölprodukte A.G.*), an organization for marketing Soviet petroleum products, was set up as a German corporation with Soviet capital. It operated some 2,000 stations in Germany.
4. *I.P.C.*, Vol. 13, No. 53, December 6, 1933, p. 1193.
5. U.S. Department of State, *Documents on German Foreign Policy* (Washington, D.C., 1949——), Ser. C, I, 450.
6. *Ibid.*, p. 717.
7. *Ibid.*, II, 81–83.
8. *Ibid.*, pp. 338–339. Rudolf Nadolny was appointed in September, replacing Dirksen, who was transferred to Japan.
9. *Vneshniaia politika SSSR: sbornik dokumentov* (Moscow, 1944–47), III, 521–526; Degras, *Foreign Policy*, II, 523–529.
10. *Izvestiia*, February 27, 1932.
11. "Iaponskii imperializm i okkupatsiia Man'chzhurii," in Mif and Voitinsky (comps.) ,*Okkupatsiia Man'chzhurii i bor'ba imperialistov: sbornik statei* (Moscow, 1932), p. 35.
12. Degras, *Foreign Policy*, II, 552–53, translating *Izvestiia*, January 17, 1933.
13. For an abridged text of the Soviet memorandum on the sale of the C.E.R., sent July 3, 1933, see Degras, *Foreign Policy*, III, 23–28, translating *Izvestiia*, July 8, 1933.
14. See *Vneshniaia politika SSSR*, III 660; Degras, *Foreign Policy*, III, 31, translating *Izvestiia*, September 22, 1933. See also Molotov's speech to the Central Executive Committee on December 28, 1933 in Degras, III, 47–48.
15. Degras, *Foreign Policy*, II, 522–523, from *S.U.R.*, March 1932, p. 56.
16. For Litvinov's comment, see Degras, *Foreign Policy*, II, 547–548, quoting *S.U.R.*, January 1933, p. 5.
17. *I.P.C.*, Vol. 13, No. 14, March 24, 1933, pp. 335–336.
18. For the Soviet regulation of April 22 see *S.U.R.*, June 1933, p. 138. See also Document 98.
19. *S.U.R.*, February–March 1934, p. 62; Degras, *Foreign Policy*, II, 53. For day to day documentation on the affair, see Great Britain, Foreign Office, *Documents on British Foreign Policy* (London, 1949——), 2nd Series, VII.

For an account by the British chargé in Moscow at the time, see Lord Strang, *Home and Abroad* (London, 1956) .

20. G. Ginsburgs and R. M. Slusser, "A Calendar of Soviet Treaties, January–December 1959," *Osteuropa-Recht*, VIII, No. 2 (1962) , 145; G. Ginsburgs, "A Calendar of Soviet Treaties, January–December 1961," *Osteuropa-Recht*, X, No. 2 (1964) , 138.

21. *Pravda*, November 10, 1932; *I.P.C.*, Vol. 13, No. 29, June 30, 1933, pp. 636–638.

22. U.S., Department of State, *Foreign Relations of the United States: The Soviet Union, 1933–1939* (Washington, D.C., continuing series) , pp. 17–18. For the initial Soviet feelers, see also the regular volumes of this series for 1931, 1932, and 1933.

23. For details of the negotiations see R. P. Browder, *The Origins of Soviet-American Diplomacy* (Princeton, 1953) , pp. 130–41; D. G. Bishop, *The Roosevelt-Litvinov Agreement: The American View* (Syracuse, 1965) , chap. i.

24. Degras, *Foreign Policy*, III, 41–43, from the *New York Times*, November 25, 1933.

25. League of Nations, Conference for the Reduction and Limitation of Armaments, *Records of the Conference* . . . , Series A, *Verbatim Reports of Plenary Sessions* (Geneva, 1932–36) , pp. 81–87.

26. *Ibid.*, Series B, *Minutes of the General Commission*, I, 122–123.

27. *Izvestiia*, June 24, 1932; *S.U.R.*, July–August, 1933, pp. 164–165; summary in League, . . . *Conference*, Ser. B, I, 128–129.

28. *Izvestiia*, June 24, 1932.

29. League, . . . *Conference*, Ser. B, I, 153–156, 203–204.

30. *Documents on British Foreign Policy*, 2d. Series, IV, 108.

31. U.S. Department of State, *Foreign Relations of the United States* (Washington, D.C., continuing series) , 1932, p. 524.

32. *Izvestiia*, September 23, 1932.

33. *Izvestiia*, September 24, 1932.

34. League, . . . *Conference*, Ser. B, I, 235.

35. Text in Litvinov, *Against Aggression* (London, 1939) , pp. 170–172, and Degras, *Foreign Policy*, III, 27–28.

36. *S.U.R.*, July–August, 1933, pp. 146–149.

37. Extracts from the speech are given in Degras, *Foreign Policy*, III, 48–61; full text in *I.P.C.*, Vol. 14, No. 1, January 5, 1934, pp. 20–25.

38. Extracts from Molotov's speech are given in Degras, *Foreign Policy*, III, 46–48; full text in *I.P.C.*, Vol. 14, No. 1, January 5, 1934, pp. 19–20.

39. K. Radek, "The New Armament Race," *I.P.C.*, Vol. 14, No. 3, January 19, 1934, pp. 70–71.

6

Intensified Efforts for World Revolution,
1932–1933

The Comintern maintained that a growing revolutionary upsurge was in evidence among the workers and toiling masses throughout the world. The Twelfth Plenum of the ECCI, which met from August 27 to September 15, 1932, accordingly emphasized the immediate prospects of a decisive class struggle and the inevitability of political disturbances and uprisings. In a report on the international situation to the plenum on August 27, Kuusinen referred to a "definite change" in the general crisis of capitalism. The accentuation of the fundamental contradictions within the capitalist world, he said, had reached such proportions that, to quote the draft Theses presented to the plenum, "at certain main points of extreme importance the antagonistic forces are almost ready for a collision." Kuusinen added:

> The relative stabilization that set in after the first round of wars and revolutions has now ended. But there is not yet an immediate revolutionary situation in the most important and decisive capitalist countries. What is taking place at present is precisely the transition to a new phase of great collisions between classes and between states, to a new round of revolutions and wars.[1]

According to the Theses, the basic task of the communist parties was the "preparation of the working class and the exploited masses" for "the impending battles for power, for the dictatorship of the proletariat" (Document 88). According to Manuilsky, speaking at the plenum, the "world crisis in the world of capitalism" and the "successes of socialist construction" in the U.S.S.R. would further the revolutionary education of the masses. The experience of the United States, for example, demonstrated that there was no such thing as "eternal prosperity"; as for Great Britain, although it had "seized and plundered hundreds of millions of alien peoples [and] subjected to itself entire continents," it had not been able to escape decay. (Document 86.)

The plenum Theses upon Kuusinen's report saw evidence of the disintegration of the capitalist countries, a situation which was bound to lead to an intensification of the antagonisms among them and ultimately to war:

> The fierce struggle which is being waged by the imperialists for markets and colonies, the tariff wars, the armaments race, have already led to the immediate danger of a new imperialist world war. French imperialism, which is developing a feverish activity in the struggle for its hegemony on the European continent, is now trying to strengthen its old military and political alliances and to form new ones (the Danubian federation). However, it encounters Germany's resistance, and also that of the United States and Italy. Germany demands for herself equal status with the imperialist powers (the annulment of reparations, parity in armament, the revision of the eastern frontiers, etc.), while Poland is preparing to seize Danzig and West Prussia. In that way Germany becomes one of the main centers of the sharpest and most intense world-imperialist conflicts.

In the Far East, the Theses continued, Japan's seizure of Manchuria and the attack on Shanghai had upset the collaboration that had hitherto existed between the United States, Japan, and Great Britain in regard to their respective spheres of influence in China. France, the Theses went on to say, was supporting Japan in its venture, as was Britain. Meanwhile, the League of Nations, "acting on the behest of France and England, supports Japan."[2]

Kuusinen maintained that in spite of the differences between the Great Powers, they all shared a common hostility toward the U.S.S.R. "It is a fact," he said, "that all these powers jointly with their vassals, and precisely in recent times, have been intensifying very vigorously their preparations for war against the U.S.S.R."

A war by Japan against the Soviet Union is being expected and desired in the camp of all the imperialists. There only remains a certain doubt as to how far Japan will be able to conduct this war with success. For this reason it has been deemed necessary to leave Japan a little more time for its war preparations. The Japanese ruling classes are themselves steering at the present time a determined course toward a war to be launched [against the Soviet Union] by the spring or autumn of 1933, immediately after the completion of the important preparatory measures which are planned by Japan.[3]

Preparations for a war against the U.S.S.R. were not limited to Japan, Kuusinen continued. The French General Staff was doing extensive work in coordinating the war plans of the general staffs of Poland and the Little Entente. In the spring of 1932, he stated, a conference of the general staffs of Poland, Czechoslovakia, and Yugoslavia was held under the leadership of the French General Staff, at which plans of army operations against the Soviet Union were discussed; one of the plans was referred to by the officers as the "Black Plan." In addition, the French General Staff was training and arming its own fighting forces for the same purpose. Since Britain did not wish to be left behind, Kuusinen reported, it was undertaking war preparations against the U.S.S.R. in the Near East, particularly in Iraq, concentrating its bombers in the airports of Baghdad, Mosul, and Basra, building a large airport in Baghdad, and laying a highway from Iraq, across Persia and Azerbaijan, to the borders of the U.S.S.R.[4]

The Comintern's interpretation of the world situation and of the alleged preparations for an imperialist attack on the Soviet Union reflected the prevailing Soviet image of the capitalist world. According to Manuilsky, the current epoch of wars and proletarian revolutions was characterized by a struggle between the dying world of capitalism and the rising world of socialism; this struggle was becoming "the key point of world politics and economics as a whole" (Document 86). The highly developed revolutionary situation demanded certain definite tasks, according to Kuusinen:

We, the communists, must make every possible effort in every country to force the bourgeoisie to give up the launching of a war. For this purpose, it is imperative to begin immediately to mobilize the broad masses of the toilers for the struggle against war. To what extent we shall succeed in preventing the carrying out of the war plans of the bourgeoisie in separate countries, we do not know. We only know that there is only one reliable guaranty against war: the proletarian revolution. Therefore, the preparation of the revolution is the most important factor in the struggle against war, just as the mobilization of the toilers for the struggle against war is at present one of the most important tasks in the effort to prepare them for revolution. These two tasks are indissolubly connected. At the present moment there is not a single capitalist country of any international significance in which these two tasks could be separated.[5]

The resolution of the Twelfth Plenum on the threat of war called on all communist parties to organize and lead workers, peasants, and all toilers for the defense of the Chinese revolution, "for the defense of the fatherland of the workers of all countries—the U.S.S.R.—against the approaching military intervention, for the defense of the toilers of the capitalist countries against a new imperialist war" (Document 91). In his final speech at the plenum, Manuilsky enjoined communists outside the Soviet Union to intensify their work. Socialism in the U.S.S.R. would "stride forward immeasurably" if aided by proletarian revolution abroad (Document 87).

Difficulties in the Policy of "Class Against Class"

The policy of "Class Against Class," inaugurated in 1928, was accompanied by the policy of the "United Front from Below." The latter aimed at winning influence over all the working masses, especially workers who belonged to social-democratic organizations, thereby destroying the latter. To this end, the social-democratic leaders were proclaimed enemies even more dangerous than the national socialists. The irreconcilable policy adopted by the Comintern was bound to bring confusion within communist ranks, especially in such countries as Great Britain, which had been accustomed for years to the principle of unity of the working class, or France, where the workers were not familiar with disciplinary tutelage from above. As a result, there seemed to be little development in the communist parties of these countries, and membership dwindled or fluctuated. The Comintern was obliged to admit that, although there was a revolutionary upsurge throughout the world and communist influence was growing, the communists of some countries had failed in the tasks given them. In particular, the Twelfth Plenum directed the attention of the sections to work among the unemployed (Document 90).

Another shortcoming of the communist parties, according to the Comintern, was "Left sectarianism in the parties and in the revolutionary trade-union movement." This attitude caused communists to withdraw from revolutionary work in the reformist trade-unions and from elective positions in them. Participation in the reformist trade-unions, however, the Twelfth Plenum stated, was the duty of every communist, although from this it did not follow that an alliance with social-democrats was to be concluded. Kuusinen said:

> The Bolshevik policy of the united front is not a bloc policy; it does not mean "making civic peace" with the social-democratic and reformist leaders (as proposed by the renegades of communism—Brandler, Trotsky, and others) . . . The united front of the communist and noncommunist workers against the bourgeoisie must be unequivocally counterposed to the social-democrats' policy of the united front with the bourgeoisie. The entire meaning of the Bolshevik united front lies, first, in the class struggle against the bourgeoisie and, second, in isolating the agents of the bourgeoisie from the masses of the proletariat.[6]

The task of the communists was, therefore, to conduct mass propaganda in favor of "soviet democracy" and to denounce social-democratic leaders. The latter, Kuusinen said, were in the habit of saying that the working class would come to socialism on the basis of democracy, but that the communists, like the fascists, were in favor of dictatorship. This was not true, according to Kuusinen, because the concept of proletarian dictatorship was absolutely different from that of fascist dictatorship, a fact which must be made clear to the masses:

> The masses are not in favor of "dictatorship in general," just as we are not in favor of it. We wish to win over the reformist workers for the proletarian dictatorship, and this is perfectly feasible. Only this has not been explained to them sufficiently. It is difficult for the masses to grasp that the proletarian

dictatorship in the form of the Soviet power is precisely the state form of proletarian democracy.

To understand this special form of democracy, Kuusinen recommended that his listeners study Lenin's Theses concerning "bourgeois democracy and the proletarian dictatorship" adopted at the First Congress of the Comintern.[7]

The efforts to make the Comintern a monolithic organization run from Moscow still encountered opposition. The French Communist Party proved to be particularly recalcitrant in this respect. Speaking at the Twelfth Plenum of the ECCI, in September 1932, Piatnitsky said:

> Bearing in mind the importance of the problem confronting the Communist Party of France, in view of the significance of French imperialism for the revolutionary workers' and peasants' world movement (for France is strangling Germany, is strangling its own colonies, is encircling the U.S.S.R. with the help of its vassals—Czechoslovakia, Rumania, and Poland— and is aiming at intervention against the U.S.S.R., etc.), we are bound to admit that the CPF has made no progress, and, on the contrary, is lagging behind more than any other section.

Piatnitsky granted that certain successes had been achieved by the CPF. On the whole, however, and notwithstanding the constant guidance given it, the CPF, and the French Red trade-unions likewise, had failed dismally in their work.[8]

The Comintern was also dissatisfied with the work of the British and American parties from the time of the adoption of the "hard" line in 1928. In 1929, a serious disagreement with the American Communist Party had occupied the Comintern, and Moscow found it far from easy to bring the members of that party to follow the line expected from them. As for the British party, in spite of (or perhaps because of) the fact that by 1929 the members who remained in the Communist Party of Great Britain were reduced to an almost slavish submission, it had failed to develop into a significant organization and enlist new members. Nor were the organizations closely associated with the CPGB, which were expected to serve as "transmission belts" between the party and the masses, doing any better—the National Minority movement, the National Unemployed Workers' movement, the United Mine Workers of Scotland, and the United Clothing Workers, the last two of which were affiliated with the Profintern. Such was the situation in the CPGB, in spite of financial assistance from Moscow and the presence of Petrovsky (Max Goldfarb, alias A. J. Bennet), a representative of the Comintern, in England. Equally unsatisfactory was the situation in the American Communist Party. S. I. Gusev, the head of the Anglo-American Secretariat of the Comintern, spoke at length on the subject at the Twelfth Plenum (Document 85).

The situation in the German party appeared much more satisfactory. "The Communist Party of Germany," Piatnitsky told the Twelfth Plenum, "has achieved considerable successes, because it has a great power of attraction for the working masses, and has added to its membership in the course of eighteen months several hundred thousand members. In addition, the party gained over five million votes during the recent elections to the Reichstag, under difficult conditions."[9]

Continued Concern with Japan and China

The Communist Party of Japan continued to suffer defeats through arrests of its members, and the Comintern continued to send new leaders to take the place of those arrested. In 1932, the CPJ received still another outline of the policy to be followed. The new Theses (Document 80), which reached Japan in June by way of the West European Bureau of the Comintern in Berlin, were prepared in Moscow with the assistance of Sanzo Nosaka, who had succeeded in making his way there after two years of imprisonment in Japan and had become the right-hand man of the permanent Japanese delegate to the Comintern, Sen Katayama.

Japan at this time was steadily extending its military occupation of China. In February 1932, Manchukuo was proclaimed an independent state, conditions on the Chinese Eastern Railway were becoming daily more precarious, and a thrust by the Japanese army into Siberia seemed imminent. The tactics prescribed for the Japanese communists were designed to remove this threat. Political disturbances within Japan would be particularly useful in this respect, and this was the plan of action for the CPJ. The Theses of 1932 proposed a policy similar to Lenin's tactics in Russia in the early 1900's. The Japanese Emperor was to be the principal target of the Japanese communists, and all signs of dissatisfaction with the existing regime among the Japanese people were to be utilized in order to do away with the "remnants of feudalism." The Theses proposed a bourgeois-democratic revolution for Japan as the first stage toward communism; no immediate proletarian revolution was to be expected. But after the overthrow of the monarchy the main task would be "the struggle for the rapid transformation of the bourgeois-democratic revolution into a socialist revolution."

Toward the end of 1932, practically all members of the CPJ's Executive Committee were arrested. Another Japanese communist was sent by Moscow, Kesami Yamamoto, and by January 1933 he had succeeded in reassembling the remaining party members. On May 3, however, he also was arrested, and more arrests followed. Thus the CPJ was soon reduced to a mere handful of revolutionaries scattered throughout the country.

By 1932–33 there was much less personal contact between the Soviet Union and Chinese communists. Pavel Mif, the last Comintern representative, was sent to China in 1931. But interest in China, if not direct assistance, was not lacking on the part of the Comintern; the Theses of the Thirteenth Plenum of the ECCI (December 1933) maintained that the soviet revolution in China had become "an important factor of the world revolution." (See Document 109. For Varga's analysis in 1932 of the situation in the Far East see Document 81.)

Attempts at a United Front of Action with Socialists

Gusev's denunciation at the Twelfth Plenum of "social-fascists" as the greatest enemies of communism was one of the strongest communist blasts directed against social-democracy. (See Document 84. For the Resolution of the Twelfth Plenum of the ECCI on the tasks of the communist parties see Document 89.) In 1933, slowly and reluctantly, the communists began to turn toward a policy of closer association with the socialists. Hitler's coming to power accelerated this change. Yet the communists continued to underestimate the significance of Hitler's rise, and maintained their faith in the eventual triumph of the German communists. *Pravda* on March 7, 1933, stated that "the 4,800,000 revolutionary proletarians in Germany who voted for the Communist Party" had given a "fitting answer to the fascist dictatorship":

> The National Socialists maintain that they have won the election. They maintain that "on March 5, the nation pronounced its allegiance to them." The greatest significance of the results of this year's election lies in the fact that in spite of

the tremendously exaggerated votes allegedly cast for the National Socialists, the proletariat of Germany has remained faithful to the end to its revolutionary flag, to the heroic Communist Party of Germany.

. . .

The knot of domestic and foreign contradictions of German capitalism is tightening. Fascist policy aggravates these contradictions in every way. There is no other class but the proletariat which could lead the country away from the state of hunger and poverty and break the fetters imposed on the toilers as the result of the criminal imperialist war. It is this class and its communist party that will say the last word in the developing class battles.

It was true, wrote Knorin in the *Kommunisticheskii International* on February 10, 1933,[10] that the German proletariat was faced with a great danger as the result of Hitler's appointment as Reich Chancellor, since the main task of the new government would be to smash Bolshevism in Germany and to fight against world communism in general. However, he added, the setting up of a fascist government in Germany was actually a sign of the weakness of the German bourgeoisie:

It signifies that the usual methods of oppressing the working masses by means of an ordinary state apparatus, in order to ensure the rule of the exploiting class, are already inadequate. It means that social-democracy is already incapable of holding back the masses from going over to the camp of the communist party, and from decisive struggle against the bourgeoisie.

This interpretation of the Nazi movement, and consequently of the aims of the new German government, determined the communists' tasks: they were to undermine the government by hampering the application of its measures, and at the same time to prepare the masses for its overthrow. The Comintern evidently did not feel that the German communists were ready for immediate revolutionary action against the new government. Continuing his evaluation of the German situation, Knorin wrote:

The Hitler government's coming to power enormously accelerates the maturing of the revolutionary crisis. Even more than before, the question of Germany is becoming the central question of the revolutionary movement of Europe, and of the entire world. Now more than ever before, the tempo of the maturing revolutionary crisis of all of Europe will depend upon the development of events in Germany.

He concluded that the next few weeks and months would "determine the course of further development of the proletarian world revolution, of which Germany is the focal point." (For an evaluation of the German situation by the Presidium of the ECCI on April 1, 1933, see Document 95.)

But despite the Nazi threat, communist leaders still insisted on "unity" of the working class on their terms. On the eve of Hitler's assumption of power, Maurice Thorez, the general secretary of the CPF, wrote in an editorial in *L'Humanité* of January 18, 1933, that his party was awaiting a response from the French Socialist Party to a communist proposal of united action: "We appeal to each communist worker, to each organization of our party, to make fraternal efforts of persuasion and to try to convince the socialist workers of the urgent need *for a united front from below* [italics supplied] to defend the daily needs, to struggle against war, and to be able to combat systematically and persistently the bourgeoisie and its supporters."

On January 31, 1933, the day after Hitler was made Reich Chancellor, the CPG issued an appeal for a general strike: "Workers! Do not permit the mortal enemies of the German people, the mortal enemies of the workers and poor peasants, of the toilers of the cities and the countryside, to carry on their crimes!" The appeal urged united action against "counterrevolution":

> Everyone into the streets! Stop all work in the factories! Immediately organize a general strike . . . Men and women workers! Young workers of all enterprises, of all trade-unions, of all workers' organizations! Arise to a general strike against the fascist dictatorship! . . . The Communist Party of Germany appeals to the proletariat as a whole, and at the same time to the all-German alliance of reformist trade-unions, to the confederation of the employees' trade-unions, to the social-democratic party and the Christian trade-unions, and calls on them to organize jointly with the communists a general strike against the fascist dictatorship of Hitler, Hugenberg, Papen, against the suppression of workers' organizations, for freedom of the working class. . . . Long live a united proletarian front against the fascist dictatorship![11]

The strike called by the communists did not take place, but a new move toward socialist unity was made on February 4–5, this time by seven left-wing socialist parties at a conference in Paris: the Norwegian Labor Party, the British Independent Labour Party, and the independent socialist parties of Holland, Poland, Germany, Italy, and France. An appeal addressed to all workers by the conference stated:

> As workers we have common interests. Whatever our differ-
> ences, we know that our first, most important task must be to
> break and defeat the attacks made upon us. So long as the
> Reaction maintains its power, not a single demand of ours, not
> even one of our aims, can be realized. The essential first duty is
> to defeat the Reaction.
> We cannot do that, any one of us, with our own forces
> singly and in isolation. Our divisions enfeeble us; our forces are
> spent on mutual struggle instead of being directed at the
> common enemy. . . . A united proletarian front of all workers
> is an imperative necessity. That is the primary condition of a
> successful fight against the Reaction and of an advance to
> achieve socialism.

On February 19, the Bureau of the Labour and Socialist International made an even clearer statement:

> The danger is too great for the universal desire of the workers
> for a common fight by the whole of the working class to be used
> for partisan political maneuvers . . . The Labour and Social-
> ist International has always been ready to negotiate with the
> Communist International with a view to common action as
> soon as this body is also ready.

On February 24, the International Committee of the Left Independent Socialist parties appealed directly to the two Internationals (Socialist and Communist) to collaborate in creating working-class unity to defeat "capitalist reaction and fascist terrorism."[12]

It was now up to the Comintern to make clear its stand. On March 5, the ECCI issued a manifesto calling for a united front of struggle against the "fascist offensive of the bourgeoisie," and above all against the German bourgeoisie (Document 93). But the manifesto accused the social-democratic parties of having exposed the international proletariat to the blows of the class enemy and allowing the triumph of fascist reaction in Germany. The manifesto then enumerated efforts made previously by the communists for united action with the socialists, and the latter's refusal to collaborate. Referring to the declaration of the Bureau of the Labour and Socialist International (LSI) of February 19, the manifesto stated that the earlier policy of the LSI justified the "Communist International and the communist parties in putting no faith in the sincerity of the declaration of the LSI Bureau." Nevertheless the ECCI called on individual communist parties to set up a united front with social-democratic workers "without waiting for the results of negotiations and agreements with social-democracy," i.e., still the "united front from below," the capture of the socialist rank and file.

Following the instructions of the ECCI, the leaders of the various communist parties proceeded to approach the socialist parties and the trade-unions in their respective countries with a view to united action. In evaluating the situation in Germany, Piatnitsky spoke of earlier communist efforts to set up a united front with the German Social-Democratic Party. On January 30 and March 1, 1933, stated Piatnitsky, the German Communist Party made a proposal to the German Federation of Trade Unions and to the German Social-Democratic Party (SPG) for a common fight against fascism. It had also proposed a general strike as early as July 2, 1932. In all these cases, however, Piatnitsky claimed, the communist proposals were rejected. Referring to the terrorist methods used by the fascists against the social-democrats, Piatnitsky said,

> One would have thought that after all this the leaders of the SPG and of the trade unions would have had to accept the proposals of the CPG to organize a common struggle against the fascist provocation and terror and call a general strike. Instead of a common united struggle the SPG and the trade union bureaucracy found a new formula of the "lesser evil." Hitler, they declared, came to power by legal means, and had been nominated by Hindenburg, and the majority of the people approved this. The SPG promised to carry on legal opposition if the fascists did not go beyond the bounds of the Weimar Constitution.[13]

It is worth noting that a year later Piatnitsky somewhat changed his evaluation of the failure of the communists and social-democrats in Germany to cooperate in 1932 and 1933:

> The reason why the CPG was unable to rouse the workers to the strikes of July 20, 1932, January 30 and March 5, 1933, is

well known. The great mistake made by the communists was that they carried on insufficiently energetic mass work, work in the trade unions and in the factories. The one thing is connected with the other. The poor mass work of the Communist Party of Germany made it impossible for the party to carry the masses with it despite the reformists, and this helped toward the fact that the call of the CPG on January 30 and March 5, 1933, at the decisive moment in the struggle against fascism, met with an insignificant response.[14]

In this passage, Piatnitsky tacitly admitted that the communists had made no effort to cooperate with the social-democratic leadership. But documentary evidence on the real communist policy in Germany is also available. One of the most revealing statements is a speech by Ernst Thälmann, the German communist leader, to the Twelfth Plenum of the ECCI, published in the English-language edition of the Comintern journal two weeks before Hitler came to power:

> Comrades, I want now to deal with the question, in how far the leaders of Social-Democracy, and their policy, have undergone a swing towards fascism. . . .
>
> Social-Democracy's policy of consistent toleration towards the Bruening Cabinet was and still is an active help for fascism. . . . the Social-Democrats kept up a talk about the "danger of a Nazi *Putsch*" . . . that a possible Schleicher-Hitler Government, and an actual Papen Government are after all better than a "pure" Hitler Government. . . . any weakening of our struggle in principle against Social-Democracy, as representing the main social support of the bourgeoisie, would be a grievous mistake, especially because the neglect of this struggle might produce new and dangerous illusions among the masses, to the effect that the Social-Democratic Party is an anti-fascist force. . . .
>
> In accordance with the Party line, and with the help of the Comintern, and of the resolutions that have been passed, our Party has of late been combating, with great success, all tendencies to weaken the struggle in principle against Social-Democracy, and has fought with all severity against all conceptions that the main offensive within the working-class ought no longer to be directed against Social-Democracy and against all deviations in this field.

After the coming into power of the Papen Government, certain tendencies to deviation from the general line of the Party in this fundamental question of our policy and tactics manifested themselves among individual comrades in Germany. . . . the proposals of the Berlin district leadership—proposals which were made to the Social-Democratic Party with a view to the holding of joint demonstrations, and which were rightly rejected by the Central Committee of our Party . . . expressed an over-estimation of the degree of maturity attained by the Social-Democratic workers, and an under-estimation of our own power among the working-class for the organisation of widespread demonstrations of the united front from below, coupled with a surrender in the face of certain sentimental feelings in favour of unity . . . The Social-Democratic workers are already beginning today to pay far more attention to the slogans of the Communist Party . . . It will be our task . . . to tear away the mass of its adherents from Social-Democracy . . .[15]

The lead editorial in the same journal three and a half months later admitted that no effort had been made to cooperate with the social-democratic leadership: the Communists "repeatedly proposed to the Social-Democratic *workers* and the *lower* Social-Democratic organisations that a united front be formed" (italics supplied). "But the mass of the Social-Democratic workers . . . being fettered by their Social-Democratic leaders . . . rejected the united front with the Communists on every occasion, and disrupted the struggle of the working class."[16]

The Central Committee of the CPF, once it received instructions for cooperation with the socialists, sent a proposal to the Permanent Administrative Commission of the French Socialist Party to hold jointly a national day of street manifestations in favor of the French workers' demands and aid to the German workers. An immediate reply was requested, but none was received. The Socialist and Labour International instructed all its affiliated branches to await its own decisions as to what course to take. The communists continued to press the point, and on March 11, Thorez declared in *L'Humanité* that the immediate establishment of a united front was necessary, possible, and indispensable. It was only because the socialist leaders were fearful of the success of such an undertaking, he argued, that they found " a million pretexts in order to be able to reject our proposals and to prevent the realization of the united front." At a session of the Executive Committee of the Socialist and Labour International on May 19, it was resolved that since contacts between the two Internationals had not given positive results, the Socialist and Labour International would advise the various parties affiliated with it to abstain from separate negotiations. The Italian communists proposed a united front with the social-democratic, Maximalist, and Republican workers and the leading committees of these parties. A draft agreement was actually drawn up by these parties and the Communist Party of Italy, but here too no further progress was made.[17]

In the United States, in line with the policy outlined in the Comintern's manifesto of March 5, the American Communist Party addressed letters to the national committees of the Socialist Party, the American Federation of Labor, and the Conference of the Progressive Labor Action (CPLA) proposing a united action against the capitalists and joint action against fascism. The A.F. of L. ignored the proposal. The National Executive of the Socialist Party discussed the proposal and decided first to set up a joint negotiation committee. The CPLA, while not making any definite agreement with the communist party, participated with it in a number of united actions.[18]

Special efforts were made to set up a united front in Great Britain. In accordance with the Comintern's instructions, the CPGB sent a letter on March 10 to the executive bodies of the Labour Party, the Independent Labour Party, and the General Council of the Trades Union Congress, as well as to the executive organ of the cooperative organizations. The letter proposed that these organizations send representatives to a conference on March 17 in order to reach a "common agreement for the carrying out of a concrete program of action against the capitalist offensive and fascism." Conditions for the agreement were outlined.[19] Only the Independent Labour Party (ILP) welcomed the proposal and expressed its readiness to participate in a conference; at its annual meeting at Derby it voted in favor of unity with the Comintern. The other organizations merely stated that the proposal would be considered, and later declined it.

On May 2 the Comintern addressed a letter to the ILP welcoming the decision to leave the Second International and approach the Communist International "with a view to ascertaining in what ways the ILP may assist in the work of the International."[20]

On May 18 the ILP sent the Comintern the text of a resolution voted at its annual conference. To this Kuusinen replied in the name of the Comintern with an outline of further steps to achieve unity of action between the communists and the ILP. If the ILP wished to join in the struggle against the bourgeoisie and the Second International, Kuusinen stated, its help would be welcome. But he warned against the idea that "the deep divergence of principle between the Second International and the Communist International could be covered up by an unprincipled rapprochement and conciliation." (Document 101.)

In response, the ILP proposed a conference of all organizations prepared to cooperate on a revolutionary socialist basis. The letter, signed by John Paton, the secretary of the party, stated:

> In our view the present disastrous position of the international working class movement is due to the failure of the policies of both the Labour and Socialist International and the Communist International. The social democratic and labour parties attached to the former have pursued policies of reformism and compromise which have proved disastrous in a situation which demanded a bold revolutionary lead and action. On the other hand, the Communist International has pursued policies which have divided and weakened the industrial organizations of the workers, and which, by treating sections of the working class outside its own ranks as enemies indistinguishable from fascists and the most reactionary capitalists, have prevented that united action by the working class which alone could have defeated the forces of fascism and capitalism.

The letter outlined a plan of cooperation and proposed to call a "world congress of all organizations which are prepared to cooperate on a revolutionary socialist basis." The invitation to the congress would be sent to the communist parties as well as to other organizations of the working class.[21] The position of the ILP was further clarified by A. Fenner Brockway in an editorial in the *New Leader* on July 14:

> We are prepared to cooperate with the Communist Party and the Communist International in the fight against fascism, war, and capitalist reaction. But cooperation does not mean identification. We have faith in our policy, our tactics, and our personnel. We want to see one revolutionary movement in this country, and one revolutionary International in the world. But the Communist Party of Great Britain is not equal to the task in this country. The British revolutionary movement will develop

from much wider elements than that, and to it the ILP is contributing much more than the Communist Party. Similarly the Communist International will have to change its tactics and organization if it is to be an adequate instrument of the international revolutionary forces outside it which will accept neither its tactics nor its organization. The task of the ILP is to bring all these forces together. If the Communist International will show greater breadth of view than the British communists are now doing, this object may be achieved during the coming year.

In reply to the proposal of a conference, the Comintern asserted in September that "nothing useful can come out of such a proposal" which was "basically the old idea of the ILP which dates back to 1920." The communists were proposing mass struggles for the defense of the vital everyday interests of the workers, for the liberation of the majority of the working class from the influence of the reformists. Social-democratic leaders did not want to struggle against the capitalists but rather to continue their collaboration with the bourgeoisie. But "we only look upon the social-democratic *parties* and the *leaders* of the reformist trade-unions as enemies, and not the trade-union organizations and the social-democratic workers." (Document 102.)

The divergence of viewpoint was now fully apparent. The Comintern's reply was definitely disappointing to the ILP. "Some evil genius seems to advise Comintern," stated an editorial in the *New Leader* of September 29:

Comintern does not want immediate cooperation of the ILP. Indeed its reply is not addressed to the National Council. It is addressed to the party membership, with the object of arousing antagonism to the National Council and splitting the party . . . [But] the effect of the Comintern's attitude has been not to draw them toward the C.I., but to make them despair of the C. I. We regret this. We shall still make a supreme effort to find a basis of cooperation. If it fails, the responsibility will rest with Comintern and those who so foolishly advise it.

Still stronger criticism was expressed in the *New Leader* on November 3: The Comintern would not genuinely apply the tactics of united action. It was inadmissible for the Comintern, the *New Leader* maintained, to declare itself ready to renounce criticism of the so-called "nonaggression pact" only in the course of joint action.

Nor should the communists attempt to build up new so-called revolutionary trade-unions in opposition to the existing ones. The Comintern should, rather, concentrate all its efforts on winning every trade-unionist for a revolutionary trade-union policy. The slogan of "social-fascism" should be abandoned. An editorial in the *New Leader* of December 8 flatly rejected dictation from the Comintern: "Refusal to be dictated to does not mean refusal to consult and to cooperate, but it must be clearly understood that it is the latter and not the former which the rank and file of the ILP agreed upon at its annual conference."

Two more years were to pass, however, before cooperation with the social-democratic leadership, and not merely capture of social-democratic workers, was sought and effected by the communists. A clearer realization of the seriousness of the fascist threat was required to make the Comintern issue orders to all its sections to cooperate with the erstwhile enemies, the "social-fascists."

The Thirteenth Plenum of the ECCI on the World Situation and the Tasks of Communist Parties

Before new tactics were adopted, the old slogans were once more vigorously restated at the Thirteenth Plenum of the ECCI, which met in November–December 1933. This was the last plenum of the ECCI. It met as usual in Moscow. The chief speakers from the CPSU were Manuilsky, Kuusinen, Lozovsky, Knorin, and Piatnitsky. They stressed the approach of a new round of revolutions and wars, emphasized the serious need of preparing communist cadres for illegal work, and called for the general intensification of communist propaganda among workers and unemployed. The "entire international situation," said Kuusinen in his report, was one of "extreme tension":

> The League of Nations, which has been abandoned by Japan and Germany, and which Italy is preparing to abandon also, cannot even serve as a meeting place for an agreement between England and France, the two imperialist powers which have leaned on it more than others. The League of Nations no longer serves as a screen to conceal the furious preparations for war.[22]

The Theses adopted by the plenum dealt with the theme of Kuusinen's speech (Documents 108–9) and called on communist parties all over the world to fulfill their duty. In propagandizing peace, Kuusinen said, communists should make it clear that their concept of peace was not that of the bourgeoisie. "Most of all it is a *Bolshevik* policy. It is a *revolutionary* peace policy, imbued with the *spirit of proletarian internationalism*." (Document 105.) The decay of capitalism and the general disintegration of the capitalist economy would not lead automatically to the collapse of capitalism, but rather to the transformation of the economic crisis into a revolutionary one. "The revolutionary vanguard of the proletariat," said Kuusinen, "must be able to take advantage most resolutely of this situation."[23]

The sections of the Comintern were to be ready for every eventuality. Hence the need of winning the majority of the workers, the need for the united front and close attention to the daily needs of the workers. "Activity in the factory is the starting point for the achievement of influence over the masses," stated Lozovsky at the Thirteenth Plenum. The task of the communists was to work in the fascist trade-unions, to "disintegrate them from within" and to "win over the workers who are in these unions."[24]

The Comintern still hoped that the CPG would be able to withstand the Nazis and unite all German workers. Piatnitsky spoke of the party's efforts during the first ten months of Hitler's regime. "Even the German fascists," he declared, "are compelled to admit that they have failed to smash and exterminate the Communist Party of Germany" (Document 106).

A significant document drafted by the Thirteenth Plenum was the resolution proposed for the eighth convention of the American Communist Party. In view of the official rejoicing expressed at that time in the Soviet press over the establishment of formal diplomatic relations between the two countries and the expected benefits, and in view of the special agreement to abstain from propaganda and all interference in the domestic affairs of the United States, the resolution drafted by the plenum is revealing. It severely attacked the New Deal of President Roosevelt, spoke of the "fascistization" of the United States, predicted the absolute inability of the American government to overcome the economic crisis, and outlined all the blessings that would accrue to the workers and the toiling people of the United States once a soviet regime had been established in that country. (Document 111.)

Finally, Knorin defined three points which would test every

communist party's revolutionary maturity, and also what was expected of every communist (Document 107).

NOTES

1. *XII Plenum IKKI: Stenograficheskii otchet* (Moscow, 1933), I, 6.
2. *Ibid.,* III, 164.
3. *Ibid.,* I, 19–20.
4. *Ibid.,* p. 21.
5. *Ibid.,* III, 120.
6. *Ibid.,* I, 31.
7. *Ibid.,* pp. 26–27.
8. *Ibid.,* II, 8–14.
9. *Ibid.,* p. 14.
10. Translation in *I.P.C.,* Vol. 13, No. 11, March 9, 1933, pp. 263–264.
11. *Iz istorii mezhdunarodnoi proletarskoi solidarnosti* (Moscow, 1957–61), V, 53–55; *L'Humanité,* January 31, 1933.
12. *New Leader* (London), March 10, 1933, p. 4.
13. *I.P.C.,* Vol. 13, No. 17, April 13, 1933, p. 388.
14. *K.I.,* No. 22, August 1, 1934, p. 36; *Communist International,* Vol. 11, No. 17, September 5, 1934, pp. 580–81.
15. E. Thälmann, "Unleash the Proletarian Rebellion!" *Communist International,* Vol. 10, No. 1, January 15, 1933, pp. 26–44.
16. "Resolution of the Presidium of the E.C.C.I. on the Report of Comrade Heckert on the Situation in Germany," *Communist International,* Vol. 10, No. 8, May 1, 1933, p. 244.
17. *I.P.C.,* Vol. 13, No. 24, June 2, 1933, p. 530.
18. *I.P.C.,* Vol. 13, No. 22, May 19, 1933, p. 484.
19. *I.P.C.,* Vol. 13, No. 16, April 7, 1933, p. 365.
20. *I.P.C.,* Vol. 13, No. 20, May 5, 1933, p. 447.
21. *New Leader,* July 14, 1933, p. 10.
22. *XIII Plenum IKKI: stenograficheskii otchet* (Moscow, 1934), pp. 13–14.
23. *Ibid.,* pp. 12–13.
24. *Ibid.,* pp. 384, 386. See also Document 110.

7

The Turn in Soviet Foreign Policy, 1934

The year 1934 was a landmark in Soviet foreign policy. Not only were closer relations sought with neighboring and other European powers, but a marked change took place in relations with France and in the attitude toward the League of Nations. There was also the beginning of a major shift in the Comintern's line, from the policy of the "united front from below" to that of the "united front from above." It would be a mistake, however, to overemphasize the significance of these changes. The old communist image of the capitalist world was by no means abandoned. It was merely that a new combination of forces and new conditions in the world situation called for new tactics to reach the same goals.

There were two major reasons for the change in tactics: The first was Japan's continued aggression in China, bringing with it constant difficulties in the functioning of the Chinese Eastern Railway, which was still under Soviet control, and, more serious, the imminent threat of an attack on the Soviet Union. The second reason was the threat from Germany. As the Nazis tightened their grip, it became clear to the Soviet leaders that they could expect no imminent collapse of the Hitler regime.

A marked stiffening in the Soviet attitude toward Germany followed, manifested particularly in the words and actions of Foreign Commissar Litvinov. The German ambassador in Moscow, Rudolf Nadolny, noticed the change in the course of a long conversation with Litvinov on January 4, 1934. To Nadolny's remark that the Franco-Soviet rapprochement might be directed against Germany, Litvinov replied that France, Poland, and the Little Entente were sincerely trying to keep the peace, and therefore the Soviet Union had moved closer to this group. When Nadolny asked whether Litvinov envisaged a broadening of the Berlin treaty of April 24, 1926, or something of the sort, Litvinov replied that the Soviet Union had no such desire. "I [Nadolny] broke off the conversation with the statement that I was very dissatisfied and concerned about the way it had turned out; Litvinov's intransigent attitude must necessarily lead to consequences that were not in the interest of the relations of either country. At that he shrugged his shoulders."[1]

But a few days later Radek was interviewed by a German journalist on the general state of Soviet foreign policy, the Soviet government's rapprochement with France, and its attitude to Germany. Radek, who for years had favored close ties with Germany, still believed that relations between the two countries might take a turn for the better as soon as there was a relaxation of tension in the Far East. Assuring his interrogator that no final decision on Soviet foreign policy had been made, Radek stressed again the Soviet desire for peace: "We do not want war, not only for tactical but also for strategic reasons. . . . technology will have made such tremendous advances in ten years at the latest that . . . all the present war materials and defenses will prove to be ridiculous."[2] In an article published in *Izvestiia* on New Year's Day, 1934, Radek analyzed the threat to peace posed by Germany and Japan, and emphasized the determination of the Soviet Union to avoid war. "*The U.S.S.R.,*" he concluded, "*will support every force that is directed against war*" (Document 113).

The unmistakable threat to vital Soviet interests posed by Nazi Germany introduced confusion and uncertainty into the formulation of Soviet foreign policy. Instead of a single voice and a single line, Soviet policy toward Germany spoke in a number of voices, following a number of different lines. Radek and Litvinov voiced similar but by no means identical views, and early in 1934 another point of view made its appearance: at the Seventeenth Party Congress, Bukharin presented an analysis of Soviet foreign policy problems which differed in important respects from those of both Radek and Litvinov. He envisaged a double pressure on the Soviet Union, from Germany in the West and Japan in the East, and added with grim humor, "It appears therefore that we shall be forced to find a place for our Union's entire population of 160 million somewhere, perhaps in one of the furnaces of Magnitostroi."[3]

The Seventeenth Party Congress

The Seventeenth Party Congress, which met from January 26 to February 10, 1934, dealt with two major points insofar as the international situation was concerned: first, the theoretical prognosis of a revolutionary upsurge among the proletariat throughout the world as a consequence of the world economic crisis, and, second, the threat from Japan and Germany. Stalin, the first speaker, dealt at length with the first point. "The working class of the U.S.S.R.," he said, "is part of the world proletariat, its vanguard, and our republic is the offspring of the world proletariat. . . . International ties and fraternal union between the workers of the U.S.S.R. and the workers of all countries represent one of the cornerstones of the strength and might of the Republic of Soviets." In Stalin's opinion the masses were not yet ready to "storm the citadel of capitalism," but the idea was maturing in the minds of the masses. Energetic efforts were needed, however, to speed up this maturing instead of waiting for the bourgeoisie to fall. "The victory of revolution," he said, "never comes by itself. It has to be prepared and won; only a strong proletarian revolutionary party can prepare and win it."[4]

Manuilsky maintained that during the five years of the world economic crisis the disintegration of the capitalist system had gone so far that the "objective prerequisites for a revolutionary crisis" had "already matured in the weakest links of the capitalist system." He spoke of the breakup of the Versailles system and of the inevitability of clashes of "tremendous force" between states and between classes. Basically, however, he defended the view that the rise of fascism in Germany signified an increase in the prospects for proletarian revolution. (Document 115.)

Voroshilov in his speech to the congress stressed the danger from Japan and the measures being taken in the Soviet Union to guard against that danger.[5] And V. K. Blücher, commander in chief of the Special Far Eastern Army, said that the party and the Soviet government had done everything possible to relieve the growing tension in the Far East, but added, "Unfortunately . . . the policy of the Japanese imperialists gives us no assurance that we will not be drawn into military complications despite all our efforts to avoid them." The Soviet Union, he emphasized, did not want to wage war against anyone; it was fully occupied with its domestic tasks under the Five-Year Plan. (Document 117.) In his final address to the congress, Manuilsky also analyzed the threat of attack on the Soviet Union from Japan and Germany, but assured his listeners that in reality the aggressive plans of the two powers were bringing closer the world-wide victory of the proletarian revolution (Document 116).

Extension of the Nonaggression Pacts with the Baltic States and Poland

To meet the threat of German aggression the Soviet leaders sought to strengthen ties with neighboring countries. On April 4, 1934, protocols were signed in Moscow on a ten-year prolongation of the pacts of nonaggression between the Soviet Union and Estonia, Latvia, and Lithuania. On April 7, another protocol similarly extended the Soviet-Finnish nonaggression pact of January 1932. And on May 5 still another protocol extended the 1932 nonaggression pact with Poland to 1945. On the occasion of signing the protocols on April 4, Litvinov emphasized that the nonaggression pacts actually were due to expire eighteen months later. "The paying of a promissory note before maturity," Litvinov said, "is evidence of the good will as well as the excellent financial position of the debtor. In the present case the premature concern of our governments with the terms of pacts which still have a considerable time to run, proves their good will and their great desire for peace." Litvinov went on to emphasize the unprecedented speed of the negotiations. "This circumstance," he said, "points also to the tremendous growth of confidence and mutual understanding between our countries."[6]

On April 5, *Pravda* stated that the prolongation of the nonaggression pacts with the Baltic states represented "a new link in the chain of victories in the policy of peace of the Soviet Union." The Baltic sector of eastern Europe, *Pravda* said, was "specially threatened by the plans of various rascals, such as Herr Rosenberg, who think of the Baltic states as a passageway and a staging area for the realization of their plans, the *Drang nach Osten*." *Pravda* voiced "profound confidence that the protocol signed in Moscow will serve the cause of the strengthening of peace in eastern Europe, and will also prove to be a firm foundation for the development of friendly relations between our country and our Baltic neighbors" (Document 118). In its commentary on the Soviet-Polish protocol, *Pravda* called particular attention to the significance of a special addition which provided that the two countries should be *"bound by no obligations and no binding declarations which would be in conflict with Article Three of the Riga peace treaty,"* i.e., the Soviet-Polish treaty of March 18, 1921, under which the two states agreed to *"renounce all claims to territory lying beyond the Soviet-Polish boundaries established by the peace treaty"* (Document 121).

The Proposal to Germany to Guarantee the Baltic States

On March 28, 1934, Litvinov proposed that in order to consolidate the peace of the world in general and of eastern Europe in particular, and to improve Soviet-German relations, the two governments should sign a protocol by which they would "assume the obligation of unfailingly taking into account in their foreign policy the maintenance of the independence and inviolability of the Baltic countries, refraining from any actions which might prove directly or indirectly harmful to this independence." The protocol was to remain open for signature by other countries.

On April 14, Nadolny informed Litvinov that his government declined the Soviet proposal (Document 119). A week later Litvinov replied that Germany's refusal to accept the Soviet proposal was in itself important, especially since the explanations given by the German government had done nothing to diminish the significance of the refusal. He also wished, he said, to point out certain incorrect explanations regarding the aims and motives of the Soviet proposal assumed by the German government, such as the suggestion that a similar proposal had first been made to Poland. What was actually proposed to Poland, Litvinov said, was a joint Soviet-Polish declaration on their "determination to protect and defend peace in the east of Europe." Nor was the protocol proposed to Germany aimed against any other countries, as no proposal had ever been made to establish a protectorate over the Baltic states. In regard to the German contention that the Berlin treaty of 1926 provided all the necessary requirements for friendly relations between the Soviet Union and Germany, Litvinov said: "The Berlin treaty, important and valuable as it is, does not cover those questions affecting the Soviet Union which have been brought into being by the new international situation and by the policy of the new German government."[7] Commenting on the German reply, *Izvestiia* on April 28 stated:

> If Berlin listened with a more sensitive ear to everything giving evidence of a threat against peace (and Berlin is not a bad place to observe the development of this danger), the German answer would not have contained the assertion, so contradictory to generally known facts, that the Soviet proposal was lacking in any foundation if considered from the angle of *Realpolitik*. The entire world press has been declaring for many months that the peace of Eastern Europe was in danger and that the future independent existence of the Baltic countries was in question . . .
>
> Under these circumstances the German refusal places a grave responsibility on Germany. German political circles must explain to themselves one very simple thing: the whole world knows and the whole world will remember that the U.S.S.R. proposed a concrete method for improving the atmosphere in Eastern Europe and that Germany rejected that method, adducing arguments therefor quite lacking in foundation and not relating directly to the matter in question.[8] [For *Pravda's* comment of the same date, see Document 120.]

The Changed Soviet Attitude Toward the League of Nations

By May 1934 a distinct shift in Soviet foreign policy had become apparent. Its most marked aspect was a more favorable attitude toward the League of Nations. The change did not occur all at once, but developed step by step. In reporting on the Manchurian situation to the Central Executive Committee on January 23, 1933, Molotov had stressed the League's inability to come to any decision on Manchuria although one commission after another had been created by it to study the situation there: "There is progress in only one respect, and that is the further discrediting of the League of Nations in the eyes of the whole world. But you are well aware of the fact that we have never tied up our hopes with the League of Nations and its commissions."[9]

But at the end of the same year, speaking at a session of the

Central Executive Committee on December 28, 1933, Molotov slightly modified his characterization: Germany and Japan had withdrawn from the League because membership was an impediment: "even the League of Nations stands to some extent in the way of 'freedom' of action for the interventionists." Such a "brake on the forces making for war must be recognized as a positive fact." On December 25, 1933, Stalin had expressed a similar view in an interview with the *New York Times* correspondent, Walter Duranty, when he said that "the League may act in some degree like a brake, retarding or preventing the outbreak of hostilities." And Litvinov was even more explicit in his report to the Central Executive Committee on December 29, 1933: "Not being doctrinaires, we do not refuse to use international associations or organizations, whether those already in existence or those which may be founded in the future, if we have or shall have reason to believe that they serve the cause of peace."[10]

A decisive step in the shift in Soviet policy towards the League occurred on May 18, 1934, when French Foreign Minister Barthou made the formal suggestion to Litvinov that the U.S.S.R. should become a member of the League and received a favorable reply. To help prepare Soviet public opinion for the change, Radek published an important article in *Pravda* on May 29 (Document 123).

Meanwhile, Litvinov at Geneva continued his efforts to secure peace through collective security. At the session of the General Commission of the Disarmament Conference on May 29, he spoke of the apparent inability of delegates even to come to a common conclusion on the reasons for failure to solve the problem of disarmament. Various Soviet proposals on disarmament or reduction of armaments had found no approval among the delegates. Irreconcilable differences of opinion on the problem of disarmament existed among the members of the conference. Now the delegates were faced with the question of the future of the conference. "Hence the question before us," said Litvinov,

> is not one of disarmament itself, since that is only a means to an end, but of guaranteeing peace. And since this is so, the question naturally arises, cannot the conference steer its way toward other guarantees for peace; or at any rate, may it not increase the measure of security for at least those states which, cherishing no aggressive designs, are not interested in war and which, in the event of war, may therefore become only the objects of attack?

Litvinov expressed himself as being in favor of such guarantees and of regional pacts:

> . . . We must not create universal pacts which would exclude any state wishing to participate or such regional pacts as would not admit all those interested in security of the particular region concerned. In measures of security of this kind, the principle of equality of all states without any exception must not arouse any doubt or hesitation.
>
> If we proceed along these lines the time and energy spent on the conference will not have been in vain and we shall not return empty-handed to the people who sent us here. . . .

Litvinov said that he did not wish to limit the scope of the Conference on Disarmament, but that he proposed something much more substantial, namely, "the transformation of this conference into a permanent body concerned to preserve by every possible means the security of all states and to safeguard universal peace. In other words, I propose that this conference be transformed into a permanent and regularly assembling conference of peace."[11] (For *Pravda*'s comment see Document 124.) And on June 4 Litvinov submitted to the General Commission of the Conference on Disarmament a draft resolution embodying the plan for a permanent peace commission (Document 126).

Closer Ties with France and Efforts for an Eastern Pact

In the field of diplomacy the Soviet Union was now tending toward a rapprochement with France and the Little Entente countries, while France, on its part, fearing Germany, was now ready to meet the Soviet Union halfway. Bilateral nonaggression pacts, however, were no longer considered sufficient by the Soviet policy-makers; their goal was now regional pacts. The establishment of closer ties with France was considered particularly important. An editorial in *Pravda* on May 28, 1934 (Document 122) spoke favorably of the French Foreign Minister's speech in the Chamber of Deputies which was devoted chiefly to Franco-Soviet relations and to the Soviet role in the struggle for peace. Not only would such a rapprochement be advantageous to the U.S.S.R., but it was also bound to dispose the small countries to seek closer relations with the Soviet Union.

Following France's new policy, Czechoslovakia and Rumania, her allies in the Little Entente, established diplomatic relations with the Soviet Union on June 9, 1934. This development, an editorial in *Pravda* on June 10 commented, "wrests a further trump from the hands of those adventurous elements who continue to oppose the guarantee of security and who are hatching military intrigues" (Document 127). But the position taken by Great Britain disturbed the Soviet leaders. "Certain circles of British imperialism," wrote Maiorsky, the *Pravda* correspondent in London on June 1, 1934, "have been working quite actively toward transforming the conference on disarmament *into a conference on armament.*" According to Maiorsky's analysis, Germany and Japan were simply being used by English imperialism to prepare for an attack on the Soviet Union. (Document 125.)

As early as 1933 the French had proposed a mutual security pact, sometimes referred to as an Eastern Locarno. French Foreign Minister Barthou discussed the idea in London on July 9, 1934, and an editorial in *Pravda* on July 16 stated that according to numerous foreign press reports and the official communiqués about the London negotiations, the pact would include the U.S.S.R., Germany, Poland, Czechoslovakia, and the Baltic states. All signatories would guarantee each other's frontiers. But to make the pact fully successful, the entrance of the U.S.S.R. into the League of Nations was imperative. The objections by some countries, the editorial said, were irrelevant, while individuals who were "critically disposed" to multilateral agreements, and those who preferred bilateral agreements, seemed "not yet to realize the significance of the changes which have taken place in the international situation" and were "continuing to live in the past." (Document 132.) Two days earlier, an editorial in *Pravda* had noted with approval a change in the British attitude toward Soviet Russia, particularly Sir John Simon's remark in the House of Commons on July 13, when he said, "We are dealing with a huge and powerful state of 160 million people which is bound to bear a profound influence on history and the development of the world."[12]

Litvinov had used every occasion to stress the need of regional pacts. The disarmament problem, he said on June 23 in an interview with Jules Sauerwein, correspondent of *Paris-Soir,* "does not lend itself to a solution," and, as to the Kellogg Pact and the League of Nations Covenant, "since both of these have already been violated with impunity, they can no longer satisfy anybody as guarantees of peace." Neither did bilateral nonaggression pacts always serve the cause of peace. "The most avowedly aggressive state may conclude pacts of nonaggression with some states in order to free its hands and secure its rear or flanks for an attack on other states." In the case of regional pacts of mutual assistance, however, every state in a given area could join and need not "consider itself encircled or subject to any danger if it shares the other signatories' desire for peace."[13]

In late July the Soviet government formally invited Germany to join. The Soviet Union was prepared to guarantee Germany's western frontiers and France's eastern frontier. The French government, on its part, would guarantee Germany's eastern and the Soviet Union's western frontiers, while Germany would guarantee the Soviet western and French eastern frontiers. Germany, however, opposed the East European pact, as was made clear in notes of September 10 to the interested governments.[14]

On September 13, *Pravda* analyzed the points raised in the German reply. The interpretation of the pact as an encirclement was groundless, according to *Pravda*. Nor could such a pact be regarded as a violation of existing normal conditions. The delay in the reply had already aroused misgivings about the sincerity of German peace declarations. "The German answer still further strengthens these doubts." (Document 134.) On the other hand, because of Germany's aloofness from any international commitments, and because of the German-Polish rapprochement, the Soviet press suspected a "crack in the French-Polish alliance" and even a possibility of Poland's withdrawal from the League of Nations.[15]

The Soviet Union Joins the League of Nations

On September 15, 1934, an invitation from thirty–four members of the League was delivered to the Soviet government. It received a prompt reply from Litvinov accepting the invitation. (For *Pravda*'s comment, see Document 135.) Litvinov's maiden speech at the League Assembly on September 18 was an effective expression of the alleged Soviet desire for peace and for equality among all nations. The Soviet Union itself, Litvinov said, was an association of different peoples uniting more than 200 nationalities which were enjoying complete equality of rights. All nationalities, he said, were naturally united by a common political and economic regime and by common aspirations toward a single ideal. "The Soviet Union has, however, never excluded the possibility of some form or other of associations with states having a different political and social system, so long as there is no mutual hostility and if it is for the attainment of common aims."

Litvinov then spoke of the peaceful coexistence of different socio-political systems under conditions of reciprocal noninterference in domestic affairs. He mentioned the already existing cases of Soviet association with other states outside the framework of the League of Nations which had shown such association to be desirable and possible.

> For its part, the Soviet government, following attentively all developments of international life, could not but observe the increasing activity in the League of Nations of the states interested in the preservation of peace and their struggle against aggressive militarist elements. . . . All this could not be without influence on the attitude towards the League of Nations of the Soviet government, ever searching for further means for the organization of peace, for cooperation in which we have been invited to come here.

Litvinov praised peace. "The organization of peace! Could there be a loftier and at the same time more practical and urgent task for the cooperation of all nations?"

> The failure of the Disarmament Conference, on which formerly such high hopes were placed, in its turn compels us to seek more effective means. . . . We must realize once and for all that no war with political or economic aims is capable of restoring so-called historical justice, and that all it could do would be to substitute new and perhaps still more glaring injustices for old ones.[16]

On September 20, an editorial in *Pravda* stated : "The entry of the Soviet Union into the League of Nations . . . represents an important and serious event, a great step in the struggle for peace." The principles which had guided the Soviet government in the decision to join the League, the editorial said, could be summarized as the struggle for peace by all available means. And the U.S.S.R. would continue this struggle and was prepared for the most far-reaching collaboration within and outside the League, "not only in the interest of its own security, but also in the interests of all of

toiling mankind, in the interests of the international proletariat."
(Document 136.) An editorial in *Kommunisticheskii Internatsional*, also on September 20, gave a somewhat clearer communist interpretation of the Soviet entry into the League. It claimed
that this step was "a new outstanding victory for the Soviet Union's
foreign policy," but in no way represented acceptance by the
U.S.S.R. of the social-democrats' policies in regard to the League.
The organization had been created by the capitalist powers; it had
limited means and possibilities. "The limits of international cooperation and its duration, as well as the grouping of forces in the
camp of imperialism, are determined by the contradictions which
are corroding the capitalist world." (Document 137.) [17]

Soviet policy-makers and spokesmen continued to emphasize
the significance of the rapprochement between France and the
Soviet Union as a powerful instrument for the consolidation of
peace. They even began to support the Versailles Treaty: "We were
never at any time in the least enthusiastic about the territorial
provisions of the Versailles Treaty," Radek declared, "but we do
not believe that the redistribution of Europe which German imperialism would like to carry out would be in any way more just"
(Document 139).

On December 5, 1934, a protocol on the Eastern Pact was signed
by Litvinov and French Foreign Minister Laval in which they
agreed not to abandon efforts for such a pact "without having first
agreed on the uselessness of pursuing them further." Should this
happen, a simple French-Soviet alliance might be considered. (For
Soviet interpretations of the significance of the protocol see Documents 143 and 145.)

Aggravation of the Situation in the Far East

Relations between Japan and the Soviet Union continued to deteriorate, as Japan's war on China threatened to involve the Soviet
Union. Negotiations on the sale of the Chinese Eastern Railway to
Manchukuo under the aegis of Japan were stalled. The communist
press interpreted the situation in the Far East basically as a struggle
for supremacy between the United States and Great Britain. On
July 20, 1934, an article in the *Kommunisticheskii Internatsional*
signed "L.I." stated that the "Pacific Ocean problem" was "one of
the most important key problems in world politics"; there the

interests and aspirations of the major imperialist powers interweave and clash (Document 133).

A TASS communiqué, published in *Pravda* on August 18, explained the difficulties and hindrances created by Japan in the negotiations for the sale of the Chinese Eastern Railway:

> The Japanese and Manchurian press are continuing their most unscrupulous anti-Soviet campaign with the purpose of influencing the attitude of the Soviet Union with regard to the sale of the Chinese Eastern Railway. The Japanese Manchurian authorities in Manchuria [continue] mass arrests of the employees of the C.E.R. and resort to other provocatory measures. . . . Hence there can be no doubt as to which party is showing obduracy and aggressiveness, and is responsible for the breakdown of negotiations on the sale of the Chinese Eastern Railway.

The Soviet leaders appeared to be preparing themselves for trouble. An editorial in *Pravda* on August 6, entitled "On Battle Duty," described the strength of the Special Far Eastern Army. On August 19, *Pravda* reported the interruption of the negotiations for the sale of the C.E.R. Later in the same month the Soviet plenipotentiary in Tokyo, K. K. Yurenev, protested to the Japanese Minister of Foreign Affairs, Hirota, about the arrest of nineteen Soviet citizens working for the C.E.R.[18] Disturbed by Japanese intransigence in the negotiations over the C.E.R., the Soviet leadership (probably Stalin personally) on November 21 used the transparent device of a TASS communiqué to restate the Soviet position on the sale of the railway (Document 140).

The relations between the United States and Japan were also of special concern to Moscow, as were the negotiations that were taking place in London on naval problems, and the final dissolution by Japan of the Washington agreement. "[The] situation is more than clear," wrote I. Erukhimovich in *Pravda* on December 26. The London negotiations, he said, had ended in *"complete failure,"* since no one wished to make concessions. In the Pacific the complex grouping of forces was portentous: "All three main imperialist powers which are fighting among themselves—the U.S.A., Britain, and Japan—are torn asunder by such profound contradictions that a possibility for more or less prolonged compromise among them . . . appears to be exceedingly problematic . . ." (Document 146.)

411

The Soviet Evaluation of Conditions in Germany

Despite the rapid progress of the Nazi revolution, Soviet analysis of German events still tended to follow the old stereotypes. When the Nazis carried out their blood purge on June 30, 1934, the image of fascism as a mere bourgeois movement, leading to an expectation of the imminent disintegration of the fascist regime, prevailed in Soviet analyses. Hitler's regime was "doomed," said an editorial in *Pravda*: "The events of the past few days . . . have shown that the social demagogy of German fascism has passed the zenith of its success. . . . For the time being the German bourgeoisie is *still* able to continue its rule, but its final collapse under the blows of the upsurge of the masses which is beginning is not far distant" (Document 129). I. Erukhimovich, writing in *Pravda* on July 1, said: "The future of the ruling classes of Germany is at stake. They do not believe that they will succeed in preventing the proletarian revolution except with the help of the still more merciless destruction of all those who stand in their way." (Document 128.) Radek also believed that the immediate consequence of the events of June 30 would be the growth of the revolutionary struggle against fascism. In the early stage of his regime, said Radek, Hitler sought and was given support by the petty bourgeoisie. But now fascism, while continuing the use of *"terror against the working class,"* was moving on to *"terror against the petty bourgeois masses, in this way narrowing its own social base and broadening the circle of its enemies."* (Document 130.)

On July 9–10, the Presidium of the ECCI held a session to discuss the events of June 30 in Germany and the tasks of the German Communist Party. Richter, a German communist, reported on the situation. He stated that social-democratic workers were slowly but definitely joining the communists. The events of June 30 marked the beginning of the crisis of fascist dictatorship, he said, and sudden developments of new events were quite possible. Richter also spoke of the great discontent that was evident among the masses. Hitler, he said, was leading the masses to catastrophe, and the communists should make further efforts to win the social-democratic workers.[19] Other speakers at the session were Piatnitsky, Pieck, Heckert, Lozovsky, and Knorin. The communist position at the time of the events of June 30 was evaluated by Knorin (Document 131).

Piatnitsky, in an article on the German situation published two months later, was still hopeful of the possibility of developing and intensifying communist work in Germany, and urged German communists to work energetically in the fascist organizations and in the factories. "After the events of June 30, 1934," Piatnitsky said, "it will be much easier to work in these organizations than it was before." He then referred to the new communist policy of the united front:

> . . . the communist party must make every effort . . . to approach the existing social-democratic groups, the activists, the former members of the reformist and Catholic trade-unions, with a proposal to re-establish jointly with them "free" trade-unions which will be class organizations, and which will immediately assume the function of organizing the struggle against the implementation of this new outrageous law, which will wipe out all the social gains of the German working class.[20]

Toward a United Front—but Not Yet from Above

The new policy in Soviet diplomacy had its counterpart in the Comintern's tactics. By May 1934, the "united front from above" began to take definite shape. It is worth noting, however, that as late as April the previous line of the Comintern, the "united front from below," was still being followed by the French communists. Thorez wrote on April 13: "All gossip about a marriage between communists and socialists is fundamentally alien to the spirit of Bolshevism. We do not want to unite with social-democracy. Fire and water cannot mix. . . . What we want is to make it easier for the development of socialist workers toward communism."[21]

Toward the end of April, Thorez, a supporter of the "united front from below," and Doriot, who opposed it, were called to Moscow. Doriot did not go, but Thorez went. About a month later, the new indoctrination of the CPF, and of other sections, became evident. On May 23, *Pravda* published a statement by Thorez and the resolution of the Politburo of the Central Committee of the CPF emphasizing the tactic of the united front.[22] On July 17, *Pravda* gave an account of developments in France. At the congress of the French Socialist Party, meeting in Toulouse on May 20, one-third of the delegates had favored the formation of a united front.

413

On May 30, the Central Committee of the CPF approached the Socialist Party of France, proposing a joint campaign for the release of the German Communist leader Thälmann and other antifascists in Germany. It also proposed a joint struggle against the threat of fascism in France. The socialist leaders advanced their own conditions and demanded additional guarantees. Soon thereafter the CPF renewed its efforts, and on July 2 a joint meeting was held in Paris between the communists and socialists. On July 15, the National Council of the Socialist Party of France voted for the acceptance of the communist offer to form a united front against fascism.[23]

On July 27, at a meeting of representatives of the communist and socialist parties of France, an agreement was signed between the Central Committee of the CPF and the Permanent Committee of the French Socialist Party with regard to joint action against fascism and war. Seven representatives were to be elected from each party to form a joint commission to settle any differences that might arise in the joint struggle. On October 15, negotiations were opened at Brussels between the Comintern and the Second International. The negotiators were Marcel Cachin and Maurice Thorez for the Comintern, and Emile Vandervelde and Friedrich Adler, the latter the exiled leader of the Austrian Social-Democratic Party, for the Second International. This was the first personal contact between representatives of the two Internationals in more than a decade. The negotiations were inconclusive, but at a conference called by the Second International on November 13, Vandervelde and Adler told Cachin and Thorez that the Second International had agreed that its branches might conclude agreements with the communist parties for joint aid to the working class of Spain.

The CPF was not alone in its bid for a united front with the socialists. On June 16, the Communist Party of Great Britain offered to form a united front with the National Labour Party; on July 15, the Czech Communist Party sent an appeal for a united front to the Czech Socialist Party, and the Czechoslovak Red trade-unions made similar proposals to the "reformist" trade-unions. Similar offers were made by the communist parties of Switzerland, Austria, and the Scandinavian countries.[24]

On June 14, Béla Kun had reported on moves by various communist parties for united fronts, and the report was printed in the English edition of the Comintern journal on July 20; with its echoes of the "united front from below," it was hardly calculated to still the misgivings of socialist leaders. Kun mentioned earlier similar proposals by the communists, and in particular the Comintern manifesto of March 5, 1933. These moves had been made, he claimed,

> in spite of the fact that after Hitler came to power the Second International forbade the social-democratic parties to organize activities jointly with the communists against Hitler's fascism. We communists do not for a minute intend to abandon our political or organizational independence, and the independence of the communist party. We do not think it possible to unite the Communist International and the Second International. But we have firmly resolved to strive with all our strength for and to ensure the unity of action of the proletariat in the struggle against the class enemies.
>
> Irrespective of how the leading social-democratic bodies reply to our proposals for unity of action, we shall call on the workers, irrespective of the party they may belong to, to undertake joint actions against capitalism, fascism and imperialist war, in defense of the vital interests and rights of the working class. We are prepared to make proposals and we are also prepared to carry on negotiations with the leading bodies of the social-democratic parties. . . . The struggle for the united front of the working class is included in the program of the Communist International, and we, whose words never differ from our deeds, take our program seriously.[25]

A clear analysis of the communist concept of the united front was given by G. Dimitroff, just after his release from jail in Germany. He, too, still urged what was essentially the "united front from below" (Document 141). An editorial in the *Kommunisticheskii Internatsional* of December 10, 1934, quoted Lenin's rejection of any real cooperation with social democratic leaders but claimed a united front was still possible (Document 144).

An analysis of the communist goal in the united front was made in a lengthy editorial in the *Kommunisticheskii Internatsional* of December 1 (Document 142). The editorial made it completely clear that the Comintern was not abandoning either its long-range goals or its basic concepts of revolutionary strategy. Destruction of the influence on the working masses of the social-democratic parties, which were viewed as the principal obstacle to the proletarian revolution, was still the major aim. In fact, the united-front tactics were to be applied in such a way that the attainment of this aim was facilitated.

The editorial recognized that the broader application of the united front was *"pregnant with dangers"* for the communist parties, particularly the danger that the social-democratic partners in the united front might influence the communists and weaken their "struggle against the bourgeoisie." "It must be admitted," the editorial conceded, "that in some places they [the social-democrats] are already doing this now, not without success."

To guard against this danger and to ensure the ultimate triumph of the communist revolution, the editorial called for maintenance of the communist parties' identity (the "party face") in the united front and for the continued struggle against social-democracy ideologically and organizationally.

NOTES

1. *Documents on German Foreign Policy,* Series C, II, 301–304.
2. *Ibid.,* pp. 333–334.
3. *XVII s"ezd Vsesoiuznoi Kommunisticheskoi Partii (B)* . . . *stenograficheskii otchet* (Moscow, 1934), p. 128.
4. *Ibid.,* pp. 36, 12. For extracts from Stalin's report see Degras, *Foreign Policy,* III, 65–72.
5. For an excerpt from Voroshilov's speech see Degras, *Foreign Policy,* III, 72–73.
6. *S.U.R.,* May–June 1934, p. 117. For extracts from Litvinov's statement see Degras, *Foreign Policy,* III, 78–79.
7. Degras, *Foreign Policy,* III, 82–83; for full text, pp. 79–83, translating *Pravda,* April 27, 1934.
8. See also *S.U.R.,* May–June 1934, p. 123.
9. *S.U.R.,* March 1933, p. 54.
10. Degras, *Foreign Policy,* III, 45, 48, 51.
11. *S.U.R.,* July 1934, pp. 156–157; complete text, pp. 154–158.
12. See also the statement in the next day's issue (July 15, 1934) by Maiorsky on the improvement in British policy and a definite inclination to participate in the proposed East European pact.
13. Degras, *Foreign Policy,* III, 84.
14. *Pravda,* July 22, 1934; *Documents on German Foreign Policy,* Series C, III, 209, 396–402, 446–449.
15. *Pravda,* September 16, 1934.
16. League of Nations, *Official Journal,* Supplement 125, p. 66.
17. For Hitler's evaluation of the Soviet Union's entry into the League of Nations, in a conversation with the Polish Minister of Foreign Affairs on August 27, 1934, see *Documents on German Foreign Policy,* Series C, III, 360–361.
18. Degras, *Foreign Policy,* III, 88–89, translating *Izvestiia,* August 24, 1934.
19. "Iz materialov zasedaniia Prezidiuma IKKI 9–10 iiulia 1934 g., posviash-chennogo sobytiiam v Germanii i zadacham KPG," *K.I.,* No. 22, August 1, 1934, pp. 16–22.

20. *K.I.*, No. 25, September 1, 1934, pp. 19–22. A Nazi law of January 20, 1934, provided for the elimination of employment contracts between employers and newly hired employees. As of September 1, 1934, employees up to the age of twenty-five years were to be dismissed and their jobs given to older unemployed persons who would be hired without contracts. Presumably those dismissed would be absorbed in military occupations.
21. *L'Humanité*, April 13, 1934.
22. Also in *I.P.C.*, No. 33, June 8, 1934.
23. *Pravda*, July 17, 1934.
24. See *I.P.C.*, Vol. 14, No. 40, July 20, 1934, pp. 1016–17.
25. *The Communist International*, No. 14, July 20, 1934, pp. 455–458.

PART TWO

DOCUMENTS

71

Izvestiia *on the Soviet-Finnish Nonaggression Pact*

"Sovetsko-finliandskii dogovor o nenapadenii," Izvestiia, *No. 23, January 24, 1932, p. 1.*

. . .

The chairman of the Council of People's Commissars, Comrade Molotov, stated very clearly in his report to the Second Session of the Central Executive Committee that the Soviet Union, which has no desire to attack anyone, is ready to conclude nonaggression pacts with all its neighbors, with every capitalist country. The idea of these nonaggression pacts is one of the fundamental ideas of the peace policy of the U.S.S.R., and its realization in relations with any foreign country would be welcomed by the Soviet government.

. . .

Among all the negotiations that are now being conducted, only those with Finland have led to the signing of a nonaggression pact, on January 21 . . .

. . . This treaty, concluded with Finland, with whom comparatively recently unfortunate disputes have taken place as a result of the provocative activities of certain anti-Soviet circles in Finland, gives reason to hope that the leading circles of Finland have really experienced a change of heart and now recognize how senseless it is to exacerbate relations with the U.S.S.R., which desires to live in peace and friendship with all peoples, including the people of Finland.

The Soviet Union on its part was especially eager to conclude a treaty with Finland. The Soviet government has great respect for the efforts of the Finnish people to strengthen their national independence. The workers and peasants of the U.S.S.R. are well aware that to the Finnish people, freed by the October Revolution from the yoke of Russian tsarism and imperialism, this national independence is especially dear. The Soviet government is fully cognizant of this in its policy toward Finland and therefore it especially emphasized its desire for peace and friendship with the Finnish people and its desire fully to respect their national independence. Soviet public opinion, therefore, welcomes the signing of a nonaggression pact with Finland and expresses its conviction that it presages the strengthening of economic and cultural ties between the two countries.

. . .

In welcoming this new nonaggression treaty, the workers and peasants of the U.S.S.R. cannot, however, forget how limited in the final analysis is the meaning of all peace treaties. The experience and lessons of the Manchurian conflict give clear evidence of this. Therefore, the signing of this treaty must in no way lower either the vigilance of the workers and peasants of the U.S.S.R. or their readiness to resist any attack, from whatever quarter it may come, against the Soviet land, which is occupied with the peaceful construction of socialism.

72

Molotov on the Danger of an Attack on the Soviet Union

Excerpts from a speech at the Seventeenth Party Conference, January 30, 1932. Izvestiia, No. 30, January 31, 1932, p. 1.

Comrades! The present conference is meeting at a historic dividing point: the year 1932 will mark the completion of the first Five-Year Plan and preparation for the second Five-Year Plan. This determines the primary tasks of the conference.

It is already evident that the instructions of the Sixteenth Party Congress to complete the Five-Year Plan in four years are being victoriously fulfilled.

. . .

Thus, despite all difficulties, the foundation of a socialist economy has been created in our country. The fundamental question of Lenin, "Who will beat whom?" has been decided against capitalism and in favor of socialism.

Therein lies our greatest world-wide historical victory. It is especially significant against the background of unprecedented world crisis and increasing unemployment and poverty which signal the beginning of the end of capitalism.

The conference will have to decide on the tasks of the second Five-Year Plan.

. . .

At the same time, special vigilance is necessary regarding the facts and tendencies which are making themselves felt more and more forcefully in the international situation, particularly in connection with the deepening world crisis and the sharpening contradictions in the imperialist camp.

The foreign policy of the Soviet Union is clear; it is a policy of peace. Everyone sees that we are completely absorbed with peaceful construction in our country and doing everything we can to thwart new imperialist attacks upon the socialist republic.

Nevertheless, provocations designed to disrupt peace continue without interruption.

The events in the Far East require from us a serious watchfulness and proper preparedness against surprises from bellicose foreign bourgeois circles.

Remnants of the White Guards, under definite foreign protection, have become busy in Manchuria. White Guardists in Manchuria and Paris are openly working to tear the Far East away from the U.S.S.R. and to create, with foreign aid, a "buffer state" in the Far East with the participation of international outcasts such as General Gaida and his gang, whom we remember from the intervention in 1918–19.

Not for nothing have such White Guard leaders as Miliukov and Kerensky gone to Czechoslovakia. In Prague, as we well know, there are people with whom they will plot new provocative wars against the U.S.S.R.

We would not be Bolsheviks if we ignored such dangers to the Soviet Union or remained passive onlookers.

Events in China, particularly the latest developments in Shanghai, speak fairly eloquently of how the imperialists are unleashing new wars.

The peculiarity of the present moment is that the dividing line between a situation of peace and war is being increasingly blurred —they creep into war and conduct hostilities without an open declaration of war.

Furthermore, they wage war, tramping under the generals' heels the sovereignty and national rights of a great people, while making speeches about disarmament and peace in the solemn atmosphere of international conferences.

All this shows that we will fulfill our duty only if we do not allow ourselves to be lulled by any talk or general resolutions on the international situation. We must display in action not only a proletarian heroism in building a new society, but also a real vigilance and proper readiness to protect the vital interests of the workers' and peasants' state.

In the first years of its existence, Soviet power was much weaker than now, yet we were victorious. Since then we have marched from victory to victory, developing our economy at a pace never witnessed in history and preparing the realization of socialism's basic task: the complete liquidation of capitalist elements and classes in general. These victories have been gained on the basis of Leninism.

Our victories have been assured by the Leninist Party and its Central Committee headed by Comrade Stalin. (Stormy applause and ovation.)

. . .

73

Izvestiia *on the Soviet-Latvian Nonaggression Pact*

"Novyi dogovor," Izvestiia, *No. 39, February 9, 1932, p. 1.*

On February 5, a new treaty was signed in Riga between the U.S.S.R. and Latvia concerning nonaggression, nonparticipation in hostile agreements, and peaceful settlement of conflicts. This treaty is another step in the peaceful policy of the Soviet government, which is regularly applying a system of measures directed at the strengthening not only of peaceful relations between the U.S.S.R. and its neighbors but also of the general peace.

The conclusion of this pact, following the signing of a nonaggression treaty with Finland and the initialing of a treaty with Poland, took place at a time when the problem of the struggle for peace has become particularly acute for the toiling masses of the entire world. In actual fact, in the Far East military operations are already in full swing and one district after another is being seized. In the apt expression of Comrade Molotov, the capitalist world "is creeping into war." At such a moment, the conclusion by the Soviet Union of an additional nonaggression pact has a significance which goes far beyond the limits of Soviet-Latvian relations, for it points out to the entire world one of the ways to maintain peaceful international relations.

At the same time, the treaty serves as one of the factors for a true strengthening of security which, as is known, is a "matter of concern" to a group of states which are included in the system of French influence and which display particular resistance to actual disarmament.

It should be noted that the Soviet-Latvian treaty was the result of fairly lengthy negotiations between the governments of the U.S.S.R. and Latvia, and that it was necessary to overcome many difficulties before the treaty was signed. The Latvian government of Skuenek was subject to very serious pressure on the part of certain foreign forces, which tried with every means at their disposal to delay Soviet-Latvian negotiations as long as possible and, if an opportunity had presented itself, actually to prevent the conclusion of the treaty. Some Latvian bourgeois circles were also working in this direction.

The text of the treaty differs somewhat from other nonaggression pacts. For example, one article which is usually present in such treaties is absent, namely the one which stipulates that one party assumes an obligation to maintain neutrality in case of an armed conflict between the other party and a third state or coalition of states. This is due to the fact that the problem of neutrality had already been settled with sufficient clearness and completeness in the peace treaty between the R.S.F.S.R. and Latvia signed on August 11, 1920, and consequently for both governments it was unnecessary to stipulate again the old and unquestionable obligations. The preamble of the treaty states that both governments agreed that all the provisions of the treaty of August 11, 1920, the validity of which is now "extended to the entire territory of the U.S.S.R.," remain "the unchanged and forever firm basis of the relations between the two High Contracting Parties." In this way, in particular, were stressed the mutual obligations of both states in regard to the maintenance of neutrality in case either party is involved in military complications with a third power.

It should also be noted that in the treaty with Latvia mutual obligations are very clearly outlined in regard to nonparticipation in any agreement hostile to the other party with one or several other states. The treaty forbids participation in any agreement, convention, or treaty directed against the independence, territorial integrity, or political security of one of the parties, or which is aimed at subjecting one of the parties to an economic or financial boycott.

Finally, it should be noted that both governments have agreed basically to the principle of the peaceful settlement of conflicts which might arise, and that they plan to conclude a special convention on conciliation procedure.

Thus the nonaggression pact with Latvia has imposed on both parties very considerable obligations, the conscientious and sincere application of which can undoubtedly play a considerable role in the task of strengthening friendly relations between the U.S.S.R. and Latvia, as well as peace in general. As far as the Soviet government is concerned, its firm desire to carry out to the full the obligations undertaken in the treaty needs no proof. In the course of the entire eleven to twelve years of peaceful relations with the Latvian Republic, the Soviet Union has proved that it maintains undeviatingly and firmly the principle of respect for the national independence of the Latvian people and the integrity of Latvian territory. The Soviet government, which carries on the policy of the working class of the U.S.S.R., is naturally alien to any aims of conquest and to any tendency toward economic domination over other countries, and in particular over the U.S.S.R.'s neighbors, with which it has been establishing broadly varied economic relations. The tendency toward domination is characteristic of the imperialist powers, and it is precisely this tendency which is one of the causes of imperialist wars. Soviet policy, however, is expressed in the struggle for peace and the establishment of relations on the basis of complete equality with all countries. That is why the Soviet-Latvian pact can actually serve as an important factor in the consolidation of general peace, and jointly with the treaty of

August 11, 1920, can become one of the bases of Soviet-Latvian relations.

74

Radek on the Contrast Between Communism and Capitalism

K. Radek, "Konferentsiia po 'razoruzheniiu': Na puti k novym voinam," Izvestiia, No. 40, February 10, 1932, p. 2.

. . .

On the fields of Manchuria, the last hope of the last blockheads that the League of Nations could prevent and wanted to prevent war has perished.

Having seized Manchuria and advanced to the Yangtze River basin, Japan has set in motion all the Far Eastern contradictions. Not one of the imperialist vultures wishes to be left behind Japan. All the imperialists are preparing for a new division of China.

The situation in western and central Europe has never been so acute as it is at present. Thirteen years have passed since the victory over German imperialism. The history of humanity knows but few such enormous victories. But now the victor, French imperialism, is confronted by the fact that the indemnities which it imposed on three generations of the German people are daily being more and more changed into a myth. Armed to the teeth, France watches with deep anxiety the growing hatred of disarmed Germany for its conqueror. Arms were taken away from Germany. She was forbidden to rearm, but a great people has tremendous powers of resistance, which will become manifest when patience is exhausted.

In southeastern Europe, Austria, Hungary, and Bulgaria are racked with convulsions under conditions in which they can neither live nor die.

Such are the problems inherited from the war. But the reshuffling of forces which are striving to hasten war has produced new and greater contradictions. The British Empire is bursting at its seams. Although a victor in the World War, it is now losing its old positions one by one. The United States has proved to be a tenfold more powerful and dangerous enemy than Germany. The revolutionary movement in the colonies has shaken the foundation of the British Empire. The dominance of the pound in world finance—that expression of the world rule of English imperialism—already belongs to the past. The British fleet no longer rules the waves. The export of English capital as a decisive factor of world politics no longer exists. The old British lion, lying down and panting after the desperate military leap, now looks around at its young competitors and shudders at the thought that it will be obliged to defend its booty with weakened teeth and muscles.

French imperialism has become satiated with reparations, it has won for itself a considerable part of the world gold supply, and now, leaning on a bag filled with gold, it even tweaks the nose of powerful American imperialism. But it is aware that it is a colossus with feet of clay.

A nation of forty million people, of whom a considerable part are peasants, cannot hold the entire European continent under its sway. The mere attempt to establish French hegemony tends to produce a coalition against France. Only in the role of gendarme for American imperialism would France be able to attempt to withstand the danger which threatens it. But it wishes to hold an independent position in regard to the U.S.A. It is becoming entangled in a network of contradictions and is arming on land and sea to an extent which surpasses its means.

Baring their teeth at one another, all the imperialist powers look with hatred and growing anxiety at the socialist world which had been born in an ocean of blood, an ocean of the suffering of the masses. Repulsing its enemies, driving them away from its path, the U.S.S.R. has laid the foundations of socialism and is building its edifice, thereby increasing its strength to resist any attack.

What will happen, the imperialists ask, when every worker in the world knows that life is best of all in the country of the dictatorship of the proletariat, that in a world of decay and ruin only this country is the kingdom of order, able to provide the popular masses with the best conditions for progress?

. . .

75

Izvestiia *Analyzes the Disarmament Conference*

"Kazhdyi za sebia i vse protiv razoruzheniia," Izvestiia, No. 47, February 17, 1932, p. 1.

It is already possible now to sum up to a certain extent the points of view of the capitalist participants at the General Conference on Disarmament. These points of view as a rule have nothing in common with the task of the limitation of armaments. Even the bourgeois press of the majority of countries has been obliged to admit that of all the statements made at Geneva, only the speech of the representative of the Land of Soviets constituted a complete and developed analysis of the problems connected with the struggle against war.

It must be said that the statements of the representatives of the capitalist governments were distinguished by an exceptional lack of coordination. . . . The first round of speeches at Geneva brought to light the extreme accentuation of interimperialist contradictions, in which each one spoke for himself and was in a hurry to ensure for himself the maximum freedom to arm. The statements of the bourgeois diplomats at the so-called Conference on Disarmament were fully and completely devoted to the struggle for the most advantageous correlation of forces for each country in a future war.

The postwar period has known a number of attempts on the part of various imperialist powers to form blocs on the basis of mutual compensation in the course of the discussions of the problems of adjusting armaments. There were times when England stretched out a helping hand to Italy. Much fanfare accompanied the Franco-British agreement of 1928. Attempts were repeatedly made to bring France and Italy into the London Naval Treaty. However, all these and many similar attempts at agreement in the armament race exerted absolutely no influence on the recent Geneva discussions.

In actual fact French imperialism, in proposing a plan for the exceptional strengthening of its military hegemony in Europe, did not even indirectly refer to compensations in the field of naval armament. The representative of Great Britain, who tried to avoid any open criticism of France, appeared to have entirely forgotten the agreement of 1928 and insisted on a proposal which was clearly directed against France by proposing to cut down the number of military trained reserves and to limit the submarine fleet. The representative of the United States, while giving no promises of any kind to the European imperialist powers, outlined a program in which all nine points were concerned exclusively with the interests of American imperialism. Of these points, the demand to prolong the London and Washington agreements and to have France and Italy join the former, but offering no compensations in return, cannot possibly satisfy the European imperialists. Nor could the continental powers favor the American demand that the use of submarines be forbidden . . . The representatives of Japanese imperialism left no doubt that Japan had no intention whatsoever of agreeing to concessions to its competitors in the Pacific.

Such is the essence of the statements made by the capitalist politicians . . . The U.S.A. is trying to make permanent that existing correlation of forces in naval armament which is advantageous to it, the conditions which existed before the crisis, in the best period of American "prosperity." France, which has become an important colonial power, tries to retain freedom of naval armament, and at the same time is making a determined effort to provide a new base for its hegemony in Europe by making use, for this purpose in particular, of its own docile allies. England tries to parry attempts to take advantage of the weakening of its international position by a new blow against English naval power. By advancing anti-French proposals, England creates a basis for bargaining with French finance capital. Italy and Germany demand for themselves "a place in the sun."

76

Litvinov Defines Soviet Policy

Excerpts from an address in Geneva to representatives from American peace and civic organizations, together with the Geneva International Club, February 20, 1932. Soviet Union Review, *Vol. 10, No. 4, April 1932, pp. 78–81. According to a note in* S.U.R., *the speech was printed there "in slightly abridged form."*

. . .

Turning to facts, I cannot see that we have more reason for optimism now than we had on the eve of the conference. The conference, it is true, has only just been born, after heavy and prolonged birth pangs, and has not yet put on weight or acquired a voice of its own, but the movements it has so far made, the sounds it has emitted, have not been such as to enable us to discern tokens of its future strength, capacity, and powers.

For, after all, up to the present we have had nothing but the general declarations of delegations. We have learned the positions taken up by the various governments in these declarations. It seems to me that anything new we have heard points rather to a retreat from these positions still further away from disarmament. While the Preparatory Commission did at least discuss limitation and reduction, we now learn, at the conference itself, that certain governments declare their entire disagreement with any reduction of armaments whatsoever, unless preliminary conditions—which, moreover, will be found to be quite unacceptable to the conference as a whole—are fulfilled. We have even heard demands for the increase of armaments, and these by no means from weak states with low armaments . . .

Those new proposals which *have* been made at the conference raise fears that the conference itself might be sidetracked. We have always held that disarmament could only be interpreted either as the abolition or the reduction of armaments, and that the conference should deal with the question of armaments. It appears, however, that this view of the task of the conference is not unanimously held. Even at the Preparatory Commission attempts were made to substitute the question of security for that of armaments . . .

No one can have anything against security, nor has the Soviet delegation, but we do say that under the political and economic conditions prevailing in most countries, nations and states will have security *only* when no one can attack them, when there are no arms with which to attack, with which to occupy foreign territory, with which to subjugate other nations. The exponents of the opposite view see security only in the more or less leveling of the chances of victory, by the redistribution or even the increase of armaments. But prewar history also knew this sort of security. Does it really amount to anything more than the time-honored principle of the balance of power, which ruled prewar diplomacy? This principle, which at the best only increased the security of some nations at the expense of others, did not save the world from the most terrible war it has ever known, from which it emerged with even less confidence in security than it had before. Was it really necessary to undergo all the horrors and disasters of the World War, to spend thirteen years preparing for a conference, to contrive all sorts of pacts and international treaties, in order to end up with the old principle of international diplomacy, merely slightly modified and modernized?

We are hearing a great deal about moral disarmament just now. Although we have not yet diminished existing military aggregates by a single unit, we are being asked to go in for moral disarmament. Again, nobody is going to say a word against moral disarmament, against the abolition of chauvinism and jingoism in the press, literature, the cinema, schoolbooks, toys, and the like, against the exposure of forged documents and the whole bag of tricks. I should be the last to object to such proposals, since there can hardly be any other country which has been the object of so much moral poison in the press, public speeches, even official documents, as the Soviet Union. . . . But all this has little to do with the abolition or reduction of armaments, and for my part I am convinced that it is precisely the existence of armaments, and of big-scale armaments and the hope, by means of these armaments and the help of alliances and treaties, of conducting profitable and successful wars, which create chauvinism, that poisoning of the wells of intelligence, which we are being invited to put an end to by administrative means alone.

Nobody will deny that profound differences—economic, political, and even territorial—exist between capitalist states. There are countries which consider that neighboring states are wrongly and illegally occupying land which belongs to themselves; hence the agitation for the restoration of infringed rights, for the revision of frontier lines, and the like. But these differences are not to be settled by the fortunate owners of disputed territory merely saying to their neighbors: "Forgive us our trespasses as we forgive you yours." Not thus is history made, not thus are international relations changed. What we have got to see is that these grievances, these dissatisfactions, should not lead to attempts to alter the situation by armed force, attempts which can be prevented only by the abolition of armaments, by the abolition of armed forces. So long as armed force exists there will be faith in it, and in the possibility of getting the upper hand of neighbors by increasing armaments and through political combinations, inside or outside of international organizations. And so long as armed force exists, chauvinism and militarism in education will continue. Moral disarmament cannot help here. It is bound to follow on actual disarmament, but can never be a substitute for it. Only when we have finished with the immediate task of the conference and achieved appreciable success with regard to actual disarmament, shall we be free to discuss measures of moral disarmament also, which then and then only are sure to be crowned with a certain degree of success . . .

I may be told that governments are often compelled by public opinion in their own countries to maintain armaments and pursue a chauvinistic policy, and that therefore as public opinion becomes more enlightened its pressure will lessen and governments will be more amenable to the idea of disarmament. I cannot share this view. Campaigns of chauvinism and national hatred, the setting of nation against nation, have never yet come from the heart of the masses. Such campaigns are always organized and artifically nourished by small groups interested in warlike preparations, the manufacture of munitions, and war industry, potential war-profiteers. They very often succeed in poisoning the minds of the masses for their own ends. Deprive these groups of their base, remove them from war industry, destroy this industry, destroy their hopes of war and of profits to be drawn from war, and these campaigns will die out of themselves, for they will become pointless. Then you will have true moral disarmament, without the need of any special administrative measures. . . . Once real soldiers have been got rid of, the world will have nothing to fear from tin soldiers. . . .

I should be sorry to leave you under the impression that we can see one point only, to the exclusion of all others. As I have already said, we do not ignore the importance of security, moral disarmament, and all other good things which may be proposed to the conference, but we are definitely against their being substituted for disarmament. The more time we spend talking about security and moral disarmament, the less we shall disarm, and the more we really do disarm, the more security and moral disarmament will be achieved.

In conclusion I should like to remark that people do not always look for the cause of insecurity in the proper place. Some delegates at the conference, for instance, even regarded the fact that the Soviet Union does not belong to the League of Nations as a cause of insufficient security. It is noteworthy that such misgivings were expressed by representatives of states themselves maintaining no relations with the Soviet Union. This is almost like trying to get a man, whose acquaintance you do not desire, to join your club. If, however, we are to look anywhere, outside of armaments themselves, for factors creating an alarming political atmosphere, mistrust, and instability, we are more likely to find them in the existence of political and economic estrangement between several states on the one hand, and the Soviet Union with its 160 million inhabitants on the other. In this respect we only have to glance at the events now going on on the shores of the Pacific, where three of the biggest Pacific countries, namely, the U.S.S.R., China, and the United States, are involved in such estrangement. It seems to me that not much imagination and political perspicacity are required to understand the extent to which this circumstance influenced, if it did not actually cause, present occurrences in the Far East, or to understand that but for this circumstance these unfortunate occurrences might not have arisen or might have looked quite different.

. . .

77

Izvestiia *on Soviet-Japanese Relations*

"Sovetskii Soiuz i Iaponiia," Izvestiia, *No. 63, March 4, 1932, p. 1.*

Already more than five months have passed since Japanese troops occupied Mukden, the capital of Manchuria, and an armed conflict began in the Far East which has assumed increasingly serious proportions. Since that time there has not been a day which has not brought further aggravation of the Far Eastern situation; there has not been a telegram which has not brought new evidence of the extraordinarily grave import of events taking place there. It is quite natural for public opinion in the Soviet Union to follow with special concern events part of which are unfolding at the very borders of the U.S.S.R.

From the onset of the Far Eastern conflict, the U.S.S.R. has maintained a position of strict neutrality. The sympathy of the toilers of the Soviet Union for the Chinese people, suffering under the yoke of imperialist exploitation, is completely indisputable. But this sympathy for the struggle of liberation of the Chinese workers and peasants has in no way interfered with the unchanging policy of strict neutrality which naturally follows from the general peaceful policy of the Soviet Union. As a result of this consistent position of the Soviet government in regard to events in Manchuria, one after another of the anti-Soviet provocations and slanders has been scattered to dust. It is enough to recall the fate of the widespread slander campaign concerning the alleged aid given by the Soviet Union to General Ma, a slander which was finally unmasked before the entire world. The Soviet policy of noninterference and maintenance of peace has received literally universal recognition, even from the adversaries of the Soviet Union. This policy conducted by the U.S.S.R. was finally acknowledged by the Japanese Foreign Minister, Yoshizawa, who stated in the Diet that the Japanese government recognized the Soviet Union's maintenance of a position of noninterference.

Nevertheless, we are witnessing a further stirring up of anti-Soviet intrigues in Manchuria. We are witnessing a whole system of provocational measures, the significance of which must by no means be underestimated. An abnormal situation is being created at our Far Eastern borders, which requires our serious attention. . . .

No impartial politician can ignore the symptomatic meaning of the fact that, during the past two months, the Japanese government has not deemed it necessary to reply to the Soviet proposal for a nonaggression pact.

. . .

The peace policy of the U.S.S.R. is not a policy of ignoring facts. We have repeatedly pointed out that the Soviet Union will not yield to provocation, that at the same time the U.S.S.R. is able in good time to uncover and break up provocations which have been prepared against the U.S.S.R. The Soviet government has conducted, is conducting, and will continue to conduct a strict policy of peace and a policy of noninterference in the events taking place in China. But this by no means signifies that the Soviet Union will permit anyone to violate the security of Soviet frontiers, invade Soviet territory, or seize even the tiniest portion of Soviet land.

"We do not want a single inch of foreign soil. But neither shall we surrender a single inch of our own territory." [Stalin, *Sochineniia,* XII, 261.]

78

Izvestiia *on the Tenth Anniversary of Rapallo*

"Rapallo," Izvestiia, *No. 106, April 16, 1932, p. 1.*

Ten years ago, in the Italian city of Rapallo, a treaty was signed between the R.S.F.S.R. and Germany in settlement of the problems which divided both countries after the end of the war. The Rapallo treaty, which restored diplomatic and consular relations between Germany and the R.S.F.S.R., laid a solid foundation for the further development of friendly relations and close economic contacts between the Soviet land and the German republic. This was the immediate content and significance of the Rapallo treaty. However, this alone by no means exhausts the historic role of Rapallo. The signing of the Rapallo treaty on April 16, 1922, was unquestionably an event of outstanding significance, not merely in the foreign policy of the Land of Soviets, not only in the postwar policy of Germany, but in the history of postwar international relations in general.

The differences which exist between the country building up socialism and its capitalist encirclement represents the basic antagonism of the world today, while the problem of the peaceful coexistence of these two systems is the main pivot around which are grouped all the cardinal problems of international politics. The historic importance of the Rapallo treaty lies primarily in the fact that it has served as a model for how relations should be established between two countries having opposing social-political systems, but with common economic and foreign policy interests during a certain span of time.

. . .

In that way Rapallo was a turning point in the relations between the Soviet republic and the capitalist countries. . . . The vitality of Rapallo is characterized by the fact that this treaty possesses enormous practical and political significance even at the present time, when the superiority of the new socialist system over the old system of capitalist relations has already been historically demonstrated. Soviet foreign policy continues to stand on the point of view of the possibility of peaceful coexistence of two systems of property until the moment when history carries out its task. Therefore Rapallo remains an important element in Soviet foreign policy.

. . .

At the present moment, ten years after Rapallo, when the imperialists are once more preparing for intervention against the U.S.S.R., and by making use of the world crisis are again attempting to enslave Germany, it is more necessary than ever before to establish the principles of Rapallo in the relations among all peoples.

79

Voroshilov Proclaims Determination to Defend the Soviet Union

Statement of May 1, 1932. "Rech' tov. Voroshilova na pervomaiskom parade," Izvestiia, No. 122, May 4, 1932, p. 1.

. . .

War has long hung over all of humanity as a fearful threat, and it will evidently threaten them for a long time to come, particularly the Soviet Union.

We, the state of the proletarian dictatorship, have created the mighty Red Army for the protection of the October Revolution and socialist construction. The capitalist rulers and political leaders are inclined to ascribe to the Red Army the role of a skirmisher of war. But this lie no longer convinces anyone, no one now believes this. All the toilers and even the best representatives of the cultural forces of the bourgeoisie are fully aware that the only reason why the second World War has not yet broken out is because of the existence of the Soviet Union, because the mighty Workers' and Peasants' Red Army exists.

The Red Army is the bulwark of peace. The Red Army has been and continues to be the defender of the borders of our state. Together with its people, together with its government, together with the Communist Party, the Red Army has never dreamed of and will never dream of a war of conquest. The Red Army has never threatened anyone and will never threaten anyone, but, together with the toilers of the Soviet Union, it will keep a sharp eye on everything that is going on at the Soviet frontiers. At the dread moment, the Red Army will be where it has to be.

. . .

Almost every day attempts are made to provoke us into war. But Bolsheviks have strong nerves, and they are able not only to fight on the military and economic fronts but also to operate their political system. We shall not be taken in by any provocation; we shall not be drawn into any wars. But if any imperialist state or group of states attempts by direct attack to destroy the fortress of the Soviet Union, they will encounter the honorable and powerful resistance of the workers' and peasants' armed forces.

. . .

80

An ECCI Directive to the Communist Party of Japan

"Theses on the Situation in Japan and the Tasks of the Communist Party" by the West European Bureau of the ECCI. I.P.C., Vol. 12, No. 23, May 26, 1932, pp. 466–472.

I. Japanese Imperialism and War

The war of plunder which has been commenced by Japanese imperialism is dragging the nations into a new historic crisis—the greatest since the end of the world war. The seizure of Manchuria, the bloody attack on Shanghai and other parts of China, together with the other military operations of the Japanese bandits, represent the first military act of one of the biggest imperialist powers during the time of the present world economic crisis. The imperialist war which has commenced is a reflection of the depth of the general and economic crisis in the capitalist world, of the tremendous sharpening of all the contradictions of world imperialism. It opens up an era of new political upheavals of terrific importance. As the result of the latest clashes between China and Japan, there has arisen an international situation of an unusually complex character. In connection with this, all sections of the Comintern, and above all the Japanese revolutionary proletariat with their communist vanguard, are faced with tasks of the greatest responsibility.

    1. The present war of expansion of Japanese imperialism is the direct outcome of all preceding stages of its development. Japanese imperialism, predatory by nature and distinguished by particular

aggressiveness, has made colonial plunder and military loot the chief sources for the accumulation of capital and its consolidation.

. . .

The growing aggressiveness of bourgeois-landlord Japan was continually upsetting the plans and aspirations of other imperialist powers. The war which Japan has commenced against China will sharpen these contradictions still further. The Pacific Ocean and particularly China, where the contradictions of world capitalism have become most entangled since the World War, is now becoming the scene of sharp clashes of the interests of the imperialist bandits. From its very commencement, the war in China has released forces which make more real than ever before the menace of a new world war, the menace of direct military clashes or intensified war preparations for such a clash between Japan and America and other big imperialist powers, if not all of them.

2. At the same time, an important fact in the policy of international imperialism at the present time is its great efforts to form a united front of imperialist powers for war against the U.S.S.R. There exists a direct danger of armed intervention by the world imperialists against the land of the dictatorship of the proletariat. The League of Nations is an instrument for this war. By means of war against the U.S.S.R., the international bourgeoisie and their social-democratic agents are above all trying to break up the struggle of the international proletariat for freedom, for a revolutionary way out of the crisis. Before the eyes of the workers of all countries, there is developing the struggle of two worlds—decaying and dying capitalism on the one hand and triumphant socialism, ever gaining in vigor, on the other hand. Against the background of the present severe world crisis, all the advantages of the Soviet system become particularly plain, especially the astounding advances of socialist construction. The industrialization of the country of the proletarian dictatorship is taking place at unprecedented speed. Tremendous successes have been achieved in the socialist construction of agriculture, in widespread collectivization and the liquidation of the kulaks as a class on the basis of the latter [i.e., by means of collectivization]. The construction of the foundations of socialist economy is complete. The preconditions have been created for the completion of the second Five-Year Plan, which will fully ensure the setting up of a classless socialist society which opens up a new epoch in the history of mankind.

For the working classes of the capitalist countries, who especially in the present economic crisis are doomed to mass unemployment, indescribable misery, and ruthless exploitation, the U.S.S.R. serves as a clear example and plain proof of the necessity to fight for a revolutionary way out of the crisis, for the overthrow of capitalism. At the same time, the plans of the imperialists are calculated to destroy socialist construction, to strangle the U.S.S.R., and to prepare the way for still more merciless exploitation of the workers and peasants in all countries, to strengthen the regime of economic and political slavery. Of special interest is the alliance of the two international gendarmes—imperialist France, the gendarme of Europe, and imperialist Japan, the gendarme of the East, who are acting as initiators in the drive against the Soviet Union.

By making an attack in the Far East, Japanese imperialism is [trying] to create the necessary conditions for a simultaneous or subsequent attack by France and its vassals (Poland, etc.) on the U.S.S.R. from the West. It is these anti-Soviet plans which best explain the support given to Japan by the other imperialist powers and the League of Nations as a whole in its war of plunder against China. Great Britain is prepared to cooperate in the dismemberment of China, and so does not oppose the seizure of Manchuria by Japan, thus partly settling accounts with American imperialism but chiefly acting as a participant in the anti-Soviet front. The U.S.A. is trying to obtain complete domination over China and is therefore openly at loggerheads with Japanese imperialism, although it has not yet openly taken active steps against Japan. On the one hand it is waiting for Japan to become weaker as the result of a long-drawn-out war, but on the other hand it fears a rapprochement between England and Japan. But like the other imperialist powers, the U.S.A. chiefly sets its hopes on Japanese imperialism undertaking the task of being the vanguard in the anti-Soviet war.

. . .

The military adventure of Japanese imperialism is directly connected with a sharp aggravation of all its internal contradictions which have deepened as the result of the severe economic crisis. Monopolist capitalism in Japan is wrapped in a specially thick web of precapitalist relations. This explains the relative economic weakness of Japanese imperialism and the exceptional sharpness of its internal contradictions. There are many survivals of feudalism in the country, the peasants are plundered in the manner of semi-serfs, the proletariat is exploited on a colonial level; these conditions, which limit the home market, have brought about a combination of the industrial crisis with the agrarian crisis and an unprecedented acuteness of the economic crisis in town and village. The landlords and the capitalists of Japan are attempting, by means of war in China, to find a way out of the crisis, to crush the growing revolutionary mass movement, to extend their colonial possessions and to open up new sources for the additional plunder of the toiling masses of China.

4. The Japanese Communists must understand the inseparable connections between the aggressiveness of Japanese imperialism abroad and its policy at home, the inseparable connection between the bandit imperialist war in other countries for the enslavement of colonial peoples and reaction at home. By means of this war, the Japanese imperialists are striving to preserve and strengthen the regime of the military-police monarchy, the regime of savage terror and violence against the workers, to strengthen the oppression of the landlords and to force down still further the standard of living of the masses.

The war will inevitably greatly sharpen the class contradictions in the country. It sets the task to the Japanese proletariat and the Communist Party of combining the struggle against war with the struggle for the vital interests of the workers, the peasants, and all the toilers against their economic and political enslavement, for the purpose of converting the imperialist war into civil war, of the revolutionary overthrow of the bourgeois-landlord monarchy. Revolution in Japan has not been deferred by the war of plunder but, on the contrary, has been brought nearer. The beginning of the war showed that, in addition to the stubborn resistance and the self-sacrificing struggle of the Chinese people for the integrity and independence of China, there has commenced a ferment against the imperialist war in the Japanese army and inside the country. This indicates the possibility of a big failure in the adventurist plans of Japanese imperialism. Under such circumstances, the *Communist Party of Japan* is called on to play a very responsible role. The course of further events and the subsequent development of the revolutionary movement depend to a great and decisive degree on the strength, the solidarity of the Communist Party, on its ability to mobilize the millions of workers around its slogans and to lead their struggle. For this reason, the question of the ideological and organizational strengthening of the Communist Party of Japan becomes of primary importance. The present conditions imperatively demand that the Communist Party should strain every effort to extend and strengthen its present extremely weak contacts with the broad masses of workers, peasants, and other sections of the toilers. At all costs, the party must cease to lag behind the growing activity of the masses and must become a real mass party, marching confidently to meet the coming revolution.

II. The Character of the Coming Revolution

5. The C.P. of Japan must realize clearly and correctly what are the relations of class forces in the country and what is the character and what are the tasks of the forthcoming revolution in Japan. It must do away with the mistaken ideas which exist in its ranks on these extremely important questions. The relationship of class forces at the present time, the character and the tasks of the coming revolution in Japan, cannot be properly estimated without an analysis and without taking into consideration the peculiarities of the ruling system in Japan, which is a combination of very strong elements of feudalism with a far advanced development of monopolistic capitalism.

1. The first starting point to estimate the concrete situation in Japan consists of the character and the relative role of the *monarchy*. . . . The monarchy is the main pillar of political reaction and all the relics of feudalism in the country. The monarchist state apparatus forms the firm backbone of the present dictatorship of the exploiting classes, and its destruction must be looked on as the first of the fundamental tasks of the revolution in Japan.

Previously in the C.P.J. the role of the monarchy was underestimated and it was contrasted with parliament and the party cabinet of bourgeois state forms "independent of the monarchy." This idea is completely incorrect. The extension of election rights for the male population which was carried out in 1925 from above under the pressure of a popular movement was a political bargain with the monarchy by the landlords and the imperialist bourgeoisie, a bargain which was calculated to strengthen the monarchist bourgeois-landlord regime for the exploitation and suppression of the workers and peasants, to trick the people by increasing their parliamentary illusions, and to bring about a closer unity between the monarchist bureaucracy and the bourgeoisie under the new circumstances of the rule of decaying monopolist capitalism. This unity was achieved in the form of an increase in the number of voters, the formation of a party cabinet of ministers, and an increase in the role of the financial oligarchy in the government, but without any limitation whatsoever on absolutism or any restriction of the rights and powers of the monarchist bureaucracy.

The war still further increases the role of the bureaucracy and especially its most aggressive and reactionary part—the military. The result of this is an increase in the role of the military leaders in the government, which means that intervention against the U.S.S.R. is brought still nearer and the police terror and violence against the Japanese workers and peasants is enhanced. It is not correct to contrast the military with the bourgeois-landlord monarchy, and it is particularly dangerous to divert the mass struggle against the monarchy in the direction of a struggle against the danger of a fascist coup which is allegedly approaching.

A few historical peculiarities must not obscure the chief and decisive fact that the absolutist regime which exists in Japan is a form of the dictatorship of the bourgeoisie and the landlords over the workers which is quite as oppressive as fascism in other countries. The party must expose the maneuvers of the ruling classes and the social-democrats, consisting of the fact that the existing monarchist regime and the growing reaction is cloaked behind the bogey of a fascist menace, to make light of the growing pressure of reaction, and thus to preserve and strengthen the dying monarchist illusions among the masses and to divert them away from the struggle against the chief enemy under modern conditions—the bourgeois landlord monarchy.

2. The second of the main component parts of the ruling system of Japan consists of *big landownership*—this backward, Asiatic, semifeudal system in the Japanese villages which fetters the development of productive forces and increases the degradation of agriculture and the pauperization of the basic masses of the peasants . . .

There is no possibility that the ruling classes of Japan will make any serious alterations in the feudal basis of the agrarian system of the country. The *agrarian revolution* should be looked on as one of the fundamental tasks of the Japanese revolution, and a determined struggle should be carried on against any underestimation of this task.

3. The third of the basic elements of the ruling system of Japan consists of predatory *monopolist capitalism*. The centralization of capital in the hands of a small group of financial magnates was greatly assisted during the last imperialist war by feverish profiteering. The capitalist concerns monopolized a large part of the national wealth of the country . . . The financial oligarchy

became closely interwoven with the whole system of the bureaucratic monarchy which is carrying out its policy.

. . . Having attained a high level of development, Japanese capitalism was and continues to be reactionary and monarchist. This is chiefly expressed by the fact that the Japanese working class, whose efficiency of labor is as high as that in Europe, is still on the level of the workers in colonial countries. Their wages are equally low and their working day just as long. The widespread system of barrack slavery exists for textile workers, miners, etc. Contract labor is used on a large scale, and there is barbarous exploitation of child labor and the labor of youth. There are no social laws. *The workers of Japan have no economic or political rights whatever.* Finance capital systematically and widely uses the relics of feudalism, home industry, and small handicraft production in order to maintain its particularly severe exploitation of the working class.

6. The above analysis shows that the whole of the political and economic circumstances in the country will drive the revolutionary movement first of all to a struggle against imperialist war, against the police and monarchist regime, against the colonial standard of life for the workers and their lack of political rights, and against the landlords and moneylending capitalists in the villages.

The Communist Party sets itself the basic task of attaining socialism and must clearly understand that the path to the dictatorship of the proletariat in present Japanese conditions can only pass through the bourgeois-democratic revolution, i.e., through the overthrow of the monarchy, the expropriation of the landlords, and the establishment of the dictatorship of the proletariat and the peasants. The power of Soviets of Soldiers', Workers', and Peasants' Deputies will be the form of the dictatorship of the proletariat and the peasants and the form of the growth of the bourgeois-democratic revolution into a socialist revolution.

Consequently, *the main tasks* of the coming phase of the revolution are: (1) the overthrow of the monarchy, (2) the abolition of parasitic landownership, and (3) the establishment of a seven-hour day and—in the conditions of a revolutionary situation—the fusion of all banks into one national bank and the introduction of control over this bank and over the big capitalist enterprises, above all, over the concerns and trusts, by the Soviets of Workers', Peasants', and Soldiers' Deputies.

This determines the character of the forthcoming revolution in Japan as a bourgeois-democratic revolution with a tendency to grow rapidly into a socialist revolution.

At the present time the chief slogans of action must be the following:

1. Against imperialist war, for the conversion of imperialist war into civil war.

2. The overthrow of the bourgeois-landlord monarchy and the establishment of a workers' and peasants' Soviet government.

3. Confiscation without compensation of the land of all land-lords, the emperor, and the churches for the benefit of the peasants. The annulment of all the peasants' debts to the landlords, money-lenders, and banks.

4. The seven-hour day and a radical improvement in the conditions of the workers. Freedom of organization and action for class trade-unions.

5. The liberation of the colonies (Korea, Manchuria, Formosa, etc.) from the yoke of Japanese imperialism.

6. For the defense of the U.S.S.R. and the Chinese revolution.

In the struggle for these slogans, the C.P. can and must rouse all the revolutionary-democratic forces of Japan, i.e., the workers, peasants, and the city poor. Therefore, the central agitational slogan of the C.P. must be the slogan: *"People's revolution against imperialist war and the police monarchy. For rice, land, freedom, and the workers' and peasants' government."*

The struggle for the workers' and peasants' Soviet republic must be closely connected by the Communist Party with the system-atic propaganda of socialism, widely using the successes of the U.S.S.R. for this purpose

. . .

In Japan the revolution may tremendously accelerate and assist the victory of the international proletarian revolution, above all the victory of the anti-imperialist and antifeudal revolution in the Eastern countries near to Japan (China, Korea, India, etc.). The economic and political brotherly alliance of Soviet Japan with the countries where the proletariat have been victorious will completely ensure the successful socialist development of Japan and of the East in general. These prospects of the socialist prosperity of Japan in close collaboration with the liberated peoples of the East must be systematically contrasted by the party with the bourgeois and social-democratic propaganda of a military and imperialist way out of the crisis.

7. The main driving force of the revolution consists of the proletariat and the poor and middle peasants.

It is not correct to say that the middle peasants are incapable of a revolutionary struggle against the landlords and the police monarchy. If the revolutionary possibilities of the middle peasants and toiling fishermen are ignored, this may lead to a break of the alliance between the workers and peasants and is extremely dangerous for the revolutionary movement. The kulaks (the village bourgeoisie) are on the side of the existing regime, being connected with them by participation in moneylending and taking advantage of land shortage and the lack of rights of the peasant masses. It is not correct to put forward the slogan of confiscating the land only from the big landlords. Failure to demand the confiscation of the land of all the parasites of the landlords is still more mistaken because at the present time the majority of peasant conflicts are directed against the middle and small landlords. Vacillations on this question will isolate the Communist Party from the rapidly developing struggle of the peasants.

Two blocs are fighting in Japan—the allied workers and peasants against the allied landlords and bourgeoisie. The workers' and peasants' revolution in Japan is directed at the present stage chiefly against the bourgeois landlord monarchy and is likewise directed against the bourgeoisie.

The successful development of the revolution can only take place if there is a close alliance of workers and peasants under the hegemony of the proletariat. The winning and consolidation of the hegemony of the proletariat is the main condition for the victory of the revolution. The workers' and peasants' revolution in Japan can only be successful if, in addition to overthrowing the military-police, bureaucratic monarchy, it removes all the exploiting classes (including the bourgeoisie) from political power in the center and the provinces.

8. The workers' and peasants' revolution can only win when it establishes the power of the workers', soldiers', and peasants' deputies.

Under the conditions of a revolutionary revolt [*sic*], the communists have the imperative task of forming everywhere soviets of workers', peasants', and soldiers' deputies in the period of a revolutionary situation, and especially at the moment of the overthrow of the monarchy. Their tasks are to fight for the complete destruction of the government apparatus of the bourgeois-landlord dictatorship (disarming of the police, the gendarmes, the officers of the army and the navy, and the arming of the workers and peasants, the formation of a proletarian Red Guard, the dispersal of parliament and the central and local organs of government, officials to be elected by the workers and peasants, etc.) .

Only the revolutionary substitution of the whole state apparatus of the bourgeoisie-landlord reactionaries by the soviets and the winning of the leading role in them by the Communist Party will prevent the Japanese bourgeoisie, especially its left social-democratic wing—Rōnō-Taishūtō [Workers' and Farmers' Mass Party], etc.—at the moment of revolutionary mass and, to a great extent, spontaneous actions from limiting the revolutionary revolt by concessions in the sphere of forms of government (declaring a bourgeois republic) while preserving the basis of the bourgeois-landlord dictatorship—the police-bureaucratic apparatus for the oppression and enslavement of the people.

After the overthrow of the monarchy by the victorious people's revolution, the main task of the Communist Party will be the struggle for the rapid transformation of the bourgeois-democratic revolution into a socialist revolution. Only the establishment of the dictatorship of the proletariat will guarantee the solution of the bourgeois-democratic tasks and will carry them to the end—the confiscation of the land of the landlords, etc. In Japan, where the material prerequisites for socialism exist and the necessity for the destruction of the capitalist system of exploitation is mature, the formation and strengthening of the power of the soviets in the course of the workers' and peasants' revolution and as a result of it, and also the winning of the leading role of the Communists in them, is *a necessary and sufficient condition to pass on to the dictatorship of the proletariat,* to a power which will guarantee the carrying out of the fundamental aim of the proletariat—the expropriation of the bourgeoisie and the construction of socialism.

III. The Present State of the Revolutionary Movement and the Immediate Tasks of the Party

9. Under conditions of the deepening of the economic crisis, the commencement of war, and the development of the attack of the capitalists and landlords against the workers and peasants, the economic struggle of the proletariat and the struggle of the peasants against the landlords becomes sharper.

The workers' movement in Japan has reached a turning point in its development from a scattered defensive struggle to mass revolutionary actions. The process of the radicalization of the masses is accelerating. The strike movement is steadily growing. It has seized all branches of industry. The widest sections of the proletariat have been drawn into the strike struggle and the activity of the most backward men and women workers is growing (increase of textile strikes). The strike struggle is taking on a more distinct class character. Strikes are becoming more stubborn and long drawn out, while the number of repeated strikes is increasing and the level of the demands is rising. Up to 1929, strikes very rarely went beyond the limits of police legality, but at the present time they are more and more frequently turning into fierce street fights against the police and they show the fighting revolutionary tendency of the movement which testifies to the attempts of the Japanese proletariat to pass on to a counterattack against the capitalists and the police regime which suppresses and hinders the struggle of the working class for its vital interests.

Previously, the majority of conflicts in the villages took place in peaceful legal forms and usually ended with peaceful arbitration or a court decision, but now the number of revolutionary clashes between the peasants and the landlords is rapidly growing every-where. There are more frequent cases of setting fire to the houses and property of the landlords and smashing up courts and police institutions (Tochigi-Niigata, etc.). In some places the discontent of the peasants and fishermen takes the form of spontaneous revolts against the local government (Chiba-Toyama, etc.).

The popularity of the slogans "Land to the Peasants" and "The Alliance of Workers and Peasants" is growing. The idea of an alliance of workers and peasants is beginning to be carried into practice in the mass movement. There are increasing numbers of cases in which peasants' movements are headed by city workers and cases in which the peasants help the striking workers.

The changes which are taking place in the masses are also expressed by the fact that the patriotism and monarchism cultivated by the ruling classes, which have up to the present been one of the chief means of dulling the class consciousness of the broad masses, are being swept away. This is shown in particular by the un-precedented cases of protest against the coronation celebrations and cases in which crowds of peasants destroyed the shrines with "holy" pictures of the Mikado. The old paternalist traditions and the whole patriarchalism are rapidly fading away. Anti-monarchist revo-lutionary feelings are penetrating into the army and navy, among the students, etc.

The correct position taken by the Communist Party towards

the war has already brought about symptomatic although weak actions by various groups of the advanced workers, peasants, soldiers, and students against war (anti-war demonstrations in Tokyo on October 17th with the participation of 1,500 workers; demonstrations in a number of towns on November 7th; repeated anti-war demonstrations of thousands of students; individual peasant anti-war meetings in the province of Toyama, etc.; unrest among the soldiers, and the formation of revolutionary soldiers' groups in some of the military units, such as the telegraph battalion, the Himeji division, and some parts of the occupation army).

Revolutionary changes are taking place among the masses of the people at the turning point of the development of the class struggle in the country, when, on the one hand, the process of the accumulation and sharpening of the internal and external contradictions of Japanese imperialism is taking place at a rapid pace, but, on the other hand, the influence of the bourgeoisie on the proletariat, which in the past was unusually strong, has only just begun to disappear on a large scale. The swing of the masses to the left is taking place under the heavy pressure of the White terror and the unbridled tyranny of the police. On the whole it is taking place spontaneously and the role of the communist party is extremely weak in the mass movement, and the social-democrats of all kinds are using the strongest opposition.

The discontent of the masses has not yet shown its real force. The social fascists, especially the Left (Rōnō-Taishūtō, the police agent Kaitcha) still have the leadership of strikes and peasant conflicts in their hands in order to betray them.

10. The policy of the bourgeois-landlord dictatorship is carried out with the active assistance of the social-democrats, who have formed an alliance with the police which puts into the hands of the bourgeoisie such a weapon as the combination of Left-democratic phraseology and police clubs, Mauser pistols and poison gases. Acting under the flag of "unity" of the labor movement, the social-democrats in reality are splitting the masses . . .

The Japanese social-democrats of all kinds have taken up the imperialist position in the present war. They are completely in the camp of the organizers of the war against the Chinese people and the U.S.S.R. and are the most active agitators for it (chauvinist agitation against the U.S.S.R.; the designation of intervention in China as a "national" and "socialist" war; patriotic demonstrations, particularly under the slogan of "Down with Currency Speculators, Make Use of the Speculators' Profits for Carrying on the War and for the Benefit of the Soldiers at the Front"; the collection of money among the workers for the war; etc.) .

The social-democrats and the leaders of the reformist trade-unions are the chief danger for the revolutionary movement of the workers and peasants. The most dangerous are the Left social democrats (Rōnō-Taishūtō, Rōnōha, which was organized by police agents from renegades from the Communist party and calls itself the "Workers' Group of the C.P.J.") , who use revolutionary phraseology, including abstract discussions on the proletarian revolution (Inomata, Yamakawa, etc.) , so as to hide their treacherous role in the war and the workers' movement, their cringing to the monarchy, and their faithful service to Japanese imperialism.

11. The circumstances in Japan are such that it is very possible for the communists to draw very wide masses of workers, peasants, and the poor of the towns into the revolutionary movement so as to revolutionize them rapidly in the course of the struggle by developing all the mass forms of struggle and protest that are possible at the present stage—mass strikes, peasant activity, mass demonstrations, etc.

As a result, big revolutionary events may take place in the near future. Many facts already show the possibility of spontaneous explosions of mass protest and struggle in the near future.

These spontaneous actions may easily be diverted from the revolutionary line if the Communist Party does not at the present time explain to the masses the causes of their misery and who is responsible for them, if it does not expose the true character and the aims of the present war, if it does not carry out in all parts of the country a systematic exposure of the policy of the government and the ruling classes and every step they take, if it does not undermine the influence of the social-fascists and become in practice the real leader of the everyday struggle of the masses, and if it does not show the masses the revolutionary way out of the crisis.

12. The tasks of the party in the struggle against war are as follows:

1. Unceasing spoken and written agitation and propaganda against the imperialist and counterrevolutionary war. The exposure of its predatory character and the role of the social-democratic leaders and the leaders of the reformist trade-unions in this war.

2. Exposure of the counterrevolutionary imperialist and antinational significance of the war slogans put forward by the ruling

classes and the social-democrats—"national interests," "protection of the life and property of Japanese subjects," "defence of the prestige of Japanese imperialism," etc.—and irreconcilable exposure of the provocational story of the "Red imperialism of the U.S.S.R."

3. A resolute struggle against the policy of the bourgeois-landlord monarchy and the social-democrats for the establishment of class peace inside the country. Stubborn and painstaking efforts to overcome the chauvinist intoxication of the masses; untiring enlightenment regarding all the misery and suffering which the war and its consequences will bring to the masses.

4. Widely developed propaganda of the successes of socialist construction, the achievements of the workers and peasants in the U.S.S.R., and the peaceful policy of the Soviet Union. Propaganda of the successes and the aims of the soviet movement in China.

5. The C.P.J. must be guided by the aim of converting imperialist war into civil war, and must put forward its slogans and carry on the antiwar struggle according to the character of the war. The slogan of fraternizing, imperative in imperialist war, must unquestionably be linked up under the conditions of the present war of imperialist Japan against the Chinese people with the demand for immediate recall of the troops from China, with appeals to the Japanese soldiers to refuse to fight, to leave the front without giving up their weapons and form soldiers' committees. The slogan of fraternization in the event of a counterrevolutionary war against the U.S.S.R. and against revolutionary Soviet China must be linked up with agitation for the soldiers to desert to the side of the Red Army.

6. In a reactionary war, the revolutionary class cannot help hoping for the defeat of its own government. The defeat of the government army weakens the monarchist government of Japan and assists the civil war against the ruling classes. In the present war of Japanese imperialism for the colonial enslavement of China, the slogan of action for the Japanese communists must be "The Struggle for the Complete Independence of China." Under conditions of imperialist war against China or the U.S.S.R., the Japanese communists must not only be defeatists but must actively fight for the victory of the U.S.S.R. and for the liberation of the Chinese people.

7. Strikes must be brought about by all means on the railroads, sea transport, and in armament factories. Mass actions and revolutionary anti-war movements must be energetically developed, with a

view to bringing about the proclamation of the general strike and its conversion into an armed rebellion.

8. In order to mobilize the widest possible masses in the struggle against war, the party must carry on special work among the youth, war invalids, and women, especially among the wives and mothers of soldiers.

9. The communists must support the partial demands of the soldiers and sailors, such as for improvement of the material situation of the soldiers and for better treatment, upkeep of their families, increased leave, commanders to be elected, the formation of soldiers' committees, political rights, etc. The communists must suitably react to the discontent in the army and help the soldiers in their conflicts with the officers. Work must be carried on to disintegrate the mass patriotic organizations of the reservists, youth, etc.

13. The Japanese communists must clearly realize that the main center of the struggle against war lies in the mass movement, in the mass struggle. It is only by working among the masses in the factories and military units, in the trade-unions and the villages, that imperialist war in practice will be converted into civil war. The success of the mass struggle against war will depend entirely on the extent to which the C.P.J. carries on work at the present time among the broad masses of workers and peasants for their urgent demands, takes over the leadership of strikes and peasant struggles, and wins the confidence of the masses by its practical revolutionary activity. *The development of the struggle for the urgent demands of the masses in close contact with the struggle against war and the monarchy must be at the basis of all the work of the party.* The practice of leading this struggle will enable the C.P.J. to train its own members for leadership of the big revolutionary events which are approaching.

The immediate tasks of the party are:

1. *All-round strengthening of the Communist Party and the extension of its contact with the workers.*

2. *Development of the economic struggle of the proletariat* for the urgent demands of the workers, the unemployed, and the clerks on the basis of the united front from below. The winning of the independent leadership of this struggle against the social traitors and the leaders of the yellow trade-unions. The strengthening of the revolutionary trade-union movement.

3. *The incitement and organization of the peasant struggle against the landlords.*

4. To lead all expressions of discontent, protest, and struggle of the masses of the people into the channel of a political struggle against war and against the ruling monarchy.

14. The Communist Party has begun to turn to work among the masses, but the contacts of the communists with the masses and their role in the mass movement are still unpardonably weak. A radical change must take place in the mass work of the party, and the everyday struggle of the workers, peasants, and soldiers must be actually led by the party. The party can only bring about this change if it finally removes from its own ranks the relics of sectarianism and opportunist passivity in practical mass work, if in practice it establishes indissoluble contacts with the broad masses of workers. The elementary basis of contacts between the party and the masses must be created—systematic personal contacts of each individual communist with the nonparty workers. The existing party forces should be concentrated on the work of forming strong party committees and the largest possible number of nuclei in the factories, especially in big factories. Finally, unhesitating recruiting work must be carried on among workers who have been tested in the struggle. It is necessary to fight against the fear of getting workers into the party, as this is a very dangerous symptom of opportunism. Workers must be energetically promoted to leading posts in all party and mass organizations. Farm laborers and poor peasants should be recruited into the party, and party nuclei should be formed in the village.

The party must carry on an irreconcilable struggle against all manifestations of Right and Left opportunism in its own ranks. The process of Bolshevization of the party, which is going on now and which is increasing, will be accompanied by an activization and sharpening of the struggle of opportunism against the party and by a still greater concealment of it. In the present prerevolutionary period, the chief danger inside the party is the Right opportunism. The most outstanding manifestations of this opportunism during the latest period are the instances of participation in money collections for the war under the pretext of preserving contacts with the masses, attempts to conceal the tasks of struggling for the defence of the U.S.S.R. on the grounds that the masses are not yet mature enough to understand it, etc. Left opportunist mistakes consist of tendencies to give up the struggle to win freedom of speech, the press, assembly, and organization for the workers; sectarianism in the Left trade-unions, which recently has been expressed by the fact that instead of recruiting and in every way drawing the workers into the trade-unions, they are presented with demands to recognize the R.I.L.U. [Profintern] and other political principles [*sic*]; etc.

It is necessary to learn to combine revolutionary illegal work with legal work in the spirit of the Communist Party among the broad masses and to take advantage of every legal possibility (every kind of open mass organization; the press; every kind of activity by the workers, peasants, students, etc.; cultural and educational work, etc.) for the class education and organizational consolidation of the masses for increasing their activity and intensifying their struggle, for winning the leadership for the communists over all forms of the organization and the struggle of the broad masses.

All communists must learn to win over the masses and organize them; to lead, extend, and sharpen conflicts; to lead struggles, guided by the experience of the mass movement, the practice and lessons of individual strikes; to lead the peasant conflicts, student risings, etc. If such training does not take place, there will be a continuation of the present condition in which everyone realizes the correctness of the tasks, such as the slogan "To the Masses in the Factories," but insufficiently puts them into practice.

Special attention should be paid to tirelessly improving the methods of conspiracy, to studying the causes when the police make successful raids, so as to take precautionary steps and especially in order to assure the continuity of the work of party organizations in case of future raids.

At the same time a ruthless struggle must be carried on against converting conspiracy into an aim in itself and against any other tendency likely to isolate the organization from the nonparty workers.

The character of the legal and illegal revolutionary press must be radically changed and it must be made interesting and understandable for the rank-and-file workers and peasants, both in language and contents.

15. The methods of party leadership in the trade-unions and all other nonparty organizations must be completely changed. Dictatorial methods must be removed and these organizations should not have the same character as the party. This leadership should only consist of the fact that communists will win the leading role in them by their energy and their ideological influence and not by claiming to be party members, etc. In every case they should win over the members to the side of revolutionary propositions by convincing them and in no other way. In order to ensure a correct

line of conduct for party members working in mass organizations, efficient communist fractions should be formed in the mass organizations and the party leadership over them and their party discipline improved.

The extremely harmful identification of the Communist Party with the Left peasant leagues was expressed very crudely in the fact that at the Congress of the "Zennō" Peasant Leagues, the communists carried on a struggle against the social-democrats, not on the question of the struggle for land and against the monarchist regime, but on the question of "a legal or an illegal party."

At the present stage of the peasant movement, in addition to increasing the work in the peasant leagues and recruiting the broad masses—especially the poor peasants—for them, it is extremely necessary to carry on a wide agitation for the formation of revolutionary peasant committees of struggle and for the formation of detachments of revolutionary self-defence.

A trade-union should be formed for the workers in the fishing industry, and also energetic work should be carried on among the large number of toiling *fishermen* in Japan. A program of partial demands should be worked out and, by leading the struggle of the small working fishermen, they should be won over to the side of the revolutionary slogans of the Communist Party.

The tremendous proportion of the *youth* and the *women* in the factories makes it necessary for the Communist Party to pay particularly great attention to the strengthening of the growth of the Y.C.L. and the all-round improvement of the work among women.

16. A struggle must be carried on for the masses against the social-democrats of all shades. This struggle has not been successful in the past, chiefly because it has not been concrete and either has not been sufficiently linked up with the direct struggle of the masses for their vital needs and with the experience of this struggle, or has in some cases been replaced by calls for a physical struggle against individual social-fascists. Neither of these has anything in common with the tasks of the Communist Party.

The essence of the struggle against social-fascism consists of the struggle for the masses against the influence of the social-fascists on them. The decisive task of the Communist Party and of all its organizations, of its press and of every individual communist, is to expose systematically, day after day and in simple popular language, the treacherous and imperialist nature of social-fascism to the workers and peasants and to tear off its mask of "friend of the people" so that in this way the masses will be wrested from its influence and won over to the side of the Communist Party. It is necessary to show up the treachery of the social-fascists, to deprive them of the confidence of the masses, not on the basis of abstract questions, but on the basis of the experience of the everyday struggle of the working class to improve its material and political situation. Only on such a basis and in close connection with the struggle for the concrete needs of the workers and peasants is it possible and necessary to expose the bourgeois nature of social-fascism on all questions of internal and international policy.

In this struggle against the ideology of social-fascism, the party must concentrate its fire of criticism against those manifestations which are most disastrous for the revolutionary movement at the given time, which have a most disastrous effect on the minds of the masses and which hinder their activity—against chauvinism, legalist illusions, etc.

17. The C.P.J. must become the party of mass political action. For this purpose, in all its daily revolutionary practical work, it must base itself on the task of initiating, organizing, and leading all expressions of discontent against the war, against the police-bureau-cratic regime of the bourgeois-landlord monarchy. The Japanese communists must respond to every political event, drawing a contrast between all the bourgeois-landlord parties or social traitors and its own revolutionary estimate of these events and its revolutionary reply to all questions which agitate the masses.

In drawing up its partial political demands, the party must clearly understand that the Japanese parliament is an integral part of the present monarchist dictatorship. While fighting by every means for partial political demands, including the fight against the existing restrictions for women and youth, the party must not under any circumstances put forward such partial political demands as would direct the attention of the masses to the struggle for improving the parliamentary system and would sow parliamentary illusions among them. On the contrary, while making full use of parliamentary elections and parliamentary work, and where possible taking part in them for the purpose of revolutionary agitation, the Communist Party must direct its work toward dispelling the parliamentary illusions of the masses. It must completely abandon the incorrect slogan of "dissolving parliament."

The program of partial economic and political demands put forward by the Communist Party must be a program calculated above all on the nonparliamentary struggle against war, against the present police-monarchist regime, against the capitalists and landlords, for the most burning demands of the working class, the working peasants and the poor of the towns.

18. The party must prepare a program of partial demands which can be changed to suit the concrete political conditions of the moment, carefully taking into account all the matters which may assist in the rapid radicalization of the masses.

The program of action of the Communist Party should include the above mentioned antiwar demands and also demands of the following nature:

1. Against the crushing of strikes and peasant activity by the military and the police; for the right to strike and the freedom of the peasant struggle; for unlimited freedom for trade-unions, peasant unions, and all other forms of organization of the toilers; against arbitration and interference by the government—law courts, police, etc.—in the struggle of the workers against the capitalists and the landlords.

2. For the immediate liberation of all victims of police violence and all political prisoners—trade-union leaders, strikers, participants in peasant conflicts, members of the Communist Party, Korean and Chinese revolutionists.

3. Unlimited freedom of assembly, speech, and press for the workers; complete freedom for political meetings and demonstrations. The formation of factory committees in all factories regardless of formalities, and their recognition; the organization of proletarian self-defence.

4. For nonpayment of rent and against the robbery of the peasants by landlords and capitalists. For the annulment of all debts of the peasants to landlords, moneylenders, trusts, and banks. Refusal to pay these debts or to pay taxes.

5. For the repeal of all anti-worker and anti-peasant laws. For really equal rights for Suiheisha;[1] for equal rights for women.

6. Against semi-slavish conditions of labor, against servitude in barracks, against contract labor, which is a hidden form of slavery for workers and youths; against the double exploitation of women, youths, Koreans, and Formosans. Equal pay for equal work. Criminal prosecution for open or concealed forms of the sale of women and children, etc.

7. Against capitalist rationalization; for the 7-hour day for adults, the 6-hour day for youths from 16 to 18 years of age and the 4-hour day for all below 16; the prohibition of child labor; the 40-hour week (but in branches of small and medium industry where the working day at present is particularly long, the 46-hour week at

first). A weekly rest day with full pay and a yearly vacation of two weeks with pay.

8. A general rise of wages, the establishment of a compulsory minimum for wages based on the cost of living of a worker's family. Prohibition of deductions from wages. Criminal prosecution for failure to pay wages in time.

9. Immediate introduction of government insurance against unemployment, sickness, accidents, and old age at the expense of the employers. Free and full control of the funds of state insurance by the workers and the unemployed. Reduction of rent for houses and the cost of electricity for workers, with the complete exemption of the unemployed for such payments. The formation of a Tenants' League for the struggle for lower rent.

10. Against the regime of economy and inflation carried out by the government at the expense of the workers. Against high prices. For a regime of economy by cutting down the expenditure of billions of public money for armaments, the police, subsidies to the capitalists and landlords, big salaries for the emperor and the nobles. For heavy taxation of banks, corporations, and trusts, the confiscation of speculators' profits and the transfer of these funds for the assistance of the unemployed and the poor in the towns and villages. For increased taxation of the rich and exemption from taxation for the workers, small peasants, poor handicraftmen and the poor in the towns.

11. For the liberation of Korea, Formosa, Manchuria, and other districts annexed from China. For the immediate withdrawal of Japanese forces from these countries. The defense of the U.S.S.R. and the Chinese people.

The whole struggle of the Communist Party for partial demands must be directed toward winning over the working masses for the basic slogans of the revolution.

By developing the struggle for partial demands and winning over the masses to its side, the Communist Party will bring nearer the outbreak of revolution. War and crisis have extremely sharpened the class contradictions in the country. The mass revolutionary struggle of the workers and peasants under the leadership of the C.P.J. will lead to the growth of a revolutionary crisis in which a crushing blow will be dealt the monarchy, and workers' and peasants' soviets will be formed, under the flag of which the C.P.J. will lead the working class and all the toilers to final victory.

WEST EUROPEAN BUREAU OF THE E.C.C.I.

NOTES

1. "Water Level Society" or Leveling League, an organization of the depressed, formerly segregated *eta* class.

81

Varga Analyzes the Situation in the Far East

Excerpt from Varga's "Economics and Economic Policy in the First Quarter of 1932." I.P.C., No. 24, June 4, 1932, pp. 506–508.

. . .

The Struggle for Hegemony in China and the Danger of Intervention

The fundamental antagonism between the Soviet Union as the center of world revolution on the one hand and all the predatory imperialist states on the other is very strikingly apparent in relation to China. The political line of the proletariat of the Soviet Union, of the Comintern, and of all the communist parties of the world, is the liberation of the Chinese people from imperialist oppression, the overthrow of the class rule of the feudal lords, landowners, militarists, and big bourgeoisie (all closely allied with the foreign imperialists) by means of a bourgeois-democratic revolution, with the perspective of a subsequent transformation of this movement into a proletarian revolution and the establishment of a Soviet China comprising the entire territory of China.

This policy of the Soviet Union and the Comintern is faced by the policy of all imperialists, which is that of continuing in one form or another to treat China as an object of imperialist oppression and exploitation.

Within the imperialist camp, again, two main directions may be distinguished:

a) The common line pursued by the bourgeoisie of those three predatory imperialist states, Great Britain, France, and Japan, which have already subjected almost all Asia to their colonial oppression. They wish to complete their work by the division of China. Naturally, the identity of their political aims merely lies in the fact that China is to be divided up; as to the manner of such a partition and the question of who is to get which particular part of the booty, there are obviously very serious differences among them.

b) The line pursued by the bourgeoisie of the greatest of the imperialist robbers, the United States, is in the direction of establishing a territorially undivided and formally independent bourgeois China, which will to all practical intents and purposes be more or less a colony of America. In the division of the world, the bourgeoisie of the United States have so far come off rather badly. Their colonial realm is in no proportion to their economic importance in the world. In case of a division of China, the fact that Great Britain, France, and Japan have already acquired powerful strategic points in and around Chinese territory would leave little for any other Power. Hence the American policy in favor of a maintenance of Chinese integrity (including Manchuria), with a view to breaking the hold of the other imperialist Powers on China, so that the United States may, by virtue of economic and political predominance, oust its competitors as in the case of South America and turn a nominally "independent" China into a semicolonial territory.

Each of these political directions is supported by different classes in China itself.

1. The policy of the Soviet Union and the Comintern is supported by the great bulk of the Chinese people, by all the exploited and oppressed classes of workers, poor and middle peasants, and the poorer strata of the urban petty-bourgeoisie whose interests this policy serves. In the soviet territory of China, workers and working peasants—led by the heroic Communist Party of China—have already taken state power into their own hands and organized the Red Army, which—actively supported by the broad masses of the population—has repeatedly vanquished the numerically and technically far superior White armies of the Kuomintang.

2. The policy of Japan, Great Britain, and France looks for support to those counterrevolutionary forces in China that desire to perpetuate the present condition of extreme exploitation of the workers and the partition of China into individual areas governed by different factions, such as the feudal landowners, and the "comprador"-bourgeoisie, militarists, and brigands. All these, and the

richest class of the national bourgeoisie, are indissolubly united with the imperialists, without whose protection their hegemony would inevitably be overthrown in a very short time by the revolution of the workers and peasantry. The uninterrupted internal struggles waged by the individual cliques against each other reflect the conflicting interests among the imperialists, who stir up such hostilities with a view to expanding their respective spheres of authority at each other's expense, while at the same time they serve the general interest of the imperialist Powers, furnishing them as they do with a pretext to advocate a partition of China as indispensable for the "restoration of law and order."

3. The policy of the United States might be expected to find its supporters not only in certain sections of the commercial, but also in the ranks of the industrial, national bourgeoisie. But whereas the workers and peasants on the one hand and the feudal lords and militarists on the other represent strong class forces, the industrial bourgeoisie of China is notably weak. It is economically and numerically weak because the industrial development of China is very slight, seeing that by far the greater part of the industry is in the hands of foreigners. But it is also politically weak, since the possession of real estate on the part of the industrialists causes them to be interested in the maintenance of the present agrarian conditions and thus allies them closely to the landowning class, so that they are averse to attempting any agrarian revolution, without which, however, the power of the landowners and militarists cannot be broken.

It would therefore appear to be in the interests of the United States to postpone their inevitable reckoning with Japan for some time to come.

The Japanese advance in Shanghai, meanwhile, is a most pronounced provocation of America. If the United States desired to postpone their reckoning with Japan until after the termination of a war of intervention, Japan, relying on its alliance with France, on the support, though vacillating, of Great Britain, and on its own indispensability as a factor of intervention against the Soviet Union, placed the United States under the necessity of a choice between two evils, i.e., either of commencing a war on Japan under extremely disadvantageous circumstances, or else of tolerating a decided strengthening of Japan's position in Shanghai, the key position to the Yangtze Valley with its 180 millions of inhabitants, and thus in China in general, which would further greatly diminish the American chances in a subsequent war with Japan.[1] The assumption of the Japanese militarists has so far proved correct, for the United States has not gone beyond mere notes of protest, preferring for the time being to avoid open warfare.

At the same time, the Japanese advance on Shanghai was intended to strike at the center of the highly effective Chinese boycott of Japanese goods caused by the Japanese campaign in Manchuria.

In this point, however, the Japanese militarists miscalculated. The occupation of Shanghai and the advance into the Yangtze Valley proved to be anything but an easy military operation, such as the occupation of Manchuria had been, but led to a regular war, in which the Japanese army met with embittered resistance on the part of the Chinese people in general and the proletariat of Shanghai in particular, and—morally, at any rate—with a severe defeat.

As a matter of fact, it was the Chinese people, and in the first place the proletariat of Shanghai, which waged the fight against the Japanese invaders, the 19th Canton Army forming no more than the organized cadre in the struggle of resistance. It would lie beyond the limits of this article to enter into a detailed analysis of the fighting around Shanghai; we shall therefore only point out the main political elements:

a) The Kuomintang government betrayed the fight from the very beginning. It fled from Nanking to Loyang, issued demagogic proclamations while at the same time sabotaging the provision of the army with money, foodstuffs, and war materiel, and sent no troops to its aid.

b) The 19th Army had repeatedly been beaten by the far worse equipped Red Army of China; its leaders, too, desired to avoid a fight against the Japanese Army. They attempted to prohibit the workers from joining their forces and taking part in the fight. It was only thanks to the determinedly militant Shanghai proletariat, under its influence and with its aid, that the rank and file of the 19th Army managed, against the will of the government and even against the will of their own generals, to offer resistance to the superior Japanese forces.

c) The fight around Shanghai has shown the proletariat of the world and the colonial peoples the great possibilities in a modern civil war in the face of great superiority of technical equipment on the part of the army of the class enemy.

d) The fight of the 19th Army against the Japanese was at bottom part of the struggle of the United States against Japan.

The small amount of help afforded the fighting Chinese army by Nanking was only given under pressure on the part of America.

In view of the vigorous resistance of the Chinese masses, Great Britain and France are interested—as is, finally, even the United States—in affording Japan the possibility of coming out of the Shanghai affair with partial success, so as to release its forces for a war of intervention against the Soviet Union. Therefore, together with the leaders of the Kuomintang, they urgently advocate a compromise and make use of the apparatus of the League of Nations to bring pressure to bear not only on China but on Japan as well.

The policy of the French imperialists is absolutely plain. Neither in the question of power nor in an economic sense are there any immediate differences between France and Japan. The French bourgeoisie therefore wholeheartedly support the Japanese policy of expansion both in Manchuria and in China itself.

Far more complicated and contradictory is the attitude of Great Britain toward Japan. Apart from the common interest in the maintenance of imperialist rule in Asia, two fundamentally important reasons range Great Britain on the side of Japan, one being the antagonism between the capitalist world and the Soviet Union and the other the antagonism between the two greatest imperialist Powers, Great Britain and the United States.

Nevertheless, Great Britain does not wholly and frankly endorse the policy of Japan. The British bourgeoisie is, indeed, between two millstones. A pronounced defeat of Japan in China might prove fatal to imperialist rule in Asia generally and to Great Britain's rule in India in particular. Too great an accession of power for Japan in Asia, and especially in China, however, would likewise be extremely dangerous for the British bourgeoisie. The trend to expansion on the part of the Japanese imperialists would by no means make a halt at the confines of British territory, since their avowed official program aims at the domination of all Asia.

The policy of the British bourgeoisie, moreover, is rendered particularly difficult by the decidedly anti-Japanese attitude of the British Dominions bordering on the Pacific: Australia, New Zealand, and Canada. A frank support of Japan in its conflict with the United States would hasten the danger of a breaking up of the British Empire and of a secession of Canada, Australia, and New Zealand to the cause of America.

Finally, we must not lose sight of the fact that there is acute commercial rivalry between Japan and Great Britain. The most dangerous and formidable competitor of the Lancashire cotton industry, not only in China but also in India and East Africa, is Japan [footnote omitted]. The boycott movement against Japanese goods—which in Farther India, East Africa, etc., where the retail trade is in the hands of Chinese traders, is carried on, if anything, even more vigorously than in China itself—is thus for the seriously menaced British textile industry a very welcome result of the Japanese attack on China and is without doubt covertly encouraged by the interested British bourgeoisie, in spite of the official British friendship for Japan.

The attitude of the United States toward Japan, again, is also to some extent ambiguous. There is a very great interchange of commodities between Japan and America, Japan figuring second (after Canada) among the countries importing into the United States, with a quota of 9.8 per cent, and fifth (after Canada, Great Britain, Germany, and France) among the purchasers of American goods, with a quota of 4.9 per cent. On the world market there is hardly any competition between the two countries. Japan exports articles of consumption, while the United States exports means of production and raw materials. Much United States capital, moreover, is invested in Japan, and the United States are the chief purveyor of rolling stock for the South Manchurian Railway.

The foreign-political differences, meanwhile, are all the more acute. Japan is the United States' greatest rival in the Pacific Ocean. Only to a certain extent and only temporarily, this rivalry is mitigated by the role played by Japan as the spearhead in the attack on the Soviet Union.

The question naturally arises as to why the United States bourgeoisie has so far tolerated the pronounced provocation practiced by Japan.

The answer lies in the present strategic superiority of Japan in Asiatic waters. True, the United States battle fleet is numerically superior to that of Japan in the proportion of 5 to 3. But in Asiatic waters, the Americans are without any up-to-date naval base.

The second main reason is that the United States bourgeoisie is fully aware that, in view of the present aggravation of interimperialist differences on all sides, a war against Japan would not be a purely Japanese-American question, but would very soon devolve into a world conflict.

All this, of course, refers merely to the present moment. In the very distant future, a war between the United States and Japan for predominance in the Pacific Ocean and for the exploitation of

China is absolutely inevitable, presuming the proletarian revolution does not in the meantime obviate all further imperialist wars. The bourgeoisie of the United States cannot allow itself to be ousted from the Chinese market, the importance of which for America grows apace [footnote omitted]. It will not leave the predominant role in the Pacific to the Japanese without a struggle. Though at the present moment the strategic position is distinctly favourable for Japan, there can be no doubt that in the long run the military forces of the United States far exceed those of Japan.

The Military Weakness of Japan and the Revolutionary Movement

Although there is no country in the world, not even France, in which the policy of the dominant classes is so greatly concentrated on the creation of a formidable military power as is the case in Japan, although in no other country are economic and cultural interests so ruthlessly sacrificed to militarism, although nowhere else do the military leaders exercise such a decisive influence on politics, although no other country has in the last few decades so persistently and perseveringly pursued a policy of military conquest, although, finally, Japan possesses an excellent fleet, a big territorial army, and a highly up-to-date armament industry, it is undeniably a weak country from a military standpoint.

The great political significance of this recognition lies in the fact that a Japanese intervention against the Soviet Union will not take place by itself alone, but (though perhaps chronologically slightly in advance) as part of an all-round intervention. This is a circumstance of the greatest importance in the fight of the communist parties against intervention.

The policy of the social-fascists aims at deflecting the attention of the European proletariat from the preparations for intervention made by the bourgeoisie of their own particular country, by depicting the danger of intervention in the East as a distant and isolated matter, at times criminally speaking of the "danger" of a war between two equally imperialist states—Japan and the Soviet Union—for the possession of Manchuria, spreading a slanderous report of the existence of an agreement between the Soviet Union and Japan, and at other times mocking at the Soviet Union for putting up with anything from Japan, intentionally drawing the attention of the proletariat to the pacifist phrases of the League of Nations and veiling the latter's real role of an organizing center for all preparations for intervention. A successful struggle against intervention is impossible without an exposure of all these maneuvers of the social-fascists and without a clear recognition of the fact that what is imminent is not a mere Japanese intervention in the Far East but a general intervention from several sides.

The military power of a country is determined by two main factors: (a) its economic strength, and (b) the stability of its social system.

Let us attempt to analyse these two factors in the case of Japan.

Economically, Japan is a poor, weak country. In this regard, we need but consider the following important circumstances:

1. The value of the internal production per head of the population is extremely small.

2. The same assertion holds good in regard to the "national wealth."

3. The financial system of Japan is wholly undermined. The stock of gold is very small, having declined from 882 million yen at the beginning of 1931 to 522 million at the beginning of 1932, although in September an export prohibition for gold was decreed. The currency is depreciated, figuring at from 30 to 35 per cent below the mint par of exchange.

4. Japan possesses no capital investments abroad capable of being mobilised for war purposes.

5. Japan proper is even in peace times dependent on the importation of foodstuffs from abroad. A general mobilization of the male population in case of war would entail an immediate pronounced recession in the production of food [footnote omitted]. At the same time, the necessity of better feeding of the troops (the majority of the Japanese peasants and workers suffer chronic starvation) would greatly increase consumption.

6. Even a relatively well-developed war industry, like that of Japan, can only cover a fraction of the requirements of a modern war. The entire metalworking, and particularly the engineering, industry must in case of war be adapted to the production of war material. In this lies one of the most serious military weaknesses of Japan. Its machine industry is very poorly developed, covering less than two thirds of the peace requirements of the country and employing (in 1928) no more than 251,000 workers [footnote omitted].

7. The weakest point in the entire military position of Japan consists in its lack of all the raw materials indispensable for war purposes, with the sole exception of copper.

There is a lack of iron ore. The iron and steel works erected for military purposes obtain their ore from abroad, for the most part from Farther India and Australia, at a distance of thousands of nautical miles.

There is a lack of steel and iron, the output of which in 1929 was as follows: iron, 1,113,000 tons; steel, 2,294,000 tons. This is not even enough for peace requirements, for in 1929 160 million yens' worth of iron and steel was imported. For war purposes it is wholly insufficient. And a considerable increase in output is out of the question in view of the absence of furnaces, ore, and cokable coal.

There is a lack of crude oil, the native production of which is quite insignificant. In peacetime, crude oil imports averaged 500,-000 tons per annum.

There is a lack of nonferrous metals, of raw materials for the chemical industry, of all textiles with the exception of silk, and so on.

In summing up, we may say that the general poverty of the country, the chaotic financial system, the lack of foreign investments capable of being mobilized, the poor development of the metal industry, and the absence of almost all raw materials render the economic basis of Japanese militarism relatively weak.

This role of a vanguard of imperialism, which Japan is thus taking upon itself, is, however, undoubtedly fraught with the most serious danger for the present dominant system.

The undeniable decay of the existing order of society, the general impoverishment of the working classes, and the extreme accentuation of class antagonisms, which necessitate the constant employment of the severest military and police terrorism for the suppression of the revolutionary movement, demonstrate the internal weakness of the present system.

All the working classes are bitterly opposed to the feudal-bourgeois class rule and to the reactionary military-bureaucratic system of government with the monarchy at its head. Class antagonism is accentuated to the utmost.

It is obvious that in the event of a general mobilization these class antagonisms will spread in a far greater measure to the army, and—together with the growing privations imposed by the war on the proletarian soldiers in the army and their relatives in civilian life—will render it increasingly unreliable.

War will not postpone, but rather accelerate, revolution in Japan. The demonstrations against the war, which have taken place in Japan in spite of the severest terrorist suppression, and the mutinies in the army and navy, show what possibilities exist for the

Communist Party of Japan to turn an imperialist into a civil war, to overthrow the government system of the monarchy, the militarists, and the bureaucrats, to wage an agrarian revolution for the liquidation of the substantial existing remnants of feudalism, and, by way of a victorious bourgeois-democratic revolution, to achieve the dictatorship of the proletariat.

. . .

NOTES

1. Japan's occupation of the Wusung forts means the control of the waterway from Shanghai into the interior of China and a further important link in the Japanese system of naval bases, henceforth forming an unbroken chain from Japan to Formosa. [Footnote in *I.P.C.*]

82

An Evaluation of the Hoover Disarmament Plan

"Sud'ba plana Guvera," Pravda, *No. 181, July 2, 1932, p. 1.*

And so Hoover's "disarmament" plan has been, as they say, "shelved" . . .

The Hoover plan, which is a caricature of the Soviet disarmament project, was perhaps not formally rejected for this very reason. However, thanks to the efforts of the three chief imperialist opponents of the United States—England, France, and Japan—it has been subjected to the procedure of being rendered "innocuous" . . .

From the point of view of the results of the five months' activity of imperialist "peacemakers" at Geneva, the fate of the Hoover plan is nothing unusual. The imperialist powers convened a conference and are postponing the time of its final fiasco because under cover of the conference it is easier for them to arm. Their whole strategy and tactics at Geneva aim at achieving military superiority and the uninterrupted growth of their own forces while disarming their rivals. The tactics of American imperialism are not different, although its projects are full of pacifist phrases.

Neither before nor since Geneva has the imperialist world ceased to arm feverishly for war, for a redistribution of the world. The crisis has not brought a standstill to this process which is natural to imperialism. In spite of enormous budget deficits (look, for example, at the current budgets of the U.S.A., France, Poland), the imperialist states continue to expend enormous sums on armaments.

The crisis has only accentuated *the unevenness in development of the armed forces of the various imperialist countries, thereby increasing both competition in the sphere of armaments and the prerequisites for new wars.*

. . .

. . . The events which have occurred in the last few days at Geneva are, in the main, a reflection of the struggle between the U.S.A. and England. The contradictions between them remain the dominating feature in international relations in the most recent postwar epoch of imperialism. And this has once again been fully confirmed at Geneva . . .

. . . French imperialism is exerting all its efforts and all its skill to weld together at Geneva, as well as at Lausanne, *a united front against the U.S.A.,* which on its part is supported by Italy, Germany, the countries of South America, etc.

The representatives of one country, the U.S.S.R., are refraining from taking part in this fight of the imperialists for this or that variant of the sabotage of disarmament. The Soviet delegation, which has revealed to the workers of the whole world the true state of affairs at the Geneva conference and which has repeatedly exposed the sabotage projects of the imperialists, carries on its own policy, which differs fundamentally from that of the imperialists. The only delegation which is really fighting for complete disarmament, for creating security from war, is the Soviet delegation. *Its task of exposing the imperialists becomes all the more important at the present time, when the five months' activity of the Geneva Conference has resulted in the still greater aggravation of imperialist antagonisms . . .*

. . .

The Geneva comedy has not changed its character as the result of the fact that from now on it has one more virtue. *It remains a means for preparing a new imperialist war, anti-Soviet intervention, and deceiving the toiling masses.* And therefore [our] task is still ruthlessly to expose the Geneva "peacemakers."

83

Izvestiia *on the Results of the Disarmament Conference*

"Protiv sabotazha razoruzheniia," Izvestiia, *No. 205, July 26, 1932, p. 1.*

After five years of preparation and six months of work, the labors of the Disarmament Conference have come to an end, having accomplished nothing. The resolution proposed by the official speaker of the conference, the Minister of Foreign Affairs of Czechoslovakia, Beneš, is nothing but a compilation of generalities. It was rejected by the delegations of the Soviet Union and Germany, with eight abstentions, including Turkey and Italy. The mere fact that this resolution was not supported by a number of large powers speaks for itself and reveals the complete futility of the conference.

What then did the Geneva conference do in the course of six months? All the capitalist countries presented declarations camouflaged in pacifist phrases which defended their own specific programs of armament. The most characteristic was the program of French imperialism. French imperialism refused to agree to any limitation on armaments and proposed instead to place the most powerful instruments of warfare in the hands of a special army controlled by the League of Nations. The French proposal did not aim at the limitation of armaments, but rather at the legalization by the League of Nations of all instruments of warfare that had been invented by postwar militarists.

In view of the fact that as a result of the Versailles Treaty Germany is the least armed of all the imperialist states, it insisted on parity in case no agreement was reached on the limitation of armament.

Italy, taking into account its difficult financial situation, was prepared to give up a number of costly modern instruments of warfare. The United States and England did not advance any special program for the limitation of armaments but simply paraded a series of humanitarian proposals for easing the burdens of war on the civilian population.

Only the Soviet Union presented a clear and exact program of disarmament, pointing out that disarmament alone will safeguard the people of the world from the unheard of calamities of modern warfare. But in view of the fact that this proposal of the Soviet Union was rejected by all the capitalist countries, the Soviet Union advanced a plan whereby armed forces were to be cut down to half their present size, and some preferential conditions granted only to small countries which fear attack by large powers. This proposal also was rejected.

After several oratorical battles at the plenum of the conference and at the sessions of the General Commission, the conference went to sleep for several months. The Technical Commissions alone held sessions. These Technical Commissions, naturally, could not make any headway because the question of disarmament is not a technical but a political one. Therefore the Technical Commissions were simply marking time, trying to find the proper definition for a dreadnought or a tank.

The situation changed when the United States put forward Hoover's proposal. This proposal was dictated by the election campaign in the U.S.A., but it also had deeper motives: the U.S. has suffered a great defeat in Manchuria.

. . .

In the years preceding the crisis, the United States was to have advanced a huge program of new armament. But at present, in view of the fact that it faces a three-billion-dollar budget deficit, the United States is trying to reach its goal by a roundabout way. It presented a program of the limitation of all armaments to one third, so that the United States would simply relinquish the construction of new naval units as stipulated by the London Naval Conference, while England and Japan would have to give up units already built. Insofar as ground forces are concerned, Hoover's proposal would even permit the United States to increase its ground forces, while Japan and France would have to cut theirs back. But irrespective of the motives of Hoover's proposal, even though it does not provide any guarantee against a new war it would nevertheless

472

lighten the burden of war expenditure which places an unheard-of burden upon the popular masses of the entire world. Consequently, the Soviet delegation supported the American proposal. But then there began a stage of the Geneva negotiations which has proved in the clearest manner to the popular masses of the entire world that the secret diplomacy of imperialism continues to be fully in force, in spite of all the outcries against secret diplomacy raised by Wilson and other preachers of a "new era in the development of the world." Having brought out their program in open session of the General Commission of the Disarmament Conference, the American diplomats then gave up the struggle for this program at the conference. Encountering opposition from England, France, and Japan, they sought to isolate one adversary from another in order to break up the front of the opposition by means of partial concessions.

The American imperialists will bargain individually with France, England, and Japan in order to see with whom they should compromise and whom they can draw over to their side. The U.S.A. is struggling not for the limitation of armaments in general, but for its own advantage, trying to create a combination of the Great Powers which would permit the American imperialists to strengthen their world position without great expense . . . The first session of the Geneva conference ended without any results. It opened the door for new behind-the-scenes machinations of the imperialist groups.

This outcome of the Geneva conference serves as a warning to the popular masses of the entire world. If at a time of unprecedented crisis, when all the powers have huge budget deficits, when thirty-five to forty million people do not know what they will eat tomorrow, the imperialist powers are not able in the course of six months to decide on even some insignificant limitation of armaments, then it can mean only one thing: all of them are preparing for war, all of them are getting ready for a new division of the world with weapons in their hands. Yes, the imperialist powers have not yet reached agreement among themselves. It will be very difficult for them to fight, with tens of millions of unemployed in their rear areas, it will be especially difficult for them to fight against the Soviet Union, in which even the most backward workers and peasants of the entire world see the leader in the policy of peace . . .

But no matter how difficult it will be for the imperialists to fight, they are getting ready for new wars and therefore do not want the reduction of armaments. The history of the Geneva conference is the history of the bourgeois diplomatic babble about peace, the history of the preparation for war. And no matter how dull it might be to rummage through the resolutions and other papers of the Geneva conference, it becomes imperative to decipher the true content of these papers and make them known to the broadest masses.

84

Social-Democracy as the Chief Enemy of Communism

Excerpts from a speech by Gusev at the Twelfth Plenum of the ECCI, September 8, 1932. XII Plenum IKKI: stenograficheskii otchet *(Moscow, 1933)*, *II, pp. 199–200.*

The clearest indication of the end of capitalist stabilization is the development of the world revolutionary upsurge, which is developing on the basis of the world economic crisis and which includes the revolutions in China and Spain; the approaching revolutionary crisis in Germany, Poland, and Japan; the huge strikes in Belgium, Czechoslovakia, England, the U.S.A.; the ripening of the revolutionary crisis in India; and a series of uprisings in South America (Chile, Peru, Brazil).

More and more the broad masses are coming over to the side of the revolution. The forces of the world revolution are growing. But at the same time the forces of counterrevolution are also coming together. "The party of revolution unites the party of reaction" (Marx). The unfolding of the revolutionary upsurge and the ripening of the revolutionary crises cannot develop in any other way. There is not and cannot be a revolution without a counterrevolution to oppose it. It is therefore incorrect to suppose that the development of fascism signifies a weakening in the development of the forces of revolution. This could be true only after the defeat of the revolution, after the ebbing of the revolution, in the period of reaction (for example, the growth of fascism in Italy in 1922–23).

But such a view is completely erroneous under the conditions of a developing revolutionary upsurge. The development of the revolutionary upsurge means the growth of the forces of revolution, not their weakening. The forces of revolution grow and launch the attack, as the result of which the forces of counterrevolution become unified and go over to the counterattack against the forces of revolution. The struggle flares up and rises to its highest stage, to revolution.

Thus the bourgeois-imperialist counterrevolution in the epoch of the socialist transformation of society is not some accidental objective obstacle for the revolution but historically inevitable. There cannot be a revolution without a counterrevolution.

The historical inevitability of counterrevolution must be emphasized because here and there in the sections of the CI the view has appeared that the development of fascism signifies some unforeseen and at the same time very dangerous additional difficulty for the revolution, as though the development of fascism signifies almost the end of revolution. Fascism itself would appear to be the result, allegedly, of the incorrect course followed by the CI and its sections. Such a view of fascism can only be described as capitulating. Since allegedly the revolution could only be victorious when the counterrevolution did not exist, the appearance of fascism is explained by the adherents of this view as the predetermined inevitable doom of the revolution. Therefore it is proposed to retreat, to capitulate to fascism. This kind of capitulationist view is contained in the recent speech by Comrade Humbert-Droz to the Swiss Communist Party, which objectively provided the platform of the international Right.

Comrade Humbert-Droz has repudiated these views, which however cannot erase the fact that such views are arising here and there, and incidentally not only in Switzerland. The source of these views is to be found in the failure to understand that it is precisely the growth of revolutionary forces which inevitably evokes the hardening of the forces of fascism.

Exactly the same failure to understand the relationship between the growth of revolutionary forces and the development of fascism in the period of the unfolding and growth of the revolutionary upsurge underlies the fatalistic theory which sprang up in the German Communist Party a year ago and which at the time was completely correctly criticized by Comrade Thälmann. What is the essence of these fatalistic theories which superficially appear so similar to Marx's thesis of the inevitability of the consolidation of the forces of counterrevolution in the course of development of the revolution, but which in reality present a crude distortion of this thesis? The essence of these fatalistic theories is that the working class must pass through fascist reaction in order to comprehend the necessity for revolution, that only the fascist dictatorship is able to bring the masses to the necessity of starting the revolutionary struggle: to put it more briefly, that without counterrevolution there can be no revolution, that counterrevolution shapes the party of revolution. This is exactly the opposite of what Marx says, not that revolution evokes counterrevolution, as Marx and Lenin taught, but the reverse, that counterrevolution evokes revolution; the point of departure for the revolutionary upsurge is thus not the growth of the forces of revolution, as Marx and Lenin taught, but the growth of the forces of counterrevolution.

The correct Marxist-Leninist formulation of the question of the relation between the growth of the forces of revolution and the development of fascism is of decisive significance for the entire strategy of the CI and its sections. The views of Humbert-Droz lead to a retreating, capitulationist strategy, the views of the German "fatalists" to a passive, waiting strategy, i.e., in reality to exactly the same capitulation to fascism as with Humbert-Droz. Yet the revolutionary upsurge cannot signify anything but the beginning of a strategic attack by the revolutionary forces, in which there may be both defensive and offensive battles.

No less significant for Bolshevik strategy than the question of the relation between the growth of revolutionary forces and the development of fascism is the question of the relation between fascism and social-fascism. This question has been worked out in detail in the theses. Nevertheless there still exists in a few sections a lack of understanding of the special role of social-democracy as the main social bulwark of the bourgeoisie and, in connection with this, a lack of understanding of Bolshevik strategy.

The Bolshevik strategy of the CI has always been in the period of the preparation and denouement of the revolution to direct the main blow against the conciliatory parties (against the social-democrats and the national-reformists). It is sufficient to look at the history of the Russian Revolution to be convinced of this.

. . .

The Bolsheviks in 1905 were accused of directing the struggle too much against the liberal-monarchist conciliatory bourgeoisie, relegating to a secondary position the struggle against the enemy, against tsarism. The Bolsheviks in 1917 were accused of directing the struggle too much against the conciliatory petty-bourgeois parties of the Mensheviks and Socialist Revolutionaries, relegating to a secondary position the struggle against the enemy, against the bourgeoisie.

Accusations of this kind simply reveal a complete failure to understand the role of the conciliatory parties and the nature of Bolshevik strategy.

Why must the main blow in the period of the preparation of the revolution and the approach of its denouement be directed against the conciliatory parties?

Because the conciliatory parties (the social-fascists and the national reformists) in the period of the approaching revolutionary denouement are the most dangerous social support of the enemies of the revolution. Because it is impossible to conquer the enemy without the isolation of these parties, without detaching from them the broad masses of the toilers.

Both fascism and social-fascism represent bourgeois-imperialist counterrevolution, but social-fascism is a special detachment of bourgeois-imperialist counterrevolution, having its own special tasks. Wherein do these special tasks lie? In striving by all means to reach a compromise, an agreement of the proletariat with its class enemy, with the bourgeoisie (in particular with fascism). By preaching compromise, and also by carrying on a bogus struggle against fascism, to restrain the workers from actions against fascism, against the political and economic offensive of capital, in short, to restrain the workers from revolutionary actions, from revolution. Thus social-fascism plays the role of a shield behind which counterrevolution can organize its forces. Therefore, in order to beat the enemy, the bourgeoisie, it is necessary to direct the main blow against its chief social bulwark, against the chief enemy of communism in the working class, against social-democracy, against social-fascism.

It may seem that in Germany at the present time, for example, the chief social bulwark of the bourgeoisie is fascism, and that therefore we should deal the main blow against fascism.

This is not correct. It is not correct, first, because fascism is not our chief enemy in the workers' movement, but social-fascism is our chief enemy in the workers' movement. What does this mean? It means that to win over the majority of the proletariat, i.e., to prepare the *basic* condition for the proletarian revolution, it is necessary to direct the main blow against social-fascism.

It is not correct, secondly, because the blow directed by us against social-fascism differs from the blow delivered against fascism. Fascism is open counterrevolution utilizing social demagogy. Social-fascism is concealed counterrevolution. Take, for example, the attitude of German fascism and German social-fascism to intervention against the U.S.S.R. The fascists are for intervention, and openly say so; the social-fascists are also for intervention, but openly talk of the defense of the U.S.S.R. (resolution of the Second International). This means that we have to strike at fascism in a manner different from that in which we would strike at social-fascism.

It is exactly in Germany at the present time that we can see most clearly the difference in the character of the blows which we deal against social-fascism and against fascism. We expose the social-fascists, but we never call for an armed struggle against them. We fight the fascists in the streets, carrying on explanatory work among the masses to the extent that the fascists still resort to social demagogy. In the period of preparations for revolution (and it is just such a period which we are now passing through in Germany, Poland, and Japan), our chief weapon is exposure, or, to use the expression of Marx, the weapon of criticism, whereas armed struggle, or as Marx expressed it, the criticism of weapons, is our secondary weapon in this period. We direct the main weapon against the main social bulwark of the bourgeoisie.

The united front with the social-democratic workers in the fight against the fascist gangs unites both kinds of weapons: the main and the secondary weapons. On the one hand, the united front is an armed fight against fascist gangs; on the other hand, the united front is the best means of exposing the social-fascist leaders in practice.

From everything that has been said it is clear that in the period of preparation for revolution we direct our main blow by our main weapon for this period against our chief enemy in the working class, i.e., social-fascism.

The main blow against social-fascism, the isolation of social-fascism, means the winning over of the majority of the working class, and also of the toiling masses of the petty bourgeoisie, urban and rural, the transformation of the toiling masses of the petty bourgeoisie from a reserve of the bourgeoisie into a reserve of the proletariat. Without this the victory of the revolution would be impossible.

. . .

85

Gusev Attacks the "Sectarian Approach to the Masses" of the British and American Communist Parties

Excerpts from a speech at the Twelfth Plenum of the ECCI, September 1932. XII Plenum IKKI, *II, 201–203, 206–207.*

. . .

. . . The sources of the sectarian approach to the masses in England and the U.S.A. are different. In England, this characteristic is explained by the fact that the Communist Party [of Great Britain] has supported the Labour Party at the elections for a number of years and the necessary transition to the tactic of "class against class" was accompanied by a stubborn intraparty struggle against the Right deviation. Therefore the tactic of the united front with the workers who belong to the Labour Party has been looked upon by a significant portion of the [communist] party members as a step back from the tactic of "class against class." On this basis, there has developed a sectarian resistance in the party to the shift to the tactic of the united front with workers who belong to the Labour Party and the Independent Labour Party. The English comrades were afraid of the united front and therefore, in spite of many favorable opportunities, the CPGB has hardly any practical achievements along this line. However, in countries like England and Germany, where there are big social-fascist parties and very big reformist trade-unions, there can be no question of winning over the majority of the workers unless the tactic of the united front is adopted and unless work is carried on in the trade-unions. Therefore the sectarian tendencies in the CPGB really mean a Right-opportunist lagging behind the mass movement, and this is the chief danger.

The situation in England at the present time is such that the CPGB could win thousands of workers from the Labour Party and the Independent Labour Party into its ranks, and into the ranks of the Minority Movement. . . . But the party does not see this task, and does not set itself this task, because it does not know how to distinguish the maneuvers of the leaders from the genuine striving of the workers. Consequently, the party repulses the workers of the Labour Party and of the Independent Labour Party who are turning to them.

Here is a very characteristic example of how this is done.

The Independent Labour Party, as is known, not long ago left the Labour Party and published its own "statute." In this "statute" there are some very "Leftist" things: "The conquest of power by the united working class," "refusal to use methods of gradual reform," "decisive transition from capitalism to socialism," "socialization of the vitally important resources of the country, including the banks and finances, the land and agriculture, the basic branches of industry and transport," etc.

All of this concerns internal affairs. In the international sphere the following program:

"The Independent Labour Party will strive for decisive counteraction by means of individual and collective resistance to every preparation for war . . . If . . . war is declared, the Independent Labour Party will demand the immediate calling of a general strike . . . The Independent Labour Party repeats its demand that England give an example of real disarmament, regardless of how the other governments act."

How did our communist party react to the withdrawal of the Independent Labour Party from the Labour Party and to its statute-program, which I have just cited?

In the first place, the withdrawal of the Independent Labour Party from the Labour Party was declared to be a "swindle." Undoubtedly, there was a very considerable element of swindle in the actual withdrawal of the Independent Labour Party. But to equate everything with a swindle means not to see, behind the physiognomies of the leaders of the Independent Labour Party, the membership masses who sincerely want to revivify or, as the members of the ILP themselves say, "rejuvenate" the ILP and transform it into a revolutionary party. This sincere Left trend of the members of the Independent Labour Party (and the Labour Party) passes unnoticed by our party. The party does not understand that the withdrawal of workers from the Labour Party is a difficult transition in their political development.

. . .

. . . The sources of the sectarian approach to the masses in the American Communist Party are not the same as in England. Sectarianism is explained here by the fact that, up to the present, the majority of the members, and especially the leading cadres of the party, have not been native-born American workers, while a considerable proportion of the cadres came from small industry and a number of them are of petty-bourgeois origin. The real nature of this sectarianism consists of a Right opportunist lagging behind the mass movement.

In contrast to the CPGB, the American Communist Party has had to its credit several big strikes which it led independently.

The above experience shows that our party and the Red trade-unions have a broad opportunity to lead independent economic struggles. However, this opportunity is utilized without any definite and consistently applied plan; it is done in the style of guerrilla warfare, episodically, disconnectedly. Therefore, it is not surprising that the strikes which are successfully led by us do not leave any trace on our party and our trade-unions . . . Take the well-known strike of the textile workers in Gastonia which brought us the sympathy of the workers in the South and gave us the opportunity to create a party organization there. But what is there in Gastonia now? Not a single member of the party. Take last year's strike in Illinois-Ohio. After the strike our union was not strengthened but weakened.

The American CP has recently led several big strikes and big revolutionary unemployed actions, but it is quite obvious that strong sectarian tendencies, especially in the question of the attitude to partial demands, still underlie this lack of plan and guerrilla-like procedure in the sphere of leadership of the economic struggles by the party. Comrade [Max] Bedacht reports that he ran into a number of cases in which our comrades, in speaking during the election campaign, offered excuses for the fact that the party was advancing partial demands. They declared that they realized, of course, that the solution of all problems would be revolution, but that the workers did not yet know this and therefore we advanced partial demands, even though this had absolutely no significance whatever. (*Laughter.*) At one meeting, at which Comrade Bedacht spoke on the question of social insurance, the workers in the auditorium told him that other party speakers had told them that our campaign for social insurance was not serious, that we did not expect to receive anything from it and were not particularly disturbed by this, since any concession would objectively patch up the capitalist system, [with the result that] the workers would be satisfied and would not wish for revolution.

The sectarian tendencies of the American CP are the chief hindrance for carrying out the tactic of the united front.

Here is one of a series of examples of how this is done.

The strike of 25,000 textile workers in Lawrence. At a meeting of the strikers, organized by the United Textile Workers' union, which belongs to the A.F. of L., there were from three to eight thousand persons. We organized a meeting on the outskirts to which 300 to 500 persons came. The result was our isolation from the basic mass of the strikers. When the reformists for the last time called a meeting, thousands of workers appeared, but there was no one to speak at the meeting, since the reformists had already decided at that time to end the strike, and they left the meeting without guidance, whereas our comrades did not know about this meeting, just as in general they take little interest in meetings called by the reformists. The strike collapsed.

One American comrade characterized the attitude of the party toward the strike as follows: they regard a struggle led by the revolutionary trade-unions as a struggle of "our workers," but a strike led by the A.F. of L. as a struggle "not of our workers."

Another American observer, Comrade Bedacht, made the following statement at the July session of the Politburo: "Our comrades divide the working class into two categories: our friends and our enemies."

"Our workers" and "not our workers"—that is the united front, American style. This sectarian formulation, however, not only does not hinder, it is the basic cause of the profoundly opportunist "gentleman's agreements" with the reformists in the "division of spheres of influence," such as took place in Illinois.

Work among the unemployed, according to the admission of the American comrades themselves (statement by Comrade Newton) "is still conducted on a narrow basis and has a sectarian character." It is therefore not surprising that it has been declining, contracting. In the first quarter of 1932 the number registered in the unemployed organization stood at 30,000 and in the second quarter at 13,000.

One of the largest mass political actions in which the party played a prominent role was the veterans' movement. It is necessary to dwell on the analysis of the party's line in this movement because of the fact that this kind of mass movement, embracing the petty-bourgeois masses along with the workers, is becoming ever more widespread in the U.S.A. and the question of the conquest of these masses by our party is acquiring the greatest significance.

The party leadership manifested toward the veterans' movement a series of hesitations, the basic cause of which is a sectarian-doctrinaire approach toward the masses. At the outset the Politburo took the decision: "To transform the veterans' march into the sending of mass delegations, chosen by former soldiers, to a number of designated cities—Chicago, Cleveland, Detroit, Pittsburgh, Philadelphia, and New York."

This decision, as the subsequent course of events demonstrated, was completely wrong and in essence was directed toward demobilizing the masses, suppressing their initiative.

The movement developed on a broad scale and could have developed much more broadly if the party from the very beginning had not taken a completely wrong approach.

But even when the movement had developed broadly and up to 25,000 veterans had assembled in Washington, the Politburo still could not rid itself of the sectarian-doctrinaire approach and adopted this decision: "The line of our comrades must be to draw a sharp class differentiation within the veterans' camp."

Instead of trying to extend the influence of our League of Worker—War Veterans and capture the leadership of the movement as a whole, the League was instructed to isolate itself from the great majority of the veterans, from the petty-bourgeois strata, and hand them over to the fascist Captain Waters, Norman Thomas from the American Federation of Labor, and the founders of the fascist blue-shirt organization of Pastor Cox.

What is the use of such a policy? This is not a line for winning over the masses; this is a line of flight from the masses.

. . .

The deepening of the economic crisis, the end of capitalist stabilization, the revolutionary upsurge, will be accompanied by huge mass movements, militant actions by *all* the downtrodden and exploited, with the most various and often contradictory demands. To fear these contradictions, to hide from them, to establish benevolent neutrality toward the petty-bourgeois masses who are entering the battle against capitalism under reactionary slogans— this means to display a complete lack of understanding of how popular revolutions take place and what our attitude toward mass movements ought to be.

. . .

To eradicate decisively the sectarian-doctrinaire approach to the mass movement, which condemns the party to Right-opportunist lagging behind—that is the central task of the English and American sections of the Comintern, which will decide everything, define everything. Without such an eradication, without a basic change in the approach to the masses, these parties will be condemned to having the masses pass them by, or in the best of circumstances they will succeed sometimes, in individual cases, in controlling individual actions of the masses, in the manner of guerrilla warfare, as was done in Burnley [Lancashire], or in Illinois, but they will not be able to establish a firm influence among the masses.

What basic conditions are essential in order to bring about a decisive change in the approach to the masses? There are two such conditions: the reorganization of the parties on the basis of intraparty democracy, and the creation of new cadres.

I am not talking about formal democracy, about that democracy which the social-democrats profess and on which they build their party. I am talking about genuine, Bolshevik democracy. What does Bolshevik democracy consist of? It consists of drawing every member of the party into the political life of the party, into the everyday work and struggle, into collective work in the preparation and leadership of mass battles, into friendly, comradely work on the basis of iron intraparty discipline, for Bolshevik democracy does not exclude but presupposes iron party discipline:

> "We understand by democracy both the raising of the activity and consciousness of the party masses, and the systematic drawing in of the party masses, not only into the consideration of questions, but into the leadership of work." (Stalin)

That is exactly the kind of genuine Bolshevik democracy which is completely inadequate in many sections of the Comintern. And this is the first, basic reason why these sections are unable to turn toward the broad masses.

. . .

The English and American parties are faced at present with four fundamental tasks:

(1) To direct the basic strategic blow against social-democracy, to win the masses away from it, to isolate it from the masses.

(2) To win over the majority of the proletariat and the poorest farmers, to train them in a series of battles and convert them into our political army.

(3) To reorganize our party into a party of the masses on the basis of Bolshevik intraparty democracy resting on iron discipline, into a revolutionary staff of this political army.

(4) To enlarge, strengthen, and renew our party commanding personnel.

In 1925, Comrade Stalin described the revolutionary perspectives as follows:

> "The world revolutionary movement at the present time has entered the stage of the ebb of revolution, but this ebb . . . must give place to an upsurge which may end in the victory of the proletariat, but also may not end in victory, and may be replaced by a new ebb which, in turn, will give place to a new upsurge of the revolution." (Stalin, *Problemy Leninizma* [9th ed.], p. 110)

The prophecy of Comrade Stalin has been fulfilled. A new upsurge of the revolution has already begun. This upsurge may end in victory. But this victory is possible for England and the U.S.A. only if the four fundamental tasks are carried out: the routing of social-democracy and social-fascism, the formation of a mass political army, the conversion of the party into the fighting staff of this army, and the formation of a strong commanding echelon.

If they succeed in carrying out these tasks, then victory will be gained in the second round of revolutions and wars.

But however things may end in England and the U.S.A., it is completely clear that the base of the world revolution, the U.S.S.R., will emerge from the second round of wars and revolutions bigger and stronger.

86

Manuilsky on the Failure of the Capitalist Countries to Solve Their Domestic Problems

Excerpts from a report to the Twelfth Plenum of the ECCI, August 27–September 15, 1932. XII Plenum IKKI, *III, 129–130.*

As is known, our epoch of wars and proletarian revolutions is characterized by the fact that the struggle between the two systems— the dying world of capitalism and the rising world of socialism— is becoming the key point of world politics and economics as a whole. In the light of this struggle, political parties, their programs, their methods of leading the masses, their words and their actions, are being tested. Political doctrines pass from the sphere of demagogic promises and assurances into actual practice, which the masses perceive through their own concrete experience. It is precisely the present world crisis in the world of capitalism and the successes of socialist construction in the first land of proletarian dictatorship which open up for the proletarian masses a wide field of observation, reflection, weighing of facts, and making political deductions. The masses are now going through the greatest political school, but they are going through it along various paths, corresponding to their own "national" conditions. One of the tasks of this plenum is to assist the toiling masses of all the capitalist countries to formulate the doubts that arise in their minds concerning traditional "sound thoughts," to make them reflect upon the entire historic result of the postwar period.

This result has been inexhaustibly rich, comrades. There is not only the experience of the proletarian revolution in Russia in 1917, but also the experience of revolutions in Austria and Germany, the experience of so-called democratic-socialism in all its various forms, such as political democracy, industrial democracy, constructive socialism; the experience of coalition governments and the experience of non-coalition labor governments; the experience of the so-called winning of a majority by legal, parliamentary methods, and the experience of dictatorship. Whatever country you take, it provides the greatest lesson for the world proletariat.

Take for example the U.S.A., the country of the most classical and pure dictatorship of the bourgeoisie in the form of bourgeois democracy, where the bourgeoisie had governed without even requiring the services of their mangy social-democracy. The bourgeoisie of the U.S.A. boasted that the U.S.A. was the incarnation of reason, justice, and the eternal existence of the capitalist system; that by its entire experience it refuted the socialist ravings of the European dreamers; that they had no social problem; that they had not only the highest profits but also the very highest wages; that in the U.S.A. every European emigrant carried, like Napoleon's soldiers, if not a marshal's baton, that of a millionaire; that there was not, is not, and never will be a class struggle in the U.S.A.; that the U.S.A. had eternal prosperity. Who now, even among the most shameless apologists of capitalism, would dare to repeat these assertions, which have been refuted by the whole course of events of the world crisis in the United States today, in this land where the working class actually enjoys no rights whatsover?

Or take Great Britain, that living example of the bankruptcy of the idea of the prosperity of a country pursuing an imperialist, predatory policy. Precisely at this time, when the bourgeoisie of all the capitalist countries, and of Japan especially, are calling for a way out of the crisis by means of war, by means of seizing new territories, by enslaving new peoples, the experience of Great Britain cries out to the toilers of all countries against this panacea with the help of which the ruling classes still fool the toiling masses. Great Britain has carried on wars, it seized and plundered hundreds of millions of alien peoples, subjected to itself entire continents, but this has not saved it from decay, which commenced long before the present world crisis . . .

And do we not gain an instructive lesson from the postwar policies of the largest party of the Second International, German Social-Democracy? German Social-Democracy rose to power on the wave of the revolution of 1918. For years they fooled the workers with promises to bring about socialism by democratic means . . . In practice their whole policy was food and drink for fascism. For years they have been paving the way for it piecemeal by their policy of the "lesser evil," until they finally surrendered all power to it without the slightest attempt at resistance. French Social-Democracy saw in the Versailles system the "natural right" of French imperialism to exploit Germany, the whole of central and eastern Europe, and the colonies, a guarantee of a privileged position for the upper stratum of the French workers' aristocracy. The consequence is the bankruptcy of Versailles, of the Dawes and Young plans, the collapse of the legend about the impossibility of an economic crisis in France.

Let us next take fascism, the spread of which in the capitalist states indicates that there are large masses who still believe in the possibility of finding a way out of the present crisis along capitalist lines. But has not fascism after ten years in Italy led to bloody persecution together with unprecedented destitution for the masses? Has not unbridled reaction in Yugoslavia, Bulgaria, and Hungary, and in Spain before the overthrow of Primo de Rivera's military dictatorship, shown to the millions of workers and peasants of Europe what fascism brings them when it is victorious? Finally, a not unimportant lesson is to be drawn from Spain with regard to the anarchist and the anarcho-syndicalist leadership of the working class in the revolution. In words, the anarchists there appeared to be the enemies of the bourgeois state, but both in words and deeds they were enemies of the revolutionary methods of the proletarian dictatorship. And therefore their leadership led the heroic working-class of Spain from defeat to defeat—politically and organizationally it disarmed it and handed it over to the force of the Spanish counterrevolution. These are just a few of the results of development in various capitalist countries.

. . .

87

Manuilsky Urges the Communists of the World to Promote Proletarian Revolution

Excerpts from a speech at the Twelfth Plenum of the ECCI, September 15, 1932. XII Plenum IKKI, *III, 143–144.*

. . .

The proletariat of the U.S.S.R., under the leadership of the CPSU (B), has assured the victory of socialism with the support of the world proletariat, but, for the time being, without the actual aid of the world proletarian revolution.

However, the cause of socialism in the U.S.S.R. would stride forward immeasurably if help came from you in the form of the proletarian revolution.

The world proletariat must know that its belatedness in regard to the world proletarian revolution has created for us many additional difficulties. The fact that our proletariat was the first to break through the imperialist front without the support of the proletarian revolution in other countries made its task particularly difficult, far more difficult than it will be for the workers of the countries who in the approaching second round of revolutions and wars will take the path of the proletarian revolution.

It is true that in the struggle for the proletarian revolution in your countries there are a number of additional difficulties which we, the Russians, did not encounter on the eve of [the] October [Revolution]. But you also have many advantages which we did not have when we marched to October.

It is true that your capitalism is more firmly established than Russian capitalism was in 1917, but your proletariat is more numerous and stronger than our proletariat was.

It is true that your bourgeoisie is cleverer, that it has utilized the experience of October, but it is also the task of the communist parties to learn from the experience of October, so as to be strong, prepared, against the cunning, deceitful, and clever enemy.

It is true that we, the Bolsheviks, had the advantage of the war situation, but you have the advantage of the world crisis.

It is true that we were saved by the enormous expanse of our territory, but you have behind you the enormous *staging-area* of the proletarian revolution and socialism in the U.S.S.R.

It is true that social-democracy is stronger in your countries, but if you have not been able to shake off the influence of social-democracy in the course of the World War, the proletarian revolution in the U.S.S.R., and the revolutions in the Central [European] empires, the present world crisis, then the fault certainly rests with you.

It is true that fascism has arisen athwart the path of the proletarian revolution in your countries, which was not the case with us, but the appearance and growth of fascism are due to the overripeness of capitalism and the belatedness of the proletarian revolution.

At the Second Congress of the Comintern we said that the

proletarian struggle for the seizure of power in the capitalist countries should be more difficult than it was with us. But, comrades, certain changes have taken place since that time. The U.S.S.R. has victoriously fulfilled its first Five-Year Plan and has embarked on a second, thereby rendering enormous assistance to the world proletariat in its struggle for power. The country that next follows the U.S.S.R. in taking the path of the proletarian revolution will have behind it not the socialist republic of 1920, the period of War Communism, but a socialistically industrialized country which has completed a Five-Year Plan. We rushed into battle alone in the sense that we had behind us neither a victorious proletarian revolution nor a country which was victoriously building socialism. We had no ready-made models of the practical construction of socialism. You have an invincible fortress—a socialist country with a firm industrial basis. Our experience of the various stages of our revolution will help you to avoid many difficulties in the sphere of relations with the peasants, the New Economic Policy, collectivization, the management of socialized industry, etc. We took a road hitherto untrodden by human feet: you will march along a beaten path. For you the building of socialism will be many times easier than it was for us, because you will inherit from the past a higher level of productive forces than our October Revolution. And if we were able to win our tremendous successes, overcoming those difficulties day by day which were placed in our path by the low level of productive forces which we had inherited, then what unprecedented rates of development and expansion will you achieve when your productive forces are put on a socialist basis!

The experience of our first Five-Year Plan and the prospects of the second, which is beginning, tell the workers of the capitalist countries who still fear the cost of the revolution and the difficulties of constructing socialism:

In 1918–19, after the end of the World War, you feared the cost of revolution, but during the past fifteen years you have suffered greater losses in preserving the obsolete capitalist system. And will it be only fifteen years? You were afraid that revolution and civil war would destroy the productive forces, but the world crisis of capitalism has destroyed them to a far greater extent. You were afraid of the convulsions which might be caused by the proletarian revolution—unemployment, depreciation of currency, fierce class struggle, bloody wars—but capitalism has brought upon you tremendous convulsions: fascism, wars, the disruption of the material base under millions of human beings. You dreamed of a "stable capitalism," but the relative, rotten capitalist stabilization which was established after the first round of revolutions and wars has come to an end. You were afraid of the difficulties of socialist construction, but capitalism has compelled you to share with it all the sufferings of its own death agony: the closing down of factories, the failures of banks, unemployment and the loss of savings of small depositors, wage cuts, the reduction and even the abolition of social insurance, the increase of exploitation.

Proletarians, you must choose between capitalism and socialism, between reaction and revolution, between the dictatorship of the bourgeoisie and the dictatorship of your own class. There are no other ways out. And we have no doubt as to the choice which the working class of the world will make: this path of the proletariat of the U.S.S.R., this path of revolution and victory! (*Stormy applause. Delegates rise and sing the "International."*)

88

The Development of the Revolutionary Upsurge, According to the ECCI

Excerpt from the Theses on "The International Situation" adopted by the Twelfth Plenum. XII Plenum IKKI, III, 165–166.

. . .

1. Since the Eleventh Plenum of the ECCI the growth of the revolutionary upsurge has become particularly evident in the following countries:

In China—a mass upsurge of the anti-imperialist struggle, the development of the soviet movement, outstanding successes by the heroic Chinese Red Army. *In Spain*—a turbulent upsurge of the mass movement, with the tendency to develop into a popular armed uprising. *In Poland*—a wave of mass strikes, numerous militant actions by peasants, and the rise of a new wave of the national revolutionary movement in the outlying regions of Poland. *In*

Germany—an increase in the mass influence of the communist party, a shift to resistance by social-democratic workers, in defiance of their leaders, against the terror of fascist gangs. *In England*—a strike by the sailors of the navy, turbulent workers' demonstrations in the autumn of 1931, the strike movement in Lancashire. *In Czechoslovakia*—a general miners' strike in northern Bohemia, a revolutionary movement of the workers and peasants in Sub-Carpathian Ukraine. *In France*—big strikes in the north, disruption of military air maneuvers. *In the U.S.A.*—big strikes by the workers, demonstrations by the unemployed, the march of war veterans to Washington, militant actions by the farmers. Of major international significance is the general strike in *Belgium*. In most countries the strike struggles were accompanied by fierce clashes with the police and strikebreaker gangs. *In Japan*—militant demonstrations of the workers, peasants, soldiers, and students which break through the restrictions of military and police terror. *In India*—an increase of revolutionary unrest in the towns and villages, stubborn mass strikes. In a whole series of countries the struggle of the proletariat is interwoven with the mass revolutionary fights of the peasants.

2. During this period the communist parties have increased their strength. In Germany, important success achieved by the party in the last Reichstag elections, development of the anti-fascist struggle under the leadership of the party on the basis of the united front from below. Growth of the mass influence of the communist parties of China, Poland, Bulgaria. In France, in spite of the fact that the communist party suffered considerable losses in the parliamentary elections and that the membership of the United Confederation of Labor has somewhat declined, there is a considerable upsurge of the anti-war revolutionary movement. In a number of countries (Czechoslovakia, Spain, Finland), development is proceeding unevenly as between one region and another. Despite the weakness of the mass influence of the communist parties in a whole series of countries, the communists in all parts of the capitalist world, in numerous fights and ordeals, under conditions of merciless terror, have shown themselves to be brave and truly revolutionary advanced fighters of the proletariat.

3. The end of capitalist stabilization, the rapid growth in the prerequisites of a revolutionary crisis in a number of capitalist states, and the new international situation in general have sharply raised the problem of solving the basic task of the communist parties at the present time: the preparation of the working class and

the exploited masses, in the course of the economic and political struggle, for the impending battles for power, for the dictatorship of the proletariat. Precisely because little time remains before the revolutionary crisis matures, it is necessary, without losing a single moment, to *intensify* and *accelerate* Bolshevik mass work for the purpose of winning over the majority of the working class, for the purpose of increasing the revolutionary activity of the working class. The opponents of the revolutionary movement have not as yet lost the support of an enormous section of organized and unorganized workers, and this circumstance, which enables them to impede the revolutionization of the proletariat, constitutes the fundamental danger with regard to preparing for its victory. Hence the necessity for ensuring the realization of the task of winning over the majority of the working class, which was placed in the forefront at the Tenth and Eleventh Plenums of the ECCI.

4. The successful fulfillment of this task demands the establishment, broadening, strengthening, of a *continuous, vital link* between each communist party and the *majority* of the workers wherever there are working masses. Necessary for this are first of all: (*a*) the genuine establishment of continuous Bolshevik work among the noncommunist working masses at enterprises, among the reformist and other trade-unions and among the unemployed, the systematic unmasking of the treachery of the social-democratic and reformist leaders, the winning away of those workers who have fallen under the influence of fascism; (*b*) defense of the everyday interests of the workers, the ability to react to every attack by the class enemy, presenting each time *concrete slogans* which are really capable of mobilizing the masses for the struggle; the systematic implementation of the line of the *united front from below;* the establishment of a union of the proletariat with the small peasants, drawing into the struggle employees and the exploited masses of the urban petty bourgeoisie under the leadership of the proletariat; (*c*) *strengthening of the communist party itself* on the basis of the formation of cadres closely connected with the masses and enjoying their confidence.

. . .

89

The Tasks of the Communist Parties Defined

Resolution of the Twelfth Plenum of the ECCI on "The Immediate Tasks of the Sections of the CI," September 1932. XII Plenum IKKI, *III, 167–169.*

1. The general task of the Comintern and its sections in all capitalist countries at the present time is to wage a concrete struggle (a) *against the attack by capital,* (b) *against fascism and reaction,* (c) *against the impending imperialist war and intervention against the Soviet Union.*

The proper conduct of this struggle against the attack of the bourgeoisie is very closely connected with *winning over the majority of the working class,* undermining and smashing the mass influence of *social-democracy.* The main link which the communist parties must grasp in fulfilling this task is the struggle for the everyday economic and political interests of the broad masses against increasing poverty, against oppression, violence, terror. This is particularly important under the conditions of the end of capitalist stabilization, the sharp contraction of the material base of reformism and the cynical betrayal of the interests of the workers by social-democracy, when the struggle for the most elementary needs of the masses brings them face-to-face with the very bases of the existence of capitalism. Only by supporting the everyday interests of the masses can the communist parties defend and strengthen the position of the working class and lead it on to ever higher forms of struggle and to the decisive battles for the dictatorship of the proletariat. When the proper conditions for it exist, the preparation and the carrying out of a *mass political strike* is one of the most important connecting links in the revolutionary struggle of the proletariat. It is necessary to conduct systematic propaganda for the dictatorship of the proletariat and to popularize the Soviet Union, where the proletariat is successfully building a classless socialist society.

2. The specific tasks of the major communist parties include:

Communist Party of Germany: To mobilize the masses of millions of toilers in defense of their vital interests, against their exploitation by monopolist capital, against fascism, against emergency decrees, against nationalism and chauvinism, and by developing economic and political strikes, by struggle for proletarian internationalism, by means of demonstrations, to lead the masses to the general political strike; winning over the basic social-democratic masses, resolutely overcoming the weaknesses of trade-union work. The chief slogan which the Communist Party of Germany must put forward to offset the slogan of fascist dictatorship (the "Third Reich") and the slogan of the Social-Democratic Party (the "Second Republic") is the slogan of the *workers' and peasants' republic,* i.e., Soviet Socialist Germany, which will also guarantee the possibility of the voluntary affiliation of the people of Austria and other German territories.

The Communist Party of France: A turn in the direction of defending the daily interests of the worker and peasant masses (against wage cuts, for social insurance, for immediate relief for the unemployed, against the tax burden, etc.), linking this defense with the struggle against Versailles, against the subjection of Alsace-Lorraine and the colonies, and against the war policy of French imperialism. Reorienting the party, the unitary trade-unions and the Young Communist League in this direction; overcoming by persistent mass work the sectarianism of its young cadres, re-educating them on the basis of a broad policy of elections and of winning the confidence of the rank-and-file masses; patiently and tirelessly to struggle for the liberation of the syndicalist and socialist workers from reformist, parliamentary, and pacifist illusions.

The Communist Party of Poland: Widening the front of economic and political strikes; destroying the mass influence of the Socialist Party of Poland; leadership of peasant actions throughout Poland; overcoming the weaknesses of the party in the big factories, among railroad workers, in the army. If suitable conditions arise, the party must take the initiative in calling a general strike. Mobilization of the broad masses of town and village against the criminal policy of an anti-Soviet war. Persistent ideological struggle against the nationalist prejudices of the Polish workers, peasants, and petty bourgeoisie.

The Communist Party of Czechoslovakia: The further development of economic and political battles on the basis of the united front from below, linking up this struggle with the exposure of the role of the Czechoslovak government as the tool of French imperialism. Intensification of the struggle against social-democracy, systematically overcoming all tendencies towards passivity and lagging behind; winning the leadership of the struggles, and organizationally consolidating the mass influence which the communist party and the Red trade-unions have won in the course of the struggle.

The Communist Party of Italy must come out from the deep underground by developing a mass struggle against the fascist dictatorship on the basis of the defense of the everyday interests of the toilers, utilizing fascist meetings, organizing impromptu meetings in the factories, penetrating into the fascist trade-unions and into cultural and cooperative organizations, preparing and carrying out strikes and demonstrations; strengthen in every way mass illegal work.

The Communist Party of Spain. Steering a course for the dictatorship of the proletariat and the peasantry in the form of soviets, create organizational support points of the mass movement of the toilers in the form of factory committees, committees of the unemployed, peasants' committees, elected committees of soldiers, overcoming sectarian aloofness and anarchist habits of work.

The Communist Party of England. Firm execution of a turn toward work in the reformist trade-unions and in the factories, rousing the working masses on the basis of the united front from below, for a struggle (1) against the new offensive of the bourgeoisie against wages and unemployment relief, (2) against the government policy of supporting and encouraging the anti-Soviet aggressiveness of Japanese and French imperialism, (3) for the independence of the British colonies and Ireland.

The Communist Party of the U.S.A. must mobilize the masses, concentrating on the struggle (1) for social insurance, against wage cuts, for immediate assistance for the unemployed; (2) for assistance for the ruined farmers; (3) for equal rights for Negroes and the right of self-determination for the Black Belt; (4) for the defense of the Chinese people and the Soviet Union. It is necessary to carry out the decision on the turn in the work of the party and the Trade Union Unity League.

The Communist Party of Japan has the task of transforming its struggle against war and the seizure of the territory of China into a real mass movement of the workers and peasants, linking it up closely with the struggle for the vital needs of the masses. Workers' and peasants' self-defense committees and the combined action of villages must be organized against the forcible collection of rents and taxes from the peasants and the seizure of land from tenants; explain to the masses the necessity for a revolutionary struggle for the confiscation of the land of the landlords, without compensation, for the benefit of the peasants.

The Communist Party of China. (1) Mobilization of the masses under the slogan of the national-revolutionary struggle against the Japanese and other imperialists, for the independence and unification of China; (2) development and unification of the soviet districts, strengthening of the Red Army; (3) struggle for the overthrow of the Kuomintang power; (4) a resolute policy of converting the Red trade-unions into mass organizations, winning over the workers belonging to the Kuomintang unions; (5) development of the guerrilla movement, in Manchuria launching slogans calling for the formation of peasants' committees, for boycotting taxes and government orders, for confiscating the property of the agents of the imperialists, for the establishment of an elected people's government; (6) popularization of the achievements of the soviet districts and the slogan of the fraternal alliance of the workers and peasants of China with the U.S.S.R.

The Communist Party of India. Strengthening the party, politically and organizationally, training Bolshevik cadres, a stubborn struggle in the reformist trade-unions, the development of a broad anti-imperialist front, liberation of the masses from the influence of the National Congress; agitational and organizational preparations for a general strike; all-round support to the peasant movement for the nonpayment of taxes, rent, and debts; popularization of the basic slogans and tasks of the agrarian revolution.

3. In regard to *organization,* the chief tasks of the sections of the Comintern are (*a*) careful concealment of communist cells in factories, combining this with completely fearless mass work; (*b*) immediate formation of strictly secret cells in military units and the militarized organizations of the bourgeoisie, in munition factories, railroads, in the ports; (*c*) a determined struggle against provocation in all its aspects and forms; (*d*) taking timely measures to ensure that the party can promptly pass to an illegal basis in case of necessity; (*e*) transformation of the party press into real mass organs which must deal with all painful questions that concern the broad mass of workers in simple language intelligible to the workers; (*f*) a thorough elimination from the leadership in all

branches of party work of *supercentralism,* the mere issuing of orders, the inflation of big central apparatuses and the stripping of local and lower party organs.

The ECCI insists on the transformation of the Young Communist League into a real mass organization, and it imposes on all communist parties the duty of securing an improvement in mass political work among the youth and the strengthening of the party leadership in the work of the Young Communist Leagues. Equally, the Comintern insists on the transformation of the sport leagues and the MOPR [International Red Aid] into genuine mass organizations. It is necessary to end decisively the underestimation of work among the female proletarian masses as an especially important task at the present time, and to develop the mobilization of working women on the basis of delegate meetings, considering this work as general party work. With regard to the education of newly recruited party members and new *cadres,* it is essential both to employ a system of schools of party education and to draw them into the day-by-day revolutionary work among the broad masses.

Internal party democracy, Bolshevik self-criticism, the discussion of the most important political problems in the lower party organizations, concrete leadership of their work, must be the basis of all party activities. These are also the necessary conditions for strengthening iron Bolshevik discipline in the ranks of the party.

A relentless struggle must be waged against all distortions of Marxism-Leninism, for the purity of party theory in the spirit outlined in Comrade Stalin's letter. Propaganda must be carried on for the principles of communism, the dictatorship of the proletariat and the Soviet state.

. . .

The crisis has shaken the capitalist system to its very foundations. In the U.S.S.R., socialism is achieving victories of world-historic importance. The forces of the socialist revolution are growing and rising all over the world. But at the same time the attack of world counterrevolution is becoming fiercer. The imperialist governments are ready to plunge the peoples into the most criminal of all criminal predatory wars.

The sections of the CI must answer this challenge of the world bourgeoisie by intensifying to the utmost their Bolshevik work, must hasten the revolutionizing of the broad masses, developing and leading the class battles of the toilers on the basis of the united front from below, leading the working class to the mass political strike, winning over the majority of the working class, directing the whole movement of the exploited classes and the oppressed peoples along the channel of the world socialist revolution.

90

The Comintern Prescribes Tactics for Organizing Workers

Excerpts from a resolution on "Lessons of Economic Strikes and the Struggle of the Unemployed" adopted at the Twelfth Plenum of the ECCI, September 1932. XII Plenum IKKI, III, 170–172.

. . .

3. Concerning Methods for Leadership in the Struggle of the Unemployed

The Twelfth Plenum of the ECCI directs the special attention of all sections of the Comintern to the tremendous and ever growing *political* significance of the *unemployed movement,* which is being aimed more and more *directly against the capitalist governments* (the struggle for food, for relief, for social insurance, against forced labor, etc.). Up till now, the struggle of the unemployed has been prepared and organized by the communist vanguard even to a much lesser degree than the strike struggle of the proletariat. The communist parties and the revolutionary trade-union organizations have not succeeded as yet in organizing serious mass actions of *the employed workers at the factories* in defense of the interests of the unemployed, even though it has been possible more and more frequently to draw the unemployed into active support of the workers on strike.

The most serious shortcoming in the mass work of the communist parties among the unemployed is the inadequate attention to the organization of the struggle for partial demands of the unemployed. At the same time, the Twelfth Plenum of the ECCI points out the extremely weak popularization of the programs of demands for the unemployed which have been worked out by a number of communist parties, the active struggle for which would mean the realization of a united front both of the unemployed themselves and between the unemployed and employed workers at the factories. The Twelfth Plenum of the ECCI declares that the decisions of the Eleventh Plenum and the Prague conference on the methods of work among the unemployed and the forms of organization for the unemployed have not been carried out, and that the unemployed movement has often been left without proper revolutionary guidance, which has been taken advantage of to a certain extent by the social-democrats and fascists. When communists and adherents of the revolutionary trade-union movement properly estimated the political importance of work among the unemployed and, broadly popularizing a program of demands of the unemployed, were able to combine this with concrete defense of the everyday interests of the unemployed, they were able in most cases to win material successes and to extend their political influence.

Systematically explaining to the working masses that unemployment is the inevitable accompaniment of the capitalist system and that it can be abolished only by the dictatorship of the proletariat, the communist parties must devote special attention to the broad mobilization and organization of the masses of the unemployed for the struggle for their everyday demands and social insurance, without, however, allowing the Red trade-unions and the Red trade-union opposition to serve as substitutes for the broad organization of the unemployed.

The communist parties must combine the defense of the interests of the unemployed with the struggles of the part-time workers, advancing for them, in addition to the general slogan of full wages, the demands for special relief, reduction of rent, reduction of charges on utilities, etc.

Using the experience of a number of communist parties, . . . the communist parties and the revolutionary trade-union organizations must head the struggle against dismissals, against overtime work and capitalist rationalization, making use of the most various forms of struggle, including seizure of the factories. Carrying on a determined fight against dismissals, the communists, when dismissals nevertheless recur, must present demands to the owners for material reimbursement for those dismissed. The communist parties and the revolutionary trade-union organizations finally must carry on a determined struggle against *mass dismissals* of young and married workers and must devote the most fundamentally serious attention to strengthening the work among unemployed women and unemployed youth.

4. Concerning Work inside the Reformist Trade-Unions

One of the chief causes of the insufficient mobilization of the masses by the communist parties and by the revolutionary trade-union organizations in the struggle against the capitalist offensive is the impermissibly weak revolutionary work *within the reformist trade-unions.*

The consistent everyday struggle waged by the communists and the supporters of the revolutionary trade-union movement for the establishment of the united front of the workers raises directly before all the sections of the Comintern and the Profintern the question of activity *within* the reformist trade-unions and of the *methods* of this work. The influence of the reformist trade-union bureaucracy, especially in countries with old and strong reformist trade-unions, constitutes one of the main impediments in the development of the class struggle—and can be overcome not by cries about the collapse of the trade-unions, which are not joined by communists, not by means of withdrawal from the trade-unions, but by stubborn work inside the reformist trade-unions, the struggle for every member of a reformist trade-union, for *every elected post* in the trade-union, for the elimination of the reformist trade-union bureaucracy and the conquest of local organizations in individual trade-unions and local trade councils in the reformist trade-unions.

The Twelfth Plenum of the ECCI calls on all sections of the Communist International to continue, with all Bolshevik consistency and determination, the struggle against capitulation to the reformist trade-union bureaucracy, as well as against the *major* danger and against those opportunist elements inside the communist parties and the revolutionary trade-union movement which in reality thus far have been opponents of the existence of the Red trade-unions and the revolutionary trade-union opposition, and the organization and conduct by them of independent economic strikes, instead of which they support the slogan: "Force the trade-union bureaucracy to carry on the struggle" (*"Zwingt die Bonzen"*).

The ECCI proposes that all sections of the Communist International explain to the party members and the revolutionary nonparty workers that the trade-union bureaucracy can only be successfully exposed and the membership masses of the reformist,

Catholic, nationalist, Kuomintang, yellow, and similar trade-unions can only be liberated from their influence if, in addition to careful everyday activity and the elucidation and advancement of their own proposals, the supporters of the Profintern speak at all meetings, assemblies, conferences, and congresses on all the questions of organization and tactics of the economic struggle, criticizing and exposing the leadership of these trade-unions for carrying on negotiations with the owners behind the scenes, for voluntarily agreeing to the worsening of working conditions, for disrupting the struggle of the masses, stifling the initiative of the membership masses and the rank-and-file members, and, when they cannot disrupt the struggle any longer, for starting it only after a delay and then capitulating to the bourgeoisie behind the backs of the workers.

The sections of the Comintern must wage a ruthless struggle against those Left-sectarian elements in the communist parties and in the revolutionary trade-union movement who take advantage of the struggle of the Comintern against the opportunist slogan of "forcing the bureaucrats," in order to avoid working inside the reformist trade-unions. The Twelfth Plenum of the ECCI calls on all sections of the Comintern to oppose most decidedly the Left-sectarian refusal to struggle for elective positions in the reformist trade-unions, which is the duty of every communist, in accordance with the decisions of the Tenth Plenum of the ECCI.

In those countries where there are *mass fascist* trade-unions, or similar mass reactionary organizations (Italy, China), and especially where the fascist trade-unions enjoy a monopoly, the communists must actively and organizedly work inside these unions, utilizing all legal and semilegal opportunities to draw the masses of the members of these organizations into the class struggle, in order to discredit these organizations in the eyes of the masses, to strengthen the position of the revolutionary trade-union movement among the masses.

. . .

7. The Development of the Revolutionary Upsurge and the Struggle against Deviations

The development of the economic struggle of the proletariat under the conditions of the end of capitalist stabilization urgently requires of the communist vanguard a clear and distinct struggle against opportunism, which becomes more dangerous in proportion to the upsurge of the revolutionary struggle of the proletariat. Adaptation to the ideology and policy of social-democracy, capitulation to the reformist trade-union bureaucracy in the task of independent leadership in the economic struggle of the proletariat, a credulous attitude toward the "Left" maneuvers of the reformist trade-union bureaucracy (in particular toward the slogan of the "demonstrative" general strike), the refusal to link up partial economic demands with general class slogans, the tactic of a "bloc" with the reformist trade-union bureaucracy instead of the policy of a united front from below, the refusal to form a Red trade-union opposition on the pretext of defending the unity of the trade-union movement, and, finally, the denial of the leading role of the communist parties in the revolutionary trade-union organizations and concealment of the aim of the communist party in economic struggles—these represent the *chief danger* at the present stage of the development of the revolutionary struggle of the proletariat.

The essential condition for a successful struggle against this chief danger of Right opportunism is a resolute struggle against "Left"-opportunist deviations, which find expression in the Leftist "theory" of the "solid reactionary mass" of workers organized in the reformist unions, in the sectarian-Leftist underestimate of the tactic of the united front, in the assertion that the reformist trade-unions are "schools of capitalism," in the sectarian attitude toward work in the reformist trade-unions, with the result that the entire work in the reformist unions leads to the destruction of the apparatus and to a bureaucratic disregard for the methods of proletarian democracy.

. . .

91

The Comintern Weighs the Danger of War and Intervention

Excerpts from the resolution "Concerning the War in the Far East and the Tasks of Communists in the Struggle against the Imperialist War and Military Intervention against the U.S.S.R." Adopted by the Twelfth Plenum of the ECCI on the report of the Japanese members, Okano. XII Plenum IKKI, III, 174–176.

1. The period of relative stability in international relations has ended. The attack by Japanese imperialism on China, which is taking place with the full and open support of France and the concealed support of England, constitutes the beginning of a new imperialist war. The struggle for the redistribution of the world, which has been intensified as the result of the world economic crisis, is expressed in the sharpening of all the contradictions within the imperialist system. The intensification of the main contradiction in the camp of imperialism between the U.S.A. and England, the sharpening of the conflict between the U.S.A. and Japan, the sharp intensification of the struggle over the Versailles system between France and Germany, and between Poland and Germany concerning the question of Danzig, the Polish Corridor, the problem of East Prussia, the sharpening of the struggle between French and Italian imperialism, and the regrouping of the imperialist powers which is taking place in connection with all the above facts are leading to the outbreak of new armed conflicts. The attitude of the League of Nations toward the Japanese attack on China plainly reveals once again that the League of Nations serves as an instrument of war and intervention in the hands of French and British imperialism. In opposing the occupation of Manchuria, the U.S.A. is pursuing its own imperialist aims of securing a "fair" redistribution of spheres of influence in the Far East. The conferences at Geneva, Lausanne, and Ottawa will not help to remove the contradictions among the imperialists.

2. The intensification of the imperialist contradictions increases the tendencies in the camp of the imperialists to settle these contradictions at the expense of the U.S.S.R. The imperialist powers, and first of all the militarists of France and Japan, are exerting every effort to extend and strengthen the anti-Soviet bloc in order to deal a decisive military blow to the basis of the world proletarian revolution—the U.S.S.R., which has consolidated its strength along the socialist path. English imperialism is supporting all the plans of intervention against the U.S.S.R. The U.S.A. is striving to provoke a war between Japan and the Soviet Union so that, by weakening both Japan and the U.S.S.R., it may strengthen its own position in the Pacific. In Poland, Rumania, and Czechoslovakia, and in the Baltic and Balkan countries, preparations for war are being carried on with the greatest possible intensity under the guidance of the French general staff. By the efforts of Japanese imperialism, supported by France and England, Manchuria has been converted into a staging area for an attack on the U.S.S.R. At the same time direct preparations for intervention against the U.S.S.R. are being carried on under the guidance of France in Poland, Rumania, the Baltic countries, etc. The threat of direct military intervention hangs over the U.S.S.R.

3. A new imperialist war, a new intervention against the U.S.S.R., will bring to the workers and toilers of the entire world suffering, privations, and bloody sacrifices such as were not experienced even during the first world imperialist slaughter. The sharpening of all forms of bourgeois dictatorship, the intensification of reaction, the growth of fascism, the persecution of the revolutionary movement, shootings and hangings, already serve as the preparation of the rear areas for the imperialist war and armed intervention against the U.S.S.R.

The Twelfth Plenum considers that the most important task of all communist parties is to organize and lead the struggle of the workers, peasants, and all the toilers for the defense of China and the Chinese revolution, for the defense of the fatherland of the workers of all countries—the U.S.S.R.—against the approaching military intervention, and for the defense of the toilers of the capitalist countries against a new imperialist war.

4. The leaders of the Second International and its parties changed their tactics during the Far Eastern war, in accordance with the demands of their bourgeoisie. At the beginning of the war against China they called on the workers to support the League of Nations, depicting the League and the Kellogg Pact as instruments

of peace. They supported the policies of their bourgeois governments, criticized only the imperialist governments of other countries, declared the attack by Japan on China to be a far-off colonial war which did not affect the interests of the working class in Europe and America, proposed to the workers as a means of struggle against war to appeal to the League of Nations and their own governments. They either passed over the threat of intervention against the U.S.S.R. in complete silence or deceived the masses outright, claiming that the U.S.S.R. was not menaced by intervention. And at the same time the parties of the Second International intensified their slanderous anti-Soviet campaign and tried to weaken the influence of the peace policy of the U.S.S.R. among the toiling masses, supporting the poorly disguised aggressive policy of the imperialist governments against the proposals of the U.S.S.R. concerning full disarmament. Reformist trade-unions sabotaged the struggle against military production and military shipments for Japan, maintaining that the war would wipe out unemployment. The Japanese social-democrats, who were connected with the Second and Amsterdam Internationals, fully and wholly supported the plunderous war of the Japanese bourgeoisie, maintaining that this war was the road to socialism. This position of Japanese social-democracy is an indication of the position which the entire world social-democracy will take on the development of a new world war.

Later on, under the pressure of the masses the Executive Committee of the Second International in Zurich has adopted a resolution formally opposing the imperialist war and in support of the U.S.S.R., shifting from the position of intervention and the support of interventionist actions against the Soviet power to a position of formal neutrality and verbal support of the U.S.S.R. In fact, however, the parties of the Second International are continuing their slanderous anti-Soviet campaign, supporting the Russian Menshevik-interventionists, sabotaging all concrete actions of the workers against military production and military shipments for Japan, continuing to sow pacifist illusions in order to divert the masses from the real struggle against the imperialist war and military intervention, boycotting the anti-war Amsterdam congress, taking part in the preparation and organization of imperialist wars and military intervention, supporting their own bourgeois government in each country.

5. The Twelfth Plenum of the ECCI greets the heroic struggle of the Communist Party of Japan against the imperialist war which was started by the Japanese bourgeoisie and landlords, and the

revolutionary struggle of the Communist Party of China against Japanese imperialism and against all imperialists.

The Communist Party of *China* must continue to exert every effort to ensure the hegemony of the proletariat in the mass anti-imperialist movement in Kuomintang China. For this purpose the party must set itself the task of further developing and deepening the soviet movement, strengthening the Red Army of the Chinese soviets, linking up the soviet movement with the mass anti-imperialist struggle in Kuomintang China, widely and consistently pursuing the tactics of the united front from below in the anti-imperialist struggle of the masses, and organizing the masses under the slogan of a revolutionary national-liberation war for the independence, unification, and territorial integrity of China against all imperialists, for the overthrow of the agent of imperialism—the Kuomintang.

The Communist Party of *Japan* must increase its work in the army and navy, especially in Manchuria, and must carry on popular agitation among workers, peasants, and the exploited urban petty-bourgeois masses, in language that can be understood by the broad masses, in order to expose the indissoluble connection between the imperialist war and the direct preparations for armed intervention against the U.S.S.R. on the one hand, and the strengthening of the military-police reaction and the increased plundering of the toiling masses of Japan itself on the other hand. Along with this the CPJ must develop the economic struggle of the workers against the capitalist offensive and must link it with the struggle against imperialist war and the preparations for intervention, must organize the peasant movement, linking this movement with the struggle of the working class and raising it to the level of an agrarian revolution, and must expose the demagogy of the fascists and the social-democrats as a means of mobilizing the masses for imperialist war and armed intervention.

The Communists of *Korea* and *Formosa,* in close collaboration with the CPJ and the CCP, must mobilize the workers and peasants of Korea and Formosa for the struggle against Japanese imperialism, for the independence of Korea and Formosa, establishing a revolutionary fighting alliance of all the oppressed and exploited for the national-liberation struggle.

6. While recognizing the undoubtedly positive results of the work of the communist parties in imperialist and colonial countries in the matter of mobilizing the masses against imperialist war and against preparations for armed intervention, the Twelfth Plenum

of the ECCI declares that the communist parties of the imperialist countries have not been able to prevent by revolutionary actions the transport of troops to China and military supplies to Japan; that they have not been able to rouse the broad working masses employed in munition factories and transport for the struggle; that the mass anti-war campaign has developed slowly, partly because of an opportunist underestimation of the war in the Far East and also because of a Leftist-fatalistic, frivolous attitude to the war.

The Twelfth Plenum of the ECCI calls particular attention to the impermissible weakness in the contact between the communist parties and the principal munition factories, the chief ports, and the key points of the railroads, and to the fact that the anti-war work of the communist parties and the Young Communist Leagues in the army, the navy, and the special fascist semimilitary organizations is in an intolerably neglected condition. The Twelfth Plenum of the ECCI emphasizes especially the weakness and backwardness of the Communist Youth International in the struggle against war and military intervention. In addition, the Twelfth Plenum states that the communist parties have not succeeded in fulfilling the urgent task of creating legal, semilegal, or illegal control committees and illegal committees of action, based on the masses, in factories, railroads, ports, and ships, and of mobilizing the broad masses of workers in the reformist trade-unions and other mass workers' organizations, on the basis of the tactic of the united front from below, for the purpose of preventing the transport of troops to China and war munitions to Japan, and in developing agitation against the imperialist war and armed intervention among the masses of peasants and the urban petty bourgeoisie. Opportunist underestimation of the war in China and underestimation of the danger of imperialist wars and armed intervention, opportunist failure to understand all the peculiarities of the present drift toward a new world war, individual pacifist deviations from the Leninist doctrine on war, opportunist passivity with regard to war, opportunist fatalistic moods, expressed in theories that revolution will automatically arise out of war, were not given a sufficiently sharp Bolshevik rejection.

7. The general tasks of all communist parties in the struggle against imperialist war and armed intervention and in the struggle against fascism, social-democracy, and bourgeois pacifism which facilitate the various methods of preparing and carrying on imperialist war and military intervention against the U.S.S.R. are as follows:

(*a*) To develop a systematic ideological struggle against chauvinism and nationalism, to carry on propaganda for real proletarian internationalism, to expose to the masses all the machinations of the foreign policy of their own bourgeoisie, to expose all the measures of the internal policy of the bourgeoisie in preparation for war, to expose the production and transport of munitions for imperialist countries, to remind the masses of all the calamities of the first imperialist war, to fight tirelessly against the militarization of the schools.

(*b*) To react vigorously against all manifestations of anti-Soviet campaigns, to increase the propaganda of the success of socialist construction in the U.S.S.R. among the broadest masses, to mobilize the toilers against the White Guards, to popularize the peace policy of the U.S.S.R., to mobilize the masses for the active defense of the U.S.S.R., China, and the Chinese soviet revolution.

(*c*) To expose, on the basis of vivid and well-known facts, all the sophisms and maneuvers of the bourgeois pacifists and especially the social-democratic parties.

(*d*) To expose broadly to the masses all the peculiar secrets of the origin and conduct of a new imperialist war (mobilization by units, formation of a cover army, preparations to purge the territories behind the front line from revolutionary elements), and, in working out the anti-war tactics of the communist party, to take into account the various new methods employed by the bourgeoisie in the preparation for and carrying out of war.

(*e*) By employing the tactic of the united front, to set up legal, semilegal, and illegal control committees [and] committees of action in munition enterprises, ports, factories, railways, ships, for the purpose of developing mass actions and carefully prepared strikes of protest, as well as economic strikes, in order to prevent the transportation of munitions and troops and to rouse the initiative of the broad masses of workers in this matter.

(*f*) To develop extensive mass work among the unemployed, among the youth, among toiling women, among emigrant workers, against imperialist war and armed intervention. To draw the peasant masses into the struggle against imperialist war. To support the national liberation movement of the colonial and oppressed peoples.

(*g*) To carry on extensive anti-imperialist work among the soldiers and sailors, among conscripts, reservists, and in the special military organizations of the bourgeoisie; to strengthen the party and all revolutionary youth organizations, bearing in mind that the whole party, the whole Young Communist League, must participate in this work; to organize the struggle of the soldiers for their everyday demands and to support this struggle by the solidarity of the workers and the toiling peasantry; to popularize revolutionary traditions and examples of the struggle against war.

The communist parties must carry on an irreconcilable Bolshevik struggle in their own ranks against an opportunist underestimation of the war danger, against opportunist passivity in the struggle against imperialist war and armed intervention, and against a pseudo-Left fatalistic attitude toward war.

The Twelfth Plenum of the ECCI imposes the duty upon the Executive Committee of the Communist Youth International and the central committees of the communist parties to check carefully the anti-war work of the Young Communist Leagues and to take all measures possible to bring about its decisive improvement.

The entire international situation imposes on the CPSU (B) a most important historic task: to continue undeviatingly to pursue the policy of peace that has been firmly followed by the Soviet government, in spite of the increasing provocation of the imperialists, and at the same time to strengthen the defensive capabilities of the U.S.S.R. and, by carrying out the great plan of socialist construction, by rallying all the toilers around the Soviet power, to strengthen the U.S.S.R. as the base and stronghold of socialism.

The communist parties must realize that the bare and empty propaganda of peace, unaccompanied by the call for and organization of the revolutionary actions of the masses, is only capable of sowing illusions, of corrupting the proletariat by imbuing it with confidence in the policy of the bourgeoisie and its agents within the working class, and of making the working class a plaything in the hands of the bourgeois governments.

In carrying on a real struggle against the preparations for imperialist war and military intervention against the U.S.S.R., the communist parties must go to the workers with Lenin's doctrine that imperialist war is caused by capitalism, that the only reliable guarantee against new imperialist wars and interventions is the transformation of the imperialist war into a civil war and the overthrow of capitalism.

92

Izvestiia *on the Franco-Soviet Nonaggression Pact*

"Franko-sovetskii pakt o nenapadenii," Izvestiia, *No. 330, November 30, 1932, p. 1.*

. . .

. . . The Soviet people greet the news of the conclusion of a nonaggression pact between the U.S.S.R. and France with the deepest satisfaction, especially since the French role in intervention left deep traces in their memory. Therefore every practical demonstration of the inviolability of this pact will call forth a response from the peoples of the Soviet Union. . . .

. . . Soviet public opinion welcomes with deep satisfaction the fourth article of the pact, which prohibits either side from taking part in economic warfare against the other. This obligation has special significance in the light of the tendency to discriminate against Soviet exports and the attempt to create special hindrances for them.

The fifth article of the treaty, including the mutual obligation not to interfere in each other's internal affairs, not to permit propaganda or attempts at intervention, not to disrupt the political [or] social system of the other party, not to permit on one's territory the development of military organizations directed against the other party, as well as organizations which arrogate to themselves the role of representation of territory under the sovereignty of the other party, has special significance in view of the practice of émigré military and terrorist groups of making France their base of action against the Soviet Union.

The carrying out of these obligations will unquestionably improve the relations between the French Republic and the U.S.S.R. As far as the Soviet Union is concerned, there will not be the slightest obstacle to carrying them out. There exist no forces in the Soviet Union directed toward disrupting the cause of peace.

Whether the same thing is true of France will be shown only by the future. The voices of the Right and nationalist French press show that there are influential circles in France whose interpretation of the nonaggression pact differs from that of public opinion in the Soviet Union, and who are manifesting a hostile attitude to the signing of this pact. From the side of the factors, interests, and desires which are reflected in the Rightist French press one can expect actions directed against the pact. We do not doubt for a single minute that not only the working masses of France but also the broadest circles of the petty bourgeoisie, which gave the margin of victory to the Herriot government in the elections exactly because they saw in him a statesman of peace, will do everything in order to ensure the effectiveness of the nonaggression pact. Its significance, its specific gravity, lies just in the fact that it is not simply a diplomatic document, but reflects the real mood and aspirations of the popular masses of France. . . .

The nonaggression pact, as far as the Soviet Union is concerned, will serve the cause of strengthening peace in Europe and the cause of developing relations between the Soviet Union and the French Republic, one of the most important countries of Europe. Therefore we welcome the fact that the majority of the German newspapers administered a rebuff to tendencies to represent this pact as a step separating the Soviet Union from the German people. In the same way that the signing by Germany at Locarno of a similar pact did not alienate those interests on which friendly relations between the German people and the Soviet Union had developed, so the policy of rapprochement between the Soviet Union and France should not damage these interests. Our relations with Germany were and are directed toward the mutual benefit of both peoples. This benefit cannot be interfered with by close relations with France; on the contrary, the strengthening of our relations with France will scotch the legend that Germany, in maintaining friendship with the Soviet Union, does so to the detriment of France. The "fraternal union of the western nations," of which some German circles have dreamed, could only have been directed against the U.S.S.R. Solid peaceful relations of all the European peoples are needed for all of them and are not directed against anyone. There can be no doubt that the strengthening of our relations with France will help in the improvement of our relations with the western countries linked with France.

The Soviet Union by its persistent policy has achieved an important victory, which is a victory for the cause of peace. The pact concluded with France is a serious political step, it means a significant strengthening of the Soviet Union, and just for that reason it is to be expected that it will evoke not only displeasure but also unfriendly acts among those elements which are interested in stirring up hostility among peoples and in preparing for war. In its struggle for peace the Soviet Union has added to the other diplomatic documents and international links one more document, one more weapon. The nonaggression pact will not paralyze those forces which create the danger of war, but it will help in fighting against them.

93

The Comintern Calls for a United Front Against Fascism

"To the Workers of All Countries," an appeal by the ECCI, March 5, 1933. "Komintern o edinom fronte," Izvestiia, No. 64, March 6, 1933, p. 2, citing L'Humanité, March 6, 1933; I.P.C., Vol. 13, No. 11, March 9, 1933, pp. 261–262.

The crisis is continuing to spread and deepen. Unemployment is increasing without interruption. Hunger and misery are seizing one section of the workers after another. The offensive of capital is growing sharper. The bourgeoisie is preparing to launch a campaign against all the political and economic achievements of the working class. Fascist reaction is spreading in one country after another. The establishment of the open fascist dictatorship in Germany has directly confronted millions of workers of all countries with the question of the necessity of organizing a united front of struggle against the fascist offensive of the bourgeoisie, and above all against the German bourgeoisie, who, step by step, are robbing the working class of all economic and political achievements and are attempting to crush the workers' movement with methods of merciless terror.

The main obstacle to the formation of the united front of

struggle of the communist and social-democratic workers was and is the policy of collaboration with the bourgeoisie, followed by the social-democratic parties, which have now exposed the international proletariat to the blows of the class enemy. This policy of collaboration with the bourgeoisie, known as the so-called policy of the "lesser evil," has led in practice to the triumph of fascist reaction in Germany.

The Communist International and the communist parties of all countries have repeatedly declared their readiness to join in a common struggle with the social-democratic workers against the capitalist offensive, against political reaction and the threat of war. The communist parties were the organizers of the common struggle of the communist, social-democratic, and nonparty workers in spite of the leaders of the social-democratic parties, who systematically disrupted the united front of the working masses. Already on July 20 of last year, the Communist Party of Germany, after the Prussian Social-Democratic government had been driven out by von Papen, proposed to the Social-Democratic Party of Germany and to the German General Federation of Trade Unions (ADGB) to organize a joint strike against fascism. But the Social-Democratic Party of Germany and the ADGB, with the approval of the entire Second International, described the proposal to organize a joint strike as a provocation. The Communist Party of Germany repeated its proposal of common action at the time when Hitler seized power; it called upon the Central Committee of the Social-Democratic Party and the Executive Committee of the ADGB to organize jointly the resistance to fascism, but this time also met with a refusal. Furthermore, when in November of last year the Berlin transportation workers unanimously went on strike against a wage cut, the Social-Democratic Party sabotaged the united-front struggle. The whole practice of the international labor movement is full of similar examples.

Meantime the Bureau of the Labour and Socialist International [LSI] on February 19 of this year published a declaration on the readiness of the social-democratic parties affiliated to this International to form a united front with the communists in order to fight against the fascist reaction in Germany.[1] This declaration stands in sharp contradiction to all previous actions of the LSI and social-democratic parties. The whole policy and activity of the LSI hitherto justifies the Communist International and the communist parties in putting no faith in the sincerity of the declaration of the

Bureau of the LSI, which makes its proposal at a moment when in a number of countries, and especially in Germany, the working class is already taking into its own hands the organization of the united front.

Nevertheless, in view of the fascist attack on the working class of Germany, unchaining all the forces of world reaction, the Executive Committee of the Communist International calls upon all communist parties to make one more attempt to set up the united front of struggle with the social-democratic workers through the medium of the social-democratic parties. The ECCI makes this attempt in the firm conviction that the united front of the working class against the bourgeoisie will be able to repel the offensive of capital and fascism and to accelerate to an extraordinary extent the inevitable end of all capitalist exploitation.

In view of the peculiarities of the conditions in various countries, as well as the differences in the concrete fighting tasks confronting the working class in them, an agreement between the communist and social-democratic parties for definite action against the bourgeoisie can be carried out most successfully within the framework of individual countries. Therefore the ECCI recommends to the communist parties of the various countries to approach the central committees of the social-democratic parties belonging to the LSI with proposals regarding joint actions against fascism and the offensive of capital. The negotiations must be based on the elementary prerequisites for a common struggle against capital and fascism. Without a concrete program of action against the bourgeoisie, any agreement between the parties would be directed against the interests of the working class. The Executive Committee of the Communist International therefore proposes the following points as a basis of such an agreement for a joint action:

(*a*) The communists and social-democrats will immediately set about organizing and carrying out defensive action against the attacks of fascism and reaction on the political, trade-union, cooperative, and other workers' organizations, on the workers' press, on the freedom of assembly, demonstrations, and strikes; they will organize common defense against armed attacks of fascist bands by carrying out mass protests, street demonstrations, mass political strikes; they will proceed to organize committees of action in the factories, labor exchanges, and the workers' quarters, as well as to organize self-defense detachments.

(*b*) Communists and social-democrats will begin immediately to organize the protest of the workers by means of meetings, demonstrations, and strikes against any wage reductions, against the worsening of working conditions, against attacks on social insurance, against the cutting down of unemployment benefits, against dismissals from the factories.

(c) In the adoption and practical carrying out of these two conditions the ECCI considers it possible to recommend that the communist parties, during the time of common fight against capital and fascism, refrain from making attacks on social-democratic organizations. The most ruthless fight must be conducted against all those who violate the conditions of the agreement in carrying out the united front, as strikebreakers who are disrupting the united front of the workers.

These conditions, which are put forward for acceptance by the LSI, apply also to those parties, such as the ILP [the British Independent Labour Party], which have proposed to the Comintern the organization of the united front of struggle.

The ECCI makes these proposals before the entire international working class and calls upon all communist parties, especially the Communist Party of Germany, immediately and without waiting for the results of negotiations and agreements with social-democracy with regard to a common fight, to proceed at once to organize joint fighting committees with social-democratic workers, as well as with workers of all other tendencies.

The communists have proved through their long years of struggle that they stand, and will always stand, not in words but in deeds, in the front ranks of the struggle for the united front in class actions against the bourgeoisie.

The ECCI is firmly convinced that the social-democratic and nonparty workers, regardless of what attitude the social-democratic leaders adopt to the establishment of the united front, will overcome all obstacles and, together with the communists, will set up the united front not in words but in deeds.

Precisely at the present moment, when German fascism has organized an unprecedented provocation in order to crush the workers' movement in Germany (the burning of the Reichstag, the forged document about an insurrection, etc.), every worker must understand his class duty in the fight against the capitalist offensive and fascist reaction.

Down with the fascist reaction and the terror against the working class!

For the united fighting front of the proletariat!

Proletarian of all countries, unite for the struggle against the offensive of capitalism and fascism!

NOTES

1. Text appears in *Le Populaire*, February 20, 1933.

94

Varga Analyzes the World Economic Situation

Excerpts from E. Varga, "Economy and Economic Policy in the Fourth Quarter of 1932," I.P.C., Vol. 13, No. 12, March 16, 1933, pp. 285–300.

. . .

The Aggravation of Inter-Imperialist Contradictions

The year 1932 witnessed the complete breakdown of those inter-imperialist understandings which formed one of the foundations of stabilization: the understanding as to the form of joint spoliation of Germany, the understanding as to the exploitation of China, and the understanding as to mutual noninterference in the exploitation of the separate powers' "own" colonies . . . The division of the world as created by the World War and codified in the system of peace treaties has been overtly upset by the military occupation of Manchuria by Japan. The fight for a redistribution of the world has thereby commenced.

The League of Nations, instituted by the victors for the purpose of perpetuating the distribution of the world resultant from the World War has, when faced with the real power of Japanese arms, found its paper resolutions to be utterly incapable of influencing the course of events. The aggravation of the antagonism between Great Britain and the United States and the united front, unreliable though it is, of the European debtor countries against America ranges Great Britain and France—the decisive members of the League of Nations, which are engaged, like Japan, in a policy of carving up and colonizing China—on the side of Japan against the United States and China, and this notwithstanding the undeniably pronounced differences between Great Britain and Japan.

This general aggravation of interimperialist antagonisms has meanwhile utterly frustrated all attempts at adapting the military armaments to the individual state revenues, so greatly reduced by the crisis. The "disarmament" proposals of the imperialist powers were one and all directed toward, relatively or absolutely, enhancing the preponderance of their own armaments by restricting the armaments of their prospective adversaries in the next world war (especially as regards those weapons most dangerous to themselves).

Under these circumstances, the only pronounced and tangible proposal of disarmament, that advanced by the Soviet Union, naturally met with no approval on the part of the imperialist robbers, and the work of the Disarmament Conference ended in the course of 1932 in complete failure. The end of relative stabilization represents the commencement of a new period of wars and interventions, in which any attempt at a concerted restriction of armaments is doomed to fail even more certainly than before. On the contrary, all efforts for the preparation of a new war for the redistribution of the world are now being redoubled. The outbreak of renewed international warfare was never so imminent as it is now at the commencement of 1933.

. . .

II. The Inter-Imperialist Antagonisms as Reflected by the Struggle over Inter-Allied Debts

"The Peace of Versailles," wrote Lenin, "represents the most serious blow the capitalists and imperialists of the victorious states could possibly have dealt themselves." (Lenin, [*Sochineniia*, 2d ed.], XXIV, p. 545.)

A decade had to elapse before the accuracy of this statement became apparent to the whole world.

The agreements concluded among the victorious imperialists to safeguard the system established at Versailles—agreements as to the methods and extent of spoliation of Germany (the Dawes plan), as to the joint exploitation of China, and as to reciprocal noninterference in their plundering of their own colonies—at the same time formed the main foundation of the relative stability of capitalism.

On this basis, the victorious imperialists began to cherish illusions as to the possibility of perpetuating the distribution of the world established by the Versailles system, of developing the League of Nations under the cloak of an "organization of eternal peace" into an instrument for the permanent suppression of the vanquished, of ensuring Germany's reparations payments and thereby also creating a basis for the defrayment of the inter-Allied debts. These agreements the governments of the capitalist countries concluded for not less than sixty-two years, just as though the Versailles system were a permanent institution and the existence of the capitalist order of society guaranteed for all eternity.

But the unequal development of imperialism permits no very lengthy fixation of the relations of power, while the general crisis of capitalism allows no long duration of relative stability. . . .

A new era of wars and revolutions is beginning. The war for the redistribution of the world has already started in Manchuria. The Versailles system threatens to crash at any moment . . .

. . .

95

The Comintern Sees Hitler Leading Germany to Catastrophe

Resolution "On the Situation in Germany," following a speech by F. Heckert, adopted by the Presidium of the ECCI, April 1, 1933. Die Kommunistische Internationale über die Lage in Deutschland (Moscow and Leningrad, 1933), pamphlet; I.P.C., Vol. 13, No. 17, April 13, 1933, pp. 377–378.

Having heard the report of *Comrade Heckert* on the situation in Germany, the Presidium of the ECCI declares that the political line and the organizational policy pursued by the C.C. of the [German] Communist Party, led by *Comrade Thälmann*, before and at the time of the Hitler coup, was quite correct.

. . .

Under the conditions of the tremendous sharpening of the economic and political situation in Germany, when, on the one hand, the Communist Party had already become a tremendous force in the working class, and a revolutionary crisis was rapidly maturing, when, on the other hand, the deep contradictions among the ruling classes themselves had become clear and the fascist dictatorship in the shape of the Papen and Schleicher government was not in a position to stop the growth of communism and find any way out of the ever intensifying economic crisis, the German bourgeoisie delegated the establishment of an open fascist dictatorship to the fascist Hitler and his "national-socialist party."

The victory of Hitler and the establishment of the power of the "national-socialists" was possible owing to the following circumstances:

German social-democracy, which had the support of the majority of the proletariat in the November revolution of 1918, split the working class, and instead of carrying the revolution forward to the dictatorship of the proletariat and socialism, which was the duty of a proletarian party, it, in alliance with the bourgeoisie and the generals of the Kaiser, suppressed the uprising of the revolutionary masses and laid the basis for a profound split in the working class of Germany. Under the flag of collaboration with the bourgeoisie and the tactic of the "lesser evil," in alliance with the bourgeoisie and with the approval of the whole of the Second International, it continued this policy of severe repression of the revolutionary movement and the line of splitting the working class right up to the most recent date. It suppressed the Red Front Fighters' League, suppressed the revolutionary workers' organizations, prohibited and fired into workers' demonstrations, broke economic and political strikes against the capitalist offensive and fascism, and supported the power of the counterrevolutionary bourgeoisie. Social-democracy concentrated the leadership of the mass workers' organizations in the hands of its corrupt bureaucratic leaders. It expelled revolutionary workers from these organizations and, by means of a network of centralized workers' organizations subordinated to it, fettered the initiative of the working masses, undermined their fighting power in the struggle against capital and fascism, and hindered them in decisively repelling the advance of the fascist dictatorship and the terrorist fascist gangs. This policy of struggle against the revolutionary masses, collaboration with the bourgeoisie, and help for reaction under the pretense of pursuing the tactic of the "lesser evil" has been the policy of the Second and the

Amsterdam Internationals as a whole, from 1914 up to the present time.

In the conditions of imperialism, and still more so in a country which has been defeated in the imperialist war and whose capitalism had been deeply undermined by the general crisis of the capitalist system, the *Weimar "democratic" bourgeois republic* could only be a reactionary dictatorship of the bourgeoisie. The labor legislation, social insurance, and democratic rights which the bourgeoisie had been compelled to give to the workers in the years of the revolution were gradually taken away by the Weimar coalition—consisting of social-democrats, the Center Party, and the "democrats"—that was in power. Continual and gradual concessions to reaction, a gradual repeal of one point of the constitution after another, of one gain of the workers after another, the gradual fascistization of the whole apparatus of the state, so greatly discredited the Weimar coalition and the Weimar republic that it lost all serious significance in the eyes of the broad masses.

The *Versailles system* plundered Germany and put the German toiling masses under the oppression of the unbearable exploitation, not only of their own capitalists, but also of foreign capital, to whom the German government had to transfer reparation payments. The oppression of Versailles, multiplied by the oppression of their "own" German bourgeoisie, led to an unprecedented fall in the standard of living of the proletariat and to such an impoverishment of the peasants and the urban petty-bourgeoisie that a section of these strata began more and more to consider as their ideal prewar Germany, in which there was not yet the general crisis of capitalism and not such an impoverishment of the masses as now. It can be understood, therefore, that at a time of the most intense economic crisis, which increased the burden of the external Versailles national oppression and when, due to the social-democrats, the proletariat was split and consequently not strong enough to carry the urban petty-bourgeoisie and the peasant masses with it, there was bound to arise, and there actually did arise, a tempestuous outburst of German nationalism and chauvinism, which considerably strengthened the political situation of the bourgeoisie and brought to the surface the most demagogic nationalist party—the party of the "national-socialists."

The communist workers organized and carried on a struggle against the capitalist and fascist offensive. They supported every, even the slightest, action of the social-democratic workers against capital, wherever such actions took place. Wishing to restore the revolutionary unity of the working class, long before the victory of fascism they repeatedly proposed to the social-democratic workers and the lower social-democratic organizations that a united front be formed for the struggle against the bourgeoisie and their lackeys, the fascists. But the mass of the social-democratic workers who carried with them the majority of the working class of Germany, being fettered by their social-democratic leaders who were opposed to the revolutionary united front, and who maintained their reactionary united front with the bourgeoisie, rejected the united front with the communists on every occasion, and disrupted the struggle of the working class. While the communists insisted on a *revolutionary* united front of the working class *against the bourgeoisie, against fascism,* the social-democrats on the contrary impelled the workers in the direction of a *reactionary* united front with the bourgeoisie *against the communists, against the communist workers,* destroying and repressing communist organizations wherever and whenever possible.

In pursuing its line of struggle for the revolutionary unity of the working class against the social-democratic united front with the bourgeoisie, the Communist Party, as the only revolutionary leader of the German proletariat, in spite of the strikebreaking tactics of social-democracy in the matter of the united front against the bourgeoisie, called on the working class for a *general political strike* on July 20, 1932, when the fascists dispersed the social-democratic Prussian government, and on January 30, 1933, when Hitler came into power in Germany, and in order to carry on this strike proposed a united front to the Social-Democratic Party and the reformist trade-unions. The development of the struggle of the proletariat against the bourgeoisie and fascism and a general strike would have caused the hesitating toiling masses of peasants and the urban petty-bourgeoisie to follow the proletariat. But the social-democrats, continuing their previous policy, and orientating themselves on further collaboration with the bourgeoisie, fettered the initiative of the masses by the network of centralized organizations which followed their lead, particularly the reformist trade-unions, and interfered with the organization of a general strike and disrupted it, thus encouraging the further attack of the fascists on the proletariat. As a result, the vanguard of the revolutionary wing of the German proletariat, the communist party, was deprived of the support of the majority of the working class.

Under these circumstances, the proletariat was in a position in which it could not organize—and, in fact, failed to organize—an immediate and decisive blow against the state apparatus, which, for the purpose of fighting against the proletariat, absorbed the fighting organizations of the fascist bourgeoisie: the storm troops, the "Stahlhelm," and the Reichswehr. The bourgeoisie was able without serious resistance to hand over the power of government in the country to the national-socialists, who acted against the working class by means of provocation, bloody terror, and political banditism.

In analyzing the conditions for a *victorious* uprising of the proletariat, *Lenin* said:

> "A decisive battle can be considered as fully mature, *if* all the class forces which are hostile to us have become *sufficiently* entangled, have *sufficiently* come into conflict with each other, have *sufficiently* weakened themselves by a struggle which is beyond their strength." *If* "all the vacillating, hesitating, unstable, intermediate elements, i.e., the petty bourgeoisie, petty bourgeois democracy as distinguished from the bourgeoisie, have *sufficiently* exposed themselves to the people, have *sufficiently* disgraced themselves by their practical bankruptcy." *If* "among the proletariat mass sentiment has begun, and is rising strongly in favor of supporting the most decisive, supremely bold and revolutionary activity against the bourgeoisie. Then the revolution has matured, and if we have properly taken into account all of the conditions mentioned above . . . and have properly selected the moment, our victory is assured." [Lenin, *Sochineniia,* 2d ed., XXV, 229; emphasis added in *I.P.C.*]

The characteristic feature of the circumstances at the time of the Hitler coup was that these conditions for a victorious rising had not yet managed to mature at that moment. They only existed in an embryonic state.

As for the vanguard of the proletariat, the communist party . . . did not wish to slip into adventurism, and of course could not compensate for this missing factor by its own actions.

> "It is impossible to win with the vanguard alone," says Lenin. "To throw the vanguard alone into the decisive fight while the whole of the class, the whole of the broad masses, have not occupied the position either of direct support of the vanguard, or at least of friendly neutrality toward it, . . . would not only be foolish, but a crime." [*Ibid.,* p. 228.]

Such were the circumstances which decided the retreat of the working class and the victory of the party of the counterrevolutionary fascists in Germany.

Thus, in the last analysis, the establishment of the fascist dictatorship in Germany is the result of the social-democratic policy of collaboration with the bourgeoisie throughout the whole period of existence of the Weimer Republic. The social-democrats repeatedly stated that they would not object to Hitler coming to power in a *"constitutional"* manner. But after Hitler assumed power, *Vorwärts* on February 2 stated that without social-democracy a person like Hitler could not have become Reich Chancellor. Wels stated the same thing on March 23, in his declaration to the Reichstag, in which he said that the services social-democracy had rendered to the "national socialists" were very great, because it was thanks to the policy that social-democracy pursued that Hitler was able to come to power. There is no need to mention Leipart, Loebe, and other social-democratic leaders who completely support the fascists. The Communist Party was right in giving the name of social-fascists to the social-democrats.

But the fascist dictatorship basing itself on armed gangs of national-socialists and the Stahlhelm and commencing civil war against the working class, abolishing all the rights of the proletariat, is at the same time smashing the social-democratic theory that it is possible to win a parliamentary majority by means of elections and to develop peacefully toward socialism without revolution. It is destroying the social-democratic theory of class collaboration with the bourgeoisie and the policy of the "lesser evil," and is destroying all the *democratic illusions* among the broad masses of workers. It is proving that the government is not a superstructure rising above classes, but a weapon of the dictatorship of the bourgeoisie, that the real state power is the armed bands of storm troops, the Stahlhelm, police, and officers, who are governing in the name of the bourgeoisie and the Junkers. The working class is actually becoming convinced that the communists were right when for a number of years they fought against democratic illusions, the social-democratic policy of the "lesser evil" and collaboration with the bourgeoisie.

Meanwhile, the unbridled dictatorship of Hitler, which has unleashed civil war in the country, cannot solve a single political and economic question of present-day Germany. The poverty and misery of the masses are increasing day-by-day. The position of industry is growing worse because the adventurist policy of the government is only accelerating the contraction of the internal and foreign market. There are not and there cannot be any prospects of a serious reduction of unemployment. There is no possibility of giving work and employment to all the adherents of the national-socialists. In place of the national-socialists who are given jobs, other workers will be dismissed. The continuation of the moratorium until October and the introduction of quotas on imports of agricultural products can only satisfy a small section of the most well-to-do peasants for a very short period, but cannot stop the growth of poverty, misery, and discontent among the broad peasant masses. The demagogic attacks on the big stores and Jewish capital cannot help the impoverished petty-bourgeoisie, whose position will grow worse proportionally with the further fall of the purchasing power of the proletariat, which will cause a further contraction of internal trade. The microscopic help given to the needy in grain and lard was only a sop for the elections. In view of the worsening economic situation, the increase of unemployment relief by two marks a month will have to be withdrawn. It is becoming clear that *Hitler is leading Germany to an economic catastrophe, which is becoming more and more inevitable.*

The national-socialist movement grew up first of all as a nationalist and chauvinist government of the petty bourgeoisie and part of the peasant masses, led by officers and government officials of the Kaiser, against Versailles. The two months of rule by Hitler has been just one long chauvinist tirade against proletarian internationalism and "world Bolshevism," a policy of aggravating relations with all countries without exception. Such a policy will not only fail to strengthen Germany but will weaken it still further and isolate it. The attempts of the government to violate the Versailles Treaty under these conditions and, even if only by means of the Anschluss with Austria, to obtain successes in foreign policy, so as to raise its prestige among the masses, whose poverty and misery it is unable to alleviate, will lead only to a further sharpening of the whole international situation and a tremendous growth of the war danger. Every day of the Hitler regime will reveal with greater clearness the manner in which the masses who follow Hitler have been tricked. Every day will show with greater clearness that Hitler is leading Germany to catastrophe.

The present period of calm after the victory of fascism is only a temporary phenomenon. *The revolutionary upsurge in Germany will inevitably grow in spite of the fascist terror. The resistance of the masses to fascism is bound to increase. The establishment of an open fascist dictatorship, by destroying all the democratic illusions among the masses and liberating them from the influence of social-democracy, is accelerating the rate of Germany's development toward the proletarian revolution.*

The task of the communists must be to explain to the masses that the Hitler regime is leading the country to catastrophe. It is now necessary to warn the masses with greater energy than ever before that the only salvation for the toiling masses from still greater poverty and want, the only way to avoid catastrophe, is the proletarian revolution and the dictatorship of the proletariat. It is necessary to strive to rally all the forces of the proletariat and form a united front of social-democratic and communist workers for the struggle against the class enemies. It is necessary to strengthen the party and strengthen all the mass organizations of the proletariat, *to prepare the masses for the decisive revolutionary battles, for the overthrow of capitalism, for the overthrow of the fascist dictatorship by an armed uprising.*

In view of all this, the Presidium of the ECCI approves the program of practical activities planned by the Central Committee of the Communist Party of Germany.

96

Izvestiia *on Extension of the Berlin Treaty*

"Bor'ba za ukreplenie mira," Izvestiia, *No. 117, May 6, 1933, p. 1.*

As the result of the exchange of ratification documents, there has entered into force the agreement signed June 24, 1931 concerning the extension of the Berlin treaty of April 24, 1926. Soviet-German relations up to this time have been based on two treaties: on the treaty concluded at Rapallo on April 16, 1922, and on the above-mentioned Berlin treaty. The Rapallo treaty put an end to the claims of both sides arising out of the World War. In spite of its limited concrete content, it represented an important historic event. Germany, burdened by reparations, still under control of the Allied officials, and the Soviet republic, which had defeated the troops of intervention but was still threatened on all sides, entered into this treaty as two equal great powers, settled old disputes in a peaceful manner, and thus cleared the way for the development of friendly relations. The content of the Berlin treaty was broader. It was concluded at a moment when Germany, having recovered to a certain extent from postwar destruction and having been temporarily strengthened by foreign loans, entered the League of Nations. . . .

The Rapallo and Berlin treaties were regarded by the other capitalist powers as a screen concealing a secret German-Soviet pact directed against the rest of the world. The more than eleven years that have passed since the signing of the Rapallo treaty, and the seven years that have elapsed since the signing of the Berlin treaty, have shown how unfounded all these accusations were. These treaties served to strengthen the economic and political relations of Germany and the Soviet Union, but they have not hindered either side from striving to strengthen its relations with other powers. As for the U.S.S.R., the treaties with Germany did not hinder the Soviet government, persistently striving for the cause of peace, from concluding nonaggression pacts with Poland and France—the best proof of the fact that the Rapallo policy was not directed against these powers.

Unfortunately, in recent years tendencies have increased in Germany itself for a deal with France or England against the Soviet Union. These tendencies, which found expression not only in broad propagandist activities of a number of groups among the German bourgeoisie, but also in the actions of certain governmental figures, did not prove to be successful. The relations of the Soviet Union to France, thanks to the peaceful policy of the Soviet government, have been strengthened to such an extent that the idea of a military alliance directed against the U.S.S.R. found no response among the leaders of French governmental policy. The elements of English imperialism which are hostile to the U.S.S.R. are occupied on so many fronts that they lack forces for an anti-Soviet adventure, no matter how dear to their hearts it might be. The attempts of German reactionary circles themselves to strengthen the position of Germany by means of the idea of intervention against the U.S.S.R. did not lead to such a strengthening. Germany at present is more isolated in foreign affairs than she has been at any time since the war. In order to be convinced of this it is sufficient to refer to the debates in the English parliament on April 13 and the commentaries on them even in that part of the

English press which previously had most zealously defended the idea of a revision of the Versailles Treaty.

The public opinion of the American bourgeoisie, which previously to a certain extent opposed the Versailles Treaty, is now in favor of preserving the status quo. There is no need to speak of France. . . . The German policy directed against friendly relations between Germany and the Soviet Union has led merely to the weakening of Germany. An external symptom of this policy was the non-extension of the Berlin treaty, which continued under various pretexts for a sufficient time to produce the impression of the liquidation of those relations which had existed for more than ten years to the benefit of Germany and the U.S.S.R. and to the benefit of the cause of general peace.

Public opinion in the Soviet Union will undoubtedly take a positive attitude towards the renewal of the validity of the Berlin treaty. In spite of their attitude toward fascism, the popular masses of the U.S.S.R. wish to live in peace with Germany, and consider that the development of Soviet-German economic relations is in the interests of both countries. Soviet policy in relation to Germany, as to all other countries, has never for a single moment gone off the tracks of peace. Public opinion in the Soviet Union has never harbored any plans directed against the integrity of German territory. It has no need to make any changes or revisions in policy toward Germany. Soviet public opinion will be pleased if the extension of the Berlin treaty by the German government produces a corresponding impression on those German circles which see a gain for Germany in a hostile attitude toward the U.S.S.R. While welcoming the extension of the Berlin treaty, Soviet public opinion is fully aware that the treaty will have that significance which is given to it by the concrete actions of both parties which concluded it.

The central idea of the foreign policy of the Soviet Union is the preservation of peace as the best condition for the development of relations between peoples. The extension of the Berlin treaty serves the policy of peace. . . . Just as in economic relations, so also in politics, only those agreements are serious which confer benefit on both parties. Friendly attitudes will evoke a friendly response, hostile actions will call forth the appropriate rebuff.

97

Radek Views the Demand for Revision of the Versailles Treaty as a Path to War

K. Radek, *"Reviziia Versal'skogo dogovora,"* Pravda, No. 127, May 10, 1933, p. 2.

. . .

Thirteen years have passed since the Treaty of Versailles was signed. Unfortunately during these years the proletariat of the leading capitalist countries has not been capable of following the road taken by the proletariat of the Soviet Union; it has not been capable so far of wresting power from the hands of the capitalist cliques and taking upon itself the solution of the problems of life and the development of the popular masses. *But the imperialists, who went bankrupt in the attempt to force upon the world the conditions of Versailles, have not been able to give the world new conditions of life fundamentally different from those of Versailles.*

The best confirmation of this is the fact that it is *the fascist governments* which have become the flag-bearers of revision, that is, the governments which most ruthlessly oppress the masses in their own countries, the governments which are based on the most medieval ideology, the governments which have outdone Herod, the governments which have deepened the imperialist theory of the mastery of the white man over the colored by the still more savage theory of the mastery of the invented Nordic race over all other peoples. *The mere fact that revision of the treaty is bound up with the victory of fascism shows how little this revision would be considered in the national interests of the masses of the nations designated by the fascists as "inferior."*

The path of revision of the predatory, tormenting Versailles peace leads through a new world war. All attempts by interested parties to represent the matter of revision merely as a peaceful resettlement of old treaties cannot deceive anyone. The diplomatic talk concerning the revision of the Versailles Treaty is simply a means of preparing for war. . . . *The word "revision" is simply another name for a new world war.* It is therefore not surprising that one of the basic demands of the revisionists is the demand for the right to those arms which are denied them by the Versailles Treaty. Discussion of revision is merely a smoke screen behind which imperialism is preparing the most horrible, the most cruel war that the human brain can conceive, a war before which all the horrors of the imperialist war of 1914–18 will pale.

. . .

What has been said is sufficient to determine *the attitude of the international proletariat to the clamor about the capitalist revision of the Versailles Treaty, and what is actually concealed behind it.* The international proletariat continues to be an enemy of the Versailles treaties. *But only its own victory could replace these treaties by peace treaties based on national self-determination*—peace treaties that would satisfy the national demands of even the most backward peoples, which would open the way for their common struggle for the transformation of the world and the common struggle against want, poverty, and ruin which have been created by postwar capitalism. *But this will be a socialist "revision."* No regrouping of the imperialist powers, no redivision of the world on the basis of the predominance of a new imperialist group over the victor powers can bring about a just peace. . . .

And only the victory of the proletarian revolution and the revolution of the colonial peoples can rid the world of the nightmare of a new imperialist war and can open the way for a truly peaceful solution of difficult problems.

Because of its attitude to imperialism, to the self-determination of peoples and imperialist wars, the international proletariat—the enemy of the Versailles Treaty—cannot side with those imperialist powers which wish to redivide the world amid the conflagration of a new imperialist war. The struggle against the danger of a new imperialist war is the central task of the international proletariat. It is connected in the most profound way with the struggle against fascism. The historical function of international fascism is the attempt to postpone the moment of the overthrow of capitalism by completely enslaving the popular masses and driving them to destruction in a new imperialist war.

. . .

. . . The imperialist powers which are making preparations for a new imperialist war are at the same time extremely apprehensive about this war. They realize that, even if they succeed in breaking the resistance of the popular masses and driving them onto the battlefield, after the first defeats the revolutionary movement will grip the masses, and that a protracted war will inevitably lead to a socialist revolution.

They fear that the Soviet Union, which would be the only haven of peace in this sea of blood, would attract the popular masses of the countries plunged into the chaos of a world war. And for this reason groups are appearing in many imperialist countries which are planning to begin the redivision of the world by means of war against the Soviet Union.

If Japan could be pushed into war against the U.S.S.R., that war might weaken the U.S.S.R., while Japan too would be so weakened that its opponents, or even "allies," would no longer have to be afraid of youthful Japanese imperialism.

If Poland could be pushed into a war against the U.S.S.R., it would be easier to persuade it to relinquish its claim on the Baltic coast region by Ukrainian compensations which it still has to conquer, and in this way provide a way out of the situation in which the German fascists find themselves.

This program of seeking the revision of the Versailles Treaty on the path of re-establishing the still worse Brest peace is the foreign policy program of German fascism. It is unnecessary to say that the "brilliant" creators of these programs were born too late. The times of Brest have long since passed, and any attempt to "revise" the Versailles Treaty at the expense of the U.S.S.R. would call into question the very existence of those capitalist powers which tried to realize such a program. *The Soviet Union does not take part in the common squabbles of the capitalist groupings. But any attempt* to turn matters against it would place on the agenda not the question of our relation to the Versailles peace or to attempts by the other imperialist powers to alter it, but the entire question of the existence of capitalism in general.

. . .

98

Radek on Relations with Great Britain

Excerpt from an article on the occasion of the suspension of trade relations between the two countries. K. Radek, "Na angliiskie melodii," Izvestiia, No. 127, May 18, 1933, p. 2.

. . . Soviet-British relations have been *constantly experiencing crises.* Not a single European state, having recognized the Soviet Union, has previously broken off relations with it. But England broke off relations with the Soviet Union in 1927, and in addition, without any apparent reason. . . . The reason was clear. The British diehards had resolved to deal a blow to the Soviet Union which was supposed to be followed by others. *The plan failed.* England's action was not followed by other powers. The blow hung in the air. It became necessary to re-establish relations. Now we are witnessing an event unheard of in the annals of history. Under the pretext of a protest against the conviction of two English intelligence agents who admitted their guilt, the English government has announced a *trade boycott* of the U.S.S.R. It has done so at the moment when on its own initiative an international conference is meeting to facilitate the course of international trade and to seek a way out of the international crisis. Where can one find people naïve enough to believe that this boycott was caused by the sentence pronounced by the Moscow court on the English intelligence agents? Who can believe that this boycott is aimed only at forcing the Soviet Union to agree to concessions in the trade negotiations? . . .

99

Soviet Draft of an Economic Nonaggression Pact

Submitted by Litvinov at the World Economic Conference in London, June 20, 1933. S.U.R., Vol. 11, No. 7–8, July–August 1933, p. 171.

The governments of the countries listed below, recognizing that the cessation of economic aggression is the most important condition for the peaceful cooperation of all nations in the sphere of economic relations irrespective of their political and economic system; believing that the cessation of economic aggression might help to dispel the present atmosphere of distrust and insecurity; and believing that in order to improve the present grave economic situation, it is necessary that all countries, in addition to refraining from war as a means of settling international conflicts, should completely renounce all open and disguised forms of economic aggression, agree on the following:

1. The contracting parties declare that they will adhere in their policy to the principle, proclaimed by the international economic conference in 1927 and confirmed by a special committee of the commission of inquiry into a pan-European union in 1931, of the peaceful coexistence of all nations irrespective of their social-political and economic systems.

2. The contracting parties will refrain from all forms of discrimination in their mutual relations. In conformity with this the parties will consider incompatible with the principles of the present protocol, the adoption and application in their countries of a special regime directed against any particular country and applying less favorable conditions to trade with that country compared with conditions obtaining for trade with all other countries.

3. In conformity with the principles set forth in Articles I and II of the present protocol, the parties solemnly renounce the application in the future, under any pretext whatsoever, as an

instrument of trade policy, of special discriminatory tariffs, applied to a single country, of general import or export embargoes applied to any single country, or special conditions for such imports and exports, discriminatory levies on mercantile vessels, discriminatory conditions for the admission of economic organizations to national territory, [and] finally, every kind of boycott established against the trade of any country by governmental or administrative measures.

4. All measures of discrimination operating in countries which sign this protocol are to be revoked from the moment this protocol enters into force for the respective countries.

5. This protocol is subject to ratification and goes into effect among those countries which announce its ratification.

100

Soviet Willingness to Sell the Chinese Eastern Railway Indicated

Summary of a statement by Soviet Ambassador K. K. Iurenev at the opening of a conference between the U.S.S.R., Manchukuo, and Japan on June 26, 1933, at the Japanese Ministry of Foreign Affairs, Tokyo. Nichi Ronenkan [Japanese-Russian Yearbook] (Tokyo, 1933), pp. 113–114.

The Soviet government attaches great importance to the continued consolidation of friendly relations with Japan as one of the most important factors of peace in the Far East and in the world in general.

Proceeding from this viewpoint and its policy of peace, the government of the Soviet Union has maintained from the time of the opening of events in Manchuria a strict position of absolute neutrality and noninterference. Taking into consideration Japan's interests, and in keeping with mutual treaties and obligations, the government of the Soviet Union has expressed its sincere readiness to ensure friendly relations with neighboring states.

At the same time, taking into account the fact that the Chinese

Eastern Railway has threatened to become the root of evil which might give rise to serious complications between Japan and Manchukuo on the one side and the Soviet Union on the other, and also taking into account the fact that various groupings of forces which interfere with the cause of peace are trying to take a path that would injure Japanese-Soviet and Manchukuo-Soviet relations, the government of the Soviet Union has decided, and has so informed the governments of Japan and Manchukuo, that it is ready to enter into negotiations for a fundamental solution of the problems by selling the C.E.R. to Japan or to Manchukuo.

As Count Uchida said in his speech, the government of Tsarist Russia built this line on the territory of a foreign country in order to serve its own aggressive imperialist plans.

The government of the U.S.S.R., in accordance with its basic principles, has absolutely no such plans or intentions.

The October Revolution nullified the significance of the railway as an instrument of imperialist aggression. But the Soviet government considers it its duty and obligation to defend the material interests of Soviet citizens, by whose labor and capital this railway was built.

We hope that the present negotiations, with the active participation of the Japanese government, will bring about the desired results.

101

Comintern Letter to the British Independent Labour Party

I.P.C., Vol. 13, No. 29, June 30, 1933, pp. 638–639; New Leader, *June 30, 1933, p. 14.*

Comrades,—We confirm the receipt of your letter of May 18 regarding the resolution adopted at the Derby Conference of the Independent Labour Party, a resolution which undoubtedly expressed the strongly increasing will to unity and struggle against capitalism among the British working class.

In conformity with your wishes, we will set out our opinion of how the Independent Labour Party would assist the work of the Communist International.

An important step in this direction is the start which is being made in the practical carrying out of the united front between the Independent Labour Party and the Communist Party of Great Britain in the struggle against the capitalist offensive, the fascist terror in Germany, and the danger of new imperialist wars. This in itself is the beginning of practical collaboration with the Communist International.

In our opinion the further steps in this direction should be as follows:

Firstly, the extension and strengthening of the actions of solidarity which have already taken place between the Independent Labour Party and the Communist Party of Great Britain, to all the important and urgent questions of the struggle of the British and international proletariat against their bourgeoisie and world imperialism and winning of the broad strata of workers, members of the Labour Party and the trade unions, for the united front in this struggle.

Secondly, the giving of real support to the struggle of the Communist Party of Great Britain against the bourgeois nationalist and reactionary policy of "National Labour," against the reformist policy of the Labour Party leaders, the leaders of trade-unions and the Second International.

Convinced by the experiences of many years, the members of the Independent Labour Party decided at the Derby Conference to follow up disaffiliation from the Labour Party by leaving the Second International. These two decisions were necessary and important steps in the struggle against reformism. But the Independent Labour Party cannot stop merely at the point of an organizational break with the Second International.

If the Independent Labour Party has seriously decided to participate in the revolutionary class struggle of the proletariat, it cannot carry this out except by a constant active struggle against "National Labour," against reformism and the reformist leaders who propagate reformist ideas, hold back and disrupt the working-class movement.

In practice, the slogan of struggle against the capitalist offensive remains an empty phrase if the party which advances it does not take any steps to mobilize the workers for mass resistance to wage-cuts, dismissals, the reduction of unemployment insurance, etc.

But the social democratic parties and the reactionary leaders of the trade unions, who state in words that they are opposed to the capitalist offensive, are in reality directing their efforts toward permitting the capitalists to carry through their merciless pressure on the workers without meeting with any resistance.

. . .

In exactly the same way, *the struggle against fascism* remains a hypocritical phrase if it is not accompanied by the organization of the united front of the working class with the aim of barring the path of the fascist attack from the very beginning.

But in every country, the parties of the Second International, including the British Labour Party, are doing everything in their power to hold back the majority of the workers from participating in the united front with the communists for the struggle against the bourgeoisie and fascism.

By their policy of collaborating with the bourgeoisie and their policy of splitting the united front of the working class, the parties of the Second International are building a road for fascism.

Before the eyes of the workers of all countries stands the example of German Social-Democracy. Under the slogan "Against Fascism and Against Communism" it consistently supported every reactionary government in Germany on the plea that it was the "lesser evil" as compared with an open fascist dictatorship, and in this way it restrained the masses from the struggle against the fascist danger.

At the same time it attempted to show the exploiters by means of all kinds of concessions to the bourgeoisie, at the expense of the workers, that they had no need to replace the "democratic" constitution by a fascist dictatorship in order to carry out their policy of attacking the standard of living of the toilers.

All the repeated and insistent attempts of the Communist Party of Germany to call on the workers for solid antifascist activity, to form a united proletarian front of struggle, were disrupted and betrayed by social-democracy and the leaders of the reformist trade-unions. In this way they succeeded in paralyzing the efforts of the communists to mobilize the majority of the working class for mass resistance to fascism (demonstrations, political strikes).

The other parties of the Second International, and the trade-union leaders of the Amsterdam International who are connected with them, follow the same path as German Social-Democracy.

Similarly *the struggle against imperialism and the wars which it is preparing* remains an empty phrase in the mouths of those who do not honestly and insistently strive to mobilize the working class for an irreconcilable struggle against the imperialism of its "own" country.

But the parties of the Second International are themselves affected through and through with the ideology of bourgeois chauvinism and are interested in the success of the robber policy of their own imperialism. Just as the social-democratic parties in every country supported their governments during the war, so are they now supporting the bloody suppression of the colonial peoples and other independent nations, and the policy of preparing new wars.

In those cases when a social-democratic party forms part of the government, it directly carries out this violent imperialist policy of the bourgeoisie (bloody repression in India and the bombing of unarmed populations under the Labour Government).

Also, in the struggle between the capitalist countries and *the Union of Soviet Socialist Republics,* the parties of the Second International have really joined in the anti-Soviet front of the capitalist world.

Therefore there cannot be any question of really serious support for the struggle of the Communist International against the capitalist offensive, against fascism, imperialism, and the menacing war danger, if at the same time the harmful role of the reformists and their hostile policy toward the working class are not exposed and if a struggle is not carried on against them at every step.

If the Independent Labour Party wishes to help the struggle of the communists against the bourgeoisie and their chief social support in the ranks of the working class—the Second International, it will give real assistance to the development of the working class movement.

But if any representative of the Independent Labour Party supposes that the deep divergence of principle between the Second International and the Communist International could be covered up by an unprincipled rapprochement and conciliation, we openly announce that this would be a most harmful delusion and an impermissible mistake from the point of view of the interests of the class struggle and the proletarian revolution.

The Second International is not acting for but *against* the class struggle of the proletariat, not for but *against* the proletarian revolution.

The members of the Independent Labour Party must clearly understand that the chief danger of the Second International consists precisely in the fact that, while representing the interests of the *bourgeoisie,* it does not do this openly, but under the cloak of defending the interests of the *workers.*

If a party like the Independent Labour Party, instead of exposing the real nature of the Second International, were to depict it as a genuine representative of the workers to which the revolutionary workers' organizations could and should reconcile themselves, it would by this merely make the deceptive maneuvers of the Second International easier to carry out.

If the Independent Labour Party were to renew the harmful attempts which it made after the war, together with several other parties, to act as an "unbiased" intermediary between the Second and Third Internationals, and if individual leaders of the Independent Labour Party were to write articles hostile to the revolutionary working-class movement (such as the last article written by Fenner Brockway), this would not be *support* for the Communist International, but for the Second International.

In practice, such attempts would be an obstacle on the path toward the establishment of the proletarian united front and the unity of the working class on the basis of the class struggle. That was the role of the Second-and-a-Half International, which held back the revolutionary development of the radicalized workers, so as to return them once more to the fold of the Second International.

What relations can be established now between your party and the Communist International?

Our opinion is as follows: Although the Independent Labour Party does not at present accept the standpoint of the program of the Communist International, nevertheless it can establish really revolutionary collaboration both with the Communist Party of Great Britain and with the Communist International.

We, on our side, declare our complete readiness for such collaboration, but, of course, retaining the right of comradely criticism when necessary.

In Great Britain there is a very great necessity for the uniting of the revolutionary forces. We see at present that many members of your party are studying the program of the Communist International and advocating a united revolutionary party. This is of serious importance.

If the members of the Independent Labour Party are really developing in the direction of adopting our program, then possibilities open up in Great Britain for the formation of a single, strong, mass Communist Party corresponding to the conditions of the country.

We are facing the greatest fights in the history of the world. A historic transition is taking place to a new cycle of revolutions and wars. The class struggle is rapidly growing in all capitalist countries. The antagonisms in the camp of the imperialists themselves are intensifying.

The picture of the capitalist world discloses the complete bankruptcy of the capitalist system. At the same time the construction of socialism in the U.S.S.R., with its mighty economic, technical, and cultural upsurge, shows that as soon as the working class organizes its forces, overthrows the dictatorship of the bourgeoisie, and shakes the capitalist parasites and exploiters from its shoulders, then before it opens up the path for a great creative work in all branches of life.

In many capitalist countries the revolutionary outlook opens up this possibility of proletarian victories. The forces of the proletarian world revolution are growing. In all capitalist countries it is the communist parties which are carrying on a determined struggle for the interests of the proletariat and for the cause of the socialist revolution.

In Germany, in spite of the raging fascist terror, the Communist Party with great self-sacrifice is successfully carrying on the struggle, and without doubt will show to the whole world that it has rallied around the banner of the proletarian revolution not only the five million workers who voted for it at the last election, but *the majority of the working class of Germany*.

If the Independent Labour Party energetically assists the struggle of the Communist International, this will be of great international significance.

We request you to inform us whether your party agrees to give precisely such support and assistance to the Communist International.

> Yours fraternally,
>
> (*Signed*) O. W. KUUSINEN
> (*For the Secretariat of the
> Executive Committee of the
> Communist International*)

102

The Comintern's Reply to the ILP

I.P.C., *Vol. 13, No. 43, September 29, 1933, pp. 953–955;* New Leader, *September 29, 1933, pp. 10–11.*

To the Independent Labour Party

Comrades,—After we had given a clear answer to the question put by your party conference as to how the Independent Labour Party might assist the work of the Communist International, we received a letter from the National Administrative Council [NAC] which made a series of absolutely unfounded charges against the Communist International and brought forward a proposal to "call a world congress of all organizations which are prepared to cooperate on a revolutionary Socialist basis."

We consider that nothing useful can come out of such a proposal. If the National Administrative Council of the ILP, together with the independent fragments of social-democratic parties, calls a world congress, as stated in its letter, nothing will come of this except an attempt, foredoomed to failure, to resurrect the inglorious Two-and-a-Half International, as was demonstrated at the recent Paris conference of these organizations.

We doubt if this idea will be received with any enthusiasm even by the members of the Independent Labour Party itself. At the Derby conference the representative of the National Administrative Council advocated the idea of an "all-embracing international" as against the resolution to approach the Communist International. But the majority decided for the latter.

We believe that the members of the ILP wish to adhere to the decision of their party conference and do not wish to be dragged into new internationals with old bankrupt policies.

The idea of a "Left Socialist" world congress, which is advocated by the National Administrative Council, is basically the old idea of the ILP which dates back to 1920.

· · ·

At the present time the radicalization of the working masses in Britain is a fact from which practical political conclusions should be drawn. We communists put forward the task of organizing the mass struggles for the defense of the vital everyday interests of the workers, for the liberation of the majority of the working class from the influence of the reformists, for rallying together the fighting front of the proletariat and organizing international united-front actions against fascism, the war danger, and the bourgeois offensive against the living standards of the working class.

But what could a joint congress of social-democratic and communist parties, such as proposed by the leadership of the ILP, give to the poverty-stricken working masses at the present time? Nothing but illusions.

The leaders of the social-democratic parties do not want to struggle against the capitalist offensive.

They want to continue their class-collaboration with the bourgeoisie, and a joint congress with them could only distract the attention of the workers from the necessity of a mass struggle in defense of their interests.

Could such a congress enlarge and strengthen the proletarian united front? It could not. The social-democratic leaders are afraid of the united front of the working masses. In all countries they prohibit their supporters from participating in any militant united-front activity with the communists.

Time after time they rejected the proposals of the communist parties for a united front. They expelled communists and other revolutionary workers, who supported the united front, from the trade-unions and from the Labour Party. They split the whole trade-unions, and in addition, when our comrades organizationally rallied together the expelled members, they shouted that it was the communists who were the splitters.

. . .

The last conference of the Second International in Paris once more demonstrated the hostile attitude of this International to the proletarian united front.

All this proves that the united front of the proletariat cannot be established by conferences from above with the lackeys of capitalism.

It will have to be forged in every separate country by the everyday cooperation of the revolutionary and reformist workers in the localities, in the factories, in the trade-unions, and by developing their joint energetic struggle against political reaction and the capitalist offensive. There is no doubt that this task can and must be carried out.

For the carrying through of these most important tasks of the revolutionary working-class movement, the assistance of the ILP in the work of the Communist International could be of exceptional value.

But some parts of the letter of the NAC to us, and statements of prominent members of the NAC (Brockway, Sandham, Jowett, etc.) during recent months, [together with] the breaking off of the united front with the communists by some leading functionaries of the ILP, give grounds for fearing that the intention of the Derby conference to assist in the work of the Communist International may be frustrated.

In view of this danger, we are compelled to put the following questions:

Firstly, at a moment when the example of German social-democracy is plainly showing to all the workers of the world how the parties of the Second International betray the cause of the working class for the benefit of fascism, what does it signify that the NAC of the ILP, instead of calling on the workers to carry on a determined struggle against the Second International, throws out the accusation against the *Communist International* that it "prevented that united action by the working class which alone could have defeated the forces of fascism and capitalism"?

This charge breaks down in face of the indisputable facts.

. . .

When the Hitler regime was in embryo, who was it that insisted on the necessity for the united action of the working class in order to break the power of fascism? Did not the Communist International make this proposal to the social-democratic parties?

Who was it that carried on a real struggle in Germany against the seizure of power by the National-Socialists? Among all the parties, it was the Communist Party of Germany alone.

In vain it approached the Social-Democratic Party of Germany and the General Federation of Trade Unions (ADGB) to carry on antifascist actions on the basis of the united front—this was done on July 20, 1932, against the coup d'état in Prussia, and on January 30 and February 28, 1933, against the dictatorship of Hitler.

More than this, the Communist Party of Germany organized a whole series of militant actions with the participation of the social-democratic workers, such as mass strikes against the emergency decree of the Papen government to reduce wages, the general strike in Lübeck for the liberation of the arrested Social-Democrats; it fought jointly with the members of the Reichsbanner against the closing of trade-union halls by the fascists (Frankfort, Düsseldorf, Hanover, Königsberg, etc.) .

But the leaders of the Social-Democratic Party and the reformist trade-unions constantly restrained the workers from this common struggle by their warnings and threats. In addition, the social-democratic ministers and police presidents suppressed hundreds of antifascist actions of the workers by police force. These are the facts.

But, writes the NAC, the Communist International is "treating sections of the working class outside its own ranks as enemies."

No, we only look upon the social-democratic *parties* and the *leaders* of the reformist trade-unions as enemies, and not the trade-union organizations and the social-democratic workers.

But the Communist International, says the NAC, is treating the parties of the Second International as enemies, "indistinguishable from the fascists and the most reactionary capitalists." No, we have always distinguished between them.

The parties of the Second International do not openly defend the dictatorship of the bourgeoisie, like the fascists, but under a democratic cloak.

By their policy of support for the capitalist offensive, they clear the path for fascism, and then the fascists do their work.

In Germany the social-democratic leaders supported, as a "lesser evil," the governments of Brüning and Papen, whose emergency decrees so impoverished the masses of the people that millions of them in despair blindly swallowed the demagogic promises of Hitler.

. . .

Secondly, at the very time when the NAC is writing us a letter on the necessity for "united action by the international working-class movement against fascism, war, and imperialism," what does it mean that the chairman of the ILP writes articles containing the worst kind of slander of the U.S.S.R., the Communist Party of the Soviet Union, and the Communist International?

The Soviet Union is the bulwark of the world proletariat and the oppressed nations against imperialism and international fascism. Therefore the hostile policy of imperialism is constantly directed above all against it. All the world knows this.

Everybody who wants at the present time to fight honestly against war and imperialism will fight first of all against the imperialist preparations for an anti-Soviet war, particularly on the part of British and Japanese imperialism.

But what does Mr. Brockway do in his notorious articles on the seizure of power by the fascists in Germany (*New Leader,* June 16, July 7)? They do not contain a word against British or Japanese imperialism, but instead of this, a senseless libel that the Communist Party of the Soviet Union bribed the other parties of the Communist International so that they came out in the alleged interests of the U.S.S.R. for "acquiescence in Japanese imperialism" in the Far East and that they also "contributed to the victory of Hitler"!

. . .

In using such dishonest means, Mr. Brockway merely displays his own desperate alarm over the fact that, especially recently, the British workers are learning more about the enormous political and economic gains of the Soviet Union and the more they learn, the more they become filled with revolutionary enthusiasm and go over to genuine socialism, an example of which is given by the victorious Soviet proletariat.

Thirdly, at a time when the ILP adopts decisions for a united front and cooperation on a national scale with the Communist Party of Great Britain, what does it mean when some district committees of the Independent Labour Party either prohibit their organizations from carrying out any united-front actions with the communists (Lancashire), or refuse in general to discuss these questions with the representatives of the communist party (South Wales)?

. . .

Allow us to state our opinion quite openly as to what it all means.

It seems to us that in your party there are *two distinct tendencies,* two political *lines.* Many members of the party are for the new line outlined by the Derby conference, but many leaders are for the old reformist line.

Many members of the party are for an uncomprising fight

545

against the bourgeoisie and the Labour Party, but many leaders are sabotaging the fight against both one and the other.

Many members of the party are firm supporters of the U.S.S.R., but many leaders are against the U.S.S.R. Many members of the party want to get nearer to the Communist International and to cooperate with it, but many leaders want to get further away from it.

In short, many members of your party are revolutionaries, but many leaders are reformists. To be more exact, they are Left reformists.

The latter are not quite the same as Right reformists, the leaders of the Labour Party or "National Labour." What do the Left reformists stand for?

They are in favor of a revolutionary policy in words, but in practice they are against it. They can accept a much more radical program than the Right reformists, but they do not cease their resistance to the revolutionizing of the practice of the party.

They talk loudly about the united front of the proletariat, but act along the lines of conciliation with the Labour leaders and continue their cooperation with the saboteurs of the united front, such as Mr. Sandham, and in this way also help the National Labourists and the National government.

Formally they are for cooperation with the Communist International, but actually they are assisting its bitter enemies in the setting up of a new international body for the purpose of holding back the masses from the revolutionary class struggle by means of deceptive phrases and Left maneuvers which are essentially directed against the communist movement.

. . .

"We also want socialism," say the Left reformists, "but by a pacifist technique of revolution." In other words, this means we do not actually want revolution, which brings all kinds of dangers.

But if socialism could be brought in without dangers and fights, either by a democratic vote in Parliament for a suitable bill, or by means of the peaceful organization of legal workers' councils, then we would have no objection to socialism.

. . .

But the British bourgeoisie are emphatically against the fate of capitalism being decided by peaceful means. It is strongly armed and is in favour of using the most merciless violence against the proletariat. Its policy is a bloody one and its "democracy" is shown up as a class dictatorship. Its state is shown up as the apparatus of class violence.

Bourgeois class violence cannot be broken by "pacifist technique," but only by the class violence of the proletariat.

The British working class will be strong enough to do this if its vanguard, its revolutionary movement, and the united front are strengthened.

For this purpose it is necessary to take advantage of all actual possibilities and practical means, including the election campaigns and the Parliamentary tribune, to activize, educate, and organize the working class, and to win its decisive strata over to the side of the revolution.

Such is the line of a genuine revolutionary policy.

. . .

We say that the political situation is *favorable* for revolutionary work. A period of great class battles for power is approaching with the inevitability of historic law. This signifies the *possibility of great victories for the proletariat.* But everything depends on how the conscious revolutionaries carry on their work *at the present time* to prepare the working class for these struggles for power.

For this purpose it is necessary, above all, to have *a clear political line.*

The path of the ILP lies forward and not backward! Backward means to bankrupt reformism. Forward means to communism, which is already leading the working class in one-sixth of the globe from victory to victory, and which will grow and conquer in all countries.

We propose that the following questions be raised for discussion in all the organizations of the Independent Labour Party:

(1) What concrete mass actions on the basis of the united front of the CPGB and the ILP can and must be carried out in the near future, with the aim of a successful struggle for a ten per cent wage increase, against the Means Test and other similar partial demands advanced by the CPGB and the ILP?

(2) Is it desirable for the Independent Labour Party to join the Communist International as a party sympathizing with communism, with the right to a consultative vote, according to paragraph 18 of the Statutes of the Communist International?[1]

We are aware that the latter question has been advanced by some members of the Independent Labour Party. We consider it timely for the party to discuss this question fundamentally.

With communist greetings, on behalf of the Secretariat of the Executive Committee of the Communist International.

(*Signed*) O. W. KUUSINEN

NOTES

1. The ECCI has the right to accept affiliation to the Communist International of all organizations and parties sympathetic to communism, such organizations to have a consultative voice. [Footnote in *I.P.C.*]

103

Izvestiia *on Germany's Withdrawal From the* League of Nations

"*Vykhod Germanii iz Ligi natsii,*" Izvestiia, *No. 254, October 16, 1933, p. 1.*

· · ·

What has caused the German government to make such an extremely serious decision?

· · ·

. . . The answer must be sought in the international position of Germany, in the internal political situation which has developed in the eight months of the fascist regime. In leaving the League of Nations, Germany apparently wished to display its foreign policy strength and resoluteness, but actually it has demonstrated the weakness of the foreign position of the fascist regime. The withdrawal of Germany from the League of Nations and from the Disarmament Conference is the result of the international isolation of fascist Germany. . . . The ruling circles of Germany have seriously aggravated relations even with the Soviet Union, which has shown no hostility whatever toward Germany, in particular by the aggressive statements of Messrs. Rosenberg and Hugenberg and other advocates of German imperialist expansion.

The fascists reckoned that the terror initiated by them against the revolutionary proletariat would draw to their side the sympathy of the capitalist world and would make it possible for them, once they had overcome the contradictions between Germany and the initiators of the Versailles Treaty, to open the way for foreign policy adventures. Having become convinced of their miscalculation, the fascist rulers retreated in their international game, and while doing so burned one of the bridges over which they had planned to launch their attack.

. . .

But Germany has not only withdrawn from the League of Nations—it has refused to participate in the further work of the Disarmament Conference. In other words, German fascism declares to the entire world that it has decided to take the path of preparation for war, the essential condition for which is the increase of armaments. The capitalist world has found itself in a deadlock on the question of disarmament. The Disarmament Conference is threatened with a scandalous fiasco. It could not have been otherwise, inasmuch as the majority of the participants in the conference refused to take the only possible path which could lead to the limitation of armaments and the strengthening of peace—the path indicated in the Soviet proposals at Geneva. It could not have been otherwise, because only the U.S.S.R. has struggled consistently for disarmament in accordance with its unchanging and consistent policy of peace.

. . .

The action of fascist Germany, confronted by the failure of its internal policy and face to face with international isolation, is threatening international peace with exceptionally dangerous adventures. The seriousness of this danger will of course be recognized by everyone who considers it his duty to struggle by all means for the preservation of peaceful relations between peoples. The withdrawal of Germany from the League of Nations is an alarm warning for partisans of peace concerning the need to be on guard.

104

Pravda *on Recognition of the Soviet Union by the United States*

"Krupneishaia pobeda sovetskoi politiki mira," Pravda, *No. 318, November 19, 1933, p. 1.*

. . .

. . . On the eve of the tenth anniversary of the first recognition of the Soviet government by the capitalist world, we mark a new and great victory of our government's policy of peace—the establishment of normal relations with the United States.

. . .

The new foreign policy success of the U.S.S.R. is an indication of the strength of its position in the struggle for peace. It is no secret for anyone that peace is threatened just now by certain imperialist powers who are determined to improve their internal affairs at the expense of foreign resources and foreign territory. The failure of the Disarmament Conference, the ominous portents in the East and the West, and the arms race among the capitalist nations indicate what indescribable sufferings threaten toiling humanity. Under just these circumstances, the new victory of our peace policy—the establishment of normal diplomatic relations between the U.S.S.R. and the U.S.A.—takes on special significance.

November 16 will mark an important date in the history of international relations of our epoch. Under the leadership of Comrade *Stalin* our party, having cleared away from its path each and every obstacle, *is victoriously leading the working class and the kolkhoz peasantry to their great historical goal.* A new stage in the competition of the two systems has been completed. The Soviet Union has become a major force by its economic and political strength, which even the most important capitalist powers cannot help but take into consideration.

The toilers of the U.S.S.R. warmly welcome this new victory of the cause of peace.

105

Kuusinen Explains the Meaning of the Soviet Peace Policy

Excerpts from the report by Kuusinen at the Thirteenth Plenum of the ECCI, November 28, 1933. XIII Plenum IKKI: stenografich-eskii otchet (Moscow, 1934), pp. 15–16.

The specific gravity of the Soviet Union in the sphere of international relations has greatly increased. The determined peace policy of the Soviet Union on the basis of the victorious construction of socialism has brought the land of the dictatorship of the proletariat, particularly in the most recent past, a series of successes which have enormous international significance.

The Soviet Union is able to carry out a consistent policy of peace because the proletariat over a gigantic territory has annihilated all causes which lead to imperialist wars. In the Soviet Union there is no lack of markets, there is no need to chase after them; the dictatorship of the proletariat, representing the vital interests of the overwhelming majority of the population of the country, is not threatened by overturn from within; there is no need for it to seek salvation in wars. The power of the Soviet Union has grown rapidly and is growing greater with every day. *Such* a country *and only such* a country is capable of pursuing a firm and consistent policy of peace.

But in connection with the successes of the foreign policy of the Soviet Union it has turned out that our communist press in the capitalist countries is not able to explain to the working masses the peace policy of the Soviet Union and its significance and to rebut convincingly the anti-Soviet calumny and sophisms of the social-fascists. However, any lack of clarity in communist agitation on this important point is absolutely impermissible. What is the cause of this lack of clarity? It seems to me that it results primarily from the fact that certain comrades understand the peace policy of the Soviet Union one-sidedly, from the fact that they envisage and explain this policy in a bourgeois-pacifist sense.

In our press it is often correctly written: "The consistent peace policy of the Soviet government," "The Soviet Union is the main factor of peace in the entire world," etc. All of this is true, but if we see nothing more in this policy and explain nothing more to the workers, we thereby simply create confusion.

There is no slogan that the bourgeoisie has abused more than the slogan of peace. The imperialist "peace policy" is the policy of the Versailles peace, of the Brest-Litovsk peace, it is that policy which serves as an instrument for imperialist rule and imperialist rivalry. Every imperialist diplomat makes use of the slogans of peace with particular zeal exactly on the eve of war. Even Hitler makes long speeches about "European peace," and Araki, the Japanese Minister of War, in his well-known pamphlet which is a sample of political hypocrisy unparalleled in world literature, has written a whole chapter entitled "The Japanese—Apostles of Peace" . . .

. . . The primary duty of the communists is to teach the toilers to see the bloody policy of the imperialists behind the sweet songs which they sing.

However, this is still not sufficient to enable the masses to understand the entire difference between the peace policy of the U.S.S.R. and the pacifist phrase-mongering of the bourgeoisie and its agents. The difference is *not only* that the peace policy of the CPSU (B) is an honest policy. A certain relationship of forces in the imperialist camp may even force this or that bourgeois government, either insufficiently strong or temporarily isolated, to try for a time to avoid war. This of course is not a consistent peace policy, but it would be completely incorrect to explain the difference between the peace policy of the U.S.S.R. and the policy of any capitalist country striving to avoid war only on the grounds that the former is a consistent, the latter an inconsistent peace policy.

The peace policy of the CPSU (B) is an honest and consistent peace policy and most of all it is a *Bolshevik* policy. It is a *revolutionary* peace policy, imbued with the *spirit of proletarian internationalism*.

In our agitation and propaganda we must dissociate in the most determined way the peace policy of the U.S.S.R. from any kind of bourgeois policy. What would the masses of the revolutionary workers think if we, the communists, were to start to confuse in our press the revolutionary peace policy of the CPSU (B) with bourgeois pacifism? Of what use would such a policy be to the Soviet Union, the workers would then ask. Why does it conclude pacts of nonaggression with the capitalist government of our country, which is simply hypocritically playing at a peace policy, which by no means intends to observe these pacts once a favorable moment arrives for a counterrevolutionary war? And in general, the workers might ask, why do the Bolsheviks conclude even temporary agreements with our reactionary government, which is secretly preparing for a war against the Soviet Union and for a civil war against the working class of our country?

Many workers, including those who sympathize sincerely with the Soviet Union, might be beset with such doubts; but in our press they do not find a correct explanation of the peace policy of the CPSU (B).

It must be explained to the workers that the peace policy of the Soviet Union may, if not avert war altogether, at all events greatly hinder the war policy of the imperialist enemies of the U.S.S.R., and may even put off the beginning of such a war, particularly if its peace policy is given real and active support by the proletariat of the capitalist countries. But to hinder and to postpone the counterrevolutionary war against the Soviet Union is in the immediate interests of the international revolutionary workers' movement. This must be explained to the working masses in every country.

But how can this be explained? In my opinion, in explaining this problem attention must be drawn to the following main points.

First, the peace policy of the Soviet Union helps to expose the war policy of the imperialists and by that hinders their aggressiveness. This is very important.

Each of the enemies of the U.S.S.R. requires and is looking for "plausible" pretexts for justifying in the eyes of the workers of their country this criminal, most highly "unpopular" war. No matter how much the bourgeois governments may wish to attack the U.S.S.R., not one of them would dare to appear openly as the attacking side (the aggressor), fearing the wrath of the popular masses in their own rear areas. Therefore a government such as the Polish, the Rumanian, and even our [sic] Finnish fascist government, cannot do without signing the pact on nonaggression or the proposal on the definition of the aggressor proposed by the U.S.S.R. It is obvious that the capitalist governments of these countries regard such a pact merely as a scrap of paper, but we, the revolutionary workers, must utilize this pact as an important document, in order to unmask the two-sided game of "our own" government and from the first moment of an anti-Soviet attack not only brand it as criminally responsible for the war but also prove this on the basis of documents. It is especially important that the Soviet Union has proposed to its most aggressive enemies, Germany, Japan, and others, that they sign pacts of nonaggression and other peaceful obligations; for them this will be a noose if only we, the revolutionary workers of every country, are able to use these documents in the broadest way in our mass agitation. Any capitalist government which refuses to conclude a nonaggression pact with the Soviet Union thereby discloses itself even more in front of the entire world as the organizer and instigator of war, just as the Japanese government has already disclosed itself before the entire world. And it is highly significant that the MacDonald-Baldwin government, the government of English imperialism, has thus far shown an extraordinarily lively interest in the freeing of the English spies who were caught red-handed in the Soviet Union, but has shown not the slightest desire to assume the obligation of nonaggression against the Soviet Union.

Second, we must declare: insofar as it is possible to secure the postponement of the counterrevolutionary war against the Soviet Union, thanks to the peace policy of the U.S.S.R., and because of the support which it receives from the toilers of all countries, this postponement is in many respects to the advantage of the international revolution. Of course, the imperialist governments also are energetically using this postponement for the perfection of their war preparations. But time is working for us if we only do not remain passive. The inevitable deepening of the general crisis of capitalism has the consequence, first, that the contradictions between the imperialist marauders become ever more acute; second, that the revolutionary crisis in individual countries continues to grow. This in turn means that there will be still more favorable objective conditions for revolutionary work, that we will have the advantage of an additional period of time in the capitalist countries for the preparation of the proletariat for the decisive struggle. This is the third consequence of the possible postponement of war against the Soviet Union. It increases our chances of being able at least in several countries to forestall the bourgeoisie and to avert the impending war by overthrowing the bourgeoisie by means of the proletarian revolution. Fourth, the movement of the allies of the world proletarian revolution, the anti-imperialist revolutionary movements of the colonial and dependent peoples, will gain additional time for further mobilization and organization of their forces. And fifth, the Soviet Union itself at the same time, on the basis of its socialist construction, will become still more powerful.

The last, of course, is the most important: the rapid growth of the power of the Soviet Union has been up till now the principal, although not the only obstacle (contradictions between the imperialist countries are also important) which has restrained the imperialists from a piratical attack upon the land of the proletarian dictatorship. They did not consider themselves sufficiently prepared for such a war. They had every reason to fear its outcome. But what kind of prospects for a successful outcome of their anti-Soviet plans can the imperialists have now, when after the brilliant fulfillment of the Five-Year Plan the relationship of forces has altered still further in favor of the Soviet Union. Now every attempt to conquer the citadel of socialism by war against it would be still more dangerous for the imperialists.

The strengthening of the Soviet Union is a major factor of peace throughout the world, but it is not only a factor of peace. At the same time, the existence of the Soviet Union is the principal factor in the development of the general crisis of the world capitalist system. The rise of the U.S.S.R. inspires the toilers of the whole world in their revolutionary struggle. For the Soviet Union is the stronghold of the world proletariat, the firm base of the world socialist revolution.

If we explain in this way the character of the peace policy of the U.S.S.R. and the significance of its successes to the working masses, it will not be difficult for us to repel the provocative attacks of the social-fascists on the foreign policy of the U.S.S.R. Every worker will understand that there is not nor can there be any conflict between the interests of the Soviet Union and the interests of the international workers' movement. The Soviet proletariat is the victorious vanguard of the workers of all countries. The cause of the working class of every country is inseparably linked with the cause of the Soviet proletariat.

106

Piatnitsky on the Failure of the Nazis to Destroy the Communist Party of Germany

Excerpts from a speech at the Thirteenth Plenum of the ECCI, December 2, 1933. XIII Plenum IKKI, *p. 194.*

. . .

Though driven underground, the party has exerted colossal efforts to publish and distribute literature on all the most important questions of the revolutionary struggle. In spite of the incredible terror, it is easier to work among the German proletariat now, in the sense that the social-democratic workers and the nonparty workers who followed the social-democrats, and also the members of the reformist unions, are becoming disillusioned in significant numbers with the policy of social-democracy.

Even the German fascists are compelled to admit that they have failed to smash and exterminate the Communist Party of Germany. Revolutionary workers who formerly belonged to other political trends are distributing communist literature, helping the communists in their work in every way. The authority of the party has grown enormously in the eyes of the broadest masses. The Communist Party of Germany has really become not only the party of the working class of Germany, but also the only party that is leading the struggle for the defense of the interests of the working class against the fascist dictatorship.

Because of the changed situation in Germany and the heroic work of the Communist Party, the communists no longer encounter the resistance in the working class which the trade-union bureaucrats and the Social-Democratic Party were formerly able to offer. Furthermore, many young members of the Social-Democratic Party are drawn toward the Communist Party and are prepared to fight shoulder to shoulder with the communists against the fascist dictatorship. In this connection it is necessary to emphasize the necessity of a determined struggle against those communists who close the doors of the communist party to such workers. Cases have occurred when social-democrats wanted to join our party, but the communists formed them into sympathizers' groups and appointed commissars over them, instead of drawing them into the party organization and giving them work to do.

However, it must be confessed that the mass work of the communist party has not yet been established on a broad scale. Word-of-mouth, individual agitation, which is needed most of all at present, is lacking. Appearances by communists at assemblies called by the fascist trade-unions are still rare, even though workers of antifascist tendency speak up at them.

. . .

To show in a popular and simple way with facts and figures at hand that the fascist dictatorship is lying is very easy, and at the same time this is of first-class importance; this lie must be demonstrated in such a way that every working family, every person working and every unemployed person will see it. There is no need to repeat here how exceptionally important at present is such an exposure of the policy of fascism on the basis of concrete examples and in order to free the petty bourgeoisie of the cities and towns and those unemployed who still believe fascist phrases. Unfortunately, however, the German Communist Party is not doing this, or is doing it badly. . . .

107

The German Question and the Communist International

Excerpts from a speech by Knorin at the Thirteenth Plenum of the ECCI, December 6, 1933. XIII Plenum IKKI, *pp. 337–341.*

Three important questions form at present the touchstone of the revolutionary maturity and class consciousness of every communist party, every communist, every revolutionary. *First,* the question of the U.S.S.R., the understanding of the role and significance of the U.S.S.R. for the international proletarian revolution, the understanding of the policy of the U.S.S.R., the understanding of the fact that the U.S.S.R. is the model for the transformation of all countries. He who does not devote all his strength to the defense of the U.S.S.R. is no revolutionary, he is a counterrevolutionary, he is an opponent of the dictatorship of the proletariat, he is an opponent of the socialist revolution. *Secondly,* the question of the attitude to the Chinese revolution and the Chinese soviet republic. He who does not devote all his strength and organizational abilities to the defense of the Chinese revolution and the Chinese soviet republic violates the international union of communists, is not fighting for the union of the proletariat of the imperialist countries with the toiling peoples of the colonies and semicolonies, is not thinking seriously about the dictatorship of the proletariat, about the soviet power in his own country. *Thirdly,* the question of the attitude to the German revolution, the understanding of its problems, the understanding of the problems and the struggle of the German proletariat. He who does not understand the German question does not understand the path of development of the proletarian revolution in Europe. He who does not devote all his powers to the support of the German proletariat is not fighting for the proletarian revolution in Europe, because the victory of the German proletariat would mean the victory of the proletarian revolution throughout the whole of Europe, the defeat of the German proletariat would retard the development of the proletarian revolution in other European countries.

Germany was and remains the weakest link in the chain of imperialist states. Germany is the country in which class contradictions are most exacerbated. Germany is the country in which all the contradictions of the capitalist world are intertwined in the most acute form. And besides this, Germany is the heart of capitalist Europe, a country which is economically and politically interwoven with all the capitalist countries of Europe. That is why the proletarian revolution is closer at hand in Germany than in any other country. And the victory of the proletarian revolution in Germany means the victory of the proletarian revolution throughout all Europe, since capitalist Europe cannot exist if it loses its heart. It is therefore clear that the German questions are the *fundamental* questions on the eve of the second round of wars and revolutions. And this places upon all the communist parties, upon all communists, a supreme responsibility for the fate of the German revolution.

The success of fascism in Germany was a great trial, in which was tested how each party and each communist understood the international situation and the course of development of the revolutionary process. The test revealed our strength and also, of course, the rotten elements which still unfortunately remain in our ranks.

First of all it is necessary to note with the greatest joy that our young *Spanish* Communist Party and its central organ, *Mundo Obrero*, which is itself in the fire of revolution, correctly evaluated from the very outset the situation in Germany, the meaning of the German events, and was able to develop a big campaign of international proletarian solidarity with the German proletariat. An energetic campaign of solidarity was also developed by the *Polish* Communist Party, which itself is struggling under the yoke of fascism. . . .

Sufficiently energetically, in proportion to their forces, the *Austrian, Belgian, Danish, Dutch* and a number of other small parties, developed explanatory work among the masses and a mass movement. Significantly weaker, i.e., not in proportion to their strength, with regard to the question of support for the German proletariat were the communist parties of the U.S.A., France, Czechoslovakia. . . . The *British* Communist Party, after a certain sluggishness in the first days, when it evidently underestimated the need for a struggle against fascism, later—and here Comrade Gallacher is correct—was able to develop a serious and continuous campaign and to take a clear political line. . . .

. . .

But, comrades, if it is possible to note a series of successes of our parties in this area, showing the growth of effective internationalism, nevertheless even where our campaign of support for the German revolution and of explanation of the meaning of the German events was most successfully carried out, it must nevertheless be considered as far from adequate. In particular, our campaign of support and defense of the German proletariat in connection with the trials of Comrades Dimitrov, Torgler, Popov, and Tanev was still far from adequate. If one compares these mass campaigns, which we are now conducting, with the campaign which was developed by the international proletariat in connection with the case of Sacco and Vanzetti, that campaign was broader than the present one. We have not been able so far to attain that level, even though the political significance of the Leipzig trial is much greater than the case of Sacco and Vanzetti. Then it was at the very beginning of the revolutionary upsurge. On the basis of the experience of the mass movement in defense of Sacco and Vanzetti we first came to the conclusion that a revolutionary upsurge, a new revolutionary upsurge, was growing. Now we find ourselves on the eve of the second round of revolutions and wars. If then it was the beginning of a new powerful movement, now this developed campaign of solidarity with the German comrades, with the Leipzig prisoners—our international struggle for the German revolution, our support for the German revolution, our mass movement against fascist terror, may become the point of departure for major political actions and movements of the working class.

The Struggle against "Left" Social-Democracy and the Right Deviation in the Communist Parties

And now, comrades, I must ask whence comes, what means the position of Gutman, who directly sabotaged the printing and popularization of the resolution of the ECCI on the situation in Germany, and also whence came the formulation of the opportunistic colleagues of Comrade Reiman from the editorial board of *Cahiers du communisme?*

These comrades have lost the revolutionary perspective, they have fallen under the influence of social-democracy, particularly under the influence of the Brandlerites and the Trotskyites, who are leading a frenzied campaign against the Comintern and the Communist Party of Germany.

At the time when the capitulation of social-democracy in Germany to Hitler was evoking indignation among the working masses of other countries, when the danger began to appear that the workers who were indignant at the conduct of the German social-democrats would go over to the communists, social-democracy attempted a big maneuver against the U.S.S.R. and the Comintern so as to discredit them in the eyes of the toiling masses. The Czechoslovak social-democrats declared that the U.S.S.R. had allegedly deceived the hopes of the German proletarians by not starting a war against fascism. This clearly provocational campaign, however, was not successful. Then a campaign was started to the effect that the U.S.S.R. was betraying the cause of the working class by maintaining normal relations with Germany. But the language of power in which the U.S.S.R. talked with Germany compelled this campaign to cease.

For us, communists, it is no dishonor if the largest and most conceited capitalist country, the U.S.A., recognizes the U.S.S.R. after sixteen years in order to strengthen the cause of peace and its own position. For us, communists, it is no dishonor if Mussolini invites Litvinov to come to Rome. The U.S.S.R. speaks to all in the language of power. For communists it is the supreme recognition when our most bitter enemies are compelled to talk with the U.S.S.R. For communists it is the supreme recognition when all the bourgeois states are compelled to reckon with the power of the U.S.S.R., with the power of the dictatorship of the proletariat.

It is now no longer fitting to talk simply of a contrast, it now behooves us to talk of the preponderance of the U.S.S.R. over any imperialist state individually and over whole groups of imperialist countries. When the campaign against the U.S.S.R. collapsed, the social-democrats put forward the slogan of boycotting German goods. Some newspapers at that time reported incorrectly that the communists were not taking part in the boycott because, they alleged, the boycott was in conflict with the economic interests of the U.S.S.R. The U.S.S.R. has no interests which are at variance with the interests of the world revolution, and the international proletariat naturally has no interests which are at variance with those of the Soviet Union.

But what could the boycott bring to the proletariat of Germany and the German revolution? An accentuation of economic war is in the interests of competing groups of capitalism. Can a boycott undermine the existence of a capitalist country? Obviously not. Why should we take part in such a boycott, for the conduct of which the social-democrats themselves undertake nothing, which the social-democrats wanted to thrust upon the communists, which was aimless and doomed to failure? . . .

. . .

Therefore, above all else, *a clear position in regard to social-democracy and above all else in regard to "Left" social-democracy, that most dangerous enemy of communism.*

. . .

There are not and there cannot be left-wingers except our party. We are the only left-wingers. This we must state clearly today. Under present conditions, in order to be a real revolutionary, it is necessary to take an open stand against counterrevolutionary social-democracy. . . .

Either in our ranks or fight against us—there is no other way. As for us, we will wage the most bitter struggle against "left-wingers," as the last line of the defense trenches of the bourgeoisie.

In order that our line with regard to the social-democrats should be clear, a determined struggle must be waged *against opportunism in our ranks.*

. . . The fact that social-democracy is undergoing a profound crisis merely shows that an even sharper struggle against it, against all its groups, and at the same time a struggle on two fronts in our own ranks is necessary.

Only thus will we be able to discharge those most important tasks which confront us.

Only we carry the communist consciousness into the spontaneously growing workers' movement. Without our stubborn work we will not be able to win over the majority of the working class for the revolutionary struggle. Only where the spontaneous movement of the workers is joined with the conscious work of the communists, only there does the revolutionary cause exist.

The most important task now for all parties, but especially for the German, Czechoslovak, and Austrian parties, is to ensure the political leadership of the masses, to react to events in good time, to issue political slogans in good time.

Only this will ensure our leadership of the masses. The second most important task is to be able to combine illegal work with the genuinely mass character of this work.

The third task is to ensure genuine continuity in the work of each party organization, beginning with the cells, ending with the Central Committee, so that events do not slip past us, so that we react to all events.

The fourth most important task is proletarian internationalism not in words but in deeds.

And in the combination of all these tasks the best, the living example so far has been and remains of all the illegal parties the Communist Party of Poland—this oldest mass illegal party.

Our tasks are difficult, but our goals are great and clear, our path is true. This we can say today with greater justification than ever before. Just think what it would be like if thirty years ago the Bolsheviks had not risen against the opportunism of the Second International, if fifteen years ago the Communist International had not been set up, if we did not exist, if the Soviet Union did not exist! In that case, the European workers' movement would lie beaten, torn apart by nationalism. Fascism would be triumphant. The working class, handed over to social-democracy, would be without prospects, without leadership.

Now there is no force which could beat us. The fate of the world workers' movement in the final analysis is in our hands. Social-democracy orients the masses in an epoch of fascism; we show that a new round of revolutions and wars is at hand. We do not know whether revolution will precede war or war will precede revolution, but even war cannot frighten us, for beyond it lies revolution. The U.S.S.R. has grown to be the greatest power in world politics. Socialism is being transformed into a reality in one-sixth of the earth. The Chinese Soviet Republic is growing. We leave this plenum with the slogan of "A Struggle for Soviet Power in the Entire World."

But what is demanded now of each of us?

What is now demanded above all of every communist is one thing—*the will for the struggle for power.*

The will to power means a stubborn, hard, self-sacrificing struggle to win over the majority of the working class, to form a revolutionary army of fighters absolutely devoted to communism.

The will to power means stubborn work in defending the everyday interests of the working class in the factories, the plants, the trade-unions, the labor exchanges.

The will to power means a hard and stubborn struggle to win allies of the proletariat in the revolution, the peasant masses and the masses of the urban petty bourgeoisie who have been ruined by the crisis, for he who does not think of allies is not facing the question of power seriously, he is not thinking seriously about the dictatorship of the proletariat.

The will to power means a struggle against war and fascism, for the defense of the U.S.S.R. and the Chinese soviets, for the defense of the German proletariat.

I recall the ancient Russian saga about Mikula Selianinovich, who possessed tremendous strength but who could not find a pulley.

"*If I could find a pulley,*" he said, "*I would lift up the whole earth.*"

We have found that pulley.

This pulley is work among the masses.

Our strength is tremendous, and if we apply this strength to mass work, if we overcome our weaknesses, apply ourselves earnestly to work in the factories and plants and trade-unions, then despite the entire world bourgeoisie, despite fascism, we will turn over the entire world and assure the complete victory for the proletariat. (Prolonged applause)

108

"Fascism, the Danger of War, and the Tasks of the Communist Parties"

Excerpts from the Theses adopted by the Thirteenth Plenum of the ECCI on the report by Kuusinen, December 1933. XIII Plenum IKKI, *pp. 589–591.*

The development of the general crisis of capitalism, after the end of the relative stabilization that was noted by the last (Twelfth) Plenum of the ECCI, has already undermined the capitalist system to a far-reaching degree all over the world.

While the U.S.S.R., the bulwark of the international proletariat and of the oppressed peoples, is developing its socialist construction and is raising its power ever higher, the economy of the capitalist world is going to pieces. The noose of poverty, ruin, and hunger is tightening. The bourgeoisie is furiously increasing its economic measures of exploitation by resorting to methods of fascist violence, the plunder of the toiling classes, and by waging predatory wars against other peoples. But at the same time the revolutionary indignation of the toiling masses and their readiness to throw off the intolerable yoke of the exploiting classes are continually growing.

The extraordinary strain of both the internal class contradictions in the capitalist countries and the international antagonisms testify to the fact that the objective prerequisites for a revolutionary crisis have matured to such an extent that at the present time the world has already *closely* approached a new round of revolutions and wars.

I. Fascism and the Maturing of the Revolutionary Crisis

1. Fascism is the open, terrorist dictatorship of the most reactionary, the most chauvinist, and the most imperialist elements of finance capital. Fascism tries to secure a mass basis for monopolist capital among the petty bourgeoisie, appealing to the dislodged peasantry, artisans, office employees, civil servants, and particularly to the declassed elements in the big cities, trying also to penetrate the working class.

The growth of fascism and its coming to power in Germany and in a number of other capitalist countries mean that

(a) the revolutionary crisis and the indignation of the broad masses against the rule of capital are growing;

(b) the capitalists are no longer able to maintain their dictatorship by the old method of parliamentarism and bourgeois democracy in general;

(c) moreover, the methods of parliamentarism and bourgeois democracy in general are becoming a hindrance to the capitalists, both in internal policy (the struggle against the proletariat) and in foreign policy (war for the imperialist redistribution of the world) ;

(d) in view of this, capital is forced to shift to open terrorist dictatorship within the country and to unrestrained chauvinism in foreign policy, signifying a direct preparation for imperialist wars.

Born in the womb of bourgeois democracy, fascism appears in the eyes of the capitalists as a means of saving capitalism from collapse. It is only for the purpose of deceiving and disarming the workers that social-democracy denies the fascistization of bourgeois democracy and contrasts in principle democratic countries to the countries of fascist dictatorship. On the other hand, the fascist dictatorship is not an inevitable stage of the dictatorship of the bourgeoisie in all countries. The possibility of averting it depends upon the strength of the fighting proletariat, which is paralyzed by the corrupting influence of social-democracy more than by anything else.

2. While the general line of all bourgeois parties, including social-democracy, is directed toward the fascistization of the dictatorship of the bourgeoisie, the realization of this line gives rise inevitably to disagreements among them as to forms and methods of

fascistization. Certain bourgeois groups, and in particular the social-fascists, who in practice do not stop at any act of police violence against the proletariat, urge the maintenance of parliamentary forms while the fascistization of the bourgeois dictatorship is being carried out. The fascists, however, insist on the full or partial abolition of these old and discredited forms of bourgeois democracy, on fascistization by means of the establishment of an open fascist dictatorship and the wide application of both police violence and the terrorism of fascist gangs. Having come to power, fascism pushes aside, splits, disintegrates the other bourgeois parties (for instance, Poland), or dissolves them (Germany and Italy). This striving of fascism for political monopoly intensifies the discord and conflicts in the ranks of the ruling classes which follow from the inner contradictions of the position of the bourgeoisie which is becoming fascistized.

3. The establishment of a fascist dictatorship in Germany has unmasked the face of *German social-democracy* before the whole world. From the bloody suppression of the proletarian revolution of 1918, through an uninterrupted chain of treachery and strikebreaking, through all the coalition governments, savage police violence against the revolutionary workers, voting for Hindenburg as the "lesser evil," to servile striving for open collaboration with the fascist gangs—such is the record of German social-democracy, the leading party in the Second International.

German social-democracy was, and still remains, the flag-bearer of all the parties of the Second International which follow in the footsteps of German social-democracy.

Social-democracy also continues to play the role of the main social bulwark of the bourgeoisie in the countries of open fascist dictatorship, fighting against the revolutionary unity of the proletariat and against the U.S.S.R., helping the bourgeoisie to prolong the existence of capitalism by means of splitting the working class. In the majority of countries, however, it is already in the process of disintegration. The radicalization of the social-democratic workers intensifies the squabbles among the leading circles of the social-fascists. Avowed neo-fascist groups are arising; "Left" fragments break away and try to patch together a new Two-and-a-Half International. Trotsky, the lackey of the counterrevolutionary bourgeoisie, is unsuccessfully trying to prevent the social-democratic workers from coming over to the side of communism by his miserable attempts to form a Fourth International and by spreading anti-Soviet slanders. On the basis of the sharp antagonisms between the imperialist countries, the international organization of social-democracy is disintegrating. The crisis of the Second International is at hand.

4. The economic policy of the finance oligarchy which tries to overcome the crisis (by the robbery of the workers and peasants and by subsidies to the capitalists and landlords), is unable to restore the stabilization of capitalism; on the contrary it contributes to further disintegration of the mechanism of capitalist economy (disorganization of the monetary system, of the budget, state bankruptcies, further deepening of the agrarian crisis), and to sharp intensification of the basic contradictions of capitalism.

In this situation all the capitalist countries continue to develop their war industries to unprecedented dimensions, adapting all the principal branches of industry, as well as agriculture, to the needs of war. The "demand" thus created for means of extermination and destruction, combined with open inflation (U.S.A., England, Japan), super-dumping (Japan), and concealed inflation (Germany), has caused in the past year an increase in output in some branches of industry in a number of countries (particularly ferrous and nonferrous metals, the chemical and textile industries). But this whipped-up production for nonproductive purposes, or the speculative spurts in production on the basis of inflation, are accompanied by stagnation or a fall in production in a number of other branches (machine construction, the building industry, the production of many articles of mass consumption), and in the future they are bound to lead to still greater disturbance of state finances and to a still further intensification of the general crisis of capitalism.

The bitter struggle *for foreign and colonial markets* has already assumed the form of a real international economic war.

5. Therefore, the social-democratic estimation of the present world situation is absolutely incorrect in assuming that capitalism has succeeded in consolidating its position, that it is allegedly on the way to overcoming its general crisis. As distinguished from the first wave of the fascistization of capitalist states which took place at the time of the transition from a revolutionary crisis to partial stabilization, the capitalist world is now passing from the end of capitalist stabilization to a revolutionary crisis, which provides different prospects for the development of fascism and the world revolutionary movement of the toilers.

When the bourgeoisie employs the most savage terror in order to suppress the revolutionary movement, once capitalism has been shaken, the advanced strata of the toilers cannot be intimidated for long or restrained from taking action; the indignation aroused by this terror, even among the majority of the workers who have followed social-democracy, makes them more receptive to communist agitation and propaganda. When the bourgeoisie reorganizes its tottering dictatorship on a fascist basis in order to create a firmly-pinned-together power, under present conditions this leads to the strengthening not only of its own class terror, but also of the elements of the disorganization of its power, to the destruction of the authority of bourgeois law in the eyes of the broad masses, to the growth of internal frictions in the camp of the bourgeoisie and to the acceleration of the collapse of its main social support—social-democracy. Finally, when the bourgeoisie tries, by means of an aggressive war policy, to strengthen its foreign position, it intensifies international contradictions and the consequent danger for capitalism to the utmost.

6. It would therefore be a Right opportunist error to fail now to see the objective tendencies of the accelerated maturing of the revolutionary crisis in the capitalist world. But the presence and operation of these tendencies, both economic and political, by no means imply that revolutionary development is proceeding upward on its own effort or unhindered, without resistance from counteracting forces. Revolutionary development is simultaneously hindered and accelerated by the fascist fury of the bourgeoisie. The question as to how soon the rule of bankrupt capitalism will be overthrown by the proletariat will be determined by the fighting preparedness of the majority of the working class, by the successful work of the communist parties in undermining the mass influence of social-democracy.

In the present situation, under the conditions of the colossal exacerbation of the antagonistic class forces, the growth of the revolutionary mass movement in individual capitalist countries can have a constant or even character even less than before. In *China,* there is war, intervention, and revolution. In *Japan,* there is the growth of the forces of revolution and the mobilization of the military-fascist forces before great class conflicts. In *Spain,* there is a clash between revolution and counterrevolution. In the *U.S.A.,* there is a wave of mass strikes of the workers and indignation among the farmers against the bourgeois program for overcoming the crisis. In *Germany,* the revolutionary hatred of the proletariat is growing at the present moment in less open forms; there, colossal revolutionary energy is being accumulated among the masses and a new revolutionary upsurge is already beginning. The strained situation in Germany greatly sharpens the class relations in the neighboring countries—in *Czechoslovakia, Austria,* the *Baltic countries,* as well as the *Scandinavian* countries, in *Holland, Belgium, Switzerland.* In *Poland* the mass strikes of the workers are accompanied by large-scale revolutionary demonstrations in the Polish countryside. In *Bulgaria,* in spite of the terror, the majority of the working class solidly follows the communist party. In *Rumania,* there is a big strike of railwaymen, with barricade fighting.

At the same time, the main stronghold of the world proletariat, the mighty *Land of the Soviets,* the land of the victorious working class, which is overcoming the final economic difficulties, raising the well-being of the toiling masses to a new, higher level, by its great socialist victories serves as an inspiration to the toilers of all countries in their revolutionary struggle.

. . .

The foundations of capitalism are already disintegrating as the result of its extremely profound, insoluble contradictions. The world economic crisis is most closely interwoven with the general crisis of capitalism, sharpening all the basic contradictions of the capitalist world to such an extent that a turn may take place at any moment, a turn which will signify the transformation of the economic crisis into a revolutionary crisis. The great task of the international proletariat is to turn this crisis of the capitalist world into the victory of the proletarian revolution.

109

"The Imperialist Preparation for a New World War"

Excerpts from the Theses adopted by the Thirteenth Plenum of the ECCI on the report by Kuusinen, December 1933. XIII Plenum IKKI, *pp. 591–592.*

The growing uncertainty of the bourgeoisie as to the possibility of finding a way out of the crisis merely by the intensified exploitation of the toilers of their own countries has led the imperialists to put their main stake on war. The international situation has the character of the eve of a new world war.

1. The flames of a new world war are flaring up in the area of the Pacific Ocean. The Japanese militarists, spurred on by the profound domestic crisis of the bourgeois-landlord monarchy, are continuing the predatory war against China, and, having subjugated northern China with the aid of the Kuomintang, are preparing a blow against the Mongolian People's Republic. English imperialism is reaching for the southwestern provinces of China— Tibet and Szechwan, the French for Yunnan. The fascist military clique of Japan is acting as the battering ram against the anti-imperialist and agrarian revolution in China. American, Japanese, and English imperialism stands behind the Kuomintang in its sixth campaign against the only people's government in China, against the Chinese soviets. The victories of the soviet revolution in China, the guerrilla war in Manchuria, the growth of the revolutionary forces in Japan, the liberation movement of the colonial peoples, create a new front in the imperialists' hinterland. The soviet revolution in China has become an important factor in the world revolution.

2. The Japanese militarists are calling on the German fascists and the English imperialists to unleash a counterrevolutionary war *against the U.S.S.R.* both from the east and the west. Pursuing a

policy of continuous provocation against the U.S.S.R., contemplating the seizure of Soviet territory, the fascist militarists of Japan are acting as an outpost in a counterrevolutionary war against the Land of the Soviets. At the same time German fascism is inviting the international bourgeoisie to buy its national-socialist mercenaries against the U.S.S.R., intriguing with the English, Italian, and Polish imperialists (German-Polish negotiations). The English imperialists at the present time have taken the place of the French imperialists as the chief organizers of an anti-Soviet war.

The Soviet Union has achieved considerable successes in its unswerving and firm policy of peace in the interests of all the toilers (a number of pacts of nonaggression, a number of new recognitions, the definition of the aggressor, forcing England to raise the embargo). The Land of the Soviets is the only bulwark of peace and of the independence of weak states against the attacks of the imperialist plunderers. By its proletarian policy, it is winning more and more the confidence of the toilers of the whole world and of the oppressed peoples. Retarding the outbreak of a new war by the powerful growth of its forces, the U.S.S.R. is calling down upon itself a new wave of hatred from the most reactionary and aggressive groups of the imperialists.

3. The fascist government of Germany, the chief instigator of war in Europe, is provoking disorders in Danzig, Austria, the Saar, the Baltic countries, Scandinavia, and, under the pretext of fighting against Versailles, is trying to knock together a bloc for a new, sanguinary carving up of Europe for the benefit of German imperialism. Imperialist blocs, headed either by France or Italy, or by England, which is intriguing behind their backs, are being feverishly reorganized around the key-points of imperialist contradictions. Europe has become a powder keg which may explode at any moment.

English and American imperialism, availing themselves of the prewar alarm in Europe and the events in the Far East, are increasing their preparations for a decisive imperialist fight for world hegemony in the Atlantic and Pacific Oceans.

4. In this situation, *social-democracy* stops at nothing in the support of the imperialist interests of its own bourgeoisie, combining this support with service to international capital against the U.S.S.R.

Japanese social-democracy and the trade-union leaders following General Araki proclaim the civilizing mission of Japanese imperialism in Asia and justify the predatory conquests of their bourgeoisie in China on the grounds of the "interests of socialism." In England the national-labourites, in conjunction with the conservatives, are pursuing the predatory policy of British imperialism; the Labour Party, deceiving the workers by its pseudo opposition to the government, is striving after ministerial posts in order to continue what is, in fact, the same imperialist policy. The French socialists (as well as the social-democrats of Czechoslovakia, Poland, etc.), carrying out the "sacred unity of the nation" under the slogans of "defense of democracy" and "defense against German fascism," are actively participating in the preparations for war against Germany. German social-democracy openly voted in the Reichstag for the national front of German fascism, which is preparing for a military adventure.

At the same time the Second and Amsterdam Internationals are adapting their policy to the prewar situation, trying to safeguard the interests of their own bourgeoisie and to ensure that the main blow will be directed against the U.S.S.R. They hypocritically cover themselves by readiness "to reply to war by a general strike and boycott," but announce in advance that they will take action only against a nation which has been declared an aggressor by the League of Nations; they simulate a trade boycott against fascist Germany, but persecute the workers for actually putting it into effect; under the slogans of pacifism, of the struggle against war and fascism, they serve as the forerunners in preparing public opinion in the capitalist countries for the counterrevolutionary war against the U.S.S.R.

. . .

The bourgeoisie wants to postpone the doom of capitalism by a criminal imperialist war and counterrevolutionary crusade against the land of victorious socialism. The great historical task of international communism is *to mobilize the broadest masses against war even before it breaks out, and thereby to accelerate the downfall of capitalism.* Only a Bolshevik struggle before the war aiming at the victory of the revolution can ensure the victory of the revolution in connection with the war.

110

The Comintern Defines the Tasks of the Communist Parties

Excerpts from the Theses adopted by the Thirteenth Plenum of the ECCI, December 1933. XIII Plenum IKKI, *pp. 593–594.*

. . .

D. The Tasks of Mass Work and Strengthening of the Communist Parties

The fulfillment of these fundamental tasks requires a genuine reorganization of the *entire mass work* of the communist parties, especially the work in the factories and trade-unions, which still represents their weakest sector. Under the conditions of great ferment among the toilers, the communists are duty bound, in taking note of the moods of the masses, to formulate *slogans and demands* in a manner that would correspond to the present level of the movement, and at the same time would show the workers the revolutionary way out.

This means:

a) to turn the content and language of *agitation and the press* toward the broadest strata of the proletariat and the toilers, showing both in agitation and in mass actions (demonstrations, strikes, and other mass actions) the *face* of the communist parties;

b) to achieve in *the shortest possible time* a determined shift in the work *at industrial enterprises,* concentrating the forces of the party organization on the decisive enterprises and raising the political level of the leadership of the everyday class struggle on the part of the factory cells;

c) to eliminate the opportunist, capitulationist neglect of *trade-union work* and especially work *inside the reformist* and mass fascist and Christian trade-unions, in accordance with the directives on work inside the trade-unions issued by the Twelfth Plenum of the ECCI;

d) to develop genuine mass *work among the unemployed,* waging a relentless struggle for social security, for every conceivable kind of community aid;

e) to strengthen revolutionary *work in rural areas,* opposing the landlord-kulak slogan of a single countryside by the class slogans of the toilers and the agrarian program of the soviet revolution; to unleash the struggle for all the partial demands of the peasantry, at the same time opposing the kulak demands which contradict the interests of the proletariat and the rural poor; establishing strong points (trade-unions of agricultural workers, peasants' committees) among the farm laborers, poor peasants, and semiproletarian elements of the village, to win over the basic masses of the small and middle peasantry;

f) to strengthen mass work among *women,* at the same time pushing ahead and training the existing women's party *aktiv,* who will be able in wartime to replace mobilized comrades in a number of cases;

g) to put an end to the *isolation of the Young Communist League,* and to turn its face definitely toward the masses of working youth, combating the forced governmental system of fascistization and militarization. The communist parties must render every possible aid to the Young Communist League in the development of work within the mass bourgeois and reformist youth organizations (cultural, sport, and others) and the establishment of Young Communist League cells at industrial enterprises.

. . .

The Thirteenth Plenum of the ECCI assigns to all communist parties, as the most important tasks, the execution of regular decisions and the constant verification of the *fulfillment of decisions,* especially on *mass work;* the organizational strengthening of their ranks; preparation for underground work, the raising of the *discipline* and fighting fitness of every party organization and every member of the party.

The whole situation demands of the communist parties timely preparation of *cadres* for underground work, serious attention to the question of *combating provocation,* the combination of methods of the strictest *conspiracy* with the maximum assurance of the best contact with the masses, avoidance of schematism of structure also in the work of the illegal organization itself.

Only the concentration of all the efforts of the party organizations on forming illegal factory cells and intensifying the work of communist fractions in all mass organizations can ensure contact with the masses and also maximum conspiracy and effectiveness.

In carrying out all these tasks the communists must utilize all legal possibilities for the development of mass work and for linking up legal and illegal work.

The Thirteenth Plenum of the ECCI calls on all sections of the Comintern ruthlessly to root out opportunism in all its forms, and above all, the Right opportunism (*Guttman, Remmele, Neumann,* and the defeatists in other countries in evaluation of the perspectives of the German revolution), without which the communist parties will not be able to lead the working masses to the victorious battles for the soviet power.

E. For the Revolutionary Way Out of the Crisis— for the Soviet Power!

1. The communist parties must set before the masses in the most determined manner the task of the revolutionary way out of the crisis of capitalism.

Against the charlatan recipes of the fascists and the social-fascists to save capitalism, which is decaying while still alive, the communists must show the masses that the ills of capitalism are incurable. Therefore, while defending in every way the everyday demands of the toilers, the communists must untiringly expose to the masses, who are suffering from starvation and exploitation, the whole truth, that their catastrophic situation will grow still worse under the blows of the further attack of capitalism, until the toilers succeed in uniting their forces for a counterblow and the crushing of bourgeois rule.

There is no way out of the general crisis of capitalism other than the one shown by the *October Revolution:* the overthrow of the exploiting classes by the proletariat, the confiscation of the banks, factories, plants, and mines, transport, houses, reserve stocks of the capitalists and the lands of the landlords, the church, the dynasty.

The *living example of the great Land of Soviets* must be increasingly popularized and explained to the toilers and the exploited in all capitalist countries; it must be shown how the Soviet economy, freed from the anarchy and the crises of capitalism, is in a position to develop unhindered the productive forces on the basis of socialist planning; how the Soviet workers and all the toilers are interested in this development and in its rapid tempo; how the Soviet proletarian government, which is simultaneously both the organization of the power of the proletariat and the ruling productive organization of society, is continually increasing social wealth and thereby the well-being of all the toilers, at a time when every bourgeois government, which is becoming more and more a social-economic parasite, is devouring and exhausting the economic strength of the nation.

On the basis of the great victories of the Soviet workers and the collective farm workers on all fronts of the class struggle and socialist construction, taking into account the special conditions of various countries, it is necessary to develop for the toilers of every country a program showing *what the Soviet power will give them in their own country*. In this connection the liquidation of unemployment and the uncertainty about tomorrow under the Soviet system must be emphasized, the continuous improvement of conditions of labor and social security along with the shortening of the working day; the liberation of the rural toilers from all vestiges of feudalism, from all slavery; the guarantee of land to the landless or small peasant, the support of the poor peasants and aid to peasant cooperatives and kolkhozes; the opening of all avenues to the cultural development of the working youth and to all the toilers, etc.

The Soviet power, the basis of which is the mass organization of the workers and the semiproletarians, offers the possibility for the broad genuine utilization of democracy by the toiling masses, previously downtrodden by capitalism.

The Soviet power is the state form of the dictatorship of the proletariat.

The Soviet power is the state form of the revolutionary-democratic dictatorship of the proletariat and peasantry ensuring the development of the bourgeois-democratic revolution into the socialist (China and others).

This is democracy for the toilers, but a grim dictatorship against the exploiters.

3. In mass work the communist parties must pose the question of *power* with all possible urgency. The major slogan of the Communist International is *the Soviet power*.

The example of the U.S.S.R. is an example of *Bolshevism*. Only *this* example shows the way out and salvation to the exploited and downtrodden of all the imperialist and colonial countries.

The example of Bolshevism is the example of proletarian internationalism. The success of the socialist revolution is possible only through the strengthening of the international ties of the revolutionary proletariat. The path of Bolshevism is the path of uniting the proletarian forces of all nationalities and races, the path of their joint struggle hand-in-hand with the Soviet proletariat against the oppressors and exploiters.

The Plenum of the ECCI imposes on all sections of the Communist International the obligation to be on the alert for every change in the situation and to devote all energies, without losing a moment, to revolutionary preparation of the proletariat for the impending decisive battle for power.

111

The New Deal Assailed by the Comintern

Excerpts from the resolution "On the General Crisis of Capitalism" drafted by the Comintern for the Eighth Convention of the Communist Party of the United States, December 1933. Theses and Decisions, Thirteenth Plenum of the ECCI (*Moscow, 1934*), *pp. 20–47.*

I. Deepening of General Crisis of Capitalism

1. The "New Deal" policy of Roosevelt was hailed by the bourgeoisie and its reformist agents as the beginning of decisive recovery from the economic crisis, the beginning of the return of "prosperity," and the ending of the misery of the masses. It was accompanied by a campaign of social demagogy through which the bourgeoisie tried to convince the masses that through the New Deal capitalism is overcoming the fundamental capitalist contradictions, is developing toward planned economy, etc. There is no foundation for all these predictions. Even in the face of the upturn of production which occurred in the summer of 1933, the misery of the masses has increased. On the contrary, all the measures of the "New Deal,"

far from solving the economic crisis, have only intensified the general crisis of capitalism.

The recent increase in production is in the main explained by: (a) war preparations, the enormous increased production of war materials, supplies, and munitions; (b) the pouring of billions of the state treasury into industry and agriculture; (c) the gigantic speculative market created by inflation (devaluation of the dollar, etc.) ; (d) the slashing of the wages of the workers, the increased speed-up system . . .

2. The intensification of the general crisis of American capitalism is indicated in the continuation of the industrial and agrarian crisis and the growing disproportion between the productive capacity and the consumption of the masses, the new forms and sharpened character of competition and anarchy in production, the enormous rise of the government deficit, the growth of inflation, the sharpening struggle for markets, as well as the rise of the class struggles within the country and the anti-imperialist struggles of the masses in the colonial and semicolonial countries dominated by Yankee imperialism.

Mass Starvation and Misery

3. Sixteen million workers stand idle outside closed factories, mines, suffering from the lack of the very things they could produce in these industries. The total income of the working class is less than 40 per cent of what it was four years ago. The oppressed Negro masses are suffering new economic attacks, and a rising wave of lynch terror. Large sections of poor and middle farmers are being driven off their land or reduced to the position of tenants and peons for the bankers and monopolies. Great numbers of the middle-class intellectuals, professionals, teachers, white collar workers, have likewise been cast into poverty . . .

New Deal—Program of Fascism and War

4. The "New Deal" of Roosevelt is the aggressive effort of the bankers and trusts to find a way out of the crisis at the expense of the millions of toilers. Under cover of the most shameless demagogy, Roosevelt and the capitalists carry through drastic attacks upon the living standards of the masses, increased terrorism against the Negro masses, increased political oppression and systematic denial of existing civil rights, and are strengthening the control of the big

monopolists over the economic and political life of the country. The "New Deal" is a program of fascistization and the most intense preparations for imperialist war. Its class character is seen in the policy of the subsidies to the railways, banks, and insurance companies, accompanied by increased parasitism, corruption, and bureaucratism . . .

. . .

Threatening War Danger

6. The capitalist class is feverishly preparing for war as a way out of the crisis. It has embarked on a naval race with its imperialist rivals, Great Britain and Japan. The army has been further mechanized, and the world's largest air fleet has been provided for, coast defense has been strengthened, army cantonments throughout the country have been provided; and the C.C.C. [Civilian Conservation Corps] has served as a trial mobilization and training ground for a great army, both for imperialist war and for civil war against the workers at home. . . .

In all the markets of the world, the struggle between Great Britain and the United States grows more acute. The Roosevelt regime, through its inflation, is engaged in a war on British goods and on British currency, in an effort to win world hegemony. The struggle for hegemony between the United States and Japan daily becomes more marked, with both nations building up their naval armaments in anticipation of a war for domination in the Pacific.

All the chief imperialist powers are clashing for the lion's share in the dismemberment of China. The imperialist aggressiveness of Roosevelt's policies is shown most clearly in Cuba, in Latin America (Bolivia-Paraguay war), and in the Philippines.

Roosevelt's policies are interlocked with the policies of world capitalism, characterized everywhere by the desperate attempt to get out of the crisis at the expense of the masses by means of fascism, war, and intervention.

7. The preparations for war are being carried through under the cover of pacifism and democracy . . .

8. The recognition of the Soviet Union by the American government, a victory for the Soviet peace policy, and the growing support of this policy by the masses of the entire world, resulting from the increasing strength of the Soviet Union, in no way indicated a peace policy on the part of the American capitalists. While extending recognition to the U.S.S.R., United States imperi-

alism continues to furnish munitions and war supplies to Japan, and tries to provoke a war between Japanese imperialism and the U.S.S.R. for the purpose of both weakening its chief imperialist rival in the Pacific, as well as the country of socialism—the workers' fatherland.

. . .

II. The Fascistization of the American Government

9. American capitalism is more and more fascistizing its rule. This is particularly being performed by the Roosevelt administration under the cover of the "New Deal." Under the mask of saving the "democratic" institutions of the United States, the Roosevelt government and the bourgeoisie are: (*a*) increasing the violence against the workers, particularly revolutionary workers and the Negro masses, against whom they have unleashed a wave of lynch terror; (*b*) increasing tendencies to suppress and deny the right to strike; (*c*) establishing labor arbitration boards with direct participation of the employers and the bureaucrats, with the object of preventing, suppressing, and disorganizing the struggles of the workers; (*d*) directly concentrating into the hands of the President almost dictatorial powers, and vesting power, formerly executed by Congress, in direct appointees of the President over matters of most vital concern to millions of toilers; (*e*) developing a wave of chauvinism and carrying through the whole N.R.A. [National Recovery Administration] campaign with the greatest emphasis upon nationalism.

. . .

IV. The Position of the Communist Party

19. Under the conditions of deepening crisis and growing revolutionary upsurge, the Communist Party has grown and extended its influence. The Communist Party alone foresaw the crisis and from the first brought to the workers a clear line of struggle.

. . .

V. The Tasks of the Communist Party

25. The central task of the party is to organize and lead the fight against the offensive of the capitalist class, against developing

fascism and the threat of imperialist war, and to develop these struggles, on the basis of the fight for the immediate partial demands of the workers, into general class battles for the overthrow of capitalist dictatorship and the setting up of a soviet government. This requires a quickening of the tempo and improvement in the quality of the work of the party, to fight for winning the majority of the working class by more quickly carrying through the decisions of the Open Letter with regard to rooting the party among the basic strata of the proletariat, in the most important industries and factories, through the application of the policy of concentration.

. . .

A. The Struggle Against the Fascistization of the Government and Against Imperialist War and Intervention

The party must arouse the masses against developing fascism in the United States and the threat of imperialist war. It must explain to the masses that in the United States fascism is being carried through under the mask of democracy by the bourgeoisie, and must combat the idea spread by the Socialists and the A.F. of L. bureaucrats and by other bourgeois agents that the Roosevelt government and its program is an alternative to fascism, as in that way they disarm the struggle against fascism in the United States . . .

. . .

The whole party must be aroused for a fight against the imminence of imperialist war and intervention. The main task consists in unmasking the pacifist cover under which war is being prepared by the Roosevelt government; in exposing the role of pacifism of all brands without alienating honest pacifists who are ready to enter into a militant fight against imperialist war; strengthening the party and the revolutionary mass organizations in the decisive war industries and in the harbors; in carrying through mass actions for stopping the shipment of arms to Japan and China; in defending the Chinese revolution to the utmost, unmasking before the masses the counterrevolutionary role of American imperialism and its oppression against the Chinese soviets (Sixth Offensive) [of the Kuomintang forces] and popularizing the heroic struggle and tremendous success of the Chinese soviet power; in increasing the political educational work in the army and navy and in the C.C.C. camps; and in widely explaining the peace policy of the Soviet Union and exposing the counterrevolutionary propaganda of the Trotskyite renegades and social-fascists. By our struggle against the danger of imperialist war, we must prepare to convert the imperialist war into civil war . . .

. . .

Every communist to carry on Bolshevik work must establish and maintain contact with nonparty workers . . .

VI. Work in the Trade-Unions

A. For a Decisive Turn in the Work of the A.F. of L.

The work of building a revolutionary trade-union opposition in the A.F. of L. and Railroad Brotherhoods has assumed greater importance at the present time, and in a number of industries is the main task of our trade-union work (miners, railroads, building) . . . .

. . .

B. Building the Revolutionary Unions

The party must strengthen its fractions in the T.U.U.L. [Trade Union Unity League] unions, and especially give attention to strengthening the independent revolutionary unions of steel, auto, marine, and textile workers among the millions of unorganized and consolidate the recent gains of these trade-unions. The communist fractions must make as one of their main tasks the drawing in of the broad masses, the Negro workers, into these unions.

. . .

VII. Building the Party

1. The key to the building of the party has been given in the definition of the Open Letter and in the control tasks which stress the rooting of the party in the factories and in the most important industries, winning especially the native white and Negro workers. This task remains in full force and must be immediately carried through . . .

. . .

3. The party must prepare to go underground, must tighten the discipline of the party, combat spies, ensure the secret function-

ing of the factory cells while maintaining the greatest contact with the masses in the factories, immediately preparing cadres for underground work. While preparing for illegality, the party must at the same time struggle against every attack upon its legal rights through the development of mass struggles.

. . .

There must be a wider issuance and circulation of literature on current political problems and propaganda pamphlets dealing with the revolutionary way out of the crisis. The mass sale of communist literature must be a normal part of the everyday activities of every Communist Party member.

. . .

VIII. The Revolutionary Workers' Government— Soviet Power—the Way Out

The Communist Party must raise before the toilers in the United States the revolutionary way out of the crisis. All members of the party must in their day-to-day work, in the fight for the demands of the workers, point out convincingly and insistently that only the destruction of the capitalist system, the establishment of a revolutionary workers' government, of the soviet power, can free the millions of toilers from the bondage and misery of the capitalist system.

The [situation in the] United States is most favorable for the establishment of socialism. Its large-scale concentrated industry and huge proletariat, its accumulated wealth and productive forces, with the enormous supplies of raw material, provide the material basis for a quick change in the life and conditions of the country. If the workers will take power, they will in a very short time radically improve the life of all toilers—industrial workers, farmers, white-collar workers, professionals, intellectuals, etc., providing a high degree of comfort and well-being for the toiling masses.

But this tremendous wealth, these gigantic productive forces, are locked away from the masses. They are the private property of a small parasitic capitalist class which has closed the factories and locked the warehouses to force growing tribute of profits . . .

There is no way out of the crisis except by breaking the domination and rule of the monopolist capitalist class and taking the road pointed out by the victorious working class of the Soviet

Union. There is no way out through the quackery of Roosevelt or the policies and practices of social-democracy . . .

The Revolutionary Workers' Government—an alliance of the working class with other toiling sections of the population—will establish a real democracy for the overwhelming majority of the toilers and a stern dictatorship against the capitalist and their agents. It will confiscate the banks, the factories, the railroads, the mines, and the farms of the big corporations—capitalist farmers.

It will immediately wipe out unemployment, provide jobs at a wage sufficient to meet the needs of the toilers. It will establish a seven-hour day, a six-hour day for workers in hazardous industries, and a system of full social insurance. It will open up the warehouses and distribute among the working people the enormous stores of food and clothing, it will open the enormous accumulation of unused buildings to those who now wander in the streets and crouch in cellars and slums.

It will wipe out the debts and mortgages now held by the bankers and monopolists upon the farmers, give land to the landless farmers, give government aid to the poor and middle farmers, will establish a seven-hour day and will raise the wages and improve the condition of the agricultural workers. The Revolutionary Workers' Government will immediately proceed to reorganize the present anarchistic system of production on socialist lines, eliminating the untold wastes of capitalism and bringing to full use the tremendous achievements of science. It will aid the farming population to unite their forces in a cooperative, socialized agriculture, thereby bringing to the countryside the advantages of modern civilization and removing the present burdens of agricultural labor.

It will establish state farms. It will grant equal rights to the Negro people and to the foreign-born and the right of self-determination for the Negroes in the black belt, exterminating all forms of chauvinism and establishing firm bonds of solidarity and fraternity between the Negro and white masses.

It will grant full independence to Cuba, independence to the Philippines and the colonies and semicolonies now oppressed by imperialism. It will establish a fraternal alliance with the great socialist brother state—the Soviet Union—and through such an alliance of two mighty socialist powers would create an unshakable force for peace and render a death blow to the world system of imperialist oppression and exploitation.

In view of the tremendous revolutionary upsurge of the masses (the heroic revolutionary armed struggle of the Austrian workers, the general strike in France, etc.), the congress calls upon all party members to increase their activity, discipline and mass work, for the Bolshevik way out of the crisis, the way of the united struggle of the working class, marching hand-in-hand with all oppressed, for crushing the power of the exploiters and establishing the soviet power.

112

Izvestiia *Welcomes Diplomatic Relations with the United States*

Editorial on the occasion of the arrival of the first American ambassador. "Druzhba mezhdu SSSR i SASSh—zalog mira," Izvestiia, No. 302, December 14, 1933.

. . . The very fact that diplomatic relations have been established between the U.S.A. and the U.S.S.R. is in itself a political fact of the utmost importance. The first American ambassador accredited to the Soviet government has correctly emphasized the historical significance of this fact by pointing out that the mission of the American representative is to "create not merely normal but genuinely friendly relations between the two great peoples." Diplomatic relations may exist between governments whose interests are basically antithetical up to the moment when the contradictions dividing them burst the shell of official relations. And if the Soviet Union has merely established normal relations with the United States, the act of recognition of the Soviet Union by the U.S.A. would not have been of historical importance.

In putting forward as his aim the creation of truly friendly relations, Mr. Bullitt indicated at the same time the basis on which the relations between the U.S.S.R. and the U.S.A. must develop. This basis is the "firm establishment of a general peace," which "corresponds to the deep desire of both our peoples." William Bullitt had the right to say that he comes to our country not as a stranger, but as one who had already demonstrated his friendly attitude to the people of the Soviet Union. In recognizing as the central task the "close collaboration of our governments in the cause of preserving peace," William Bullitt has once again shown his understanding of the spirit animating the popular masses of the U.S.S.R. The popular masses throughout the world, particularly the popular masses of the Soviet Union, are filled with hatred for war, for the new extermination of millions. There is no better basis for the rapprochement of peoples than the mutual effort to preserve peace. The public opinion of the Soviet Union welcomed the appointment of William Bullitt as ambassador to the U.S.S.R. as proof that the government of the U.S.A. desires to cooperate with the Soviet government for the maintenance of peace. If William Bullitt succeeds in furthering this aim—and we are convinced that he will succeed—then history will justify the confidence he has expressed in the importance and historical significance of his mission.

The American ambassador said that the peoples of the U.S.A. and the U.S.S.R. are "surely linked by the bond of common youthful energy, a readiness to seek new ways to solve new problems, and the courage to face the future unafraid." This common spirit animating both peoples will help strengthen and deepen the relations between the two countries and create a basis for successful joint economic work. The cultural growth of the Soviet Union creates tremendous demands, both material and intellectual. The participation of the U.S.A. in satisfying these demands will make the relations of both states invaluable for the broadest masses of both countries.

. . . The energetic, determined president of the United States has shown in deeds that he believes in the great future of Soviet-American relations. The pioneer of Soviet-American relations whom he has chosen to carry out the mission of strengthening these relations, Ambassador William Bullitt, has begun his work with words which prove that he understands the great tasks which must be carried out in the immediate future—a time of exceptional danger. Soviet public opinion fully supports the statement of the chairman of the Central Executive Committee of the U.S.S.R., Comrade Kalinin, who assured the American ambassador of help from the Soviet government in carrying out his mission. He can rely on this help also on the part of public opinion in the U.S.S.R., which sees in the strengthening of Soviet-American relations an important guarantee of peace.

113

Radek Analyzes German and Japanese Plans for Expansion

K. Radek, "Podgotovka bor'by za novyi peredel mira." Izvestiia, *No. 1, January 1, 1934, p. 2.*

The course of world politics in 1933 deepened and sharpened the general trends of international development that had been evident since the *seizure of Manchuria by Japan.* Japanese expansion on the Asian continent marked the beginning of an armed struggle for the *change in the correlation of forces established by the Washington agreement of 1922.* At that time England found it necessary under the pressure of the United States to give up its alliance with Japan, which forced the latter to give up its plan of the seizure of Shantung and eastern Siberia, and of expanding in general on Chinese territory. The Washington agreement indicated that the imperialist powers were abandoning the plan of the further division of China, and that each of them would be satisfied with the possibility of economic expansion, for which the principle of the "open door" was to be maintained, i.e., equal opportunities to all competing powers. By seizing Manchuria and withdrawing from the League of Nations, Japan showed that she has no intention of taking into consideration any longer this correlation of forces established by the great powers, and that she has freed her hands for further steps.

The world constitutes a single entity. The violation of the correlation of forces at one end of the world is bound to have repercussions in all the other sectors. The reactionary circles of France, which had insisted on the correlation of forces in Europe established by the Versailles Treaty, and which at first welcomed the "bold initiative" of Japan and praised her as the gendarme of East Asia, capable of establishing order in "anarchistic" China, were soon compelled to realize that they had made a mistake. It is quite instructive to compare the articles of the reactionary French press at that time, headed by M. Pertinax, with the articles which are being published now in the German fascist press with regard to events in the Far East. We limit ourselves to references to two articles. Thus the serious economic weekly *Wirtschaftsdienst* published on September 22 [1933] an article under the instructive title, "A Danger for International Peace," in which one can read the following:

[The article recommends that if the United States, Great Britain, Russia, France, The Netherlands, and Portugal wish to halt Japanese expansion in the Far East, they should come to an agreement with Germany.]

If one deciphers the meaning of this article, it becomes quite clear. England and America cannot possibly remain for a long time onlookers at the Japanese struggle for hegemony on the Asian continent. But if war breaks out simultaneously in Europe, England will be tied down in it and unable to defend her interests either on the side of Japan against the United States, or with the United States against Japan. . . . If she wishes to purchase freedom of action in the Far East, let her act as a mediator between Germany and France, and insist on the abrogation of the Versailles Treaty. But if England prefers to sacrifice her position in Europe, and transfers the center of her attention to the Far East, leaving France to its own devices, then German imperialism would understand the meaning of such a step and would utilize the struggle in the Pacific to bring about a change in the alignment of forces on the Rhine.

[Radek cites a second article, from the Berlin *Lloyd-Zeitung* of December 1, entitled "Decision in the Far East."]

. . .

The German imperialist bourgeoisie believes that great historical decisions are to be taken soon, and while "not throwing themselves into utopia," i.e., not anticipating events, they are preparing for them. Thus the most important characteristic of the present international situation is that *two world powers are exerting every possible effort in order to effect a change in that very unstable equilibrium which was established after the war or between the capitalist countries and between the capitalist world and the first socialist state.* Japan is trying to bring about a change in the situation in the Far East, i.e., a change not only in its relations with China but also in its relations with the United States and England, not to speak of the secondary imperialist powers in the Far East.

Germany is trying to modify its relations with the Versailles victors. Both Germany and Japan are trying to modify their relations with the U.S.S.R. As to the Japanese militarists and the German fascists, who are outlining openly a program for an attack against the U.S.S.R., there is no need to waste words here on proofs.

But even if one examines the official program as expressed in the pacifist speeches of the Reich Chancellor, Hitler, there emerges *a program of a federal unification of Central Europe, from the French border to the Berezina, from Memel to the Balkans, under the aegis of German imperialism.* This is how the official press organs of German fascism and publicists who are called upon to provide the theoretical basis for the tactical maneuvers of the German government interpret this program.

. . .

Dreams of Neutrality and the Danger of a World War

German fascism and Japanese imperialism have placed on the agenda the struggle for the redivision of the world, *directed against the U.S.S.R., against France, Poland, Czechoslovakia, Rumania, against the Baltic countries, against China, against the U.S.A.*

English imperialism cherishes the dream that the struggle can be directed *exclusively against the U.S.S.R. This is a childish dream.* Such a redivision of the world would cost first of all the political head of Poland, the most important ally of France. Then it would strike at all the positions of France. In the Far East, it would strike at the U.S.A., which would lose every possibility of economic expansion in the Pacific, not to speak of *China,* which represents a great potential force. Furthermore, English imperialism would soon feel the consequences of such a policy on its own skin in Australia, in the approaches to Singapore. The question now stands as follows: *no matter where war starts, it will become worldwide and will draw into its slough all the powers. Now only one thing is possible: either to coordinate all actions in order to prevent the outbreak of war or to allow the avalanche to start rolling which no one will be able to stop.*

. . .

Yes, there is no doubt that the policy of Roosevelt directed at the avoidance of "any" war is more farsighted. Only such a policy can ensure peace for the U.S.A. and relieve it from the danger of being drawn into war. If war cannot be avoided, then it will be a world war, irrespective of the number of stages through which it would pass. In this war, world capitalism will risk its own head. This is a very considerable risk, and, therefore, it is most important for the capitalist world to strain its head to the utmost—while it is still intact—in order to prevent the catastrophe.

The U.S.S.R. will support every force that is directed against war. It meets the new year under the banner of the struggle for peace, which is the old banner of October.

114

A Recapitulation of Clichés

L. Magyar (Madiar), "War, Fascism, and the Policy of the Soviet Union," I.P.C., Vol. 14, No. 8, February 9, 1934, pp. 227–228.

. . .

Every Bolshevik knows that sooner or later the imperialist world will make an attack on the first, and at present the only, proletarian state. But it is the duty of every Bolshevik to do his utmost to prolong the hard-won peace as long as possible, for the sake of socialist construction in the Soviet Union, to give time for the maturing of the revolutionary crisis, for the organization of the forces of revolution, for the maturing of the national revolutionary movements in the colonies. Leninist policy calculates upon time, place, comparative forces, and imperialist antagonisms.

Lenin taught us that the task of foreign policy is: (1) to strengthen the Soviet Union as the basis of the world revolution; (2) to win over the masses of the workers and peasants of the capitalist countries; (3) to gain the confidence of the small states and oppressed people; (4) to gain where possible the sympathies of the petty-bourgeois masses and the intelligentsia; (5) to utilize the imperialist antagonisms in the interest of socialist construction.

Lenin's best disciple, Comrade Stalin, leads the foreign policy of the Soviet Union on the lines thus inherited from Lenin. This policy has achieved huge successes and has secured the prolongation of the period of peace. These successes have been made possible by the fact that the economic, political, and military strengthening of the Soviet Union is such that an attack on the Soviet state would represent the greatest danger to the aggressor. The Red Army is a convincing argument for the peace policy of the Soviet Union. These successes have been made possible by the fact that the policy of the Soviet Union has combated the extreme war parties in the capitalist countries and has rendered their criminal activities more difficult; by the fact that the policy of the Soviet Union has taken into account that the extreme war parties have not yet gained the upper hand in all countries, and that the tendency to form blocs against the Soviet Union is hampered by the antagonisms in the camp of the imperialist powers, and even by their struggle for the League of Nations; and by the fact that the peace policy of the Soviet Union has gained for it not only the support of the working class and the working peasantry, but at the same time the confidence of the small states and oppressed peoples, and even the sympathies of certain strata of the petty bourgeoisie. We are well aware that the League of Nations is an instrument of imperialist policy. But a situation has arisen in which precisely that imperialist group which *at the present moment,* for various reasons of imperialist policy, is *not* in favor of immediately letting loose the dogs of war, has decisive influence in the League of Nations. A realistic proletarian policy must take even this circumstance into account, in order to render more difficult the criminal activities of the warmongers.

The Hitler bandits are speculating that Japan's counterrevolutionary war against the Soviet Union will set the war machine going in Europe. They are speculating that the war cries of German fascism against the Soviet Union will secure for German fascism the support of the whole world bourgeoisie. This speculation will prove false. German fascism is preparing for war, hoping to overcome its difficulties at home by adventures abroad. The policy pursued by German fascism is driving German capitalism to disaster.

115

Manuilsky Evaluates the Prospects for Revolution

Excerpts from a statement at the Seventeenth Party Congress, February 1934. XVII s"ezd Vsesoiuznoi Kommunisticheskoi Partii (b) . . . stenograficheskii otchet *(Moscow, 1934), pp. 306–308.*

. . .

Capitalism, it would seem, has passed the lowest point of the economic crisis, and since 1932 it has been marking time. However, even if it has succeeded in temporarily scrambling up to the stage of depression, or even a little higher, nevertheless there will be neither "prosperity" [in English in original] nor the restoration of capitalist stabilization. And in this respect capitalism of the period of depression, and even of a stage a little higher, would be different from capitalism as it was when it entered upon the world economic crisis in 1929. Five years of this crisis have still further shattered the world system of capitalism and made its general crisis more profound, the more so because the economic, political, and military strength of the Soviet Union has grown during these five years, because a new outpost of the world proletarian revolution has been formed on the shores of the Pacific in the shape of the Chinese soviets, and because there has been a growth of other political factors which accelerate the growth of the revolutionary crisis: the war in the Far East and the setting up of a fascist dictatorship in Germany. And this must be specially emphasized, for it is of great significance in determining the revolutionary perspectives of the world workers' movement. The stage of depression would not, for example, give German fascism that breathing space which Italian fascism enjoyed in the period of partial capitalist stabilization.

During the five years of the world economic crisis the shattering of the capitalist system has gone so far that the objective prerequisites for a revolutionary crisis have already matured in the weakest links of the capitalist system, the colonies and dependent countries;

they have almost matured in Central Europe (Germany, Austria, Czechoslovakia), in the Balkans, in Poland, in the Baltic states; they are maturing in the strongest links of the capitalist system which occupy the commanding heights in it—in the United States, France, England.

. . .

In the sphere of international relations the world economic crisis has likewise sharpened all imperialist contradictions.

Before the crisis, imperialist contradictions were steadily growing from year to year. The Sixth Congress of the Comintern, in the summer of 1928, called attention to the fact that the third period of the postwar development of capitalism, which had already commenced, would inevitably lead states and classes toward clashes of tremendous force. Now imperialist contradictions have matured to such an extent that the question of the redivision of the world has again been raised, with even greater sharpness than in 1914.

Capitalism at present cannot permit itself the luxuries of the democratic-pacifist era, as it could at the beginning of the period of capitalist stabilization. Imperialist war is on the order of the day for all capitalist governments of the world.

Evidence of this is the fact that in a number of capitalist countries the most extreme war parties have come to power—I have in mind Japan, Germany, England.

This is shown by the frenzied growth of the war industry in those capitalist countries which are preparing for war most feverishly (Japan and Germany). At the present time the world is mined on all sides with explosive material through which the insane governments and their agents of the type of Van der Lubbe dash by underground passages with lighted torches.

A sign of the approach of war is the rupture of those treaties by which the ruling classes regulated their mutual relations in the international arena during the period of the first round of wars and revolutions. What remains of the Versailles Treaty at the present time?

One would have to go crazy to imagine that Germany will pay reparations, said Comrade Stalin at the Sixteenth Party Congress. Germany has indeed gone crazy, having seated the fascists on its shoulders, but it has ceased to pay.

Germany was disarmed before the crisis. It is arming now, today it can raise a million-strong army.

At Versailles Germany was thrown a beggarly portion of territory on which the German bourgeoisie and its agents, the [social-democratic leaders such as] Wels, lived quietly up to the crisis; now fascist Germany, like a smuggler, is thievishly sneaking across frontiers, sowing sedition and counterrevolutionary anarchy everywhere. Germany has become the main instigator of war in Europe. The general staffs of all capitalist governments already have their fingers on the electric button which will set the monstrous machine of war in motion.

What has become of the Washington agreements by which the imperialist powers regulated the balance of forces in the Pacific? The Washington Nine-Power Treaty established "the principles of the open door and equal opportunities" in China for the imperialist robbers. But now the Japanese imperialists, without waiting for leave, are extending their sphere of opportunities, acting on the principle of the bandit who by night in the streets strips the passer-by naked, snatching from him everything possible. In the beginning —in the autumn of 1931—Japan grabbed Manchuria, then the province of Jehol, then Chahar; at the present time it is sneaking toward the frontiers of Outer Mongolia, closing the "open door" in Manchuria, Jehol, and Chahar in the face of an astonished America. The Japanese generals care little about the other point in the Washington agreement—the "territorial integrity" of China. Japan has converted not only this point but the whole Washington agreement into a scrap of wrapping paper with which the Japanese corporal wipes off the blood from his bayonet in Chapei.

The partition of China by the imperialists has begun. The struggle around China, as one of the principal elements of imperialist contradictions, is giving rise to the great Pacific Ocean conflict which is already bursting the bounds of the other Washington agreement—the Five-Power Treaty on the correlation of naval forces.

Who headed world reaction before the crisis? Imperialist France, which acted as the main initiator of the policy of intervention against the U.S.S.R. and stood guard over the Versailles Treaty.

Who is heading world reaction at the present time? England. England is assuming the leading role in the preparation for war against the U.S.S.R. because she knows that wars with such imperialist opponents as the U.S.A. will lead to the partition of her colonial dominions, because she knows that a new imperialist war of the capitalist powers among themselves will disrupt that balance of power which gives England her dominating position. England wants a counterrevolutionary war against the Land of Soviets so that in this way, as its diehard politicians think, it may escape revolutions in capitalist countries and improve the affairs of English capitalism at the expense of the tremendous natural wealth of the U.S.S.R.

The English diehards are backing up Germany and Japan at the present time, surreptitiously directing their hands against the U.S.S.R. England comes forward in the capacity of a broker, trying to smooth out the contradictions between France and Germany in order to create a united front against the U.S.S.R.; it would have liked to disrupt the work of consolidating peace which has resulted from the rapprochement between the U.S.S.R. and France and the recognition of the U.S.S.R. by America. And in order to carry out this counterrevolutionary policy, the English bourgeoisie has not chosen a lord, but has found its "Pu-Yi"[1] among the leaders of the Second International. Every epoch gives birth to its own hero. . . . [ellipsis in original]

And thus the eve of a war among the imperialists is already at hand in the international arena—especially insistent, precipitate preparations for a counterrevolutionary war against the Land of Soviets are at hand. But the growing contradictions have not yet burst out in a warlike collision, because the bouregeoisie for the time being is still restrained by the threat of world proletarian revolution and petrified by fear of the growing strength of the U.S.S.R.

But, comrades, what is the meaning of the war against the U.S.S.R. which the English bourgeoisie is preparing together with Japan and Germany? It is the continuation in the international arena of that civil war which the bourgeoisie of all the capitalist countries is waging against the workers, although with varying degrees of violence in different countries.

Before the world economic crisis the bourgeoisie in a number of capitalist countries was already fighting the communist movement with terrorist methods. Today the number of these countries has grown and the methods have become still more barbarous. And just this alone testifies to the deepening and sharpening of the general crisis of capitalism and to the ripening of those conditions from which the revolutionary crisis is growing. In almost all the capitalist countries, in one form or another there is evident a national crisis of the "upper strata," which with the exception of China and Spain has not yet led to revolution, but which has resulted in the fascistization of all bourgeois political parties, including social-democracy. In a few countries, like Germany, it has resulted in the establishment of a fascist dictatorship.

Why has this happened? This has happened because the forces of the proletarian revolution have not yet matured, while the world bourgeoisie, taking into account the lessons of the defeat of the Russian bourgeoisie in October 1917, are directing all their forces against the proletariat at a moment when it cannot yet join in the decisive battle. The forces of the proletarian revolution have proved temporarily weaker in various capitalist countries than the forces of bourgeois reaction. They have proved weaker because social-democracy has split the proletariat; because it has placed at the service of capital the huge mass organizations of the working class which grew especially strong after the first round of revolutions and wars; because it has systematically demoralized one part of the working class, which has followed it by its calls to defend bourgeois democracy, i.e., the bourgeois dictatorship; because it helped the bourgeoisie disarm the working class, as is evident from the examples of Germany and Austria. But this split working class was confronted by monopolistic capital and the big landowners, who temporarily overcame their internal contradictions by the establishment of a fascist dictatorship and the concentration of the forces of the bourgeoisie into a single striking fist in the face of the proletarian revolution which threatens them. The split of the working class had the further harmful consequence that it also weakened to an enormous extent the influence of the proletariat in the reserves of the proletarian revolution—the basic masses of the peasantry, the lower strata of the petty urban bourgeoisie and employees. In Germany, as a result of this, a significant part of the peasantry, the petty urban bourgeoisie, and employees wavered to the side of bourgeois reaction.

In the course of years social-democracy by its corrupting propaganda against the proletarian revolution and the socialist construction in the U.S.S.R. prepared the shift, even though temporary, of these strata to the right. . . .

NOTES

1. P'u-i ("Henry Pu-yi") , the puppet emperor of Manchukuo.

116

Manuilsky Analyzes the Prospects of Fascism

Excerpt from a speech at the Seventeenth Party Congress, February 1934. XVII S"ezd, *pp. 311–312.*

· · ·

If one draws up an account of the present condition of the world revolutionary movement, the following conclusions will have to be drawn.

First, there is to be observed such a shattering of the capitalist system in its weak links that a crisis of the "upper strata" is maturing in some of the countries and in others has already matured, and this crisis is beginning to develop into a nationwide revolutionary crisis. But there is not yet such a shattering of the capitalist system as a whole as would create a situation favoring the immediate rupture of the imperialist chain in its weak links. The political domination of the bourgeoisie is being undermined every-where, but unevenly. Least of all has it been undermined for the time being in the U.S.A., in France, and to some extent in England, most of all in the colonies and the fascist countries. The setting up of a fascist dictatorship represents an intermediate stage in the further maturing of the revolutionary crisis.

Secondly, comrades, there is to be observed such profound discontent among the masses, such indignation on their part against capitalist bondage, as is already threatening the bourgeoisie today with the overthrow of its dictatorship. This discontent is being displayed unevenly, at different times, in the most varied forms of the revolutionary movement, from small scattered demonstrations and economic strikes in Germany to guerrilla warfare in the colonies, to unrest in the army and open armed uprisings. However, in the overwhelming majority of capitalist countries the state apparatus of coercion has not yet been so shattered, the mass basis of the bourgeois dictatorship has not been destroyed to such an extent, while the mass revolutionary movement is not yet strong enough to be able to break its way forcibly through the bayonets of the bourgeoisie's armed forces, which are beginning to waver. As a result of this, the bourgeoisie is driving the discontent of the masses underground by terrorist methods, but precisely in doing this it is creating the conditions for outbursts of tremendous force, which may at any moment hasten the growth of the revolutionary crisis. This factor of "unexpectedness" and "suddenness" of revolutionary outbursts is an especially characteristic feature of the whole present situation.

Thirdly, there is everywhere to be observed an active participation of communists in the front ranks of the revolutionary movement of the masses. In a number of cases the communist parties have given the revolutionary movements independent leadership. But there is not yet a political and organizational growth of the communist parties sufficient to assure the isolation of social-democracy in the colonial powers and of national-reformism in the colonies, representing the main hindrance to the revolutionary movement of the masses. In the overwhelming majority of capitalist countries the communists have not yet won over the majority of the working class. In a number of capitalist countries the communists are already leading considerable sections of the peasantry under the hegemony of the proletariat—for example in Bulgaria and Poland, not to mention China—but they have not yet achieved this hegemony over a significant part of the toilers in town and countryside in all capitalist countries.

But all this taken together is evidence that the most important conditions for a revolutionary crisis of the world capitalist system are not yet present, that the forces of the proletarian revolution have not yet matured for the decisive battle in individual capitalist countries.

And it is just because these conditions for the revolutionary crisis are not present, though they are maturing every month and every day, that the bourgeoisie is hastening to let loose the fury of war, in order to find a way out of the contradictions which are throttling it. And it is just because the forces of the proletarian revolution have not yet matured in individual capitalist countries, though they are maturing every day and every hour, that the bourgeoisie, preparing its rearguard for war, is unleashing the fury of fascism.

II. WAR, FASCISM AND REVOLUTION

Japan and Germany—Factors in the Collapse of the Capitalist System

But imperialist war and fascism are not only products of the accentuation of imperialist contradictions and the disintegration of capitalism. They in their turn, as Comrade Stalin emphasized in his report, are still further deepening the general crisis of capitalism, still further disintegrating the capitalist system. Into this system, already a prey to disintegration, they are introducing still more elements of chaos and disorder.

The two most reactionary governments in the world—Japan and Germany—are at present acting as objective factors in the destruction of the capitalist system, accelerating by their adventurist counterrevolutionary policy the maturing of the revolutionary crisis. Japan and Germany at the present day are the striking fist of world bourgeois reaction. Japan has already become the gendarme of the Far East; fascist Germany wants to become the gendarme of the capitalist order in Europe. Both the ruling cliques of Japan and Germany are acting as crusaders against world Bolshevism, opposing the fascist whip and axe to the Soviet hammer and sickle. Both governments desire expansion at the expense of the U.S.S.R., both are fighting with the same methods against "dangerous ideas," both are dragging the capitalist world into adventures for which the bourgeoisie of all capitalist countries will have to pay.

The whole experience of world history teaches us that the most reactionary governments most frequently pave the way for the greatest revolutions. Russian tsarism with its bloody repressions did not destroy the revolutionary workers' movement: it evoked among the masses such a burning hatred for the ruling classes of old Russia that its consequences are still being felt by the whole capitalist world. Tsarism too, like German fascism, attacked the working class and the Bolsheviks, but it was not tsarism which routed the working class and the Bolsheviks—it was the Bolsheviks at the head of the working class which routed tsarism. (*Applause.*)

(*Roisenman:* "Correct!")

Tsarism, just like imperialist Japan, wanted to disrupt revolution by means of wars, but the revolutions of 1905 and 1917 disrupted the wars of tsarism. Tsarism, just like Germany and

Japan, wanted to be the gendarme of capitalist order, but the proletarian revolution has converted the most reactionary and backward country in the world into a mighty sentinel of the socialist order. (*Applause.*)

The military clique in Japan wants a war against the U.S.S.R. because there is a growing threat of revolution of the Japanese workers and peasants. Imperialist Japan is being torn asunder by its inner contradictions.

"At the present time, as before a thunderstorm, the whole sky is darkened by storm clouds. It is the calm before the storm," declared General Araki in an interview after the big maneuvers in October 1933. And the Japanese militarists want to dispel these storm clouds by the thunder of cannon at the frontiers of the U.S.S.R.

The firm, unswerving policy of peace pursued by the Soviet Union, reinforced now by a number of nonaggression pacts, by the recognition of the U.S.S.R. by the North American United States, has hitherto disrupted the provocational policy of the Japanese militarists. But counterrevolutionary adventurism is void of political reason. An attack on the U.S.S.R. by imperialist Japan cannot be ruled out as a possibility.

But what would a counterrevolutionary war by Japan imperialism against the U.S.S.R. mean? This would not be a war between Paraguay and Bolivia,[1] this would not be a war of two capitalist states against one another. This would be a war of the most reactionary capitalist state against the bulwark of the world proletarian revolution. And it could not but lead to the setting in motion of the whole force of the world proletarian revolution.

Lenin wrote of the war of 1914 that it created a revolutionary situation in Europe. But in 1914, capitalism was not entering the war after five years of a world crisis which has already inflicted more losses upon capitalism than it sustained in the world imperialist war of 1914–1918. Capitalism today is approaching a new imperialist war when it is already in the throes of a general crisis, which was not the case in 1914. In the individual capitalist countries and throughout the capitalist world as a whole elements of revolutionary crisis are already maturing today which were unknown to the world in 1914. Today the bourgeoisie cannot buy itself off from revolution by means of reforms, as it did in Austria and Germany in 1918. Today the working masses in a number of capitalist countries have already had experience of the "democratic socialism" of Hilferding and Otto Bauer. Today the masses have been taught by the bloody experience of the fascist movement to understand the meaning of revolutionary violence. Today there is the Leninist-Stalinist Communist International, which did not exist in 1914. (*Prolonged applause.*)

Today at Japan's flank there stands the 350,000-man Red Army of Soviet China, which, if war breaks out, will set into motion a nation of 400 million against the imperialist yoke. (*Applause.*)

Today there is the U.S.S.R., the armed section of the world proletariat. (*Applause.*)

Let the bourgeoisie today try to arm the masses in the capitalist countries, as they armed them at the end of the world imperialist war—they will understand then what the armed people signify for the fate of capitalism and how the armed people will speed up the development of the revolutionary crisis. (*Applause.*)

Let the Japanese military clique, comrades, stir up racial chauvinism with some success. But if thirty thousand persons have been arrested in Japan since 1929 for "dangerous thoughts"; if the illegal *Sekki,* the central organ of the Communist Party of Japan, comes out not in Geneva and Paris, like *Proletarii* and *Vpered,*[2] but in Tokyo every five days in an edition of up to 60,000 copies a month; if, notwithstanding the bloody murder of communists, a significant part of the Tokyo students consider themselves communists; if communist ideas have penetrated into the higher aviation school; if village teachers in an enormous number of the Japanese prefectures act as supporters of communism; if the peasant movement grips entire provinces—for example, Tottori: then it is completely clear that successful wars are not waged with this kind of home front, one can fight against Chiang Kai-shek with this kind of home front but not against the U.S.S.R.—the fatherland of the toilers of the entire world. (*Voice:* "Correct!" *Applause.*)

The victory of the U.S.S.R. and the world proletariat over the imperialism of Japan will be the victory of the Japanese workers and peasants over the Japanese monarchy, over Asaki, Mitsui, and Mitsubishi; the victory of the colonial revolution in Asia; the victory of the soviets in all China; the decisive blow against the whole of world reaction, opening the doors to the proletarian revolution in other capitalist countries.

But if the imperialist clique of Japan is digging the tank traps for capitalism, fascist Germany is undermining it in the center of Europe, on the banks of the Rhine. If Japan is laying down the dynamite of war against the U.S.S.R., in order to disrupt the relationship of forces between the proletariat and the bourgeoisie in the international arena, fascist Germany is mining the ground for a revolutionary explosion at home. From this home, however, which today is reminiscent of an insane asylum, the powder train leads to all corners of Europe. The German bourgeoisie, like a losing gambler at Monaco, is now throwing down onto the table its last card—fascism. But with this card it risks not only its own fate but the fate of all of capitalist Europe. Today with full justification, it can say, paraphrasing Louis XV, "After Hitler, the deluge." The German fascists wanted to stir up all of Europe against the Bolsheviks, but so far they have only succeeded in forcing France and Poland—the hammer and anvil between which fascist Germany is spread—to turn under the threatening danger of a new imperialist war toward the U.S.S.R., the real revolutionary sentinel of peace between peoples.

Today Germany is bankrupt, deprived by the fascists of the sympathy and support that the world proletariat showed the German people which had been plundered by Versailles. Today not a single proletariat in the world would lift a finger in the event of war to support *fascist* Germany in a struggle against Versailles. The German fascists wanted by bloodletting to break the desire for revolutionary violence on the part of the German proletariat, but by shattering the democratic illusions and the authority of bourgeois legality among the social-democratic workers they have made the German proletariat an advocate of armed uprising against the bourgeois dictatorship.

The German fascists wanted to destroy Marxism, but they have achieved the decisive turn of the social-democratic workers to the side of communism. The German fascists wanted to destroy communism, but they have brought its victory closer by rousing class hatred among millions of workers of the entire world toward not only the German bourgeoisie but also the entire international bourgeoisie. The German fascists wanted to isolate the communists from the masses by the burning of the Reichstag and the Leipzig trials, but in fact they have covered themselves with shame in the eyes of the entire world.

The German fascists, in order to disrupt the influence of the communist party, wanted to pulverize the proletariat, but in fact they have brought about the united front not only of the German but of the world proletariat, rising to the defense of Dimitrov and the other Leipzig prisoners at the call of the communist party.

The German fascists wanted to paralyze the influence of the communists among the peasantry and the petty bourgeoisie, but, in fact, by activating these strata politically they are preparing their shift to the side of the proletariat as the result of disillusionment with fascist demagogy.

. . .

NOTES

1. Between 1932 and 1935 Paraguay and Bolivia fought a war over the Gran Chaco.
2. Illegal Bolshevik publications in the period before 1917.

117

Blücher Pledges the Red Army's Preparedness to Meet Japanese Aggression

Excerpts from a speech by V. Blücher, Commander in Chief of the Special Far Eastern Army, at the Seventeenth Party Congress, February 1934. XVII s"ezd, pp. 629–630.

. . .

The Far Eastern region which I represent here is one of the most remote sectors of our country. It is located in a vital area of present-day international political events, and borders directly upon Japan, which is feverishly preparing for war. There is no need for me to dwell at length on the situation which confronts us in the Far East. Comrade Stalin and Comrade Voroshilov have characterized with exhaustive clarity the situation which has developed in the Far East. I want only to emphasize that in the situation in the Far East we have felt particularly clearly that wise, cautious, and at the same time firm policy which our Leninist Central Committee is following, a policy directed toward the prevention of war and the utilization of capitalist contradictions for the benefit of socialist construction. In the Far East we have felt this especially strongly. We have seen that the Central Committee has taken all measures to smooth away the growing sharply concentrated tension in our relations with Japan. Unfortunately, however, the policy of the Japanese imperialists gives us no assurance that we will not be drawn into military complications despite all our efforts to avoid them.

The fact is that there exists a tremendous difference between the official policy of the Japanese government toward the U.S.S.R. and its actions. Despite the expressed, apparently peaceable assertions of the official leaders of Japanese policy, we observe—as Comrade Voroshilov has already described in detail—that feverish preparations are being made for war, that northern Manchuria has become a military base which Japan is setting up with desperate energy and by straining its entire state organism in order from that base to make a thrust into our Soviet Far East.

Comrade Voroshilov in his speech has already given the most important details of these preparations. I want to confine myself here only to those measures which clearly reveal that, despite the assurance by all official policy makers of the Japanese government, their preparations are being made not for defensive purposes but for launching an attack on the Soviet Union.

I want to present just three facts which prove without doubt that these preparations are directed against our Soviet Far East.

What are these indications?

The *first* and decisive fact is the tremendous strategic railway construction which has been carried on feverishly by Japan within the last two years. I must tell you that within these two years they have succeeded in laying down more than a thousand kilometers of railway track. Of these 1,000 kilometers of track which lead up to our frontier, not more than 30 to 35 per cent can be justified on economic grounds. This is the first indicator which shows in what direction will develop the military events, for the preparation of which Japan is now actually investing all its national wealth.

The *second* indicator is the network of roads. During these two years Japan has built 2,200 kilometers of unpaved roads. If we observe the direction of these roads we shall see that they are laid either in the district near our frontier, or that they lead from inner Manchuria directly to our frontier points, in those directions which would be most favorable for future strategic operations.

The *third* indicator is the construction of air bases. The Japanese have built about fifty airdromes and air bases. If we look at their position on the map, they are all situated to the north of Mukden, they are all concentrated in the triangle *Mukden-Harbin-Tsitsihar,* and north of this area.

In an interview on February 3, Japanese War Minister Hayashi, modestly reducing his forces in Manchuria, accused us of an enormous concentration of troops on our borders. He said: "We, the Japanese, occupy in Manchuria an area equal to the territory of France, Germany, and Belgium taken together and have only 50,000 troops there, whereas you have piled up 100,000 men and 300 planes on the Far Eastern border alone." This incorrect information must be dispelled. We are in the possession of absolutely exact data [indicating] that if before the occupation of Manchuria the Japanese forces numbered only 10,000 men, at the present time there are 130,000 there, that is, more than a third of the entire Japanese army. To this must be added from 110,000 to 115,000 men in the Manchukuo army and 12,000 White Guardists capable of bearing arms, who are being equipped and organized by the Japanese. To this it should be added that during this period the Sungari flotilla has been increased by 24 units.

Mr. Hayashi complains in his interview that the Soviet government has concentrated 300 airplanes in the Far East. We shall not quarrel with him; perhaps more, perhaps less. I will say only that if it becomes necessary, our party and government will be able to concentrate so many planes that they will certainly exceed those of the Japanese. (*Voice: "Correct." Prolonged applause.*) However, for all Mr. Hayashi's modesty, I must nevertheless state that the Japanese have 500 planes in Manchuria— (*laughter*) —although they modestly keep silent about them.

Comrades, every one of us can understand the significance of the measures which have been enumerated. They testify, without doubt, to preparation by the Japanese imperialists for a large-scale war. We are perfectly well aware that both the growth of the military budget and the growth of the productivity of the military industry of Japan may be directed against us at any moment.

If we look at the direction of the strategic construction of railways and roads, the network of airdromes, the locations of supply stores and bases, and at the scope of these preparations, it becomes obvious that all these have not been planned for the defense of Manchuria, but for attack on the Soviet Far East.

As you see, in words the Japanese official policy makers speak of their desire for friendship with the Soviet Union, but actually this desire is not supported by a single fact. However, we would like to see facts, not words.

This same Hayashi says, "We have no idea of fighting the Soviet Union if the Soviet Union doesn't attack us." I believe that I express the general opinion of the congress when I say that we are not thinking of attacking them, that there is no need for us to do so.

We need no new territories, or mineral wealth from you, for we have enough of them; it will be sufficient probably for hundreds of years, even with increased utilization. Before us stand the grandiose tasks of the second Five-Year Plan. We have to build mines, blast-furnaces, foundries, railways, power stations—not engage in war.

It is perfectly understandable, comrades, that, observing the military measures of Japanese imperialism, we could not and cannot remain indifferent to them. Therefore, by a decision of the party and the government, measures have been taken for the defense of the Soviet Far East.

What are these measures?

First of all, the strengthening of our border. We are padlocking our border. Our border, as Comrade Voroshilov said here, is girdled with reinforced concrete and is sufficiently strong to withstand even the most powerful teeth. This fortification will break any imperialist head gripped by military phantasy. (*Applause.*)

Second, a number of measures have been taken to strengthen and fortify the army itself. The army has been strengthened by the best cadres. There is no need to cite the figures or the corresponding percentages of its growth, but I can assure you that it has been brought both in quantity and quality to such a level that we can continue our work here in complete tranquility. (*Applause.*)

Furthermore, as we all know, our party and our leader Comrade Stalin, if they ever begin something, carry it through to the end. And the defense of the Far East will be carried through to the end in this way. (*Applause.*)

We are also strong technically, in tanks and aviation. If it is necessary to measure strength, if we are forced to do that, I think we will emerge victorious from these clashes in this branch of the forces, as well as in the army as a whole. (*Applause.*)

Our tanks and our aviation are the offspring of our first Five-Year Plan. I think that this offspring of the first Five-Year Plan will be able to fulfill its socialist duty to the Soviet Union not only on the borders, not only on the front, but also anywhere deep in the rear areas of the imperialist antagonist. (*Applause.*)

War, comrades, does not enter into the plan of our second Five-Year Plan. (*Laughter.*) At least, in listening to the speeches by Comrade Molotov and Comrade Kuibyshev, I did not notice the inclusion of any point or paragraph about war. (*Laughter.*)

We do not want to fight, but if we are compelled, forced, we can bravely measure our strength, and then let our neighbor not complain if he is well and truly beaten by our army, which is tested in battle, strongly organized politically, united and devoted to our party, and by the offspring of our first Five-Year Plan, tanks and aviation. (*Applause.*)

What is the fundamental difference between the measures taken by the Japanese military command in Manchuria and ours in the Far East? The difference is that everything which we are doing in the Far East is subordinated only to the defense of our Far Eastern border, whereas the measures of the Japanese military command pursue the goal of attack. We are doing everything for defense, they are doing everything for attack. This is the fundamental difference.

Comrade Stalin, in discussing the Far East in his speech, said:

We are not only not prepared to give up the Far East, but on the contrary, we shall strive there to develop further the cause of socialist construction.

And when I report to you today in the name of the Army that we shall not give up the Soviet Far East, my confidence rests not only on the power of the Red Army, not only on its technical equipment, not only on its personnel, which is devoted to the cause of the revolution and to our party, but also on the enormous changes in the economic aspect of the region itself.

In the first Five-Year Plan we invested larger funds in the Far Eastern region than had been invested during the entire existence of the Tsarist government; the second Five-Year Plan for the Far Eastern region will be an enormous program of the *socialist industrialization* of this region.

. . .

The task of transforming the Far East into one of the powerful industrial regions confronts us in the first place with the task of accelerating the settlement of the region and the creation of a powerful base for animal husbandry and agriculture.

The decision of the Central Committee concerning [tax] immunities, which is historic for the region, together with correct Bolshevik work on the part of our Far Eastern party organization and the daily aid of the Central Committee by directives, tractors, capital investments, seeds, will create all the prerequisites for the solution of these tasks in the second Five-Year Plan.

We, the men of the Far East, must take note with special satisfaction here, in front of the congress, of the correctness and exceptional significance of the decision on immunities which was taken on the initiative of Comrade Stalin. This decision has inspired the Far Eastern kolkhoz peasantry to militant work in mastering the region. It has created all the prerequisites for the rapid growth of an animal husbandry and agricultural base.

The Far East party organization realizes its responsibility to the party, to the nation. . . .

Finally, comrades, the entire personnel of the Far Eastern Army understands the enormous share of responsibility which it bears in the situation which has developed in the Far East.

Understanding this, we began the current training year with the firm resolve conscientiously and honorably to master military affairs in the shortest possible time, to master the enormous technical means which the party and the government have given us.

. . .

In conclusion I, as the commander in chief of the Army, in the name of the Army organization, the Red Army men, the command and the political staffs, assure the congress of our party:

If military events break out in the Far East, the Special Far Eastern Red Army, from Red Army man to commander, as supremely faithful soldiers of the revolution, under the immediate direction of the beloved leader of the Workers' and Peasants' Red Army and Navy, Comrade Voroshilov, of the Central Committee of our party, of the great leader of our party Comrade Stalin, will reply with a blow which will shake the foundations of capitalism and in places bring it down in ruins. (Stormy applause; cries of "Hurrah!")

Long live the leader of the Workers' and Peasants' Red Army, Comrade Voroshilov. (*Prolonged applause.*) Long live the Leninist Central Committee of our party! (*Applause.*) Long live the great Leninist, the leader of the party, the strategist of the world proletarian revolution, Comrade *Stalin!* (*Stormy applause; all the delegates rise; cries of "Hurrah!"*)

118

Pravda *on the Extension of Nonaggression Pacts with the Baltic States*

"Sovetskii soiuz—oplot mira," Pravda, No. 94, April 5, 1934, p. 1. *An excerpt from Litvinov's speech on this occasion appears in* Degras, Foreign Policy, *III, 78–79.*

On April 4 there took place in Moscow the signing of a protocol which extends for ten years the nonaggression pacts between the Soviet Union and Estonia, Lithuania, and Latvia. As is known, the proposal to extend the pacts was made by the Soviet government two weeks ago, and it was met with the complete approval and support of the governments of the above-mentioned Baltic countries. The protocol signed in Moscow was formalized within a period whose shortness is unprecedented in the history of diplomatic relations.

The extension of the nonaggression pacts with the three Baltic countries represents a new link in the chain of victories in the policy of peace of the Soviet Union.

The Soviet Union fights systematically for peace. It does not substitute wishes and declarations for its struggle against the danger of war. The toilers of our country know very well what efforts are needed to defend the cause of peace, especially now under conditions of the sharpest contradictions among the imperialists, under conditions of the growing threat of a new imperialist war and an attack on the Soviet Union.

It is quite natural for the Soviet government to give special attention to the consolidation of peaceful and friendly relations with its neighbors. This is illustrated by the numerous nonaggression pacts signed on the initiative of the Soviet government with our neighbors on the western border. The peace policy of the U.S.S.R. is testified to by the nonaggression pacts signed with numerous other countries, and in particular with Turkey and France. In signing in

Moscow the protocol for the extension of the nonaggression pacts with the three Baltic countries, the Soviet Union has made another and important contribution to the great cause of the maintenance of peace.

The enemies of the Soviet Union have often tried to speculate on the assumption that the Soviet love of peace results from the weakness of the country of the proletarian dictatorship, and from the weakness of its defensive capabilities. Now even the stupidest enemy of the Soviet state would hardly dare to assert that the peace policy of the U.S.S.R. is a sign of weakness. . . .

The U.S.S.R. has repeatedly shown its desire for peace. Beginning with the proposal for universal and complete disarmament advanced by the Soviet delegation at the Genoa Conference in 1922, the Soviet Union, after this offer had been declined, proposed a plan of partial disarmament, but this plan was declined likewise. The Soviet Union did not abandon its struggle for peace. It signed nonaggression pacts and strengthened them with the convention on the definition of aggression which has recently come into force among all the countries which adhered to it. Every move which the Soviet Union has made undoubtedly contributes to the consolidation of peace.

The significance of the protocol signed yesterday in Moscow is exceptionally great; it can be correctly understood if one takes into consideration the existing international situation. It was brilliantly characterized by the Commissar of Foreign Affairs, Comrade M. M. Litvinov, in his speech.

"The threat of war"—said Comrade Litvinov—"which menaces all five continents of the world is talked about and written about daily, but scarcely anything is heard of the possibility and the means of averting this impending catastrophe for humanity. Governments, governmental people, regard it with a kind of fatalism, as something completely inevitable. The only thing they can think about is general rearmament—that armaments race which in the past not only did not avert wars but stimulated them."

And, in fact, what remains of the conference on disarmament? A pile of papers. In the entire capitalist world, a frenzied armaments race is under way—in some countries openly, in others secretly. The filthy wave of chauvinism and nationalism is rising higher and higher. The fascist "saviors of mankind" speak openly of the necessity of bloodletting; under the mask of various "racial theories," a savage persecution of the toilers by the ruling classes is going on, the unrestrained setting of one people against another.

The small states are the first objects of the attempts on the part of these unbidden "saviors." And in this warlike clamor more and more clearly are heard calls, often reminiscent of the fighting of savage beasts, for "a struggle against Bolshevism." At this moment the Soviet Union strengthens the chain of its activities directed toward the defense of peace by the new powerful link, which is the protocol signed yesterday.

It is not accidental that the Soviet government approached its Baltic neighbors with its proposal. This sector of eastern Europe has been specially threatened by the efforts of various rascals, such as Herr Rosenberg, who think of the Baltic states as a passageway and a *staging area* for the realization of their plans, the *Drang nach Osten*. The Soviet Union is interested in the maintenance of peace on its borders, in the maintenance and consolidation of the independence of the Baltic countries. The toilers of the Soviet Union express their profound confidence that the protocol signed in Moscow will serve the cause of the strengthening of peace in eastern Europe, and will also prove to be a firm foundation for the development of friendly relations between our country and our Baltic neighbors.

However, it is quite obvious that peace in the Baltic sector of eastern Europe may be violated by other states. That is why the protocol which was signed would gain additional force if other states also adhered to the initiative of the Soviet government. Whatever may be the policy of other states, however, and independently of it, the Soviet Union will continue the struggle for the maintenance of peace. This was clearly and expressively stated by Comrade Litvinov in his speech, which was cited above.

"The Soviet Union"—said Comrade Litvinov—"which is a stranger to chauvinism, nationalism, militarism, racial or national prejudices, sees its governmental tasks not in conquests, not in expansion of territory; it sees the honor of the people not in education in the spirit of militarism and thirst for blood, but simply in the fulfillment of that idea for which it came into existence and in which it sees the whole meaning of its existence, namely, the building of a socialist society."

The Soviet Union has once more given an example of the struggle for peace. The toilers of the U.S.S.R., confident in their own strength, have proved once more that they represent the greatest bulwark of peace.

119

The Proposal for a German-Soviet Guarantee of the Baltic Countries, March 28, 1934

Statement by TASS. Pravda, *No. 118, April 27, 1934, p. 1.*

On March 28, the People's Commissar of Foreign Affairs, Comrade *M. M. Litvinov,* in the name of the Soviet government, through the German Ambassador in Moscow, Herr Nadolny, proposed to the German government, for the purpose of strengthening the general peace, and in particular peace in eastern Europe, and also to improve the relations between Germany and the U.S.S.R., the signing of a protocol, in which the governments of the U.S.S.R. and the German Republic would assume the obligation of unfailingly taking into account in their foreign policy the maintenance of the independence and inviolability of the Baltic countries, refraining from any actions that might prove directly or indirectly harmful to this independence.

The protocol should remain open so that other countries interested in this problem might join it.

On April 14 Herr Nadolny informed Comrade Litvinov that the German government had turned down the Soviet proposal, in connection with which Herr Nadolny made the following statement:

Answer of the German Government

If the Soviet government desires to do something concrete with the aim of restoring relations of confidence between Germany and the Soviet Union, we naturally can only greet this with satisfaction. We have ourselves unequivocally emphasized on every available occasion our own desire to bring this about, and therefore it was difficult for us to understand and at the same time regrettable to us when Mr. Litvinov, in his well-known speech of December 28 of last year,[1] and in his important interview with the German ambassador on January 4 of this year, expressed such a negative and openly distrustful attitude. We must regretfully point out that the procedure proposed by Mr. Litvinov for the realization of his object does not, for a variety of reasons, appear to us to be suitable to this purpose. . . .

. . . We are able to see the true cause of the regrettable alienation in German-Soviet relations only in the attitude of the Soviet government toward the National Socialist regime in Germany. For this reason we can only emphasize again that the difference in the internal order of the two states should not affect their international relations. Of this we are firmly convinced. The successful development of these relations is in the final analysis a question of political desire. In the field of foreign policy there are no real developments which might interfere with this desire. On the contrary, numerous common interests of the two states point in this direction. For this reason, everything depends on relations being built not on artificial foundations but on the natural and constructive foundation of the Berlin treaty.

This treaty provides for the two governments' maintaining friendly contact with one another in order to ensure agreement on all political and economic problems affecting both countries. The German government is fully prepared to discuss with the Soviet government, in accordance with this agreement, the question of the restoration of relations of confidence useful to both countries.

On April 21, Comrade Litvinov in turn informed Herr Nadolny orally in the name of the Soviet government of the following . . .[2]

NOTES

1. For this speech see Degras, *Foreign Policy*, III, 48–61.
2. For the text of Litvinov's statement see *ibid.*, pp. 79–83.

120

An Analysis of Germany's Refusal to Guarantee the Independence of the Baltic States

"Otkaz nemotivirovannyi, no otkrovennyi," Pravda, *No. 117, April 28, 1934, p. 1.*

The Soviet government has proposed to the German government the signing of a joint protocol concerning the non-violation of the independence and integrity of the Baltic states. As interpreted by the Soviet government, the protocol could be adhered to by any interested third state. After two weeks' deliberation the government of fascist Germany has declined the peace initiative of the Soviet Union.

The German refusal to strengthen, in the form of a protocol, the simple obligation to respect the right to independence of the small Baltic peoples and not to undertake anything that might prove directly or indirectly harmful to this independence, reveals with particular force the tense situation existing in eastern Europe.

It should be added that the German refusal becomes even more striking if one recollects that it followed soon after all four Baltic states agreed willingly and quickly to the proposal of the Soviet Union for an extension for ten years of the nonaggression pacts. And, in turn, in the light of this refusal the well-known facts of the subversive work carried on by the German fascists and their agents in all the Baltic countries acquire new significance.

German diplomacy has been unable to conceal the differences between the deeds and words of fascist Germany, between their program of expansion to the east and their statements about the benefits of peace and the harmfulness of war, which are destined for export and which do not fit in the least the newly born fascist pacifists. In its reply to Comrade *Litvinov,* the German government simply did not advance—and, in fact, could not advance—a single even partly convincing argument against the Soviet proposal: it was unable to motivate its refusal.

However, the diplomatic sophistry which accompanied the German refusal to accept the peace proposal of the U.S.S.R. is so characteristic and it so openly reveals the line of German policy in eastern Europe that this reply deserves more careful study.

The first "argument" of the German reply represents not so much a policy as a political intrigue. Please, say the German diplomats, did you not already propose some such obligation to the Polish government? Why, then, do you now propose it to us, Germany? The German diplomats are pretending in vain that they are badly informed; the difference between the Soviet proposal to Poland and the Soviet proposal to Germany, which was actually very clearly explained by Comrade Litvinov in his reply to the German ambassador, was, of course, known to Berlin. But something else is important: it has apparently never occurred to the ruling circles of Germany that the proposal made to them by the Soviet Union, together with the proposal to Poland, together with the extension of the pacts with the Baltic states for ten years, together with a whole series of other peace efforts by the U.S.S.R., is one of the measures which "in serving a single aim and being part of a single system, supplement rather than exclude one another" (reply of Comrade Litvinov).

Equally groundless is the second "argument" of the Berlin answer. It is allegedly not yet known what position will be taken by the Baltic states themselves in regard to the Soviet proposal. Will they not take it as a kind of Soviet-German protectorate over the Baltic countries?

This fascist concern for the national sentiment of our Baltic neighbors sounds truly touching on fascist lips, and it deserves better application.

First of all, as Comrade Litvinov has explained, the Soviet Union would not conclude any obligation which concerns the Baltic countries without first asking their opinion. Second, never yet has the recognition of the independence of any state, or even the guarantee of its frontiers, been considered as a protectorate over that state. Finally, the German diplomats know very well that the very concept of a protectorate, which is closely connected with the international practice of the imperialist states, is incompatible with the basic principles of Soviet foreign policy, which are well known to the whole world.

However, if the Berlin diplomats still have some doubts in

regard to the attitude of the Baltic states to the Soviet proposal, we recommend that they study their responses, which we are publishing today, in which they welcome the peace initiative of the Soviet Union and correctly evaluate the true meaning of the refusal of fascist Germany. No, indeed, the role of defender of the Baltic states does not suit fascist Germany!

The third "argument" likewise will not stand up to criticism: "The Soviet proposal is void of any real political basis; the independence and integrity of the Baltic states are not exposed to any threat."

The authors of such an unexpected statement would have done well to inquire first of all about the opinion of the Baltic states themselves and to acquaint themselves with these states' own interpretation of the systematic provocative and subversive work of fascist agents in Estonia, in Latvia, in Memel, etc.—"work," the main purpose of which is to clear the ground for foreign aggression, for the liquidation of the independence of the Baltic countries.

This *most real* threat cannot be treated with indifference by the Baltic states, by the Soviet Union. For *"the violation of peace in this sector of Europe might prove, and very likely will prove, a prelude to the outbreak of a new world war. The Soviet government, which is concerned with the maintenance of peace in general, must give particular attention both from this general point of view, and from the point of view of the security of the Soviet Union's own frontiers, to the cause of the maintenance of peace particularly in this sector of Europe"* (from Comrade Litvinov's answer).

And, besides, is there to be found today in the entire capitalist world, which is openly preparing for a new world slaughter, even one small corner of the earth—and especially if one is speaking about the small states—where peace is not threatened? Truly, one must have a peculiar sense of humor to come forward with such careless "pacifist" statements about the absence of the threat of war, under present conditions and, in addition, in the name of fascist Germany!

Finally, could it be that the German government has forgotten some of the literary exercises of *its own* ideologists, exercises which have not been consigned to the archives but which are continually being made in the German press, which fairly often, and depending on the mood and the situation—each time in some variation, and so far on paper only—remake the map of eastern Europe?

But let us assume for a minute that the German government is sincerely convinced that there is no threat to the peaceful existence of the Baltic states, and does not take seriously the statements even of its own authoritative statesmen. *Why, then, in that case, does it not wish to confirm this fact in the form of a bilateral or multilateral international obligation, and acknowledge formally the independence and integrity of the Baltic states?*

In vain shall we seek the answer to this question in the German government's reply!

Finally, the last, the fourth "argument": The Soviet proposal allegedly does not lead in any way to the improvement of Soviet-German relations; these relations have deteriorated because of the negative attitude of the U.S.S.R. to the National Socialist regime; there are no reasons for a new political treaty between the U.S.S.R. and Germany; it is necessary to develop these relations on the basis of the Berlin treaty and to desire their improvement.

Of course, the peoples of the Soviet Union take the attitude to the National Socialist regime in Germany which it deserves. But when entering into normal diplomatic and economic relations with the capitalist countries the toilers of our Union realize perfectly well that they are dealing with countries in which in one or another form—concealed or open—the dictatorship of the bourgeoisie is being practiced. Normal relations between the U.S.S.R. and a number of capitalist countries exist inasmuch as the maintenance of such relations is in the interest of both sides, in the interest of peace. This is as well known to the German government as are the reasons which caused the "unfortunate deterioration of German-Soviet relations," reasons which come *entirely from the German side and which have nothing in common with the spirit of that Berlin treaty to which the German reply refers.*

The Soviet government has proposed a concrete way for putting in order and improving German-Soviet relations. The German government could not fail to realize that the acceptance of the Soviet proposal *would have provided considerable reassurance to the Baltic states,* which fear for their own independence and which now have another reason to fear for it *in Soviet-German relations.*

The absence of any convincing argument in the German refusal forces us to reach the conclusion that *there exist* other, *more real, motives, not mentioned in the German answer, which prompted this refusal.*

The basic motive is, obviously, *the desire of German fascism not to bind itself by any obligations which would interfere with its aggression against the Baltic countries.*

The exchange of opinions between the governments of the
U.S.S.R. and Germany has revealed with exceptional clarity and
unexpected frankness the driving forces and motives of German
foreign policy. For this reason alone the U.S.S.R.'s peace initiative
has not been in vain.

121

Pravda *on Extending the Nonaggression Pact with Poland*

*"Novyi shag ukrepleniia mira," Pravda, No. 123, May 6, 1934, p. 1.
For the text of the protocol see, ibid., p. 5.*

On May 5, the People's Commissar of Foreign Affairs, Comrade
Litvinov, and the Polish Ambassador in Moscow, Mr. Lukasevic,
signed a protocol prolonging the Soviet-Polish nonaggression pact
for ten years, or to be more precise, until December 1, 1945.

Thus the Soviet government's proposal to prolong for ten years
the pacts which are in force between the U.S.S.R. and its western
neighbors has been realized. The basis of peaceful relations between
the Soviet Union and the Baltic states, and also between the
U.S.S.R. and its most important western neighbor, Poland, has been
strengthened and consolidated.

There can be no doubt whatever that the successful realization
of the Soviet Union's initiative will serve the cause of strengthening
peace in eastern Europe and the consolidation of the independence
of the Baltic countries.

As is known, the proposal to extend the nonaggression pact
between the U.S.S.R. and Poland for ten years was made by the
Commissar of Foreign Affairs, Comrade Litvinov, to the Polish
Minister of Foreign Affairs, Mr. Beck, at the time of his visit to
Moscow on February 13 of this year. The negotiations which began
in the closing days of March between the Soviet and Polish governments on this proposal led to the signing of the protocol on May 5,
which extends the nonaggression pact for ten years and provides for

its automatic extension after this for another two years if one of the parties does not withdraw from the pact six months before the indicated date.

The extension of the nonaggression pact between the Soviet Union and Poland for ten years will be met with profound satisfaction by the toiling masses of the Soviet Union and the entire world, as a new factor for strengthening peace in eastern Europe. The value of this fact increases immeasurably if one takes into account the sharpening of imperialist contradictions and the threat of a new war. There is not the slightest doubt that in this situation the extension of the pact between the Soviet Union and Poland will contribute to the cause of the stabilization of peace.

It is necessary to emphasize with particular force that the extension of the nonaggression pact between the U.S.S.R. and Poland for such a long period has provided a firm foundation for the all-around good neighborly and friendly relations between the Soviet Union and the Polish republic. The sincere aspiration of the toilers of the Soviet Union for the strengthening and development of peaceful and good neighborly relations between the Land of Soviets and its neighbors has received a new confirmation.

A special feature of the instrument signed between the Soviet Union and Poland on May 5 is that in addition to the basic document—the protocol on the extension of the pact—there is a special final protocol, the value of which is extremely great.

In the first paragraph of the final protocol the parties state that *they are bound by no obligations and no binding declarations which would be in conflict with Article Three of the Riga peace treaty.* As is known, Article Three of the Riga treaty provides that the Soviet state, on the one side, and Poland, on the other, *renounce all claims to territory lying beyond the Soviet-Polish boundaries established by the peace treaty.*

The statement about the absence of agreements in conflict with the obligations assumed by the parties under the peace treaty is extremely timely and valuable in view of all kinds of rumors which have been reaching the world press recently regarding secret agreements of a contrary nature.

In the Soviet-Polish negotiations on the extension of the pact, a definite place was occupied by the question of the note by Chicherin to the Lithuanian government on September 28, 1926. Chicherin's note was sent to the Lithuanian government in connection with the signing of the nonaggression pact between the U.S.S.R. and Lithuania. In this note the Soviet government confirmed its point of view, which had been expressed earlier in the Riga peace treaty, that the problem of the Vilno region should be solved by peaceful means between Poland and Lithuania. The Polish government pointed out that Chicherin's note permits various interpretations.

The Soviet government confirmed its old point of view, which has found expression in various documents, that in its opinion disputable territorial questions should be settled by agreement between the parties. It goes without saying that the Soviet government will welcome the amicable solution of the existing territorial dispute between Poland and Lithuania. The final protocol with Poland confirms once more this old point of view of the Soviet Union.

The protocol signed between the Soviet Union and Poland on the extension of the nonaggression pact, together with the statement of the parties concerning the absence of obligations in conflict with the Riga peace treaty, has a significance which far exceeds the framework of Soviet-Polish relations, and is a factor of immediate significance for the strengthening of peace.

The instrument signed yesterday undoubtedly represents a new success in the policy of peace undeviatingly pursued by the Soviet government.

122

Pravda *on the French Rapprochement with the Soviet Union*

"Franko-sovetskie otnosheniia i bor'ba za mir," Pravda, No. 145, May 28, 1934, p. 1.

The statement of the Minister of Foreign Affairs of France in the Chamber of Deputies has aroused exceptional interest throughout the world. This is due primarily to the fact that a considerable part of Barthou's speech was devoted to Franco-Soviet relations and to the international role in the struggle for peace which, as has been duly acknowledged by the French government, is played by the Soviet Union.

Barthou's statement that "French policy aims at a sincere rapprochement with the U.S.S.R.," which is evidence of the strengthening of the change in the attitude of the ruling circles of France toward the Soviet Union, has been met with much satisfaction by the toiling public of our country. Truly, there is hardly any clearer example of the rapid and radical change in the relations between the U.S.S.R. and a large capitalist power of Europe—in relation to the growth of the internal and international strength of the Soviet Union—than the development and consolidation of Soviet-French relations during the last two years.

The signing of a nonaggression pact, the signing of a trade agreement, the visits to the U.S.S.R. of leading political and scientific representatives of France—such were the landmarks of the change in the attitude of leading French circles to the U.S.S.R., a change which coincides, and not by chance, with the successful completion of the first Five-Year Plan of large-scale construction. This change, as has been confirmed again by Barthou's statement, which is now supported by all, or by at least the overwhelming majority of the French parliament, is all the more significant since it is being strengthened during a most complex and threatening international situation, when the aggressive forces which have made war the order of the day are growing and grouping themselves.

. . .

In the same speech the French Minister of Foreign Affairs announced France's interest in inviting the U.S.S.R. to join the League of Nations. He mentioned that he had had a talk concerning this subject with Comrade Litvinov during his recent meeting with him at Geneva, which aroused lively comments in the press all over the world. The French press more than once through a number of its influential organs expressed itself in favor of the French government's taking upon itself the initiative of inviting the U.S.S.R. to join the League of Nations.

In a number of other countries, mainly small countries which fear that they may be drawn into the fight among the large imperialist powers and become victims of this fight, the idea has recently gained increasing popularity that only the participation of the U.S.S.R. in the League of Nations could change it from an organization which certain great powers attempt to utilize for their own imperialist aims into an organ which would help at least to some extent the struggle against the danger of war. And, in fact, the withdrawal of Japan and Germany from the League of Nations, i.e., the countries which do not consider it necessary to conceal their determination to satisfy by means of rearmament, annexation, and war, their imperialist lusts, has raised the question whether the League of Nations could not become to a certain extent a place of meeting of forces which, irrespective of their motives, are willing at present to halt, in one way or another, the bloody settlement of contradictions and to help even if only to some extent the strengthening of peace.

The dialectic of the development of imperialist contradictions has led to the situation in which the old League of Nations, which had been planned as an instrument for imperialist enslavement of the small, dependent, and colonial countries and for the preparation of anti-Soviet intervention, has become in the process of the struggle between imperialist groupings an arena on which "those tendencies which are interested in the maintenance of peace appear to be winning out, and this perhaps explains the profound changes which are apparent in the composition of the League" (Litvinov, speech at the Fourth Session of the Central Executive Committee of the U.S.S.R.).

Barthou's speech, the first in which it was publicly stated in the name of the French government that "the entrance of the Soviet Union into the League of Nations would be an event of considerable significance for the cause of European peace," indicates to what extent the French government has become aware of the threat to the cause of peace, and how seriously concerned it is with the finding of new means to strengthen it . . .

. . .

The very fact of the raising of the question of inviting the Soviet Union to join the League of Nations is a new indication of the growth of the international power and prestige of the Land of Soviets, the country of the victorious construction of a socialist society, the country whose invincible strength represents the most important factor of peace. . . .

123

Radek Indicates Possible Soviet Willingness to Join the League of Nations

K. Radek, *"Dialektika istorii i Liga natsii,"* Pravda, No. 146, May 29, 1934, p. 2.

. . .

The League of Nations has proved incapable of becoming the political expression of an "organized" capitalist world, to coordinate the interests and direct the expansion of that world against the U.S.S.R.

What does the *League of Nations* represent *today? The two powers have withdrawn* from it *which are the chief representatives of the tendencies of imperialist expansion in the present historical period,* the two powers which now aim at a redistribution of the world.

There remain in it first, the *small nations* which know that in case of a new imperialist war, they will be its first victims. These small nations tremble at the thought of a new imperialist war and try to make the League of Nations an instrument which could at least delay the development of the war danger.

There also remain in the League France and the countries connected with it by alliance, against which is directed the predatory policy of fascist Germany and the countries which are drawn to it. France, understandably, is defending the interests of French capitalism. France is defending what remains of its position in Europe and its standing as a world power. *But the defense of this position demands the defense of peace,* since France can hardly expect that in case of war all the powers that assisted it in defending its position during the world war of 1914–1918 will again side with it.

Finally *there remain in the League of Nations Great Britain and Italy,* which, while preparing themselves for participation in the struggle for the redistribution of the world, believe that the time has not yet come to stand openly on the side of those powers which are making ready for a new world slaughter (Great Britain), or which hope (Italy) that they may succeed in having their demands satisfied by making use of the contradictions between the leading imperialist countries.

The League of Nations, or what remains of it, has proved unable in the present historical period to play the role of the organizer of an international campaign against the Soviet Union. The danger of a war against the U.S.S.R. does not come at present from the League of Nations, but from its open adversaries or from the English diehards. *The League of Nations has been unable to reduce armaments, to safeguard the peace,* it proved to be unable to guarantee peace, to remove the danger of war. Everything that the Bolsheviks said on this subject when the League was formed has been fully confirmed. But in the ranks of the League *there are some powers which are interested in the maintenance of peace.* Therefore, Comrade *Stalin,* in reply to the question of the American journalist Duranty—"Will your attitude and policy toward the League of Nations always be exclusively negative?"—answered:

> No, not always and not under all circumstances. You perhaps do not fully understand our point of view. Notwithstanding the withdrawal of Germany and Japan from the League of Nations—or perhaps just for that reason—the League may become to some extent a brake to delay the development of military actions, or to prevent them. If this is so, if the League might prove to be an obstacle in that path, so that it might even to a small degree hinder the cause of war and facilitate to some extent the cause of peace, then we would not be against the League. Yes, if that proves to be the course of historical events, then it is not out of the question that we will support the League of Nations, notwithstanding its colossal defects.

That is how sharply the historical development of the role of the League of Nations has changed. *The bourgeois powers* which were preparing a united attack against the Soviet Union have *fallen apart. The Soviet Union has become a mighty international force, dangerous to its foes and capable of rendering assistance to its friends.* The Soviet Union has proved that it pursues a *policy of peace,* that any idea of annexation is alien to it. The Soviet Union has forced its neighbors, who have been constantly directing slander against it concerning Soviet imperialism, to recognize this fact. By signing nonaggression pacts proposed by the Soviet government, by signing detailed definitions of an aggressor, proposed by the Soviet government, almost all the Soviet Union's neighbors have recognized its peace policy. The Soviet Union, as the defender of the cause of peace, has not only won the confidence of the popular masses of the whole world, but has also made all those who are threatened with imperialist aggression look to the first state of the workers and peasants.

The speech of the French Minister of Foreign Affairs, M. Barthou, calling for the entrance of the Soviet Union into the League of Nations in the name of the cause of peace, shows the influence of the strength of the Soviet Union and its peace policy even upon the Great Powers, to the extent that they are interested in the strengthening of the cause of peace.

124

Pravda *on* Litvinov's *Disarmament Proposals at* Geneva

"Iasnaia programa bor'by za mir," Pravda, *No. 148, May 31, 1934, p. 1.*

The Soviet delegation summed up in the speech of its chairman, Comrade *M. M. Litvinov* at the session of the General Commission of the Disarmament Conference which opened on May 29 in Geneva, the results of the more than two years of activity of the conference. The results are pitiful.

The Geneva conference has suffered complete failure *as a conference on disarmament.*

In the two years which have elapsed since the beginning of the conference, the capitalist countries, particularly the most aggressive of them, have achieved great success in the domain of *armament*. It is not unknown that Japan and Germany left the conference in order to carry on armament without any hindrance and with the aim of imperialist conquests, thereby dealing a blow to the idea of disarmament. The armaments race continues with ever increasing speed and in truly gigantic proportions. The propagation of militarism and chauvinism have acquired monstrous proportions. War is being openly preached on the pages of fascist newspapers and journals in Germany and Japan, and is being inspired by certain circles of English imperialism. The danger of a second imperialist war for the new division of the world is now stronger than ever before. There is nothing surprising in the fact that the fate of the conference is being questioned.

The responsibility for the failure of the conference falls entirely upon the capitalist world, and in particular on those imperialist countries which are preparing a new war in the near future or which are already waging it on the territory of the long-suffering Chinese people.

The Soviet Union has been and continues to be a supporter of *the most radical measures of struggle against the danger of imperialist war.* It has been and continues to be a consistent supporter of *universal and complete disarmament,* in which it sees "the most effective means for the destruction of the institution of war." The toilers of the Soviet Union as before are convinced that "there can be only one kind of peace—a disarmed peace," and that "an armed peace is merely an armistice, an interval between wars, the sanctioning of war in principle and in fact."

But, as is known, all the proposals of the U.S.S.R. concerning complete and concerning partial disarmament were rejected at the Geneva conference, and the capitalist countries are continuing to arm. Even now, after the failure of the Geneva conference is obvious, the Soviet Union declares, through Comrade Litvinov, that it is prepared to discuss any plan of disarmament which would have a chance of being accepted by all countries. The experience of the Geneva discussions, the rich experience of two years, shows that there is no hope that *all* countries will accept such a plan.

The situation as it has come to exist calls for corresponding conclusions. If disarmament, as *a means to guarantee peace,* has suffered defeat, then naturally it becomes necessary to find other means, because the Soviet Union is concerned, as it had been in the past, with the *guaranteeing of peace.* If the Geneva conference proved incapable of strengthening the general peace by such a means as disarmament, it by no means follows that the Geneva conference should be buried, as is suggested by the German fascists, Japanese imperialists, and the militant groups of other capitalist countries. No, whoever is interested in guaranteeing peace is duty bound to do everything possible so that the conference can *"search for other guarantees of peace, or, at least, increase the security measures of those states which, not having any aggressive designs, are not interested in war and which, in case of war, can only become the objects of attack."*

The conference needs a new, concretely realistic program of struggle for the strengthening of peace. *This program has been outlined in the speech of Comrade M. M. Litvinov* at the session of the General Commission.

The Soviet delegation's proposals are based on a realistic estimate of the situation. The danger of war and attack on the U.S.S.R. grows out of the intensification of imperialist contradictions. These contradictions have also resulted in a split in the anti-Soviet camp. There are now countries in the capitalist world which are actively aiming at war and which are openly preparing an attack on the U.S.S.R. There are countries which, although they do not wish to be drawn into war, are actually preparing the path for it, by pushing forward and giving encouragement to the warmongers. And finally, there are countries which are not interested in war now, which would prefer to avoid it, and which therefore are prepared to collaborate with those who are interested in the strengthening of peace. Such is the concrete situation which makes it possible to combine the efforts of several—actually the majority —of countries for the guaranteeing of the general peace by *new means.*

In rejecting the plans of complete or partial disarmament which were advanced by the Soviet Union, the capitalist countries proceeded from their class interests. Here two worlds met, two policies, two classes. In signing nonaggression pacts with the Soviet Union, pacts on the definition of aggression, these or other capitalist countries were also proceeding from capitalist motives. But here the contradictions between the imperialist countries came into play. A great many capitalist countries which had declined Soviet projects of disarmament, and *thereby rendered inevitable the failure of the Geneva conference in the first stage of its existence,* were obliged to meet halfway one or another peace initiative of the U.S.S.R., inasmuch as they themselves were threatened by danger and could not ignore such a tremendous factor for the strengthening of peace as our country represents. Therefore, it is completely possible that *effective guarantees may be taken,* even if one or another country does not approve of them, because "this should in no way prevent the others from coming even closer together in order to carry out measures which would increase their own security."

Comrade Litvinov offered a number of such measures. They were, first, *the acceptance of the Soviet proposal concerning the definition of aggression;* second, *one or another sanction against violators of the peace;* third, *separate regional pacts of mutual assistance, embracing one or another group of countries, proposed at the conference at one time by the French delegation.*

But the Soviet delegation offers at the same time something more than separate measures, separate guarantees. It proposes *to retain the conference, making it into a "permanent organ which is concerned in every way with safeguarding the security of all states, with safeguarding the general peace," into "a permanent peace conference meeting periodically."* "Up till now," says Comrade Litvinov, "peace conferences were convened mainly after a war and had the purpose of dividing the spoils of war, forcing hard and humiliating conditions upon the vanquished, redistributing territories, carving out states, and thus sowed the seeds of new wars. *The conference which I have in mind should be created for the prevention of war and its terrible consequences. It should work out, broaden, and perfect methods for strengthening security,* respond in time to warnings of growing war dangers, to the calls for help, to the 'S.O.S.' of the threatened countries, and *render the latter in good time all possible assistance, whether moral, economic, financial, or other."*

The program of the struggle for peace outlined by the Soviet delegation is *clear* and realistic, and it will find undoubtedly a wide response among the toiling masses not only of the Soviet Union but of the entire world. The danger of war threatens all toiling humanity. There is no country which can consider itself free of danger. Sooner or later it will touch the toilers of all countries. Let not the ruling classes of England or some other countries situated at the threshold of eastern Europe lull themselves with the illusion that they could succeed in directing the war into channels favorable to them. The marauders' calculations will not be justified, and these countries may find themselves the first in "hot water."

The statements of the Minister of Foreign Affairs of England, *Simon,* and the speech of the Minister of Foreign Affairs of France, *Barthou,* are brilliant illustrations of the estimate of the situation given by Comrade Litvinov.

The oratorical attempts of Simon did not conceal from anyone the fact that he, as the defender of German fascism, was against

Comrade Litvinov's proposal, which the French Minister of Foreign Affairs, Barthou, had supported. . . .

Simon's speech shows where the forces can be found which are pushing mankind toward a new catastrophe. The speech of Barthou shows that there are at present in the capitalist world also forces which are trying to prevent this catastrophe.

The Soviet Union has pronounced its weighty word. It has outlined its program of struggle for the strengthening of peace and security against the warmongers. This program corresponds to the interests of all toiling mankind, against which are directed the designs of the fascist enslavers and the militarist cliques. We do not doubt that this program will meet with complete approval by the broadest popular masses of the entire world and will be supported by the power and authority of our entire motherland, all of whose faithful sons stand on guard for peace, security, and prosperity.

125

Pravda *Sees a Desire for War in Certain English Circles*

Maiorsky (London correspondent of Pravda), "Raskrytye karty," Pravda, No. 149, June 1, 1934, p. 5.

"The great" London press does not conceal its annoyance at the impression created by the speech of Comrade Litvinov in Geneva.

After all, it is well known that certain circles of British imperialism have been working actively toward transforming the conference on disarmament *into a conference on armament*. The decisive role in this transformation was played by Britain when it made the question of Germany's arming the basic foundation of its position in Geneva.

The annoyance caused among English circles by the Soviet delegation's proposals was so great that they openly revealed the real nature of their position, which earlier they had camouflaged in polite diplomatic phrases.

. . .

The question of what is to be done with the Geneva conference has been discussed at length within the English ruling circles. After some private conversations, in the course of which the differences between the contending parties proved to be no greater than those between "a blue and a yellow devil," a decision was taken to liquidate the conference. Geneva has become embarrassing for carrying on diplomatic machinations behind the stage. Having made a mockery of the "parliament of sixty-four nations," English ruling circles have begun to prepare for a new chapter of diplomatic history, leading more closely and directly to the beckoning goal—a crusade against the U.S.S.R.

In this atmosphere of pleasant anticipation of the desirable outcome, peals of thunder were suddenly heard. It became known that the countries which are interested in the maintenance of peace had no intention of dispersing and abandoning the further struggle for peace. The speech of the French Minister of Foreign Affairs, *Barthou,* in the Chamber of Deputies has revealed France's interest in the entry of the U.S.S.R. into the League of Nations. The question of security and the entry of the U.S.S.R. into the League of Nations began to be discussed in the international press.

For the definition of the real foreign policy position of English ruling circles this discussion played the same role which litmus paper plays in chemistry.

. . .

A similar situation exists in the Far East. Not to mention China, which is being completely abandoned to being torn to shreds by Japanese imperialism, England demands the first sacrifices from the United States. By strengthening Japan morally and materially, England is driving the United States out of its positions in Asia.

But with the fact that still greater sacrifices are expected from *the small states* for the realization of the militaristic plans of certain British circles, the lordly masters of historical destinies have in general no intention of concerning themselves. Geneva fell into the disfavor of London to a considerable degree because of the necessity of taking into account "the little people of this earth," whereas war against the U.S.S.R. is inconceivable without the destruction of a number of powers, which could only lose in war. No matter what the outcome of war might be, they are doomed to destruction by English policy. Is it strange, therefore, that these states find it necessary to insist on a guaranteed peace?

In reality, English policy is creating a hopeless situation for Germany and Japan themselves. They are expected to carry out the most difficult work. They are being pushed forward under fire. Meantime a powerful air weapon is being built and Singapore [is being strengthened militarily], as a guarantee that in the future it will be possible to dictate whatever is suitable to the weakened performers of tasks which were actually beyond their strength.

But no matter what deceptive dreams someone may dream, sober reality speaks an entirely different language. The Soviet Union is in a favorable position and is confident of its forces. In the struggle against those who are preparing to attack it, it is assured of the sympathy and support of the toilers and the exploited of the entire world. An attack on the U.S.S.R. would be equivalent to an act of suicide for the attacker. The Soviet Union will vigorously and systematically struggle for the general peace, searching out the friends of peace wherever they exist.

126

Litvinov's Plan to Transform the Disarmament Conference into a Permanent Organization

Draft resolution proposed to the Conference on Disarmament, June 4, 1934. Soviet Union Review, Vol. XII, No. 7, July 1934, pp. 160–161.

On the basis of the report of the chairman of the conference and on documents circulated by him, bearing evidence to the fact that "parallel and supplementary negotiations," which took place between various governments after the last session of the General Commission in October 1933, did not remove obstacles which previously prevented the General Commission from drawing up a draft convention acceptable to all nations, and did not create conditions from which to expect a successful outcome of the discussion and drafting of a conversation at the present time,

Taking into account that "the general political atmosphere, which was not particularly favorable before the opening of the conference, has hardly improved during the existence of the conference" (see the speech of the chairman of the conference on May 29),

Continuing to recognize the tremendous importance of a reduction in armaments and its necessity as a measure in the general system of guaranteeing the security of nations and lessening the danger of war,

But considering that the further prolongation of the discussion on a reduction in armaments cannot at the present moment be expected to produce any effective results,

Maintaining a firm decision in no event to abandon efforts to attain a unanimous decision for a reduction in armaments, as soon as circumstances permit,

Noting that the present international situation is full of menacing symptoms of a growing danger of war and that the people, alarmed by this danger, expect from the conference the speedy adoption of effective measures for the preservation of peace,

Taking into account that the Disarmament Conference has included among its tasks not only the drafting of a disarmament convention, but the adoption of other measures of security for all nations, and that in its decision of February 25 it provided for the examination of all questions serving the "organization of peace," and that the lack of results up to the present time in the work in the field of disarmament and the political situation which has caused this lack of results, demand the most speedy adoption of all possible measures of security,

The General Commission decides:

First, immediately to resume the interrupted work on the consideration of existing proposals for pacts of mutual aid and defining aggression,

Second, to recommend to the plenary session, in view of the special importance acquired by the universal and uninterrupted organization and guaranteeing of peace at the present time, to declare the Conference for the Reduction and Limitation of Armaments a permanent body, renaming it the Peace Conference, with the following tasks:

a) Continuation of the work to reach an agreement on the

drafting of a convention for the reduction and limitation of armaments;

b) Drawing up an agreement and deciding on measures for creating new guarantees of security;

c) Taking every kind of preventive measure for the avoidance of military conflicts;

d) Control over the carrying out of the convention and decisions of the conference;

e) Consultation in the event of violation of international agreements for the preservation of peace.

NOTE: The renaming of the conference in no way infringes the former relations existing between the conference and the League of Nations.

Third, to instruct the bureau of the conference to work out rules for the conference in accordance with its extended tasks and submit them for discussion to a plenary session of the conference.

127

Pravda *on Recognition by the Little-Entente Powers*

"Uspekh sovetskoi politiki mira," Pravda, *No. 158, June 10, 1934, p. 1.*

On June 9 there took place the exchange of letters concerning the establishment of diplomatic relations between the *U.S.S.R.* and *Czechoslovakia* and *Rumania,* carried out between Comrade *Litvinov,* on the one side, and the Ministers of Foreign Affairs of Czechoslovakia and Rumania, Beneš and Titulescu, on the other. This diplomatic act acquires particular political significance in the tense and threatening situation which has arisen at present in Europe.

The Geneva "disarmament" talks, as their unfortunate course has proved, have so far contributed very little to the strengthening of the cause of peace. The frenzied armament race of all the imperialist countries is an indication that the storm clouds of the danger of war are closing in not only over the Far East but over Europe as well. Against this background the new act of peace which has been completed in Geneva represents one more link in the long chain of measures carried out undeviatingly by the Soviet Union for the strengthening of peace. The establishment of diplomatic relations between the Soviet Union and two states of the Little Entente wrests a further trump from the hands of those adventurous elements who continue to oppose the guarantee of security and who are hatching military intrigues.

It should be kept in mind that until recently no contact whatsoever existed between the Soviet Union and Rumania, and that it was only on July 3, 1933, during Comrade Litvinov's visit to London, that a convention on the definition of aggression was signed in which Rumania also participated. Between the U.S.S.R. and Czechoslovakia, in addition to the participation by the latter in the analogous convention signed in London on July 4 of the same year, treaty relations have existed already since June 5, 1922, when a provisional Soviet-Czechoslovak agreement was signed.

Nevertheless, the reactionary circles of Czechoslovakia have offered bitter resistance for many years to the establishment of normal diplomatic relations with the U.S.S.R. These circles, which have maintained close connection with the White emigration, hating the proletarian state, dreaming of an armed struggle against it, deliberately and systematically, to the detriment of the political and economic interests of their own country, disrupted the normalization of Soviet-Czechoslovak relations. The forces in Rumania hostile to the Soviet Union were still more active, exerting strong influence on its foreign policy and attempting to push it into anti-Soviet adventures.

The decisive changes which have taken place in Europe recently forced the leading circles in Czechoslovakia and Rumania to revise their position with respect to the Soviet Union. They became aware of the fact that the postwar structure of Europe, which had appeared firm and stable, has begun to undergo a process of disintegration. In the forefront of foreign affairs there is an increasing activity of imperialistic factors which are trying to bring about a new division of the European map by armed force.

The struggle of conflicting interests of the big capitalist powers threatens with fatal results a number of countries which might fall victims to imperialist expansion. It is not accidental that in the offices of the leaders of German fascism there hang maps of the future "Central Europe" which incorporate entire states which are now independent. It is not accidental that in the columns of fascist newspapers and journals there is a discussion of the fate of countries which "have no right to existence." The Danube Basin has already been transformed into a staging area, for the seizure of which a bitter struggle is being waged and over which the storm clouds are gathering ever more thickly. For this part of Europe the danger of war is no longer a question of the remote future. The atmosphere of instability caused by the approaching storm is beginning to affect the policies of the countries of southeastern Europe.

At the same time the economic and military power of the Soviet Union, which is playing an increasingly important role in international politics and which is making use of its influence in order to strengthen peace and combat the danger of war, has grown immeasurably. If a short time ago the proposals of the Soviet Union in the struggle for peace were ignored and were received with hostility, now the importance of the Soviet Union as the decisive factor of peace has become clear to everyone who has no interest in the preparation for a new war and who can expect nothing positive from it.

. . .

. . . The consistent policy of peace of the Soviet Union is already bearing fruit. And it is no accident that while the World Economic Conference in London of July 1933 was turning out to be a complete failure, Comrade Litvinov signed there the pact on the definition of aggression—a definition which played a major role in strengthening security. In the same way, the exchange of notes on the establishment of diplomatic relations between the U.S.S.R. and Czechoslovakia and Rumania in Geneva acquires particular importance against the background of the fruitless "disarmament" discussion, behind the scenes of which feverish arming is taking place and weapons are being forged for the approaching war.

. . .

128

Pravda *Sees Signs of Failure of the Dictatorship in Germany*

I. Erukhimovich, "Politicheskii smysl sobytii v Germanii," Pravda, No. 179, July 1, 1934, p. 2.

The signals of the growing internal political crisis of the fascist dictatorship in Germany follow one after another. After the Marburg signal of Papen, thunder in Berlin![1] Only thirteen days have passed—but how rapidly events are maturing and how hurriedly the fascist dictatorship is revealing itself and appearing in all its repulsive nakedness!

. . .

On June 30, 1934, the fascist dictatorship itself admitted *the failure of its policy*. It again resorted to machine guns, but this time *against its own guard*. No other way remains to it, even if the shots fired in Berlin and in other large centers of Germany at the same time destroy the confidence which the broad strata of the petty bourgeoisie had reposed in the fascist regime.

The fascist top leadership did not agree with a light heart to *open capitulation* before the "reactionary cliques" of which Goebbels was making fun only yesterday for demagogic purposes. This "great" chatterbox of the Third Reich has shut off the fountain of his eloquence (or was he shut up?) and has retreated. Goebbels more than any of the other fascist leaders had gambled on the word "socialism." It was he who introduced into circulation the current expression, "a socialism of action." Now his hour has come, the fascist dictatorship faces the masses *without masks* in its true image of counterrevolutionaries, finished and brutalized by fear and inner weakness. The contradictions between the fascist top leadership and its mass base have destroyed the demagogic cover of the fascist regime. It has broken up with a bang and has revealed what lay beneath it: *the mailed fist of finance capital.*

There is no doubt whatever that the hurry with which the Hitler-Goering group is acting *can be explained first of all by its critical position.* The speech of Papen, quite apart from the governmental stature of this personality, sounded an ominous warning to Hitler as the executor of the will of finance capital.

Finance capital, of course, is grateful to Hitler for his struggle against the working class, against the toilers. It is grateful to Hitler for creating the conditions for shameless exploitation and impoverishment. But it has become increasingly convinced that social demagogy in the form in which it was used is *an extremely dangerous weapon under present-day concrete conditions.*

That tens and hundreds of thousands of toilers deceived by fascism should become a weapon of struggle against the revolutionary proletariat—finance capital has nothing against this. It is even prepared to recognize the services of those same fascist leaders who are now swimming in their own blood; at an earlier time they carried out brilliantly the task which had been assigned to them. *Then* the dangerous playing with fire was justified, since fascism was able to captivate the embittered petty-bourgeois masses and certain strata of the backward workers by slogans of "dividing up the banks," the big department stores, etc.

Now the situation is different. Now these deceived masses demand that the fascist dictatorship *honor its own promissory notes.* But as Goebbels admitted in his speech in Essen, not a single one of these promises can be fulfilled. Papen demanded a turn to a "conservative counterrevolution" *before it is too late, before the toiling people of Germany demand a trial for their oppressors.*

In essence, Hitler was presented with an ultimatum: either obedience or a struggle. Papen could speak in those terms because behind him in this case stand the circles of heavy industry, the banks, and the Reichswehr. Hitler accepted the ultimatum, as is indicated by his orders and by all the measures taken yesterday, especially the order to "Maintain a loyal attitude toward the Reichswehr."

Hitler was forced to do this all the more expeditiously because *in the womb of the dictatorship itself an open struggle for power has begun.* In this atmosphere the danger has developed, as can be understood from the official reports, that *the squabbling groups within the fascist camp itself will eliminate each other. The group of Hitler-Goering was in the greatest danger during these days.* Formally, Hitler has liquidated the advocates of the so-called "second wave of revolution"; in reality, by the shooting of

Schleicher and scores of the most important leaders of the storm troopers, Hitler has tried to prevent a transfer of power into the hands of this group, which at a moment of internal crisis tried to oppose the group of Hitler, *making use for this purpose of the dissatisfaction of the storm troopers.* In the hour of confusion Hitler evidently did not forget the warning words of Papen about the danger of an "uprising from below"; in his ears echoed the words of the Vice-Chancellor: "Whoever irresponsibly plays with such an idea (of a "second wave," i.e.) should remember that following a second wave a later third one may easily follow . . ."

Hitler has forestalled his adversaries. For the time being their heads have rolled. But the fascist dictatorship now enters a new stage of its existence with its prospects for the future greatly impaired. What is happening in Germany merely reveals how insecure is the position of the ruling classes and how strong is the pressure of the masses. The future of the ruling classes of Germany is at stake. They do not believe that they will succeed in preventing the proletarian revolution except with the help of the still more merciless destruction of all those who stand in their way.

But where does this road lead?

The events of the last few days reveal the exacerbation of the situation in Germany and the discontent of the broad masses. The dictatorship is searching for a way out of the situation. It received a blow in Marburg. This was the first signal of the final days. Yesterday's events were a second signal. But German history moves on, it is approaching that turning point when the third and final signal will be given.

This time is already not far off.

NOTES

1. On June 17, 1934, Franz von Papen, the vice-chancellor of Germany, in a speech at Marburg University made an unfavorable reference to the minister for propaganda, Joseph Goebbels, who would not permit others to make any criticism of the Nazi regime.

129

Pravda *Considers Hitler's Regime Doomed*

"Obrecḧennyi rezhim," Pravda, *No. 180, July 2, 1934, p. 3.*

The fascist dictatorship in Germany has been dealt an irreparable blow. This does not mean that it has lost *all* possibilities of maneuvering. The events of the past few days, however, have shown that the social demagogy of German fascism has passed the zenith of its success and that it is now faced with an extremely dangerous descent on brakes.

During these days German fascism once again revealed itself as the agent of finance capital. The class-conscious workers were already aware of this fact. Today, however, even the backward sections of the workers are in a position to see clearly *who* it was that put Hitler's party into power, *whose* interests he is defending. They can now more easily understand the *price* of the refined and at the same time extremely crude demagogy with the aid of which the fascist dictatorship has deceived the toiling masses for seventeen months.

The Hitler regime created for finance capital incomparably more favorable conditions for the ruthless and unlimited exploitation of the proletariat and the working masses than ever before. But what has been done in this connection up to the present was only the *beginning* of the carrying out of the program for further plundering of the toilers by the capitalists and the landlords. Today the German bourgeoisie is making especially desperate efforts to extricate itself from the crisis at the expense of the millions; it is squeezing the last penny out of the German worker's wages. It requires a mute slave, humble and undemanding.

German imperialism is preparing for foreign political adventures and already, in the absence of large reserves of gold and foreign exchange, it is carrying on an intensified and dangerous trade war, for the purchase of raw materials through the securing of markets or in the hope of obtaining foreign credits. The toiling masses are already doomed to an existence of hunger similar to the war and blockade period. Millions of toilers are doomed to monstrous privation in order to provide the Krupps and the Thyssens, the stock exchanges and banks, with funds to be able to maneuver. *The basic meaning of the entire program of finance capital at the present moment comes down to this, the further robbery of the toilers.*

. . .

The general deterioration of the internal and external situation of the fascist dictatorship has led to an obscure struggle within its own ranks. The ferment became more and more dangerous as it spread more strongly and deeply within the ranks of the storm troopers. They all demanded with increasing persistency the fulfillment of the promises made to them and, first of all, *the checking of the predatory lusts of the financial magnates.* The mass base of the fascist dictatorship began to crack in a threatening fashion. The storm detachments put increasing pressure on "the leaders," demanding a struggle against "capital"; they had actually taken seriously the demagogic and inflammatory speeches of Hitler, Goering, Goebbels, and their own commanders! Having been a *bulwark of the apparatus* of the fascist dictatorship, the mass of the storm troopers gradually was transformed into a *hindrance* to the execution of the program of attack of monopoly capitalists. The moment came when the fascist dictatorship had to make a decision on a drastic change—to dissolve the storm troopers and to rout their leadership.

Hitler succeeded in isolating the Roehm group and in physically destroying it. But millions of deceived storm troopers still remain. *It is not possible to "liquidate" them all, but it is also becoming more difficult to deceive them.* The crack in the façade of the dictatorship will therefore continue to widen, the breach between it and its mass base will increase, *and this will lead to and is pregnant with all kinds of surprises in the isolation of the fascist dictatorship itself from its mass base.*

The fascist regime is slipping. In this respect the events of June 30 are extremely significant. The fascist dictatorship itself is devouring its "best men" . . . Their death will alienate from fascism those who believed sincerely in its demagogy. Today Hitler is balancing on the dead heads of his oldest companions, but he has shown the way and the methods for reprisals against other fascist groups. Hitler, of course, is no Caesar, and modern Germany has little resemblance to ancient Rome. The events of June 30 are more reminiscent of the customs in Ecuador and Panama. But Germany is not Ecuador, and *these murders will hardly be without their effect.*

The situation which has developed in Germany indicates that it is becoming increasingly difficult for the fascist dictatorship to prevent a dangerous alliance between the mass resistance of the working class against the plundering program of finance capital and the ferment among the masses of the petty bourgeoisie.

Fascism has shown itself to be the most deadly enemy of the petty bourgeoisie, whose hopes it exploited to the full in the struggle against the revolutionary proletariat. Considered from this standpoint, *the events of June 30 represent the biggest defeat of fascism, not only in Germany but also far beyond its frontiers.* The petty bourgeois masses honestly believed that fascism would secure a peaceful and comfortable life for them, expressing the words of Marx, "behind the back of society, by a private path." Today they are in a position to see that *for them, too, there is no other way out* but a struggle shoulder to shoulder with the proletariat under the leadership of the communist party against capitalist society and its gendarme, fascism.

The broad masses of the German population regard the Hitler dictatorship in a different light from that of February-March 1933 and before the event of June 30. Hitler, it is true, is still Reich Chancellor. For the time being he speaks in the name of Germany. But the master of the situation is that force of finance capital, the Reichswehr. All the "vital forces" of German imperialism in the broadest sense are grouping themselves around the Reichswehr—this is not merely an army in the narrow sense of the word; it is now the most tried armed support of the ruling classes, it is at the same time their political staff and their most trusted military instrument. *And it is by no means accidental that this instrument was sent into action at the moment when it became necessary to settle accounts with the leaders of the storm troopers.*

But what is to come next?

The mass basis of fascism has been seriously shaken. The fascist dictatorship is revealing itself more and more openly as the agent of exactly those "reactionary cliques" about which only a few days ago the fascist agitators were speaking with foam at the mouth. At the same time there is taking place an obvious *leftward* turn of the broadest masses. The former storm troopers are as yet unorganized and dismayed. *But they will find their way into the antifascist organizations.* This reshuffling of class forces is the characteristic of the approaching period, which will set its stamp on the tactics and maneuvers of the Hitler-Goering group.

The *old forms* of demagogy have proved unsuitable, but at the same time fascism is facing still more serious problems. The broadest offensive against the standard of living of the working class is impending. The fascist dictators are well aware that the German proletariat will offer stubborn resistance in one form or another to the predatory offensive of capitalism against its existence. Big class struggles are inevitable.

But fascism is facing a further test. The financial situation is rapidly deteriorating. Germany is moving toward inflation, and *this will bring with it the ruin not only of the proletariat but also of the broadest strata of the petty bourgeoisie.* It is therefore not impossible that the fascist dictatorship, whipped on by its own situation, will again resort to its favorite measure, social demagogy, *with a different content, for the purpose of holding the masses in check with demagogic promises, relying on the bayonets of the Reichswehr.* Undoubtedly fascism is also counting on its reserves—the kulaks and other strata among the rural population which still follow Hitler.

Now, however, after the events of June 30 the fascists have still less reason to hope for any prolonged success from their demagogic promises. The burden of taxation and the expenses of the economic policy of finance capital will weigh upon the toiling masses still more heavily. The economic position of Germany is *not improving,* but is *growing worse,* and this fact will determine in the last analysis the *acceleration of the toiling masses' move from the hitherto passive forms of resistance against the policy of robbery and oppression to open mass class struggle.*

But if this is so—and this is the direction in which the situation is developing—then new collisions *within the Hitler-Goering group* itself are by no means impossible, a repetition of the events of June 30 is by no means impossible. Such are the prospects for development.

German fascism will still try to maneuver. It will try to lean upon its tried weapon of mass deceit, adapted to the new situation. But this will only lead to increased vacillation of the deceived masses, at the same time curtailing the maneuvering possibilities and narrowing the base of the dictatorship.

The events of June 30 have shown that all the hopes of turning

Germany, this great country, the heart of Europe, into a fascist graveyard, have completely failed. For the time being the German bourgeoisie is *still* able to continue its rule, but its final collapse under the blows of the upsurge of the masses which is beginning is not far distant.

130

Radek Evaluates the Nazi Blood Purge

K. Radek, "Predvaritel'naia istoricheskaia proverka," Pravda, No. 181, July 3, 1934, pp. 3–4.

Many days will pass, and even weeks, before the world learns in detail what has just happened behind the scenes of the fascist dictatorship in Germany . . .

But the *historical meaning of the events* is already completely clear and was established by the entire world press on the publication of the very first reports about the events of June 30. It consisted of the fact that *German fascism, which from its very beginning has been a tool of the monopolistic bourgeoisie, which was able to come to power only under the mask of a "national" movement to save the petty bourgeoisie from ruin, has been forced to strike at its mass social base—at the petty bourgeoisie.*

This side of the affair is absolutely clear, and will soon appear in striking actions of economic policy. It would be naïveté to think that the stunning events of June 30 would be understood *immediately* by the petty-bourgeois masses and that German fascism has completely dropped the mask of "savior" of the popular masses. But the direction in which German fascism is moving—this will become clearer with every day to even the backward masses of the petty bourgeoisie. The decay of the petty-bourgeois basis of fascism, the further struggle within the fascist camp, will facilitate the development of the struggle of the proletariat—this *basic* force of the liquidation of fascism.

. . .

The events of June 30, 1934, in Germany have shown that *the coming to power of fascism is possible in the most highly developed capitalist country of Europe, in the country with the oldest, the most disciplined workers' movement*. It is true that the specific position of Germany as a vanquished country played a certain role here. It helped the fascists to utilize nationalist demagogy.

The German workers' movement is the strongest in comparison with the workers' movement in other capitalist countries. But in comparison with the strength of the German bourgeoisie, its organized character, multiplied by the elemental force of the millions of petty bourgeoisie ruined by the crisis and embittered by their miserable condition, seeking salvation in the utopia of the "Third Reich," the strength of the split social-democracy of the German proletariat proved insufficient to halt fascism from coming to power.

The German experience has not only proven the possibility of the coming to power of the fascists, but has also shown that a fascist power in the center of Europe can resort to savagery, to medieval violence, of a kind which even the gloomiest phantasy could hardly have admitted. The orgies of German fascism, the smashing of the legal workers' organizations, the destruction of science and art in Germany have had a *stimulating effect on fascist tendencies in all countries*.

. . .

Why is it that German fascism, having smashed the legal organizations of the working class, should now destroy its own petty-bourgeois base? It is obliged to do so because *it did not succeed and could not succeed in defeating the true revolutionary workers' movement. German fascism broke up all the legal organizations of the proletariat, it threw into jail and into concentration camps tens of thousands of revolutionary workers, thousands were slaughtered.* But even the savage forms of the fascist terror, public executions, the unheard-of savagery in the concentration camps—everything, which suggests some kind of madness, was the result of the conviction of the fascist leaders themselves that they had not succeeded and would not be able to succeed in getting the better of the workers' movement.

. . .

The savage debauchery of terror against the revolutionary workers *did not halt for a moment the struggle of the vanguard of the proletariat, the struggle of the communist party*. It is alive, it has preserved part of its old cadres, it has formed new cadres, and the struggle continues. But fascism has not only failed to get the better of the cadres of the working class, *it has also failed to get hold of the backward strata of the workers.*

The most profound discontent is growing among the social-democratic workers who have been shamefully betrayed by their leaders. *Under the blows of the fascist lash they are maturing the idea of the dictatorship of the proletariat.* . . . The idea of a single revolutionary front against fascism, the idea of the struggle for the dictatorship of the proletariat, will strengthen itself and grow.

· · ·

And what is the result? The result is a workers' mass of more than ten million, hostilely disposed toward fascism, drawn into the struggle against it, a mass which in the future will unite under the banner of the struggle for the dictatorship of the proletariat.

Classes are not divided by a Chinese wall from one another. The hostility of the proletariat toward fascism, the strengthening of the actively struggling core of the proletariat, *are bound to have a revolutionizing influence on the petty bourgeoisie* with which the proletariat comes into contact. It is bound to influence it all the more since fascism is forced to increase the exploitation of the petty-bourgeois masses. The petty bourgeois, who looked for salvation from fascism and who is becoming convinced that he has been the victim of a new deception, will now listen very attentively to every allusion, every opinion of the workers, especially when he knows that they have not capitulated.

· · ·

. . . The fear of demagogy because of its possible consequences has augmented the suspicion of the fascists toward their own mass organizations. Some of them were dissolved even before the events of June 30. But then the entire dissatisfaction of the petty-bourgeois masses was bound inevitably to center in the one mass organization which was still in existence—the storm trooper units. The time came when German fascism had to put an end to the storm trooper units.

· · ·

Together with terror against the working class, fascism now moves on to terror against the petty-bourgeois masses, in this way narrowing its own social base and broadening the circle of its enemies. Its strength will be less, that of its enemies will increase. One of the reasons why the working class of Germany was unable to render an armed resistance to the coming of fascism to power was the fact that the petty bourgeois leaned toward fascism. The withdrawal of part of the petty bourgeois masses from fascism, the vacillation of another part, will put an end to the political isolation of the proletariat . . . On the other hand, one of the reasons why monopolist bourgeois capital called fascism into power was that it is only possible to struggle against a mass revolutionary movement in a highly developed country with the help of a mass counterrevolutionary movement.

. . .

Even these immediate consequences will lead to the growth of the revolutionary struggle against fascism. This is inevitable, even if fascism is not forced to suppress new conspiracies by resort to arms, new attempts and new splits in its ranks. *The murder of Schleicher does not mean the removal of the actual competitor.* General Schleicher had lost the leadership of the Reichswehr, the trust of the landowners and of Hindenburg, and besides he was a very sick man. The struggle will have to be waged at the very top of the fascist leadership, men who, like Goering, are more capable of making organic contact with the old leading groups than can the petty-bourgeois elements. The struggle will have to be waged with the representatives of the *old bureaucracy and the generals,* who will take into account the growing disintegration of fascism and will gradually concentrate power in their own hands.

It is difficult at present to foresee the concrete development of events, but one thing is beyond doubt: *fascism, which was supposed to create an "iron authority" concentrated in a few hands, the power of one party,* power *without* a rift, has *proved incapable of this.*

All of this has happened to German fascism even though it has not yet entered a period of great pressures. But can it be said that the atmosphere of revolutionary movements or the atmosphere of war will eliminate the contradictory tendencies, consolidate German fascism into that concentrated force which it dreams of becoming? *Strong pressures strengthen a socially uniform body* and accelerate the breakup of socially contradictory ones. Therefore the dictatorship of the proletariat becomes stronger in battle, whereas the dictatorship of fascism will break apart.

Those who hoped to create in German fascism a steel hammer

that would pulverize the power of the German proletariat, and would fall upon the Soviet proletariat and its state, have now every reason to reflect. The international proletariat will do the same and will probably reach results which are not very favorable for German fascism in particular and for fascism in general.

131

Knorin on the "Crisis" of German Fascism and the Tasks of German Communists

Excerpts from a speech at the session of the Presidium of the ECCI, July 9–10, 1934. K.I., No. 22, August 1, 1934, pp. 23–29; The Communist International, *No. 16, 1934, pp. 537–539.*

. . .

We must state that on this occasion, in June 1934, the communists were not yet sufficiently strong to drive a serious wedge between the contradictions in the fascist camp so as to develop an immediate struggle against fascism. Nevertheless, they proved to be sufficiently strong to be able to utilize these contradictions in order to intensify their work among the masses and to draw to their side the elements who are now breaking with fascism.

The opinion is sometimes still expressed that the communists cannot seriously draw the petty-bourgeois masses to their side, that there is a deep gulf between the communists and the petty bourgeoisie. Talk can still be heard to the effect that the communists can only promise the petty bourgeoisie a number of years of civil war, collectivization, and the destruction of small-scale trade, while the petty bourgeoisie allegedly want to have their own farms, their own little stores, their own workshops.

The most determined struggle must be carried on against such interpretations. The fact that the petty bourgeoisie supported the fascists in 1932–1933 was *only* the result of the split within the workers' movement, the result of the fact that the proletariat was unable to develop the struggle and attract the masses of the petty bourgeoisie and peasantry to its side. But the masses of the petty bourgeoisie and the peasantry have become disillusioned with fascism, with all the parties of the bourgeoisie, and it is quite possible that now they will turn in the direction of communism, or at least will adopt a neutral position. It is not for nothing that the *Völkischer Beobachter* headed its editorial on June 30, "Hitler or Stalin."

. . .

How do matters stand with regard to attracting these strata to our side in Germany? Unfortunately, it must be admitted that recently the German Communist Party has carried on practically no work among the petty-bourgeois masses of the cities and the peasantry. On the eve of the fascist dictatorship a fairly good beginning was made for our work in the villages and among the middle strata in the cities, especially in 1931, but this beginning has been almost forgotten. The present crisis of the fascist dictatorship, which is casting the broad masses of the petty bourgeoisie and peasants into the opposition, requires from us a serious organization of this work. Meetings of storm troopers are being broken up, many of them have been arrested, they are forbidden to wear their brown shirts. Why? Because the masses of the storm troopers have reflected the real discontent of the toiling part of the petty-bourgeois masses, because at one time they seriously believed in the fascist demagogy, and now demanded the fulfillment of the promises given them. They have now realized that they have been duped. What should we do now? We must say to them, "You followed the enemies of the people, and together with them you murdered those who wanted a better future for the people; you, with your lack of consciousness, broke up the organizations of the working class; now you see that your behavior was harmful and disgusting. You can make amends for the severe crimes which you have committed against the toiling masses by carrying on jointly with all antifascists the struggle for the overthrow of the fascist dictatorship. There is still much which separates you from genuine revolutionary fighters. We can join together, however, on the basic thing: on the struggle against Hitler, who broke up your organization, on the struggle for the overthrow of the fascist dictatorship. Organize illegally, don't give up your weapons, prepare for the *real revolution of the people, for the proletarian revolution.*" The CPG has now adopted this line, and it seems to us that on the basis of this line considerable masses of storm troopers will actually come over into the ranks of the revolutionary fighters.

The party must do everything to make this path smooth for former storm troopers, in order to create a reserve for the proletarian revolution out of them.

Discontent is growing in the villages. The economic crisis hits the peasant with special force. But almost nothing is heard about our party work in the village. Of course, this is an exceptionally difficult task. It is understandable that up to the most recent past the party had to strengthen itself in the basic industrial centers—without this it would be impossible to go forward. But now already we must say, "The village must not be neglected, work in the villages must not be disdained now." If we do not do this now, organizations will be formed in the villages without our participation. The German comrades remember very well the peasant movement headed at one time by Klaus Heim. What kind of a movement was it? Recently I had occasion to read a detailed description of this movement. This was a spontaneous movement which rejected all parties, but which finally went along with the National Socialists. If we do not make a change, we will be faced by new organizations of the same type. Conditions now are favorable for us. There is not a single bourgeois party which has not proved bankrupt. We alone are the only force which has not deceived the peasant, the force which can save him. We must say this to the peasant. But in order to say this, the first condition is *the extension of our party work* in the peasant districts.

The most important thing is the organization of the proletariat, the strengthening of the communist party

I have already stated that the contradictions within the bourgeoisie, the opposition mood among the nonproletarian classes, the conflicts between these nonproletarian classes and the dictatorship of finance capital, constitute merely the indirect reserve of the proletariat. *Only a strong party can make use of this reserve*—therefore, all forces for the strengthening of the party! The German party has been able to go underground, to create a mass organization underground, numbering at least sixty thousand persons. It has been able to organize the publication and distribution of illegal literature on a scale previously unknown in history. But this is not all. The party has its cells in the industrial enterprises; a relatively larger number of party members now work at the enterprises than before the fascist revolution. But these cells still work weakly. Each party member carries out the responsibilities assigned to him, and carries them out heroically. But the cells do not get together, they do not discuss the questions of the workers' life in the factories and

plants. Therefore many questions which are exceptionally important for the working masses slip past the communists. There are
district committees, but they also do not work collectively. They do
not discuss the questions which interest the working masses of the
district, they do not display sufficient initiative. Of course, it is very
difficult and dangerous now to hold conferences, but an exchange of
opinions among members of the party is essential. Without this
there can be no real leadership of the party organizations, without
this the party organs will not be in touch with the interests and
inquiries of the broadest masses. Within the German party the
center of gravity of the leadership has now been shifted to the
instructor apparatus. This is good from the viewpoint of carrying
out centralized decisions from above, but it bureaucratizes party life
and makes the party cumbersome. Therefore there must be a
change in the direction of strengthening initiative from below.

The situation is that every day brings important events: new
fascist laws appear, directed against the workers; the fascist apparatus changes; actions by the masses in the factories and plants may
begin. Rapid response is demanded from the party organizations; it
is demanded that *the party formulate the public opinion of the
masses* in regard to each new decision of the fascists.

Unfortunately this still is being done to an inadequate degree;
the slogans of the party are correct, the formulation of general goals
and the definition of prospects are correct, but they do not sufficiently analyze concrete occurrences at the factory, at the plant.
This situation must be radically changed. Now the most important
task is to react in good time to all new occurrences in the workers'
life, to all the measures of the fascists. Then the party will obtain
significant big success. For this purpose the party apparatus must be
reorganized; notwithstanding the terror, the masses must be given
the opportunity to manifest initiative in the party organizations.
Everything indicates that this is possible.

Concerning the United Front

The most important question facing the CPG, as well as the other
parties, is the question of the tactics of the united front. It is true
that German social-democracy has been smashed. There is no
centralized social-democratic party left at present in Germany. Even
Stampfer says that social-democracy has seemed dead up to the very
recent past. . . . But *local social-democratic organizations have
been maintained, and in some cases they are mass organizations.*

They have no clear program, they have no centralized leadership. Right now discussions are taking place on the program question, on the question of cadres, on the question of leadership. This is the most favorable moment for us to approach the social-democratic workers and *help them find the way to communism.* Therefore, the German Communist Party must use widely the tactics of the united front, *propose to the local social-democratic organizations to carry on a joint struggle against fascism, and, as we draw nearer to them, take a line toward unification on the basis of the program and tactics of the Communist International.* In some places this has been done, with great success. But in many cases our party organizations have little interest in attracting former social-democrats into the ranks of the communist party. In many cases our comrades have feared to draw them into the ranks of the party on the grounds that they still have many social-democratic ideas, that they do not agree with our formulations. This, of course, is true. Former social-democrats cannot become communists all at once.

In order to win social-democratic workers over to the side of the communist party, it is necessary for every agitator seriously to think through his entire argumentation against social-democracy. But it is exactly here that we encounter a great oversimplification.

For example, an orator demands that the social-democratic workers accept our correct formulation, that social-democracy and fascism are twins, and applies this formula to the present illegal social-democratic workers' circles, which have been organized for the struggle against the fascist dictatorship. For example, an agitator demands that the social-democratic workers accept our correct international formula that social-democracy is the chief social support of the bourgeoisie and in this connection argues that this is the case now in Germany with regard to the illegal social-democratic workers' circles, which have been organized for the struggle against the fascist dictatorship.

If these agitators were to think through their argumentation seriously, they would arouse the hatred of the masses for the entire social-democratic policy, they would convince the workers that the communists were right in calling fascism and social-democracy twins and the leaders of social-democracy social-fascists, but by over-simplified argumentation they often hinder the united front and the approach of these workers toward communism.

To whom is it not clear now that Wels, Severing, Loebe are guilty of torturing the German workers? To whom is it not clear now that without them and many other social-democratic leaders there would be no fascism, there would be no dictatorship of the bourgeoisie in general? Without social-democracy, fascism could not have triumphed. But it is also true that monopoly capital resorted to open fascist dictatorship because the social-democratic leaders were no longer able to restrain the growth of the revolutionary upsurge of the masses, in their own organizations as well, and to ensure the implementation of the measures of finance capital. For that reason the bourgeoisie fired Wels, Severing & Co. But they broke up the mass organizations of social-democracy because they feared them as workers' organizations, which might go over to the side of revolution, because they could no longer rely on them.

The fascist dictatorship in Germany rests not on social-democracy but on the Reichswehr, the police, and the mass fascist organizations. Wels and Severing, of course, are willing to serve the bourgeoisie in the future also, and it is for this purpose that Wels is seeking for contacts with the working masses in Germany.

He will try to utilize the social-democratic tendencies that still survive among the masses. It is necessary, therefore, to carry on a struggle against these survivals. Wels will try to hold back the social-democratic groups from a united front with the communists, so we must intensify the struggle for the united front.

The situation in Germany has changed. But even now it is correct to call Wels a social-fascist, it is correct that the fascists and social-democracy led by Wels were twins.

But the illegal social-democratic groups which are now carrying on work in Germany are not social fascists and do not constitute the social support of the bourgeoisie: they are on the road toward communism, they must be won for the communist party . . .

If a few sectarian errors are corrected, then without question our party will have big successes in employing the tactic of the united front. Our tactic of the united front has brought important successes in a number of countries, particularly in connection with the campaign to free Comrade *Thälmann. Comrade Thälmann can be saved only by the struggle of the broad masses for his release, first of all in Germany itself, in England, in France and the United States.* Our struggle for the release of Comrade Thälmann must be strengthened by every means. But in addition to its immediate goal, the release of Comrade Thälmann, this struggle also has major general political significance. If the broad masses of the social-democratic workers rise for the struggle for the release of the leaders of the communist movement, Comrades *Dimitrov* and *Thälmann*, that means that in the future they will listen to the words of these leaders of ours and will follow them. The struggle for the release of Comrade Thälmann, like the struggle for the release of Comrade Dimitrov, *is a struggle for winning over to our side new broad masses of workers.*

. . .

132

Pravda *on the Importance of an East European Locarno*

"Vostochno-evropeiskoe Lokarno," Pravda, *No. 194, July 16, 1934, p. 1.*

. . .

As the result of the London negotiations [between France and Great Britain], two realistic prerequisites have been created for the establishment of regional security pacts. The leading circles of England have come to the conclusion that under the present correlation of forces, the best solution of all the problems which at present aggravate the relations between the major states of the European continent would be the establishment of a system capable of establishing security.

Italy has also taken a favorable attitude to the Eastern Locarno. Thus the most important powers have come out in favor of the strengthening of security.

The statement by the English Minister of Foreign Affairs, *Simon,* in the House of Commons, and also the speeches of English statesmen so well known to our country as Austin Chamberlain and Winston Churchill, indicate that the ruling circles of England have decided to support France's efforts. Thus we are able to note the progress of the idea of peace and security. Simon, Chamberlain, and Churchill have all supported in the House of Commons the project of an East European security pact. From the rostrum of the English parliament in the words of the most important political figures of England, it was recognized, in connection with the discussion of the results of the London negotiations, that "the U.S.S.R. is undoubtedly interested in the maintenance of peace." All these facts are a witness to a certain change that has taken place in favor of peace, which it is impossible not to welcome.

Wherein lies the significance of the East European pact, the draft of which is being discussed by the entire world press? Its significance lies in the fact that it provides a basis for the defense of peace and for the strengthening of normal relations among the East European states.

There can be no doubt that the East European pact would also play a very important role in the consolidation of peace not only in Europe.

As can be seen from the numerous reports of the foreign press and from the official communiqués about the London negotiations, the draft of the pact envisages the adherence to it of the U.S.S.R., Germany, Poland, Czechoslovakia, and the Baltic states. All states which sign the pact guarantee the integrity of each other's frontiers. The draft of the pact presupposes that, in order to make it fully successful, the entrance of the U.S.S.R. into the League of Nations is imperative. As is known, both France and England have spoken in favor of the U.S.S.R. entry into the League.

During the London negotiations between Barthou and representatives of the British government, the question of the agreement between the U.S.S.R. and France was also touched upon. According to this agreement, both parties guarantee each other's frontiers. There is no doubt that such an agreement would provide a new powerful guarantee of security and peace in Europe.

As is known, the English reservations required as an absolute condition for the East European Locarno, first, that Germany should be drawn into it and, second, the principle of complete reciprocity of guarantees given each other by the U.S.S.R., Germany, and France. These reservations did not meet with objections during the London negotiations, and they will undoubtedly not meet with objections when the question of concluding the pact is posed on a realistic basis.

It is not difficult to understand the situation which would be created in Europe by the realization of those plans which were discussed in London. There is no doubt that the world [or "peace" —*mir*] will gain by it. And after all, this is the most important factor for the popular masses of all countries.

But it is known that the aspirations and expectations of the popular masses do not always coincide with the intentions of the ruling circles. Some countries, the people of which have had sufficient bitter experience of all the horrors of past wars, find it possible to advance various objections against the idea of the regional security pacts, and particularly against the East European pact. These objections deserve attention.

It is being maintained that the complete equality of all participants is an indispensable condition for joining the East European pact. But is it not clear that the East European pact actually provides *complete equality for each of its members insofar as security is concerned?* All participants have an *equal right* to share this blessing, and *the pact grants them this right to an equal degree.*

The East European pact should be instrumental in providing the prerequisites for reducing *the burden of armaments* which the popular masses have to bear. It in no way serves as a pretext for a new arming.

But there are other claimants to objections against the draft of a West European pact. It cannot be said that these objections are in any way better grounded than the first. These critics to whom we refer, who do not formulate their objections openly, nevertheless make it sufficiently clear that their agreement to the draft of a West European pact depends upon the acceptance of a number of conditions that concern prestige, *which have no direct bearing on the East European pact.*

These critics even go so far as to state that they are "critically disposed" to the system of multilateral agreements. They prefer "the path of realistic, concrete bilateral treaties." These "critically disposed" individuals seem not yet to realize the significance of the changes which have taken place in the international situation, and are continuing to live in the past. In any case they do not realize either the popularity which the idea of an East European pact has *already* acquired or the negative effect that their stubborn advocacy of their own unfounded notions is bound to produce. Any country that wants peace and security cannot fail to appreciate the significance of the regional East European pact.

As to the toilers of the Soviet Union, they can only welcome every step taken that brings closer the realization of this undoubtedly important factor of peace. The Soviet Union is guided unalterably in its foreign policy by the interests of preserving peace. Our government follows strictly the instructions of our great leader, Comrade Stalin: "If the interests of the U.S.S.R. demand a rapprochement with one or another country which is not interested in the violation of peace, we shall agree without the slightest hesitation . . . We stand for peace and will defend the cause of peace

. . . Whoever wants peace and seeks business-like relations with us will always find support in us . . . [ellipses in original]

"Such is our foreign policy." [Stalin, *Sochineniia*, XIII, 302–303, 305.]

Such are the principles which predetermine the position of our country in regard to the East European security pact.

133

An Analysis of Far Eastern Tensions

L. I., "Bor'ba Iaponii, SShA i Anglii za Tikhii okean," K.I., No. 20 21, July 20, 1934, pp. 30–31.

The Pacific Ocean problem is one of the most important key problems in world politics. On the Pacific the interests and aspirations of the major imperialist powers interweave and come into collision with one another. In the basin of the Pacific Ocean and in the regions adjoining it are found the most important colonial possessions of England, and also of France and the U.S.A. As for Japanese imperialism, all the paths of its grasping policy run through the Pacific Ocean, in the various sectors of which its aggression is increasingly manifested. The most important sector of the Pacific Ocean basin at the present historical stage is undoubtedly China. The struggle of the imperialist powers for the gigantic Chinese market, for "spheres of influence" in certain regions of the country, or for their outright seizure, is becoming increasingly acute. On the other hand, the resistance to the imperialist seizures by the national-liberation movement of the toiling masses of China is growing. The existence of the soviet districts in China, which are growing stronger, serves as a guarantee that in the future the Chinese proletariat and peasantry, having taken the path of liberation simultaneously from the chains of foreign imperialism and enslavement by their own "national" bourgeoisie and landlords, will lead China out of the condition of being a passive "object" of Pacific Ocean politics.

For the Soviet Union, with its extensive sea and land frontiers on the Pacific Ocean and in the Far East, the problem of the Pacific Ocean is of tremendous political significance and is closely connected with the vital interests and defense of our country.

Imperialist Japan, pursuing its annexationist policy on Chinese territory—with unequivocal encouragement by English imperialism—is simultaneously making increased preparations for an attack on our Union. All of this makes it obligatory and highly important for us to watch very carefully all changes in the Pacific Ocean situation, the development of contradictions between the imperialists, and in particular, the strategic situation and the immediate preparations of the imperialist powers for war on the Pacific Ocean.

The most recent events have signalized the unprecedented intensification of the contradictions and the growth of the war danger. The declaration of the Japanese Ministry of Foreign Affairs in April 1934, notwithstanding the "reassuring" explanation made later, means nothing less than an official claim by Japanese imperialism for a protectorate over all of China. Contrary to the Nine-Power Treaty concluded at Washington in 1921, the signatories of which promised to support the "Open Door policy" in China, Japan now claims control of both the political and the economic relations of China with other states, under the pretext of Japan's "mission" to "defend the seas" in the Far East. In that way Japanese imperialism aims to ensure for itself a monopoly of new territorial acquisitions in China and at the same time to cut off China's contacts with other powers. Tokyo considers as particularly undesirable America's financing of China, which, it is true, is limited at present, and the planning of aviation routes and airlines in China with American assistance. Likewise, Japan imposes beforehand its "veto" on the comparatively modest projects of financial assistance to the Nanking government proposed by the League of Nations. The recent incident in regard to the "disappearance of Kuramoto" shows that the annexationist intentions of Japan are not limited to the northern sectors of China only and that the other regions of the country are likewise their object.

In pursuing its annexationist policy in China and preparing for war against the U.S.S.R., Japan is building up its armed forces on land, on the sea, and in the air at frenzied tempos.

The reply of the U.S.A. to Japanese aggression in the Far East is an equally accelerated strengthening of its armament and the adoption of a new program for military, naval, and air construction.

Great Britain, likewise, is taking "precautionary" measures with respect to all possible adversaries.

Thus the Pacific Ocean situation is becoming ever more entangled and exacerbated. It differs sharply at the present time from the situation which existed in the period of the relative stabilization of capitalism, which was expressed in the system of the Washington agreements, which at present have been nullified in fact.

. . .

The situation is bound to become even more aggravated and complicated in the future, in 1935, first, because the withdrawal of Japan from the League of Nations becomes effective and, second, because a new naval conference is to be held. The former means that the "mandate" given Japan by the League over a group of islands in the northern Pacific (the Mariannas, the Carolines, and the Marshalls) will no longer be valid (these islands belonged to Germany before the war, and were seized by Japan during the war). In spite of the "delicate" situation which will thus arise, Japanese imperialism has announced in advance its firm intention to hold the islands, which constitute an important strategic position on the Pacific Ocean, regardless of future decisions of the League of Nations on this question.

At the naval conference, the Washington and London agreements on the limitation of naval armaments are to be re-examined. The very fact that at present the political basis of these agreements no longer exists (it rested on the Nine-Power Treaty on China concluded at that time in Washington, which has been actually torn up by Japanese bayonets) makes the possibility of the renewal of the naval agreements highly improbable. . . .

134

On Germany's Rejection of the East European Pact

Dzh. G., "Germanskii otvet," Pravda, *No. 253, September 13, 1934, p. 5.*

Yesterday there appeared in the press a communiqué of the German information bureau to the effect that the German government had made known to interested states its position in regard to the conclusion of an East European pact.

Germany is the one of the proposed participants in the East European Locarno which has expressed its attitude to the Eastern pact with considerable delay. The German government had sufficient time for that "careful study" of the draft of the Eastern pact to which the communiqué of the German information bureau refers. In view of this the public opinion of the entire world had a right to expect a reply of exhaustive clarity to the question which was in fact posed with absolutely exhaustive clarity.

However, the German reply has not justified these expectations. Actually this reply merely sums up all those arguments that have already been given repeatedly in the German press, arguments which cannot be regarded as substantial or as reflecting a genuine and sincere desire for peace and the strengthening of the security of central and eastern Europe.

What, then, was the question that was raised before the proposed participants in the East European pact? If one formulates it briefly, this question is as follows: *For or against the strengthening of peace and security?*

The question was raised in exactly this way because the significance of the East European pact lies in the fact that it provides the basis for the defense of peace, for the strengthening of normal relations between the states of eastern Europe.

The distinguishing feature of mutual aid pacts is that, "possessing equal rights and responsibilities and an equal measure of security, not a single participant of such a pact should be considered as encircled or exposed to any danger, if only he shares the desire for peace of the remaining participants" (Litvinov).

Mutual aid pacts really cannot be considered as the encirclement of anyone, inasmuch as all states of a given region may participate in them. Hence it follows with complete obviousness that every state which is truly interested in the maintenance of peace and the strengthening of security would *reply by unconditional adherence* to a proposal for a mutual aid pact, leaving the question of the solution of this or that detail to later discussions.

And it is characteristic that the majority of the proposed participants in the East European pact have acted in exactly that way. The statements of *Estonia, Lithuania,* and *Latvia,* which were published at the time, expressing the willingness of these states to join the Eastern pact, did not in any way close to these states the path of further negotiations, for the purpose of taking into consideration the special conditions of each country individually.

The German reply, however, advances a whole series of arguments *against the pact, and does not contain a statement of Germany's willingness to join it.* This can only mean that the German government actually declines the pact, and simply hesitates, or does not wish to state this openly before the entire world.

Instead of stating its readiness to support a measure which is directed at the strengthening of peace and security, the German reply raises beforehand the question not of the maintenance of normal relations but of their violation. This cannot but arouse perplexity, to say no more. The French press has already evaluated the German answer as a definite unwillingness to assist in the strengthening of peace. . . .

The German answer in reality gives sufficient ground to think that the real aspirations of German policy are those objections of the German press which are based on premises directed not toward the strengthening of peace, but at the exact opposite. We may recall the arguments of the influential economic organ, *Wirtschaftszeitung,* which stated openly that the new pact might be an obstacle to the "freedom of movement" of Germany in the east. We may also recall the documentation of the *Börsenzeitung,* which wrote that Germany should not participate in the Eastern pact because the guarantee of the western borders of the U.S.S.R. would alleviate the position of the latter vis-à-vis Japan.

The delay in Germany's reply on the question of its attitude to the Eastern pact had already aroused misgivings among all sincere advocates of peace and doubts about the sincerity of the peace declarations of the German government. The German answer still further strengthens these doubts.

135

Pravda *on Soviet Entry into the League of Nations*

"SSSR prodolzhaet bor'bu za mir," Pravda, *No. 257, September 17, 1934, p. 1.*

Telegrams from Geneva of September 15 report that the majority of powers which are members of the League of Nations have approached the Soviet government with an invitation to join the League of Nations in order to strengthen its struggle for the consolidation of peace. This invitation was the result of the initiative of the French government, which approached the other powers with indications of the necessity of drawing the U.S.S.R. into the League of Nations in view of the general aggravation of the international situation.

The contradictions among the European powers which were expressed in Germany's withdrawal from the League of Nations and in its rearming, in the conflict between fascist Germany and Austria which led to the mobilization of Italian troops on the Austrian border, and the growth of contradictions in the Far East leading to the seizure of Manchuria, to the enormous Japanese rearmament, to the growth of Japan's aggression against the U.S.S.R., to the sharpening of the naval armament race, to the withdrawal of Japan from the League of Nations—all these facts are the signs of the growing war danger. It finds expression in the fact that from the moment of the opening of the Conference on Disarmament to the beginning of 1934, expenditures on armament have increased by one billion rubles!

Imperialist tendencies are inherent in all capitalist countries. But not all capitalist powers find themselves in the same situation. Those powers which came out of the World War most enriched materially and territorially are not aiming at the present time at a new redistribution of the world. Other powers, which were defeated in the World War, or which did not receive everything they were striving for, which are suffering more from the crisis of capitalism, having no reserves which would allow them to hope to extricate themselves from the crisis, are aiming at present at a redistribution of the world as a means of healing their own wounds at the expense of other states. They think first of all of expansion at the expense of the U.S.S.R., and they are putting forward a plan for an anti-Soviet war, hoping for the support of the entire imperialist world. But war against the U.S.S.R. would lead to the explosion of all the imperialist contradictions. It might prove to be that stone which sets in motion the avalanche of a world war. Therefore, in spite of their hostility to the Soviet land which is building socialism, in some capitalist powers there have arisen apprehensions that the anti-Soviet enterprises of the adventurist imperialist elements might serve as the beginning of a new world war directed also against a number of the imperialist powers.

Thus it happened that after the withdrawal of Germany and Japan from the League of Nations, which up till that time was an organization that united all the capitalist countries with the exception of the U.S.A., there remained in the League of Nations in a majority the large and small powers which fear a policy of the impetuous development of war. These powers have proved incapable of preventing the aggressive policy of Japan and the rearmament of Germany. Now, in the face of the growing threat of war, they are looking for new forces capable of struggling against the war danger, prepared to participate in the organization of the defense of peace, ready to assume responsibility for this defense. In spite of their hostility to socialism, their gaze is now fixed upon the U.S.S.R., the power which has shown its firmness and its determination in the struggle for the maintenance of peace.

Only the Soviet Union has striven for the realization of the basic goal of its foreign policy—the strengthening of peace. And it has achieved important successes on this path. The turn toward the better in our relations with many capitalist countries, and first of all the improvement of relations with France, the establishment of relations with the U.S.A., the numerous nonaggression pacts signed by the Soviet Union with its neighbors, the pacts on the definition of the concept of aggression—all this shows how step by step our country has won victories in its struggle for peace. What were the reasons for the change in the relations of our country with many countries of the capitalist world? *"First of all, the growth of the strength and power of the U.S.S.R. In our time it is not customary to take account of the weak; account is taken only of the strong"* (Stalin).

The Soviet Union has not rejected a single measure which might help to one degree or another the strengthening of peace. The great role which the U.S.S.R. has played as an active participant in the Preparatory Commission for the Conference on Disarmament and at the conference itself is well known. The strivings of the U.S.S.R. for peace have been imprinted in the numerous speeches of Comrade *Litvinov* at Geneva. By its struggle for disarmament, the Soviet Union has won enormous popularity among the popular masses of the entire world. And although the proposals of the U.S.S.R. were not accepted, they played no small role in the cause of the struggle for peace.

The Soviet Union has not rejected any kind of collaboration with those elements of the capitalist world which under present conditions were interested in not permitting a new war.

Already in December 1933 Comrade *Stalin* had given an exhaustive reply to the question of the *New York Times* correspondent Duranty concerning the U.S.S.R.'s attitude to the League of Nations.

. . .

The position of the Soviet Union has been made completely clear by Comrade Stalin. It is completely obvious that the attitude of the Soviet Union toward the League of Nations is determined by the attitude of the members of the League of Nations to the U.S.S.R., their attitude to aggressive plans no matter whence they emanate, by the capability of the League to play the role of that "obstacle" of which Comrade Stalin spoke. On this has depended primarily the readiness of the Soviet Union to support the League of Nations, "in spite of its colossal defects."

The Soviet Union, in giving its positive answer to the appeal of the thirty-four powers, is continuing its tested policy of the struggle for peace. The Soviet Union is entering the League of Nations as a great power, as a mighty factor of the struggle for peace, as an important international force. It is entering the League of Nations in the desire to utilize even the smallest possibility for preventing war.

Entering the League of Nations and setting themselves the task of the further undeviating struggle for peace, the toilers of the

Soviet Union will continue the cause of strengthening the economic, cultural, and defensive power of their great motherland.

136

Pravda *on Limitations and Possibilities in Soviet Participation in the League*

"Sovetskii Soiuz v Lige natsii," Pravda, *No. 260, September 20, 1934, p. 1.*

In his profound speech published yesterday in *Pravda,* Comrade *M. M. Litvinov* outlined before the plenum of the League of Nations the unanimous opinion of the toilers of our country on the significance of those events which have led to the entry of the U.S.S.R. into the League. Comrade Litvinov gave a thorough evaluation of the successful efforts of the majority of states which are members of the League of Nations, and in particular of the efforts of France aimed at bringing the U.S.S.R. into the League.

The first speech of the representative of the great proletarian power at the plenum of the League of Nations was awaited in Geneva and throughout the entire world with great anticipation. And this is not accidental. The entry of the Soviet Union into the League of Nations, the unanimous decision taken by the plenum of the League to choose the U.S.S.R. as a permanent member of the Council, represents an important and serious event, a great step in the struggle for peace.

The toilers of the Soviet Union, soberly evaluating the significance of the events which have taken place, note with satisfaction the important success of the peace policy of the Soviet government, a success which reflects the inner strength and power of our great country.

Comrade Litvinov outlined in his speech the basic principles which have guided our government in accepting the invitation of the thirty-four powers. These principles can be summarized as *the struggle for peace by every means which leads to this goal.* The

toilers of our country warmly welcome and approve the program of
the struggle for peace which was set forth in Comrade Litvinov's
speech, the program of collaboration within the framework of the
League of Nations in the name of the struggle against the threat of
a new war. *The U.S.S.R. will carry on this struggle as it has done up
to the present, being prepared for the sake of the maintenance of
peace to enter into the most far-reaching collaboration both within
and outside the League of Nations.* In doing so, the U.S.S.R. is
acting not only in the interest of its own security, but also in the
interests of all of toiling humanity, in the interests of the international proletariat.

In joining the League of Nations, the Soviet Union is well
aware of the fact that it is the only representative there of a new
world, the world of socialism. We understand perfectly well that in
inviting the U.S.S.R. into the League, the capitalist countries were
prompted by their class interests and were guided by their practical
political considerations. The peculiarity of the present situation,
however, lies in the fact that these considerations, independent of
their premises, *objectively help our proletarian state struggle for the
maintenance of peace.*

The Soviet Union understands very well that it is entering an
organization founded by the capitalist powers. It therefore does not
assume in any way responsibility for those decisions of the League
and for those points in its Covenant which have been adopted
without its participation and consent.

*The Soviet Union enters the League of Nations as a state of the
victorious proletariat, not renouncing any special features of this
state, true to its aspirations and ideals.* It enters the League of
Nations because the objective situation and the many assurances
given by the majority of the members of the League of Nations have
provided our country with reason to consider that this form of
international collaboration will permit the Soviet government to
struggle even more actively, even more energetically, for the attainment of the goals for which it strives: *the organization of peace, the
active and effective struggle for the guarantee of security, against
the threat of war which constitutes the greatest danger for all
peoples and which cannot be averted by invocations and prayers.*

But it seems that each serious occurrence also has its comical
side. One cannot of course treat in any other way the conduct of the
Swiss delegate *Mott,* the Portuguese delegate *Mat,* the delegate of
Holland, and so forth. In the strictly business-like atmosphere of
Geneva they introduced in recent days an element of the pompous

provincialism of European and non-European out-of-the-way places. The great statesman-like mind of M. Mott and his colleagues was utterly incapable of grasping the events which had taken place! It is not so difficult to guess whose orders these gentlemen were following when they spoke against the invitation of the U.S.S.R. into the League of Nations; there are still enough elements hostile to the U.S.S.R. in the capitalist world. The hysterical malice against the proletarian state of these political shopkeepers who are hardly noticeable on the international arena, and who only make themselves known by their specific odor, can only evoke a smile from us.

At present, a question is being settled which concerns the essential interests of all toiling mankind—whether there will or will not be a new bloody slaughter which is being actively prepared by two or three bellicose fascist-militarist powers, whether a war is or is not to take place which threatens equally almost all the capitalist countries, because this war will concern a new redistribution of the world.

The Soviet Union is fully aware of how limited are the means and possibilities of the League of Nations, but it declares through Comrade Litvinov its conviction that *"with a firm will and the harmonious cooperation of all its members a great deal can be done at any given moment for the maximum reduction of the chances of war."* If this is actually the aspiration of the majority of the members of the League of Nations, it will encounter on the part of the U.S.S.R.—the great proletarian power—the warmest support, and will find in it a consistent and powerful collaborator in the task of ensuring peace.

The Soviet Union evaluates fully and seriously the meaning of the events of September 18, 1934. But the toilers of our country know that the limits of international collaboration and its continuity, as well as the grouping of the forces within the camp of imperialism, are determined by the contradictions which corrode the capitalist world.

The elements which are hostile to our country, which are hostile to the cause of peace, have by no means laid down their arms. They will make every possible effort to organize new blocs against the U.S.S.R., to explode from within the present correlation of forces in their own camp.

Therefore, the untiring care for the strengthening of the economic and defensive power of our Land of Soviets is, as before, the most important and essential part of our further struggle for peace and security.

137

Comments on Soviet Membership in the League

"SSSR i Liga natsii," K.I., No. 26–27, September 20, 1934, pp. 3–11.

The entrance of the U.S.S.R. into the League of Nations has become a fact. To the invitation by thirty-four states headed by France, England, and Italy, the Soviet government responded by agreement, after which came the formal acceptance of the U.S.S.R. as a new member of the League of Nations and the assignment to it of a permanent seat on the Council of the League. September 18, 1934, is a date of great international significance, it is a major victory for the peace policy of the U.S.S.R.

But whereas this event has been almost universally appraised as a new outstanding victory for the Soviet Union's foreign policy, the *interpretation of the motives* which prompted a number of leading imperialist powers to invite the U.S.S.R. to join the League of Nations and of the motives which prompted the U.S.S.R. to accept this invitation, and in particular the evaluation of the *consequences* which may ensue from this entrance *differ radically* among, on the one side, the imperialists, the reformists, and the social-fascists, and, on the other, the communists—the true exponents of the interests of the broadest toiling masses. Even in the camp of the imperialists, rent by internal contradictions, the greatest disagreement exists on this score.

Equally apparent is the attempt of the Second International to interpret this step by the U.S.S.R. as an alleged acceptance by the Bolsheviks of the social-democratic policy toward the League of Nations (see the social-democratic press of Czechoslovakia, France, and Germany, which is discussed below) .

Likewise there is the completely analogous self-deception on the part of the bourgeois press (*Le Temps* of September 17) , which alleges that a sharp turn has occurred in "the foreign and even the internal policy of the Soviet Union," an assumption which merely shows the extent of the bourgeoisie's desire finally to see a "new," i.e., a bourgeois Russia. Comrade Litvinov hit the nail on the head in regard to those who console themselves with such hopes when he emphasized in his speech of September 18 that the U.S.S.R. was entering the League of Nations as the representative of a new social and economic system of states, fully retaining its independence and the independence of its policy, relinquishing none of the characteristics of its government; that the U.S.S.R. bore no responsibility for the former actions of the League of Nations; that in the future it would not only refuse to participate in, but would oppose decisions and actions directed toward the oppression of peoples; that in general *"every new member entering an organization is morally responsible only for those decisions which are taken with its participation and with its consent."*

. . .

For the revolutionary proletariat the misinterpretations of the policy of the U.S.S.R. and the discordances in the camp of the imperialists in their evaluation of September 18 should serve as a warning against hasty conclusions, against unnecessary exaggerations and harmful illusions, of which the most harmful is the illusion that the entrance of the U.S.S.R. into the League of Nations disposes of the danger of war.

The Soviet Union understands very well that it is entering an organization created by the capitalist powers; it realizes how limited are the means and the possibilities of the League of Nations; it knows that the limits of international cooperation and its duration, as well as the grouping of forces in the camp of imperialism, are determined by the contradictions which are corroding the capitalist world.

We should not forget that not only in those countries which opposed the acceptance of the U.S.S.R. into the League of Nations, but even in the countries which were in favor of it, among the bourgeoisie and even among the ruling circles, there are passionate opponents of a rapprochement with the U.S.S.R. which conducted before September 18 and will continue to conduct after September 18 a frenziedly violent struggle for the organization of a war against the U.S.S.R. It must not be forgotten that Poland, having signed a pact of nonaggression with the U.S.S.R., thereupon immediately made an agreement with Germany, which is openly preparing an attack on the U.S.S.R., and that this same Poland, while it follows the three great powers in favor of accepting the U.S.S.R. into the

League of Nations, stubbornly opposes the conclusion of an Eastern pact. The double game must not be forgotten which England is now playing in relation to the two powers who are equally the chief warmongers at present: her attitude to Germany, her differing attitude to Japan. (Incidentally, two days after the entry of the U.S.S.R. into the League of Nations, the London *Times* came out with some sharp anti-Soviet attacks.) *We must not forget the possibility of all kinds of unexpected turns in the policies of individual governments,* the conduct of which depends on the most varied fluctuations in these countries' domestic and foreign situation, for the development of which the times of stability or confidence in the future have long since disappeared.

Equally harmful, however, would be any underestimation of the importance of this major event, any oversimplified interpretation that in reality "nothing has changed," since this too would be an underestimation of the possibility of a sharper, more active struggle for peace on the part of the U.S.S.R. thanks to the new position that it has won.

For those tens of millions of toilers whose life hangs on the gamble of a new war, even the smallest step toward prevention represents a major achievement. For the revolutionary vanguard of the proletariat the defense of the Land of Socialism is the first-priority task and at the same time the necessary condition for a victorious revolutionary struggle against capitalism in their own countries. For the revolutionary vanguard in exactly the same way, even the mere postponement of the approaching war, by giving them the opportunity for further struggle to delay it or prevent it by means of the proletarian revolution, constitutes a great success for the entire world revolutionary front.

In order that the international proletariat will be able to utilize the new position which the U.S.S.R. has won for the cause of peace and for the realization of its class aims, it should clearly understand two questions.

First, what new conditions, what changes in the international situation, forced the overwhelming majority of the capitalist countries, headed by the Great Powers—France and others—*to seek at the present moment a rapprochement with the Soviet Union* in spite of their ineradicable hostility to the Soviet system?

Second, what reasons have led to *the agreement by the U.S.S.R. to join the League of Nations,* the evaluation of which by the U.S.S.R. has invariably come down to two factors: the characterization of its nature as a clearly expressed imperialist organization, and the conviction of the complete uselessness of its laborious efforts to organize a capitalist "order"?

The first question can be answered easily if one takes into account the extreme sharpening of the contradictions between the imperialists—in connection with the deepening of the crisis of capitalism—and the greatly increased power of the Soviet Union, the strongest factor of peace. The offensive of Japan against China, the seizure by Japan of Manchuria, have created a direct threat to the sphere of influence of the U.S.A. in China, and this, together with the growing power of the Land of Soviets, was the reason for the change in the policy of the U.S.A. toward the U.S.S.R., a change which led to the re-establishment of diplomatic relations between the two countries. In addition, the coming to power of fascism in Germany—which increased to the extreme the expansionist, annexationist tendencies of German imperialism, leading to the feverish rearming of Germany in spite of the Versailles Treaty, the accelerated preparations for the annexation of Austria and the Baltic states by means of pressure from within and from without, the efforts to convert the Soviet Ukraine into a [German] hinterland by means of an anti-Soviet war, creating as the result of all this a direct threat to the hegemony of France on the European continent and the threat of a war of revenge against France in the future—compelled France to alter its policy toward the U.S.S.R. and led to the invitation to the U.S.S.R. to join the League of Nations.

Hitler's coming to power in Germany was also bound to introduce serious changes into the policies of England and Italy. . . .

. . .

Such was the configuration of conditions which forced the bitterest enemies of the dictatorship of the proletariat to seek for rapprochement with the Soviet Union and bring about its entry into the League of Nations.

Turning to the question why the U.S.S.R. agreed to join the League of Nations, we must point out first that the entry of the U.S.S.R. into the League of Nations was the natural continuation of its consistent and successful policy of peace. The policy of the capitalist world toward the U.S.S.R., in particular in the form of the policy carried out by the League of Nations during the first fifteen years of its existence in the attempt to strangle it on the pretext that it allegedly pursued the goals of "Red imperialism," or at worst to draw it into the struggle of one imperialist group against another, was a failure. One after another the legends of the war plans of the Soviet Union, of a military alliance between it and Germany or Italy, have broken down. At the same time, by its systematic unmasking of the war plans of the imperialists, the Soviet Union was able on more than on one occasion to disrupt plans that were already prepared.

In the world situation which has developed, when Japan, having turned Manchuria into a military staging-area against the Soviet Union, resorts daily to war provocations, when German-Japanese rapprochement for the purpose of war has become a fact, there is no need to rack one's brains for an answer to the question of what caused the Soviet Union to accept the invitation to join the League of Nations.

The Soviet government, the proletariat of the Soviet Land, and the revolutionary workers of all countries harbor no illusion in regard to the League of Nations. But they recognize, on the one hand, the significance of that change in the attitude to the Soviet Union which has taken place as the result of the tremendous weakening of the capitalist world, the sharpening of contradictions among the imperialists, and the growing power of the Soviet Union. On the other hand, they realize that the attitude of the League of Nations toward war depends also on who composes it at a given time. For those imperialist cliques which, like Germany and Japan, have already made war the order of the day, the League of Nations, headed by those who at present are not moving toward war, has proved to be a hindrance on the road to the immediate unleashing of war, and even if only a small, only a formal one, nevertheless a hindrance. Influential in this respect were the growing contradictions in the imperialists' camp within the League of Nations, leading to the withdrawal from it of Japan and Germany, which left the League in order to free their hands for war.

The entry of the Soviet Union into the League of Nations will undoubtedly significantly enhance the League's role of a brake, which it has begun to play in the most recent past. In joining the League of Nations, the U.S.S.R. has in no way changed its basic attitude to the Versailles system; as before, it is against this system. But it is also against the revision by means of war of boundary lines fixed by the Versailles Treaty. It is against having a new counter-revolutionary war against the U.S.S.R., and an imperialist war for a new redistribution of the world, break out under the pretext of the revision of the Versailles Treaty. And by joining the League of

Nations the U.S.S.R. will have the opportunity to struggle even more actively, even more effectively, against the counterrevolutionary war directed at the U.S.S.R. and against the imperialist world war for a new redistribution of the world.

First, the entry of the U.S.S.R. into the League of Nations will contribute to the isolation of the chief warmongers—Germany and Japan—and will strengthen the position of those who, due to one consideration or another, at this time are against war but are vacillating.

Second, by entering the League of Nations the U.S.S.R. will be able, by means of multilateral agreements, to organize resistance to the warmongers.

This policy of disrupting the war plans of the most aggressive imperialist governments by means of a correct evaluation of all changes in international relations is the most genuine policy of peace, based on the interests of socialist construction, on the vital interests of the proletariat of all countries, on the interests of the proletarian revolution.

. . .

The French, German, and Czech socialists are simply lying when they attempt to prove that the Bolsheviks, in the form of the Soviet Union and the communist parties of all countries, now see in the League of Nations a bulwark of peace, a genuine pledge against war. This is not true. We, the communists, see in the participation of the Soviet Union in the League of Nations only a modest chance of delaying the approach of war, and we believe it would be a crime against the entire international proletariat to ignore this chance, no matter how modest it might be. Neither those thirty-four states which invited the Soviet Union, nor even the powers which were the sponsors of this invitation, and still less the states which voted against the admission of the Soviet Union, can be in any way the guarantors of the maintenance of peace. Both outside the League of Nations and inside it the imperialist contradictions will increase. The specific weight of the Soviet Union within the League of Nations, and consequently its chance of influencing the development of events, will depend on the forces which stand behind the representatives of the U.S.S.R.—the growing socialist construction and the power of the Red Army in the Land of Soviets, and the revolutionary united antifascist, anti-war front in the capitalist countries.

. . .

138

The Comintern Calls for World Revolution

Appeal of the ECCI "To the Men and Women Workers of the Entire World, To All Toilers, All Oppressed Peoples," October 11 1934. K.I., No. 31, November 1, 1934, pp. 3–8.

Comrades, class-brothers!

Seventeen years have gone by since the time when the Russian proletariat under the leadership of the Communist Party of Bolsheviks, under the leadership of *Lenin*, overthrew the power of capital, the government of the bourgeoisie and landlords, and took power into their own hands.

The October socialist revolution, opening a new era in the development of humanity, won by means of the *armed uprising* of the Russian workers with the support of millions of peasants. It was prepared for by the heroic *struggle* for many years of the proletariat under the leadership of the Bolsheviks against the ruling classes. It was prepared for by the fact that the Communist Party of Bolsheviks, in irreconcilable *struggle against the conciliatory, reformist parties* of the Mensheviks and Socialist-Revolutionaries, won over to its side the majority of the working class and led it to the decisive struggle against oppression, hunger, and imperialist war, for the establishment of the dictatorship of the proletariat, for socialism.

The power of the working class in alliance with the peasantry, *the power of the Soviets* of workers', peasants', and Red Army men's deputies, constitutes a stern dictatorship against the exploiting classes. The Soviet power at the same time constitutes broad democracy for the toilers. This power was organized by the masses for the struggle against the furiously resisting exploiting classes, against the military intervention of the imperialists. It ensured victory for the proletariat in the civil war. It led the Land of Soviets along the path of industrialization. It achieved the victory of the kolkhoz system in the village. The dictatorship of the proletariat, under the leadership of the proletariat, assured the victory of the first Five-

Year Plan; it is leading on to victory in the second Five-Year Plan, to the building of a classless, socialist society.

The Soviet Union, the country of the victorious proletarian revolution and the dictatorship of the proletariat, demonstrates graphically to the entire world what the *working class* can achieve, even in a technically and culturally backward country, when power is in its hands.

In the countries of capitalism, where the bourgeoisie is in power, the cruel economic crisis has brought greater destruction than the recent four-year imperialist war. Even the most advanced capitalist countries have been set back by many years. The partial rise in production which has set in during the past year has not improved the situation of the toilers: millions of workers are condemned to hopeless unemployment, millions of peasants and farmers have been ruined, millions of young people entering life have been thrown out onto the streets, without work, without bread, without hope for the future. The want and poverty of the toilers are continually growing.

The dictatorship of the proletariat in the Soviet Union, carried out under the leadership of the Communist Party, has created the conditions for the uninterrupted growth of the well-being and culture of the toiling masses. It has converted [this country] into a land of socialism where there is no unemployment, where the wages of workers and employees rise continuously, where the broadest system of social insurance has been established, where every worker is firmly convinced of the coming day, where work has become a matter of honor and valor for the toilers. The socialist reconstruction of agriculture has annihilated poverty in the villages. It ensures the elevation of the entire kolkhoz peasantry to a prosperous and cultured life. The Soviet power has freed all the previously oppressed nationalities and has united them into a fraternal union.

The workers and collective farm workers of the U.S.S.R. are providing a brilliant example of selfless devotion to the cause of socialism, an example of genuine international solidarity with the oppressed and exploited of the entire world. The militant example of the toilers of the Soviet Union has already been followed by the worker and peasant masses of China, who have created the soviet power on part of the territory of their country. The Chinese soviets point to the sole road of salvation for the entire Chinese people and the toilers of all colonial countries from imperialist enslavement and the oppression of their own exploiting classes.

The exploited and oppressed of the entire world are defending the Soviet Union—the fortress of victorious socialism, the stronghold of peace, the great foundry of a new, socialist culture, *the base and support of the world proletarian revolution, the socialist fatherland of the workers of all countries and the oppressed peoples of the entire world, a bright beacon lighting the way for tortured humanity fighting against capitalist slavery.*

Over the toilers of the entire world hangs the threat of a new imperialist war. The capitalist world is feverishly arming, preparing new and previously unknown weapons of mass destruction. Japan and Germany are directly striving to provoke war. But war can be postponed only by means of the union of all the forces of the proletariat into a united front for a determined fight against capitalism. War, a new bloody extermination of the toilers, can be blocked only by means of a complete break by the workers with the compromising policy of social-democracy, only by means of the victorious struggle for the dictatorship of the proletariat.

In order to find a way out of the crisis in which the capitalist world is struggling, the bourgeoisie is still further intensifying the plunder of the workers, the farmers, the peasantry, the colonies, and the economically weak countries. It is trying most of all *to smash the working class, to deprive it of its last remnants of democratic rights, to cut down still further its beggarly wages, to make its situation still worse, to exterminate its revolutionary vanguard.* Fascism has come to power in Germany and Austria, it is in power in Italy and Poland, it threatens the toilers of all countries. As the storm detachments of the bourgeoisie against the working class, fascism first of all tries to organize an attack on the shock brigade of the world proletariat—the Soviet Union.

But the proletariat and the toiling masses will be able to repulse the attack of fascism if the proletariat establishes a *fighting united front* of its ranks and together with all the toilers carries on a *determined struggle* against capitalism.

The policy of conciliation with the bourgeoisie which was carried out by the leadership of the social-democratic parties tore away the victory of the proletarian revolution in Germany, Austria, Hungary, and Italy in 1918–1920. The policy of class cooperation of the social-democrats tied the hands of the working class, split its ranks and undermined its forces in the face of the attacking class enemy. The policy of conciliation with the bourgeoisie led to fascism in Germany and Austria.

There is no peaceful road to the power of the proletariat.

There is no peaceful road to socialism.

True to its historic mission—the preparation of the masses for the conquest of state power by the proletariat—the Communist International more than ever before calls on the workers to join together in a *united front for the organization of joint actions of all the workers against fascism and the threat of war, it calls on the workers of all countries to unite for the overthrow of the power of the bourgeoisie, under the tested red banner of Marx-Engels-Lenin-Stalin, under the banner of the Communist International.*

The idea of the storming of capitalism is maturing more and more in the consciousness of the masses. Social-democratic workers are breaking away from reformism and conciliationism with the bourgeoisie and are entering the path of the class struggle. In February of this year the heroic workers of *Austria,* having broken away in fact from the social-democratic policy of class collaboration, rose in arms in order to block the way to fascism. But they failed because the social-democratic party which was leading them disarmed them politically, did not prepare them for the decisive struggle, and did not lead them into the attack on capitalism. In France the working class in the February days gave an initial rebuff to fascism by a general strike. But this struggle against advancing fascism will be successful to the extent that the French proletariat outgrow their democratic illusions and form together under the banner of communism.

In October the toilers of Spain, headed by the working class, rose in arms to defend their bread and freedom, to beat back the attack of fascist reaction. The workers of Asturia, under the leadership of the communist party, went into battle for the power of the workers and peasants.

Ever more frequently, the workers who are organized in the social-democratic parties are beginning to break away from the policy of collaboration with the bourgeoisie, ever more frequently social-democratic workers together with the communists are beginning to join in the struggle against fascism, capitalism, and war.

Brother-proletarians!

The Communist International appealed to the Socialist International with the proposal to organize immediately joint actions by the communist and socialist parties in all countries in the defense of the struggling Spanish people. But at the moment when government artillery was destroying the mines of Asturia, burying alive the worker-miners who had taken shelter underground, at the moment when military planes were bombarding the cities and towns of Spain, when every day, even every hour, was costing the lives of thousands of heroic workers and peasants of Spain . . . *at that moment* the official leaders of the Socialist International, under a formal pretext, postponed the discussion of the question of joint action for three weeks.

The Communist International is continuing its policy of the united front. Proletarians of all countries, display your solidarity with the struggling Spanish workers! Come out as one man against the Spanish bourgeoisie, which is throwing all its forces into the bloody suppression of the working class and the peasantry! The Spanish workers who have entered into battle against capitalism are sons of our class. The workers of Asturia who have raised the banner of the struggle for the power of the workers and peasants are our brothers.

Their cause is the cause of the entire world proletariat.

Class-brothers! Comrades!

Strain all your forces in order to establish as soon as possible the united front of the working class for the struggle against fascism and imperialist war, for the struggle for bread and freedom, for the struggle for power, for socialism!

Social-democratic workers! Workers of all political tendencies! Unite under the banner of the Communist International! Follow that revolutionary path on which the Russian proletariat won the October Revolution, on which alone the working class can be victorious!

All for the struggle against fascism and war!

All for aid to the heroic workers and peasants of Spain!

Defend the Soviet Union—the socialist fatherland of all the toilers and oppressed, the bulwark of socialism and peace among peoples!

Defend the Chinese Soviets!

Long live the united front of the working class! Long live the fighting alliance of workers and peasants of the metropolis[1] and the colonies.

Long live the victory of the world proletarian revolution!

Long live the dictatorship of the proletariat in the entire world! Long live socialism!

EXECUTIVE COMMITTEE OF THE COMMUNIST INTERNATIONAL

NOTES

1. Used here in the sense of "colonial powers."

139

Radek Evaluates the Rapprochement with France

K. Radek, "Tenth Anniversary of the Establishment of Diplomatic Relations between France and the Soviet Union," I.P.C., Vol. 14, No. 57, November 10, 1934, pp. 1508–9.

. . .

The Soviet government is not a signatory to the *Versailles Treaty*. However, one must look facts in the face. What is left of the Versailles Treaty today? The provisions of the Versailles Treaty which burdened the masses of the people most heavily, namely, the *reparations*, have already disappeared. The provisions which prohibit Germany's rearmament and which the German bourgeoisie considers as the most onerous discrimination do not move us unduly. Our aim is to persuade all states to join in the work of consolidating peace and thereby to make possible *a reduction of the burden of armaments* which presses heavily on all peoples. In any case, the complaints of the German bourgeoisie against discrimination in the question of armaments are absurd for the simple reason that Germany long ago rejected in practice all those armaments limitations imposed by the Versailles Treaty. All that is now left of the provisions of Versailles are the territorial provisions.

We were never at any time in the least enthusiastic about the territorial provisions of the Versailles Treaty, but we do not believe that the redistribution of Europe which German imperialism would like to carry out would be in any way more just. When the states of Europe have made war more difficult and its consequences more dangerous and more problematical, then there will be time to think of measures to diminish the existing national antagonisms. At the moment, any appeal to the national question in Europe is nothing else but a cloak for fascist warmongering and a pretext for war.

On the tenth anniversary of the establishment of normal diplomatic relations between the Soviet Union and France, the peoples of the Soviet Union are openly in favor of *the further consolidation of these relations and in favor of close cooperation with France against the danger of war* and for the consolidation of the peace of the world. The closer the relations between the two countries become and the clearer and more definite their joint actions for the impeding of war become, then the more securely will peace be maintained both in Europe and in the Far East. *The rapprochement between France and the Soviet Union can be made into one of the most powerful diplomatic instruments for the consolidation of the peace of the world.*

140

Tass Explains the Reasons for Delay in the Sale of the Chinese Eastern Railway

"K peregovoram o KVZhD," Pravda, No. 320, November 21, 1934, p. 1.

In spite of the detailed explanation in the TASS communiqué of October 31 of this year concerning the actual state of the negotiations on the C.E.R., incorrect information continues to appear in the Japanese and Manchurian press on the course of these negotiations. On the other hand, in international circles a completely understandable interest has appeared on the question why, in spite of the attainment of agreement on the price of the C.E.R., negotiations on other conditions of the sale of the line are delaying the conclusion of a final agreement. In connection with this, TASS has assembled from well-informed circles additional information on the state of the negotiations regarding the C.E.R. which gives a correct idea of the reasons for this delay.

It turns out that with regard to a number of conditions connected with the sale of the C.E.R., the Japanese side has displayed extreme obstinacy and unwillingness to meet halfway some of the most natural demands of the Soviet side. This concerns first of all the legitimate wish of the U.S.S.R. to be given a guaranty that the price for the C.E.R. will be paid; as is known, the price is conceived in the form of obligations to be given by Manchukuo, to be guaranteed by Japan. Unfortunately, the Japanese side has not changed its position on this highly essential point of the agreement since the publication of the TASS communiqué of October 31 of this year.

The Japanese side meets Soviet business-like arguments with the principle of "confidence" in Manchukuo and the promise to "mediate" in case of difficulties in the payments from Manchukuo. Moreover, the Japanese side, and in particular the Japanese-Manchurian press, tries to interpret the Soviet insistence on a guaranty as a sign of distrust, as almost an insult to Manchukuo and Japan from the Soviet side. This position has evoked great bewilderment among well-informed Moscow circles, where it is pointed out that in the entire world it is a commonly accepted practice to provide guaranties in concluding deals of this kind. In the present case, which concerns the sale, under conditions of extended payments; of a great economic enterprise which, more-over, is to come into the possession of its new owner immediately on conclusion of the agreement, this usual demand for a guaranty should be taken all the more for granted.

As to "lack of confidence," it is quite obvious that the Soviet side would not have insisted on the guaranty by Japan if it did not believe in the effectiveness of such a guaranty, and if it did not consider that the Japanese government would not permit, in its own interest, anyone to violate the obligations guaranteed by the Japanese side. Thus the giving of a guaranty by Japan should ensure the normal functioning of the agreement.

Proceeding from the same desire to eliminate in advance, in the interest of strengthening normal relations between the U.S.S.R. and Japan, the possibility that quarrels and conflicts during the carrying out of the agreement might become the source of new complications between both states, the Soviet side advanced the demand for arbitration trials of possible disagreements in the delivery of goods on account of sums due on the railway, in which connection if it should prove impossible to agree concerning the choice of an impartial president of the arbitration court, the Soviet side pro-posed that the latter should be named by some foreign chamber of commerce with a solid international reputation (the chambers of commerce of England and the U.S.A. were named). The important significance of this question arises from the fact that, as is known, the Soviet Union has agreed to receive two-thirds of the payments in

Japanese and Manchurian goods. At the same time, to meet the wishes of the Japanese side, the U.S.S.R. agreed to widen the nomenclature of the goods, including among them, together with industrial equipment, also such goods as textiles, silk, tea, soy beans, rice, etc.

However, the Japanese side objected to an arbitration court with the participation of a foreign president. Instead they proposed to use in the capacity of an arbitration court a representative of the Japanese Ministry of Foreign Affairs or the Japanese Ministry of Trade. This proposal was, of course, declined, inasmuch as Japan cannot be regarded as a disinterested "third" party in a possible dispute between the U.S.S.R. and Manchukuo. The Japanese refusal to settle possible disagreements between the U.S.S.R. and Manchukuo by means of the application of the principle of arbitration is all the stranger since Japan resorts to this principle itself in the settlement of economic disputes with other countries, as can be seen from the fact that it is a participant in the international treaty on commercial arbitration.

The irreconcilable position taken by the Japanese side in the above question attracted attention in Moscow also because the Soviet government in the latest statements of Comrade Iurenev to Mr. Hirota, on October 30 and 31 and November 6, made a number of new substantial concessions on other points in dispute.

Without dwelling on all the unsettled questions in the negotiations, it is essential to point out that the negotiations are being obstructed also by the continuing rejection by the Japanese side of agreements which had previously been reached on individual points. It is sufficient to cite as an example that despite the agreement already reached on July 23 of this year on the question of immediate settlement with employees of the C.E.R. of the terminal payments and pensions due them, recently the Japanese side unexpectedly declared this question to be still not agreed upon.

In well-informed circles special attention is drawn to the fact that in the course of the negotiations there appeared the differing approaches of the Soviet and the Japanese sides to the desirable content of the agreement. The Soviet side consistently desires that the agreement on the sale of the C.E.R. should not only remove once and for all the possibility of using the problem of the C.E.R. for aggravating relations between the U.S.S.R. and Japan, but should contain in itself a guarantee for normal and satisfactory fulfillment, thereby aiding the strengthening of the political and economic relations between the two countries in the interests of general peace. On the other hand, a number of Japanese proposals are of such a nature that if they were used as a basis for the agreement they would open the possibility of new attempts to use the question of the C.E.R. as a source of conflicts between the two countries even after the sale of the C.E.R.

In well-informed Soviet circles it is pointed out that giving the agreement on the C.E.R. a character of that kind might perhaps serve the interests of some circles in Japan which would be able to change this treaty from an instrument of peace into material for the preparation of new conflicts, however, such a character of the agreement would obviously contradict the interests of strengthening normal and good neighborly relations between the U.S.S.R. and Japan, and in that way would contradict the interests of peace in general. Therefore, in the aforementioned Soviet circles the hope is expressed that the Japanese government will show its good will and thereby will ensure the satisfactory conclusion of negotiations in which Japan cannot but be interested. (TASS)

141

Dimitroff on Ideological Struggle Against Social-Democracy in the United Front

Excerpts from G. Dimitroff, "The Struggle for the United Front!" I.P.C., Vol. 14, No. 59, November 24, 1934, pp. 1582–83.

. . .

In all the capitalist countries the workers are more and more beginning to understand the necessity for restoring their unity and are more and more supporting the initiative of the communist parties in the organization of the united front. *The question of the united proletarian front is becoming the central question and the most urgent task of the working class movement of all countries.*

. . .

The question of the united front brings internal differentiation and struggle into the ranks of the social-democratic parties and other noncommunist workers' organizations. The right-wing elements in these parties who are closely connected with the bourgeoisie are exerting every effort to prevent the organization of the united front. The advanced social-democratic workers, on the other hand, are more and more boldly coming to the united front, to the struggle together with the communists. The "left" elements of the social-democratic parties are trying by means of demagogic phrases to keep the hesitating social-democratic workers from realizing the united front and thus to hinder the further revolutionizing of the social-democratic masses.

As the united front develops and extends, this more or less lengthy process of differentiation inside the social-democratic parties will develop, the internal struggle in the ranks of the social-democratic parties will become more intense, in some cases going as far as the splitting away of right-wing groups and drawing still closer to the bourgeois parties, and, on the other hand, leading to the uniting of some of the groups and organizations of the revolutionizing social-democratic workers with the communist parties.

We have already seen a fact of tremendous importance, which was not to be observed during recent years, that the social-democratic workers and the social-democratic organizations in a number of countries are marching together with the communists even to the armed struggle against fascism. We have seen how the advanced social-democratic workers in *Austria*, having rejected the conciliatory policy of social-democracy, took up arms hand-in-hand with the communist workers and at the last moment tried to stop the offensive of fascism. At the present time the Austrian working class, taking to heart the lessons of the February fight, are establishing unity on the path of the revolutionary struggle. In *Spain*, the communists, socialists, and anarcho-syndicalist workers took up arms against the attack of fascist reaction. Not long before the beginning of the armed struggle the Communist Party entered the *Workers' Alliance*, making it into an organization of the united front. It was solely the united front, which only began to be carried out in the course of the struggle itself, which made it possible for the working class of Spain, even without drawing in the reserves of the peasant revolution, to carry on such a stubborn, such a lengthy struggle, which in some districts led to the establishment of the power of the workers and peasants.

During the last few months a rapid development of the united front has taken place in *France*. The Communist Party and the Socialist Party concluded a pact for a joint struggle against fascism and the bourgeois offensive. Rallying in the united front and beginning to combine in united trade-unions, the French working class is successfully beating back the provocative onslaught of fascism. The strivings of the workers toward unity in the struggle are growing in all countries.

But these are only the first steps. In spite of the resistance to the united front by the leaders of the Second International and of a number of social-democratic parties, it is necessary to go further toward widening and strengthening the united front among the masses. The united front is first and foremost *the wide mobilization and uniting of the masses from below,* in the factories, around the united organs of struggle formed by the masses themselves. The immediate task of the united front is now to form *elected organs of the united front* from below, chiefly in the factories and mills. An equally important task for the further widening of the united front is also the *uniting of the trade-union organizations* of the working class, as organs of the class struggle against the bourgeoisie.

The further successes of the united front depend primarily on the all-round strengthening of the communist parties, on the correct policy and energetic mass work of the communists themselves, because it is precisely they who are the real initiators of the united front and its chief organizing force.

When carrying out the tactics of the united front, two kinds of hindrances are met with, which make themselves felt to a greater or less extent, according to the concrete conditions in various countries. *First,* there is a failure to understand the importance and urgency of organizing the united proletarian front, a sectarian fear of the masses, a fear of wide mass political action. Consistent and lengthy work among the masses for the organization of the united front is sometimes reduced merely to a formal approach to the social-democratic party. The refusal of the social-democratic leaders to undertake joint action merely causes some comrades to breathe a sigh of relief, instead of making them work with redoubled energy, utilizing this sabotage by social-democratic leaders and in spite of their resistance, to draw closer to the social-democratic workers and lead them to the united front.

Sometimes the whole tactics of the united front are looked upon by some comrades simply as the immediate transition of the social-democratic workers into the ranks of the communist parties. However, it is a more or less lengthy process for the social-democratic and other noncommunist workers to come over to the path of the revolutionary struggle, and during this process we must fight for each individual worker.

Secondly, in their efforts to reach an agreement with socialist parties or to preserve an existing agreement, our comrades may sometimes slur over the difference in principle between our ideology and that of the social-democrats or may restrict the struggle of the united front simply to the limits of the agreement, not making the mobilization of the masses themselves the chief center of the united front. It must be understood that the struggle for the organization of the united front, for its strengthening and widening, does not exclude but on the contrary presupposes constant ideological work for explaining to the working masses the difference in principle between the communists and social-democratic parties, between communism and social-democracy, between the line of irreconcilable class struggle and the line of class collaboration with the bourgeoisie, between the path of Bolshevism, which led to the victory of socialism in the U.S.S.R., and the path of social-democracy, which led to the victory of reaction and fascism in a number of countries.

The conclusion of an agreement with the social-democratic parties for a joint struggle against the capitalist offensive, against fascism and war, which is one of the means of practically carrying out the united proletarian front, by no means signifies that we shall stop or weaken our struggle against social-democratic ideology—the ideology and practice of compromise with the bourgeoisie.

On the contrary, in the interest of the united front itself, this ideological struggle must be intensified. Our propaganda must be linked up with our proletarian policy. It is necessary to avoid the replacement of a concrete policy by abstract propaganda. It must not be forgotten that the Communist Party is the *political party* of the proletariat, and not a society for the propaganda of communism. While fighting for the formation of the united proletarian front, the communists must not for a moment lose sight of their revolutionary perspective, must be able to link up the tactics of the united front with the strategic task—the struggle for the victory of the proletarian revolution, for the dictatorship of the proletariat.

Successful work for the formation and widening of the united proletarian front is impossible unless a constant struggle is carried on against the above-mentioned two chief hindrances. The chief blow must be directed against the hindrance which, at the given moment and in the given concrete situation, at the given stage of the struggle, is the *chief hindrance* toward carrying out and strengthening the united front. It is particularly necessary to avoid the schematic application of the tactics of the united front, without taking into account the correlation of class forces and the concrete conditions in each country, the mechanical transfer of the experience of one country—France, for example—to other and sometimes absolutely different conditions in another country—England, for instance. Such a stereotyped, uncritical transfer of political and organizational experience from one country to all others has frequently led to failures which have cost the working class very dear.

The *Communist International,* taking as its basis the growth and consolidation of its sections, the revolutionizing of the masses of workers in the social-democratic parties, the reformist trade-unions, and other organizations, considers the most important task of the day to be the organization of the joint struggle of the communist, social-democratic, anarcho-syndicalist, and other workers against the offensive of capital, against fascism and the war danger. For the formation and strengthening of the united proletarian front is now the *main link* in the preparation of the world proletarian revolution.

142

The Comintern Analyzes Fascist Victories and Prescribes Tactics for the United Front

"Ot rasshatyvaiushcheisia stabilizatsii ko vtoromu turu revoliutsii i voin," K.I., No. 34, December 1, 1934, pp. 3–19.

Six years separate us from the Sixth Congress of the Comintern. During these six years, the face of the world has changed, and the changes have proceeded in the *direction* predicted by the Sixth Congress.

The Sixth Congress of the Comintern met in 1928, at a time when the partial stabilization of capitalism still existed; when the intensified splicing-together of the social-democratic parties and the reformist trade-unions with the state apparatus and the employers' organizations was taking place; when "social-democracy had passed from the shamefaced defense of capitalism to its open support" (Theses of the Sixth Congress of the Comintern); when social-democracy, drawing after itself the majority of the working class, was still extending its influence everywhere; when the leading social-democratic party, the German party, was still in the government.

Under these conditions, social-democracy predicted that capitalism would continue to thrive for many years and preached "industrial peace," "economic democracy," "organized capitalism," as the path of the "peaceful transformation of democracy into socialism."

The prognosis and the aims outlined by the Comintern were quite different.

. . .

And the Sixth Congress, announcing the beginning of the third postwar period and outlining its characteristics, foretold the disintegration of capitalist stabilization, the revolutionary upsurge, "a new period of imperialist wars and wars against the U.S.S.R., national-liberation wars against imperialism, and gigantic class battles."

History has completely shattered the hopes and predictions of social-democracy and has fully confirmed the prognosis of the Comintern.

Since the Sixth Congress of the Comintern, the basic contradiction of the contemporary epoch has deepened to an enormous degree—that between the U.S.S.R. and the capitalist world. The U.S.S.R. in the last six years has achieved a victory of world-historical importance.

During this very same period, during the past six years, the capitalist countries have revealed to the world a picture of the growing decay, the disintegration of capitalist economy, the shattering of the very bases of capitalism. An economic crisis unprecedented in depth and scope has developed. In 1932, capitalist industrial production reached its lowest ebb, after which a certain increase of production began, but this increase of production actually was a "special kind of depression" which is not leading to a new upturn and a new revival of industry, although it is not swinging back to the level of the previous greatest decline, and which is being attained at the cost of robbery of "the workers, farmers, peasants of the colonies and economically weak countries" (Stalin).

The basic dynamic characteristic of development during the period since the Sixth Congress of the Comintern is the disintegration of capitalist stabilization, *the ripening of the revolutionary crisis,* even though it is not proceeding equally in various countries or in a straight line in each country. Together and in close connection with the maturing of the revolutionary crisis, and the answer to it by the bourgeoisie, a new wave of fascism and an increased threat of war has arisen.

It will be necessary for us to outline at the Seventh Congress of the Comintern a clear-cut answer to the problem of the *ripening of the world revolutionary crisis, of the conditions for its ripening, of the weakest links in the imperialist chain, of the prospects of the revolution,* in order to determine *the basic aims* and tactical tasks of the Comintern in the immediate future. . . .

. . .

Why do we speak of the ripening of the revolutionary crisis even though the revolutionary development is not proceeding evenly or directly? For the following reasons:

First reason. The "special kind of depression" which set in during 1933 does not lead to the expectation of an industrial upsurge, and still less of the stabilization of capitalism . . .

Second reason. The change to a "special kind of depression" has not only not weakened the class struggle, but on the contrary, as experience has shown, this struggle has become still further intensified.

Third reason. The bourgeoisie is feverishly preparing for an imperialist war, and first of all for a counterrevolutionary war against the Soviet Union. But the sympathies of the broad masses for the Soviet Union are increasing daily. Therefore the preparation for a war against the Soviet Union hastens the maturing of the revolutionary crisis, and when the war breaks out, it will inevitably be transformed into a civil war in the capitalist countries because of the present Bolshevik work of our parties.

Fourth reason. The ever spreading wave of reaction, fascist violence, and fascist terror not only does not hinder but on the contrary hastens the revolutionary development, arouses the indignation of the masses, imbues them with the idea of [launching] an offensive.

Fifth reason. Social-democracy—that chief social bulwark of the bourgeoisie in the industrial countries—is now undergoing an ideological and organizational crisis which will grow continually more serious and which—if we follow a correct policy—will facilitate the shift of the social-democratic working masses to the side of communism.

Finally, the *sixth reason*, which is of tremendous and prime significance. The Soviet Union won a victory of world-historical significance in the first Five-Year Plan, and in the second Five-Year Plan is successfully solving and will definitively solve the food problem, the problem of supplying the toiling masses, and thereby will trump the last card of the bourgeoisie in its anti-Soviet propaganda, proving to even the most backward strata of the workers that the path of October is the only way to salvation for them.

The maturing of the world revolutionary crisis is evidenced by the developments of the last few years.

First, in two countries we have already experienced a revolution in the course of a number of years.

In Soviet China, the victorious revolution represented by the heroic Chinese Red Army, having defeated five campaigns of the counterrevolutionary Kuomintang, at the end of the sixth campaign, the most carefully prepared, by skillful maneuvers *has retained its vital strength and in retreating from certain districts has successfully seized others.* The soviet revolution in China has exerted and is exerting a tremendous influence on all colonial countries, in which extensive regroupings of class forces—the national bourgeoisie and the proletariat—have taken place during the last six or seven years. Now, not only in China, where the hegemony of the proletariat has already been established on a territory of considerable size, under the democratic dictatorship of the proletariat and peasantry in the form of soviets, but also in Indochina, India, and a number of other colonies, the proletariat is waging an intensified and not unsuccessful struggle for hegemony in the anti-imperialist and antifeudal revolutionary movement, and is raising in those countries the banner of the soviet revolution. The soviet revolution in China is an important factor of world revolution. The soviets of China represent the most dangerous revolutionary rearguard against the armed attack on the Soviet Union which is being planned by Japanese imperialism.

At the other end of the old world, in Spain, a revolution is also taking place which in the entire course of its development has raised the question of power. The general strike in Spain, launched to meet the threat of a fascist coup, has been transformed in the industrial northern regions (Asturia and Biscay) into a mass armed uprising. For the first time, soviets have appeared in Spain.

In this particular encounter the winner was the counterrevolution, but the forces of the Spanish proletariat have not been routed. A regrouping of forces is taking place to prepare for new decisive battles. The revolution in Spain is hastening the maturing of the world revolutionary crisis.

Second, it is exceptionally symptomatic that *revolutionary events are occurring here and there all over the world,* even in such "peaceful" countries as Holland and Switzerland, that in the industrial countries, not to speak of the colonies, we see demonstrations not only by the workers, but in some localities even by the peasants, and that vacillations are evident within the armed forces.

. . .

All of this speaks for the maturing of the *world* revolutionary crisis in spite of the great unevenness in the revolutionary development.

Third, the movement is now assuming very *acute forms.* Economic strikes rapidly develop into political ones, they are accompanied by strikes of solidarity, general strikes break out much more frequently than formerly . . .

The most symptomatic thing is that the workers now are beginning to take up arms (Spain, Austria).

Fourth, completely new is the general strong urge of the social-democratic workers to the united front of struggle together with the communists, and in places the coming over not only of social-democratic workers but even of entire social-democratic organizations to the camp of communism.

The world revolutionary crisis is maturing, but the process of its ripening is developing not in a straight line, but in zigzag fashion. Especially where the fascists have succeeded in seizing power, we have a temporary slowdown of the movement. . . . After the temporary defeat in Germany, after the establishment there of an open fascist dictatorship, and in connection with this, we have seen in Central Europe a temporary weakening of the movement. In Germany under the Hitler regime strikes have had and still have at present a short-term and almost always spontaneous character. . . .

This victory of fascism and the resultant temporary weakening of the movement in several industrial countries of Central Europe was prepared and at the decisive moment made possible in reality by the treachery of social-democracy. But a certain share of the responsibility for this—for the fact that we were not able to paralyze the treacherous actions of social-democracy—falls on us also, falls on our parties, their slowness, their mistakes. The Comintern has frequently noted this slowness and these mistakes: for example, in connection with the fascist revolution in Finland, recently in connection with the fascist revolution in Bulgaria. In Germany also, on the eve of the fascist revolution, at the Twelfth Plenum of the ECCI, members of the Executive Committee of the Comintern, including the leader of the Communist Party of Germany, Comrade Thälmann, subjected the slowness and mistakes of the CPG to criticism. The mistakes and slowness of the parties must now be subjected to the most intensive self-criticism by the leadership of our parties. But at the same time we must not forget that regardless of zigzags, the revolutionary movement is going ahead, on an ascending line, and that it is compelled to do this not only by objective conditions but also and to a very considerable degree by our parties and the Comintern. If international social-democracy is now undergoing a crisis, if the social-democratic parties in Germany and Austria have been smashed after the establishment there of open fascist dictatorship, while our parties, which have been far more terrorized, remain at their post, while in Austria precisely at present our party is tempestuously growing, this obviously is the result of the good work of our parties.

The process of the maturation of the revolutionary crisis is developing *unevenly*. At present, after the victory of Hitler, we have a lull in the mass movement in Germany, and at the same time an upsurge of the mass movement in various degrees and in various forms in the strongest industrial countries: in France, in England, in the U.S.A. But, in speaking of a lull in the mass movement in Germany, it must not be forgotten that large-scale mass strikes, and especially a general strike, would be of an entirely different character and have entirely different consequences in Germany from mass strikes and general strikes taking place in France, or, even more, in the U.S.A. In Germany a general strike, regardless of its outcome, would signify the beginning of revolution. Therefore in Germany a much greater piling up of forces is required, a much greater accumulation of revolutionary discontent and revolutionary enthusiasm, for a general strike to break out there; but when it does break out, it will develop in incomparably more stormy forms.

These processes of the discrediting of authority and the accumulation of revolutionary forces are even now taking place in Germany. And this is being extraordinarily facilitated by the bankruptcy of the demagogic economic promises of Hitler. These processes will be significantly accelerated when the communists succeed there in calling partial, quickly changing, and even small strikes and flying demonstrations in various places. These processes are already being accelerated by the upsurge of the revolutionary movement in neighboring "democratic" countries, not even to mention the enormous influence of the world-historic victories of socialism in the U.S.S.R. It is by no means necessary to expect a long road to revolution for Germany on the basis of the temporary lull there. This lull is very deceptive: it is the lull before the storm.

Such are the conditions of the ripening of the world revolutionary crisis, such are the prospectives of the revolution.

Confronting us, however, is still another prospect, the prospect of war; it is, however, inevitable that out of war also revolution will develop, besides which, under present conditions, the transformation of war into revolution will occur much more rapidly than it did during the first round of wars and revolutions.

In the period of partial stabilization of capitalism, "pacifism" prevailed; a certain equilibrium was evident in the relations of the imperialist countries on the basis of treaties for the division of the world after the war; a "breathing space" characterized the relations of the U.S.S.R. with the capitalist countries. After the Sixth Congress of the Comintern, the era of pacifism ended. An imperialist war is approaching, and still more so the counterrevolutionary war against the U.S.S.R. that has been discussed for a considerable time quite openly by both the Japanese military group and the German fascists.

Very recently, however, we have witnessed in this connection certain zigzags. The invitation of the U.S.S.R. to the League of Nations, and its joining the League, undoubtedly indicate some difficulties experienced in launching a war. However, it would be a harmful and a dangerous illusion to believe that this is a *guarantee* against war, particularly against an anti-Soviet war.

First, it is not at all necessary for the launching of an anti-Soviet war to be preceded by the formation of a broad anti-Soviet bloc. The warmongers hope that once they present the other imperialists with an accomplished fact, the latter will change their positions.

Second, the entire capitalist world is far from pleased with the prospect of the successful completion of the second Five-Year Plan of the Soviet Union.

Third, the tenseness of the imperialist contradictions is evidence of the danger of an imperialist war. Therefore, the prospect of an imperialist and especially of an anti-Soviet war has by no means been eliminated, while the fact that this prospect is linked with the prospect of the victory of the revolution in a number of countries has been sufficiently eloquently explained by Comrade Stalin at the Seventeenth Congress of the CPSU (B).

Thus we are at present experiencing the eve of the second round of revolutions and wars. One of the peculiarities of the maturing of the second round of revolutions and wars is the fact that it is now taking place under the conditions of the growth of fascism and the crisis of social-democracy.

The coming to power of fascism, the change from the concealed parliamentary dictatorship of the bourgeoisie to an open fascist dictatorship in Germany, Austria, and other countries, means a very serious blow against the proletariat and its communist vanguard. The fascist dictatorship is the most savage, the most odious form of the dictatorship of the bourgeoisie. This is the dictatorship of the most terroristic, the most reactionary, the most chauvinistic, the most imperialist strata of finance capital, which under contemporary conditions has grown out of the concealed parliamentary dictatorship of the bourgeoisie.

But in what way and to what extent does the coming to power of the fascists have a bearing on the maturing of the revolutionary crisis? Especially, what does it mean that the bourgeoisie now is everywhere placing its *bets on fascism?* This is evidence of the growing danger of revolution, in the face of which the bourgeoisie is no longer able to rule by the old methods of parliamentarism and bourgeois democracy. *The bet of the bourgeoisie on fascism is evidence of the weakness of the bourgeoisie.* The fact that fascism *was victorious* in a number of countries, that the bourgeoisie in a number of countries was able to establish an open fascist dictatorship, is an indication not only of the weakness of the bourgeoisie but also an indication of the weakness of the proletariat as the result of the treachery to the working class of social-democracy, which cleared the way for fascism. But the fact that the bourgeoisie consciously set its *course toward fascism* is explained by exactly its weakness. It felt and feels itself forced to this, even though it realizes that this is connected with dangers for it. In the first place, fascism, in destroying parliamentarism and unleashing civil war, involuntarily contributes to the process whereby the proletariat undergoes a revolutionary education, more rapidly outlives its democratic illusions and is trained in the forcible overthrow of the bourgeois system. In the second place, fascism, having created for itself by means of social and nationalist demagogy a mass basis among the ruined petty-bourgeoisie and in part among déclassé workers, among strata of the population which are permeated by anti-capitalist sentiments, after coming to power is forced to manifest and is already manifesting complete inability to fulfill its demagogic promises, which must inevitably lead sooner or later to a mutiny of the deceived petty-bourgeois masses and the déclassé workers, *on condition that there is present a sufficiently strong communist movement among the workers.* This is already taking place in Germany. Therefore the bourgeoisie, setting its course toward fascism and bringing fascists to power, realizes that it is running a great risk.

When the fascist dictatorship was established in Germany, social-democracy and the renegades of communism, and following them a few unsteady elements within the communist parties, advanced the thesis that an entire *historical epoch of fascism* had begun, in the sense that fascism was *inevitably* bound to triumph, that the resistance of the proletariat had been smashed, and that there were no revolutionary prospects. The facts have proved that this capitulationist, fatalistic theory was doubly incorrect. In the first place, the very fact of the establishment of a fascist dictatorship in Germany, the frightening example of the Hitlerite terror, caused great alarm among the broadest strata of the proletariat of various countries and gave the impulse for a stormy counterattack of the proletariat against native fascism in these countries. Let us recall the grandiose February battles in France, the heroic armed struggle of the Austrian workers against fascism, the general strike and armed uprising of the Spanish workers in response to the inclusion of fascists in the government—battles in which no small role was and is played by the passionate desire of the French, Austrian, and Spanish workers to avoid the fate of the German proletariat. In the second place, in Germany itself the Hitlerite regime with its rabid terror and unrestrained demagogy, even though it has created great difficulties for the development of the mass struggle of the proletariat, has been unable to destroy the communist movement, while the Hitlerite economic measures have already evoked a certain resistance by the working class, which found expression in the election of proxies in the factories and plants. The results of these elections have been described by the fascists themselves as "a blow in the face of the National Socialist idea." Shortly after this there began the mutiny of the petty-bourgeois masses, who have been deceived by fascism. Serious disturbances began among the storm troopers, who demanded the fulfillment of the demagogic promises of Hitler at the same time that the real bosses of Germany—the Thyssens and Krupps—demanded the further offensive of capital. This, and in part also the conflict between the Reichswehr and the storm trooper officers, led to the sanguinary events of June 30, though far from indicating the collapse of German fascism, which will set in only under the blows of the proletariat, nevertheless indicates *the onset of its crisis.*

German fascism has consolidated its state and military apparatus, and still further consolidated them after the events of June 30, but at the same time it is more and more losing its mass basis. This is a good confirmation of the Comintern thesis that fascism not only strengthens but at the same time undermines the position of the bourgeoisie. It must not be forgotten that the present wave of fascism, unlike that which took place on the eve of and during the period of the partial stabilization of capitalism, developed not as the result of the defeat of the proletariat but out of the profound impoverishment of the middle strata, the revolutionary upsurge of the proletariat, and the bourgeoisie's fear of the approaching revolution. Nor must it be forgotten that industrial Germany is not Italy, that the German proletariat is far stronger than the Italian, that the present-day Communist Party of Germany is incomparably stronger in all respects than the Communist Party of Italy at the time of Mussolini's coming to power.

. . .

II

"The revolutionary crisis is maturing and will continue to mature." But "the victory of the revolution never comes by itself. It must be prepared and won. And it can be prepared and won only by a strong proletarian revolutionary party." (Stalin, [*Sochineniia,* X, 345]).

What, then, is our situation in regard to the existence of a strong proletarian revolutionary party? In the period of the first round of wars and revolutions, the sections of the Comintern, with the exception of the CPSU (B), did not constitute such parties, and the Comintern as a whole only to a weak degree constituted a single world party of the proletariat of a new type. At that time it was such only in an embryonic condition. After the Sixth Congress of the Comintern, in the period 1928–1930, it was possible to confirm the consolidation of the majority of the sections of the Comintern and the transformation of the Comintern itself into a monolithic world party of the proletariat of a new type. The results of the Bolshevization of our most important sections, their consolidation, and the transformation of the Comintern into a single world monolithic party soon made themselves apparent. Immediately after the Tenth Plenum of the ECCI in 1929 we were able to note the rapid growth of the political influence of our parties and a series of most important successes obtained by the strongest of them: the German, the Chinese, the Polish, the Czechoslovak, etc.

. . .

The present period is characterized by sharp and sudden changes. Such changes call for changes in tactics. But under the conditions of such sudden changes and tactical turns, vacillations in separate links of the party, or in one or another party, are possible and even inevitable. The difference between the present situation and the past, when our parties were not yet consolidated, is simply that these vacillations and mistakes are corrected and outlived faster now, and that they do not result in party crises as happened in the past.

At the present time there are big changes in connection with the establishment of open fascist dictatorships in Germany and Austria and the offensive of fascism in other countries, in connection with the increasing danger of war, in connection with the maturing of the world revolutionary crisis, in connection with the revolutionizing of the mood of the broad proletarian masses, in connection with the deep crisis of social-democracy, in connection with the attraction of the social-democratic masses toward the united front of struggle together with the communists. All this requires that we advance as the central political slogan, the slogan of "Soviet Power," and this has already been done by the Thirteenth Plenum of the ECCI. At the same time all this demands from us a change in tactics of the united front so as to adapt them to the new and changed situation. We change the tactics of the united front not because our former tactics were incorrect, as social-democracy and the renegades of communism are now trying to prove. Notwithstanding individual mistakes made locally, and sometimes by the party leadership, our former tactics were absolutely correct. We now change the tactics of the united front because the situation has changed.

The nature of the changes in the tactics of the united front was indicated already in the appeal of the ECCI to the workers of all countries on March 5, 1933, "concerning the establishment of the united front of struggle of the communist and social-democratic workers against the attack of capital and fascism." In this appeal, it was recommended that our parties "refrain from making attacks on social-democratic organizations *during the time of the common fight* against capital and fascism," provided the social-democrats observed two conditions: a genuine struggle against fascism and against the lowering of the living conditions of the workers and the unemployed, and on condition that they conduct "the most ruthless struggle against all those who violate the conditions of the agreement on conducting the united front of the working class, as strikebreakers who are disrupting the united front of the workers." This tactic for conducting the united front is the new one which corresponds to the new situation. In the past we applied it only in individual instances (in July 1932 and in January 1933 the CPG appealed to the social-democratic leadership with the proposal of a united front; in 1922, also, in Lenin's lifetime, in a different international situation, the Comintern participated in a conference with the Second and Second-and-a-Half Internationals). This new tactic of the broad application of the united front of 1934 has already led to a number of important successes: it helped our French comrades, who had taken the initiative of launching a counter-offensive against fascism in the February days, draw the socialist workers to their side, and gave a great sweep to the movement; it helped our small Austrian Communist Party triple its strength and greatly increase its influence on the working class, in connection with the armed battles in February, to the detriment of the bankrupt social-democracy; it helped our French Communist Party overcome the resistance of the Socialist Party to the establishment of a united front, and gain that party's consent to it; it helped our Dutch Communist Party develop revolutionary fights of the unemployed in the July days of 1934; it helped our American comrades carry out a successful general strike recently in San Francisco, etc.; it helped our Spanish comrades create better conditions for the contact with the masses and for their mobilization by joining the "Alianza Obrera"; it helped our Spanish comrades carry out jointly with the socialists both a general strike and an armed struggle in Spain. However, when the movement [in Spain] reached a higher level— the struggle for power, and for the soviet power (in Asturia and Biscay) —it became apparent that the socialist organizations, which were ready for the struggle as long as it concerned the defense of the republic, began to put obstacles in the path at this higher stage of the struggle.

The above-enumerated facts represent only the first steps in the application of the tactic of the broad united front. Its further development opens broad perspectives before us. If we correctly apply this tactic, we shall be able to link ourselves more closely with the social-democratic working masses who are undergoing a process of radicalization; we shall be able to mobilize on a broad front the struggle against fascism, the attack of capital, and the danger of war; we shall be able to increase the confidence of the working class in its own strength and the confidence of [its] allies in the strength of the working class; we shall be able to bring these masses to the decisive battles for power. But in order to apply the *tactic* of the broad united front correctly and to avoid the dangers connected with it, we must have *a clear concept of our aims.*

We are at present on the eve of a new round of revolutions and wars. *But no people's national revolution can be victorious at the present time unless it is launched under the banner of the soviets,* no matter what the slogans are under which this revolution might start, and no matter what character it has, whether it is a democratic or a proletarian revolution. The Thirteenth Plenum of the ECCI, marking the ripening of the world revolutionary crisis and the approach of the eve of a new round of revolutions and wars, at the same time advanced *the slogan of "Soviet Power" as the central political slogan for the present time.* It is clear to us that this slogan must become the central political slogan today even in countries which are backward in the revolutionary sense, because there too the workers should know beforehand what path they should take. But millions of the masses of the workers in the capitalist countries have not yet grasped the meaning of the slogan of soviet power. Their sympathies for the Soviet Union, with its consistent policy of peace, are growing every day, every day they are becoming more convinced that genuine socialism is being built in the U.S.S.R. Nevertheless the majority of the workers in the capitalist countries, due to the prolonged influence exercised upon them in the past by the social-democratic agents of the bourgeoisie, are still not certain that an armed uprising, the establishment of the dictatorship of the proletariat in the form of soviets, is the *only* way to socialism, that there is no other way to victory, regardless of the special characteristics of this or that country. They must be *led* to the struggle for the soviet power. For this it is necessary everywhere tirelessly to propagandize the slogan of soviet power, clothing this propaganda in concrete forms corresponding to the special characteristics of each country. But propaganda alone, even the broadest, is completely inadequate for this. The masses will be more easily and quickly convinced of the correctness of the policy of the communists and their slogans on the basis of the experience of their own struggle. The events of the past year have provided many vivid examples showing that the social-democratic and nonparty worker masses under present conditions can best be led to the struggle for the power of soviets by means of the broad application of the tactic of the united front of struggle against fascism, the attack of capital, and the danger of war. The greater the development during this year of the struggle of the masses by means of the united front, the more receptive they have become to our slogan of soviet power, the more rapidly they have outlived social-democratic prejudices (France), the more rapidly their tug toward communism has grown (Austria), the more rapidly, finally, in the presence of a revolutionary situation they themselves have taken part in the struggle for soviet power (Asturia). It is for exactly that reason that the problem of the united front is now being given so much attention by the Comintern.

But the struggle by the united front against fascism, the attack of capitalism, and the danger of war will lead the social-democratic and nonparty masses to the struggle for soviet power *only under certain conditions*. We must remember, first, that the united front, by the very meaning of this term, presupposes the existence of at least two parties in the working class. When the communists fight shoulder to shoulder with other communists or with Komsomol members, or the members of the Red trade-unions, we do not call it a united front. But the proletariat can only carry on successfully the direct struggle for soviet power under the leadership of *one party, the communist party, leading the majority of the working class*. We must remember, second, that social-democracy agrees to join the communists in the united front only to the extent it carries out a *defensive task*—to repulse by united antifascist efforts the attack of fascism, to defend from the fascist attack the democratic rights of the workers, to hamper and delay war. Social-democracy agrees to the united front with the communists while remaining on the basis of bourgeois democracy. *But we are pursuing not merely a defensive but an offensive task,* we wish not only to repulse the attack of fascism, or to win back this or that position which it has seized, but to smash fascism and *the class rule of the bourgeoisie in general,* and to establish the dictatorship of the proletariat in the form of soviet power. And this we can achieve not in a bloc with social-democracy but in a struggle against it. *Hence it follows that the struggle by the united front can lead the social-democratic and nonparty masses to the struggle for soviet power only if we, in the process of the struggle in the united front, win to our side the majority of the working class and liquidate the mass influence of social-democracy.*

For this, first, the initiative for the struggle by the united front must come from us. For this, second, we must unmask not only those social-democrats who oppose the establishment of the united front but also those who try to substitute for the slogan of the united front the slogan of "Organized Unity," which has the purpose of obliterating the distinction between communism and social-democratism and of diverting the communist workers onto the social-democratic path of compromise. For this, third, in joining the united front we must not hide the face of the party, we must not tie our hands, we must not renounce the revolutionary initiative in the battles which are developing, and at the same time, in relation to the strengthening and broadening of the united front, we must extend in every way the demands made by us upon the united front, we must present it with demands for the ever greater sharpening of the struggle. Only in this way will we succeed in speeding up the process of differentiation in social-democracy—speeding up the sifting out from the united front of those social-democrats who cannot and who do not want to break with the policy of class cooperation, and bringing more closely to us the majority of the social-democratic workers and more social-democratic organizations, or those social-democratic functionaries who are ready to fight with us to the end.

Comrade Stalin said at the Fifteenth Congress of the CPSU (B):

"Only when the petty-bourgeois parties of the Socialist Revolutionaries and the Mensheviks finally disgraced themselves in regard to the basic questions of the revolution, only when the masses began to be convinced of the correctness of our policy—only then did we lead the masses to an uprising. . . . [ellipses in original] There lies the basis of the united front. The tactic of the united front was used by Lenin only to make it easier for the millions of the masses of the working class, contaminated by the prejudices of social-democratic conciliation, to come over to the side of communism."

For us the united front is not a maneuver. We make it easier for the social-democratic masses to come over to the side of communism by showing them in deeds, in the practice of the united front, that we alone fight consistently against fascism, against the attack of capital, and against the danger of war. But we do not conceal the main goal of the united front.

This main goal of the united front is to make it easier for the social-democratic masses to come over to the side of communism for winning soviet power. This has been our aim, and it is now under the new tactic of the united front.

What are the changes needed in the tactic of the united front to meet the new changed conditions? Here we must distinguish three factors.

1. As is known, on the eve of the Sixth Congress of the Comintern, the Ninth Plenum of the ECCI advanced the slogan of "Class against Class." This slogan, of course, did not and does not mean that the class of the bourgeoisie was to be opposed by only one class—the proletariat—without allies. This slogan simply sharpened the struggle against the conciliators. The slogan "Class against Class" was advanced at first only in accordance with the tasks of the French and British communist parties in connection with the change in the election tactics of these parties proposed by the Ninth Plenum of the ECCI . . . But it would be a crude error to consider that the most important thing in the slogan "Class against Class" was limited to a change in election tactics. That is how the renegade Doriot now interprets this slogan, and on this basis he maintains that we now, having changed our election tactics in France, thereby have tacitly abandoned the slogan "Class against Class." Doriot's point of view merely testifies to his parliamentary cretinism . . . We were unable to lead a mass struggle of the working class without "taking the line of sharpening the struggle against social-democracy," which at that time had the capacity to place and did place enormous obstacles in the development of the mass struggle.

At that time the Comintern understood the slogan of "Class against Class" to mean the need for a struggle against our enemy, the bourgeoisie, and *first of all,* for the intensification of the struggle against social-democracy and the leadership in the reformist trade-unions. This followed from the situation as it existed then, when the top strata of the workers' organizations led by social-democracy were effecting a rapid unification with the state apparatus and the entrepreneur organizations, when the leading social-democratic party—the German one—was still in the government, and when other social-democratic parties were either participating in bourgeois governments or expected to be; when this chief social prop of the bourgeoisie was not yet shaken up and corroded with inner differences—as the result of which it was necessary to undermine this barrier *first of all* in order to be able to develop the mass struggle. The workers at that time evaluated correctly the slogan "Class against Class." And to this we owed the big success in the parliamentary elections of 1928 in France, when for the first time we applied this slogan there. In those elections we received 1,069,000 votes (20 per cent more than in 1924). In those elections the influence of our party grew particularly in the industrial districts, our party became the strongest party in the proletarian quarters of Paris and its suburbs. Tens of thousands of workers came over to us from the socialists at that time. [Footnote omitted.]

Since that time the situation has greatly changed. Social-democracy is now experiencing a crisis, and in some countries (Germany and Austria) has been defeated and has gone bankrupt in the eyes of the broad masses. At the same time fascism has grown greatly and continues to grow, drawing to its support the broad petty-bourgeoisie masses and a few déclassé strata of the workers, and which in a number of countries has captured the governmental apparatus, which it uses for the terrorizing of the workers. At the same time, the mood among broad strata of the working class, particularly among those strata which formerly followed and which still follow social-democracy, has undergone a change. Among broad strata of the social-democratic and nonparty workers there is a growing inclination toward the united front with the communists for the struggle against fascism, or an inclination toward communism. Under these circumstances, the slogan "Class against Class" still remains valid just as it remains valid that the bourgeoisie is our enemy, and that our goal is to develop a mass struggle against the bourgeoisie. But it is much easier for us now to develop the mass struggle, applying the broad tactic of the united front, in which connection we must now, without weakening the struggle, *change the form of the struggle against social-democracy*. We must now mobilize all antifascist forces for the struggle against fascism—in order to offer resistance to the attack of fascism, in order to draw away from fascism the masses which follow it—setting as our goal the complete routing of fascism, which can be accomplished only by the victory of the proletarian revolution and the establishment of the dictatorship of the proletariat. As to social-democracy, we will be best able to liquidate its influence upon the masses by the successful and correct application of the tactic of the united front in the struggle against fascism (and war), *in the process of this struggle,* and in the process of the struggle for the *complete destruc-*

tion of fascism and for the victory of the proletarian revolution, which under no conditions shall we be able to accomplish in a united front with the social-democratic conciliatory parties, but without them and against them, although with the help of considerable strata of the social-democratic workers, part of the social-democratic organizations, and some social-democratic functionaries, whom we shall succeed in drawing to the revolutionary struggle against the bourgeoisie. In all of this lies at present the application of the slogan "Class against Class."

2. Earlier, at the time of the Sixth Congress of the Comintern, the tactic of the united front was expressed in the fact that, using this tactic for the struggle against the bourgeoisie, for the mobilization of the masses for this struggle, encountering at the first steps the determined resistance of social-democracy, which led the majority of the working class, we were forced to begin with the ruthless unmasking of social-democracy. Now we also unmask the compromising policy of social-democracy. But now, because of the crisis of social-democracy, because of the very strong inclination of social-democratic workers toward a united front with us, we can and must, by means of the tactic of the united front, mobilize the broad masses, unmasking social-democracy best of all *in the process of the struggle*. This means that *we must apply the tactic of the united front in such a way that the social-democratic workers would in no way be able to regard it as a maneuver on our part, which we are actually not carrying out.*

3. The Sixth Congress of the Comintern proposed "to transfer the decisive center of gravity to the united front from below." This decision did not exclude in principle the simultaneous application of the united front from above. But at that time, during the Sixth Congress, the necessary prerequisites did not exist for the application of the tactic of the united front from above. *Now, still keeping the center of gravity on the united front from below, we cannot at the same time reject the combination, or attempts at the combination, of the tactic of the united front from below with the tactic of the united front from above, when this can be achieved without sacrificing principles and, despite all the changes regarding the criticism of social-democracy which follow from this, while maintaining the criticism itself.* We must do this because conditions have substantially changed since that time. At the time of the Sixth Congress it was impossible to count on success in making any social-democratic parties, or even social-democratic party organizations, or even a prominent social-democratic functionary, agree to even a

limited united front with the communists, and *this fact made it difficult for us to approach the social-democratic masses.* Now, however, the oppositional pressure of the worker masses on social-democracy from below has increased so greatly and the fear of the savage fascist terror even by the social-democratic leaders is so great that the social-democratic parties or organizations are not only forced to resort to "left" maneuvers to an unprecedented extent, but certain social-democratic parties, while not refusing to co-operate with the bourgeoisie, are forced to come to an agreement on a united front with the communists in the struggle against fascism and war, and some social-democratic organizations and some influential social-democratic functionaries are even ready to come over and have already come over to the camp of the communists.

The new situation now is such that we must move *with complete boldness for broadening the tactic of the united front* if we wish to utilize the favorable objective situation in order to draw into our struggle the broadest possible strata of the social-democratic workers who today are still not ready to become communists, if we wish to utilize the favorable situation for winning over the majority of the working class, for bringing together all antifascist forces, for mobilizing the broad masses for the struggle against fascism and the war danger, for drawing these masses into the decisive battles for power, for soviet power, which are approaching.

. . .

Is this new tactic of the broader application of the united front pregnant with dangers? Unquestionably it is. We must not forget that if a social-democratic party as a whole, a social-democratic party as such, has agreed or agrees tomorrow to conclude a pact on the united front with a communist party, the goals, if not the immediate ones then the more distant ones, at which it aims and at which we aim are different in principle, *they are irreconcilable with one another.* They, in concluding with us an agreement on the united front of struggle against fascism, have as their ultimate goal the restoration or strengthening of the regime of bourgeois democracy, which is one of the forms of the dictatorship of the bourgeoisie. We, however, in concluding such an agreement, being ready to fight energetically for the defense or re-establishment of even the smallest democratic rights of the workers, for the defense of even the smallest economic demands of the workers, have as our ultimate goals the destruction of any form of the rule of the bourgeoisie and the establishment of the dictatorship of the proletariat.

In view of this opposition of the ultimate goals and the consequent differences in principle in tactics and organizations, the socialist parties may use an agreement on the united front with us against us, in order to weaken our struggle against the bourgeoisie. And it must be admitted that in some places they are already doing this now, not without success.

We must now carry out the tactic of the united front with complete boldness. But in order to avoid the dangers connected with this tactic, we must, in using this tactic, not for a moment lose sight of the revolutionary prospects; we must link this tactic most closely with our strategic task—the conquest of the majority of the working class for the immediate struggle for power, for soviet power; we must subordinate this tactic to our strategic task, not for a moment losing sight of the latter.

This means in practice that in applying the tactic of the united front we must not conceal our party face, we must not limit ourselves, thanks to the agreement, in the conduct of mass strike battles; we must not confine our activity within the limits of the agreement; we must not make difficult for ourselves the possibility of leading the masses independently. This means that, having concluded an agreement with the social-democratic parties and having made a number of concessions as the result of this agreement—for example, refraining from mutual attacks where we are waging a joint struggle—we must not, while carrying out this obligation conscientiously, abstain from determined, ruthless criticism when this agreement is violated or sabotaged; we must not abstain from criticism which, directed toward the broadening of the tasks of the united front of struggle, by its form does not threaten to disrupt the agreement; we must not abstain from organizing the struggle from below, from disrupting the too narrow framework of the agreement; we must also not abstain—for the sake of recruiting new members of the party, for broadening our influence among the masses and for the leadership of their struggle—merely from propagandizing our platform, but must not abstain from criticism, criticism unclamorous yet concise, clear, and principled, of the program, strategy, and tactics of those with whom we are concluding the agreement, etc.

· · ·

143

Pravda *Evaluates the Laval-Litvinov Protocol on the East European Pact*

"Franko-sovetskoe soglashenie o vostochnom pakte," Pravda, No. 337, December 8, 1934, p. 1. The text of the protocol is given in Degras, Foreign Policy, III, 96–97.

. . .

There is no doubt that all sincere supporters of peace in all countries would welcome the realization of an East European pact. Tranquility and a stable peace in eastern Europe are the essential conditions for the strengthening of peace not only on the entire European continent, but also far beyond its borders. This is understood very well by those imperialist groupings which are striving for new military adventures and which are therefore interested in every possible way in the failure of the idea of an East European pact.

These groupings which are hostile to the cause of peace are making no small efforts to attain their goal. Especially worthy of notice are their attempts, on the one hand, to make it appear that the U.S.S.R. and France have changed their points of view on the significance of the pact, and, on the other hand, attempts to sow distrust between the U.S.S.R. and France and to undermine the basis of the pact.

The agreement signed between People's Commissar of Foreign Affairs, Comrade *Litvinov,* and the French Minister of Foreign Affairs, M. *Laval,* is of great importance *exactly because* it brings complete clarity into the question of the nature of the East European pact.

Wherein lies the meaning of the agreement?

First, the agreement testifies to *the firm intention of the governments of both countries to continue to work for the realization of the pact, for the strengthening of peace and normal good-neighborly relations among all the interested states of eastern Europe.* Both governments continue, as before, to believe that the

East European pact is an *indispensable condition* for the attainment of these goals.

Thus the agreement deals a crushing blow to those who have attempted to speculate on their own inventions regarding the position of the U.S.S.R. and France.

Second, the agreement should put an end to any intrigues directed toward sowing distrust between France and the U.S.S.R. We know that not a few efforts have been made and no little eloquence has been expended by some political "traveling salesmen" of definite imperialist groupings in order, by means of intrigues, to complicate the realization of the pact. The Franco-Soviet agreement shows that these intrigues are doomed to failure. At the same time it testifies to the further strengthening of friendly relations between both countries.

Third, the agreement should also put an end to all attempts by these same groupings to replace the East European pact by a less effective agreement which would impose no obligations of any kind on anyone, or which might even pursue opposite purposes.

That is why the communiqué on the conclusion of the Franco-Soviet agreement should give deep satisfaction to all champions and supporters of peace.

144

The Comintern Defines the United Front

"Za edinyi front bor'by mezhdunarodnogo proletariata," K.I., No. 35, December 10, 1934, pp. 10–12.

. . .

It is necessary with even greater energy than before to organize, consolidate, and widen the united proletarian front of struggle. The threat of a new war has increased. The offensive of capitalism and fascism has gathered strength. The bourgeoisie is concentrating its forces in order to forestall the maturing revolutionary crisis. More than ever before it is necessary to oppose the reactionary front of the fascist bourgeoisie with a *united front of struggle* of the international proletariat. *In proposing to the Second International the establishment of a united front of struggle in defense of the Spanish workers, the Comintern was guided by the conviction that in spite of existing differences on all questions of program, strategy, and tactics, in spite of the difference of aims pursued in the establishment of a united front by the parties of the Second and Third Internationals, it was possible in a number of countries to establish a united front of communist and socialist parties.*

Notwithstanding the refusal of the Second International, the communist parties will continue with all revolutionary determination *to develop in breadth and depth the united front of the struggle of the proletariat.*

In those countries where the leadership of the s.-d. parties is against an agreement on the united front, the communist parties, in accordance with the example of the Comintern's appeal of October 11 of this year, will appeal again and again, in connection with specific attacks of capital and fascism, to the leadership of the s.-d. parties, to their local organizations, to the s.-d. workers, with practical proposals for joint actions in the united front. Most important: without waiting for an answer, the communists will immediately develop independently the struggle of the workers against the specific forms of the offensive of the bourgeoisie. The communists will not let themselves be driven from this path by any refusals of the social-democratic leadership.

In those countries where it has been possible to reach an agreement on the united front, between the communist and socialist parties, the communists will strive for the *consolidation, deepening, and broadening of the united front* . . .

Very urgent for our struggle for the united front are the instructions given by *Lenin* in connection with the conference of the three Internationals in 1922. The delegation of the Comintern (Radek, Bukharin, *et al.*) made a concession to the representatives of the Second and Second-and-a-Half Internationals (Vandervelde, Adler, *et al.*), agreeing to the presence of representatives of the Second and Second-and-a-Half Internationals at the trial of the Social Revolutionaries and promised that the Soviet government would not apply the death penalty to the Social Revolutionary terrorists. This concession was considered by Lenin to be a concession to the *reactionary bourgeoisie,* and he considered the role of the leaders of the Second and Second-and-a-Half Internationals to be "the role of extortionists of political concession." Concluding his article, Lenin wrote:

The representatives of the Second and the Second-and-a-Half Internationals need a united front because they hope to weaken us by making us agree to excessive concessions; they hope to work their way into our communist establishment without giving up anything on their part; they hope by means of the tactic of the united front to convince the workers of the correctness of reformist tactics and the incorrectness of revolutionary tactics. *We need* the united front because we hope to convince the workers to the contrary. We will shift the mistakes made by our communist representatives onto them and onto those parties which make these mistakes, in order to teach by the example of these mistakes and to ensure that they will not be repeated in the future. Under no circumstance, however, shall we lay the blame for the mistakes of our communists on the masses of the proletariat, which throughout the entire world is confronted with the attacks on it of offensive capital. For the sake of helping these masses struggle against capital, helping them understand "the cunning mechanics" of the two fronts in the entire world economy and in the entire world politics, for the sake of that, we have accepted the tactic of the united front, and we shall carry it on to the end. [Lenin, *Sochineniia*, 2d ed., XXVII, 280.]

In their entire struggle for the united front the communists are fulfilling in deeds these instructions of Lenin, and in spite of all hindrances and obstacles raised by the enemies of the united front in the Second International, they will carry on this struggle to the end. The communists will not allow themselves to be forced off this path by any attempts to replace the united front of *struggle,* immediate joint actions, by discussions of the unity (organic, political) of the working class in general. Neither will the communists allow themselves to be forced off this path by the opportunists in their own ranks, who hide individual mistakes made by communists from the masses; they will fight ruthlessly against both "Left" sectarianism and against the Right opportunist danger as the greatest danger at present. In consolidating and broadening the united front of the struggle of the international proletariat, the communists will convince the masses of the proletariat, in the process of the struggle of the united proletarian front, of the correctness of the entire policy of the Communist International, and, at the head of the majority of the working class, will lead the millions of the masses of toilers to a victorious struggle for the soviet power throughout the entire world.

145

A Soviet Evaluation of the Eastern Pact

"Vostochnyi pakt—garantiia mira," Pravda, No. 349, December 20, 1934, p. 1.

We have spoken already more than once (see *Pravda* of December 8 and 9) of the meaning, significance, and purpose of the Franco-Soviet protocol signed at Geneva on December 5. Now, when the text of this protocol is in our hands, it will be useful to return once more to this question.

The protocol has a threefold significance. *First,* it indicates the futility of attempts to sow distrust between France and the U.S.S.R. *Second,* it testifies to the readiness of the governments of France and the U.S.S.R. to guarantee *the continuity and efficiency of Franco-Soviet diplomatic collaboration. Third,* it constitutes, together with the successful completion of the visit to Moscow of the French Minister of Trade, M. *Marchand,* an indication of the further rapprochement between France and the U.S.S.R.

In vain a part of the reactionary French press (and not only the French) has tried to interpret the signing of the protocol in the sense that it ties the hands of the governments of France and the U.S.S.R., that it represents a step backward, etc. This is absolute nonsense! The Franco-Soviet protocol is *a step forward and not backward.* It is a step forward inasmuch as it testifies to further Franco-Soviet rapprochement, and thereby *improves the prospects for the realization of an East European pact.* It is a step forward for the strengthening of peace *inasmuch as it deals a palpable blow to each and every intrigue directed against it, against France, against the U.S.S.R.*

The French Minister of Foreign Affairs, M. *Laval,* spoke on all these questions, which are of the greatest importance for the fate of European peace, when he reported to the Senate on December 18. He gave their due to Franco-Soviet relations and the Franco-Soviet protocol signed at Geneva. M. Laval also touched on Franco-German relations. He stated that "the Franco-Soviet rapprochement within the international framework constitutes an effective guarantee of peace."

Agreement with Germany is essential, and both France and the U.S.S.R. are striving for it. The point of view of the Soviet Union has been exhaustively set forth in the statement made by Comrade Litvinov on December 7. Pointing out that the U.S.S.R. and France seek the best possible relations with Germany, Comrade Litvinov stated: "The Eastern pact would make possible the establishment and further development of those relations between these three countries, as well as among other participants in the pact, and would introduce that pacification into the international situation which is so much desired by the peoples of Europe and North America."

Such an agreement with Germany, within the limits of the Eastern pact, would undoubtedly prove useful and would provide relief to all peoples. We stress—*such an agreement,* because it is clear that there can be all kinds of agreements. It is necessary to dwell on this question in the interests of peace. The position of the Soviet Union is absolutely clear. It fights for peace, for universal security. Frequently the organs of the English and German press attempt to frighten the whole world by the Franco-Soviet "military alliance." They have selected this bugaboo not accidentally: their aim is to defame the peaceful character of Franco-Soviet collaboration.

In reality, the Soviet Union is not in favor of military alliances against third states; it strives for a collective agreement in the defense of peace and security for all countries.

In this connection, inasmuch as the question of the necessity of an agreement with Germany has been raised, the situation should be stated as it is. It seems that we have not yet heard any similar proposal coming from that side, nor do we know of any such steps being taken by Germany which would indicate the readiness of the leading circles of fascist Germany to sign a collective agreement for the struggle for peace and for ensuring security for all countries, or at least along Germany's entire border.

On the contrary, the leading circles of Germany openly decline the East European pact, giving preference to "bilateral agreements." Therefore an impression is gained that all their statements pursue not peaceful aims, but on the contrary, *the realization of old adventurous plans.*

At present all of this must be said quite openly so that there will be no lack of understanding on the question of the purposefulness of German foreign policy. Germany realizes that it cannot fight on two fronts, that for the time being (but only for the time being!) it cannot venture to settle accounts with its western neighbors. Hitler therefore stated in a conversation with the representatives of the French fascists Maxime Gouas and Robert Monnier: "In the west the density of our population is 237 persons to one square kilometer. Is it conceivable that we intend to win back territory with such a density of population in order to complicate our situation still further?" In this case we are not touching upon the value of such arguments. It is significant to note that Hitler immediately added: *"Several problems on our eastern frontiers have a different character"* (*Le Matin,* November 18) .

In the programmatic work of the National Socialists, *Mein Kampf,* the following is stated in black and white:

> No matter how strongly we now recognize the necessity of coming to terms with France, these terms in general and as a whole will bring no results, if we make use of them in our entire foreign political plans. The coming to terms can and will make sense only if it would serve us as a support and a cover for the expansion of our territory needed for the livelihood of our people in Europe.

This idea was expressed even more clearly by one of the literary henchmen of German imperialism, Karl Mergala, when he wrote, *"It is not possible, of course, to fight everyone at once!"* With everyone—no, but to beat one's neighbors one at a time—yes! That is the meaning of the German policy of bilateral agreements.

If that is the situation, however, then it is against such dangerous plans that *serious guarantees* are needed. And the best guarantee is the East European pact. It is imperative to understand clearly that *at present there is not and cannot be any more reliable guarantee of peace and security than this pact.* In proposing to Germany to join the East European pact, France and the U.S.S.R. ask *nothing except a guarantee of peace.* If Germany is for peace, it should give this guarantee.

That is the whole situation. And this should not be forgotten for a minute. At any rate, the Soviet Union is not forgetting about all this.

146

Pravda *on the Failure of the London Naval Conference*

I. Erukhimovich, "Podgotovka voiny na Tikhom Okeane (neudacha Londonskikh morskikh peregovorov i rastorzhenie Iaponiei vashingtonskogo dogovora)," Pravda, No. 355, December 26, 1934, p. 3.

I

On December 19, for the first time in the entire course of the negotiations in London, the delegations of England, the U.S.A., and Japan met for the first time in one sitting—up till that time, only *bilateral* negotiations had taken place. This was the last meeting. "All aspects of the naval problem were discussed sincerely, fully, and harmoniously. Now it is necessary to postpone the negotiations in order to make it possible for the delegates to discuss the situation with their governments. It is hoped that the negotiations will be resumed in the near future." Thus reads the official communiqué, which, as is proper on such occasions, does not misuse either clarity or precision.

And yet the situation is more than clear. The London negotiations have ended in *complete failure.* Not a single party wished to make any concessions to the others. Or to be more exact, they were *not able to do it.* The demand put forward by Japan—parity of naval forces—and the draft of a future naval agreement proposed by Japan contradict so much the interests of the U.S.A. that it refused point blank to accept them. Great Britain, which tried as long as possible to remain in the position of "mediator" between the U.S.A. and Japan, likewise did not venture to accept unconditionally all the demands of the latter.

The contradictions between the three largest naval imperialist powers disrupted the negotiations in London. . . .

The delegates of the U.S.A. and Japan had hardly had time to notify their governments of the postponement of the London negotiations when a second and even more stunning blow was struck. On December 22 the Japanese government took a decision in accordance with which Japan is to be considered free of the obligations of the Washington naval treaty, while the treaty itself is abrogated. The official communiqué is to follow before the end of 1934, i.e., within a few days. This event is undoubtedly one of high importance, and it is pregnant with far-reaching consequences.

Between the time of the announcement by Japan of the abrogation of the Washington treaty and its complete annullment two years must pass, during which the treaty will still be in force (till December 31, 1936). But this is the formal aspect of the affair. The essence lies in the fact that the *entire system of the "balance of power" in the Pacific is crashing down,* the system favorable to American imperialism which arose after the World War and which was consolidated in 1922 in Washington.

Fourteen years later not a stone is left standing of this imposing edifice. The imperialist contradictions in the Pacific have now reached such a depth that all the participants in the struggle for the monopolist right to rob and exploit the multimillion masses inhabiting eastern Asia, as well as their land, now find themselves once again at the starting point of the struggle, but under completely different conditions. The Washington treaty has proved, therefore, to be a summit which, in Herzen's witty phrase, crowns the mountain . . . with nothing.

. . .

III

. . .

The complexity of the grouping of forces which has come into existence in the Pacific is obvious. All three main imperialist powers which are fighting among themselves—the U.S.A., England, and Japan—are torn asunder by such profound contradictions that a possibility for more or less prolonged compromise among them that would satisfy all three powers appears to be exceedingly problematic. At the same time, the possibility of a durable Anglo-American alliance directed against Japan is almost excluded; the latter is making every effort to renew the alliance with England, which has so far not indicated its readiness, believing that *the closer the Japanese-American fight, the more advantageous will be the key position of Great Britain.* This is a bet on the aggravation of Japanese-American contradictions.

There can be no two opinions that if England had spoken firmly and decisively against the abrogation of the Washington treaty, Japan would not have decided to take this step. Japan is acting with assurance and boldness exactly because *it considers the abrogation of the Washington treaty as one of the most necessary and most important prerequisites for the re-establishment of the Anglo-Japanese alliance.*

Japan regards the abrogation of the Washington treaty as an essential link in a long chain of measures aimed at bringing about *naval parity between Japan and America, strengthening for itself the decisive positions in China, in order to put an end to the America policy of the "Open Door."* In exactly this way Japan, in the words of its Minister of Foreign Affairs, Hiroto, intends to ensure its "security and establish the principle of nonaggression." Japan wants to take revenge for Washington.

. . .

If the Washington treaty in itself was the expression of the unceasing competition among the imperialist powers in regard to naval armament in "peace" time, then the abrogation of this treaty is an expression of *the monstrous armaments race at sea, on land, and in the air on the eve of war.*

. . . The further exacerbation of contradictions among the imperialist countries will accelerate the military denouement on the Pacific Ocean, which the denunciation of the Washington treaty by Japan indicates to all friends of peace.

BIBLIOGRAPHY

AND INDEX

SELECTED BIBLIOGRAPHY

Works cited and others which are especially pertinent to this period are listed. For more detailed listings see T. T. Hammond, *Soviet Foreign Relations and World Communism: A Selected Bibliography;* W. C. Clemens, Jr., *Soviet Disarmament Policy, 1917–1963: An Annotated Bibliography of Soviet and Western Sources;* and W. S. Sworakowski, *The Communist International and Its Front Organizations.*

The names of periodicals are given in full, with the exception of *I.P.C.* (*International Press Correspondence*) and *K.I.* (*Kommunisticheskii Internatsional*).

GENERAL

Academy of Sciences, Institute for Chinese Studies. *Sovetsko-kitaiskie otnosheniia; sbornik dokumentov* (Soviet-Chinese relations; a collection of documents). Moscow, 1959.

———. Pacific Institute. *Krizis kolonial'noi sistemy: natsional'no-osvoboditelnaia bor'ba narodov Vostochnoi Azii* (Crisis of the colonial system: national-liberation struggle of the peoples of East Asia). Moscow, 1949.

Acton, H. B. *The Illusion of the Epoch: Marxism-Leninism as a Philosophical Creed.* Boston, [1957].

Airapetian, M. E., and G. A. Deborin. *Etapy vneshnei politiki SSSR* (Stages of foreign policy of the U.S.S.R.). Moscow, 1961.

———. *Komintern i vneshniaia politika* (The Comintern and foreign policy). Moscow, 1962. 47 pp.

———. *Leninskie printsipy vneshnei politiki sovetskogo gosudarstva* (Leninist principles of foreign policy of the Soviet state). Moscow, 1957.

Agrarnyi vopros na Vostoke (Agrarian question in the East). Moscow, 1933.

Aleksandrov (pseud.). *Kto upravliaet Rossiei? Bol'shevistkii partiino-pravitel'stvennyi apparat* (Who rules Russia? Bolshevik party-government apparatus). Berlin, 1933.

Aleksandrov, V. "Iugo-zapadnaia Afrika" (Southwestern Africa). *Kolonial'nye Problemy,* Sbornik II, 1934, pp. 212–227.

Ali, M. "Razvitie rabochego dvizheniia v Indii [1928–1929]" (Development of the workers' movement in India [1928–1929]). *Revoliutsionnyi Vostok,* No. 7, May 29, 1929, pp. 255–271.

Ardzheno. "Prichiny vosstaniia v voennom flote v Indonizii" (Reasons for the mutiny in the [Dutch] navy in Indonesia). *Kolonial'nye Problemy,* Sbornik I, 1933, pp. 108–112.

Arsenev, E. *Podzhigateli voiny: 4 pokusheniia na polpredstvo SSSR v Varshave* (Fomenters of war; four attempts on the U.S.S.R. embassy in Warsaw). Moscow, 1931.

Avarin, V. Ia. *Bor'ba za Tikhii Okean: agressiia SShA i Anglii, ikh protivorechiia i osvoboditel'naia bor'ba narodov* (The struggle for the Pacific Ocean: aggression of the U.S.A. and England, their differences, and the liberation struggle of the peoples). Moscow, 1952.

———. *Bor'ba za Tikhii Okean; iapono-amerikanskie protivorechiia* (The struggle for the Pacific Ocean: Japanese-American differences). Moscow, 1947.

———. *Imperializm v Man'chzhurii* (Imperialism in Manchuria). 2d ed. Moscow, 1934.

———. "Natsional'no-osvoboditel'naia voina i klassovaia bor'ba v Man'chzhurii" (National-liberation war and the class struggle in Manchuria). *K.I.*, No. 17, June 10, 1933, pp. 33–48, and *Kolonial'nye Problemy*, Sbornik II, 1934, pp. 116–137.

———. *Raspad kolonial'noi sistemy* (Disintegration of the colonial system). Moscow, 1957.

Beloff, M. *The Foreign Policy of Soviet Russia, 1929–1941.* 2 vols. London and New York, 1947–49.

Bishop, D. G. *The Roosevelt-Litvinov Agreements: The American View.* Syracuse, 1965.

——— (ed.). *Soviet Foreign Relations: Documents and Readings.* Syracuse, 1952.

Bogolepov, I. "Anglo-iaponskaia ekonomicheskaia voina" (Anglo-American economic war). *Kolonial'nye Problemy*, Sbornik II, 1934, pp. 98–115.

Bonch-Osmolinsky, A. *Angliia i Soedinennye Shtaty v bor'be za mirovuiu gegemoniiu* (England and the United States in the struggle for world hegemony). Moscow and Leningrad, 1930.

"Bor'ba dvukh mirov" (The struggle of two worlds). Editorial, *Revoliutsionnyi Vostok*, No. 1–2, 1932, pp. 5–35.

"Bor'ba Iaponii, SShA i Anglii za Tikhii Okean" (The struggle of Japan, the U.S.A., and England for the Pacific Ocean). *K.I.*, No. 20–21, 1934, pp. 30–37.

"Bor'ba za edinyi front proletariata na Vostoke" (The struggle for a united front of the proletariat in the East). *Krasnyi Internatsional Profsoiuzov*, No. 11–12, 1933, pp. 5–15.

Brewer, F. M. *Russo-Japanese Relations.* Washington, D.C., 1944. Reprint from *Editorial Research Reports*, Vol. II, No. 16, November 3, 1944, pp. 279–292.

Briand-Kellogg Pact. *The General Pact for the Renunciation of War; Text of the Pact as Signed; Notes and Other Papers.* Washington, D.C., 1928.

Browder, R. P. *The Origins of Soviet-American Diplomacy.* Princeton, 1953.

———. "Soviet Far Eastern Policy and American Recognition, 1932–1934." *Pacific Historical Review*, Vol. 21, August 1952, pp. 263–273.

Bukhartsev, D., *et al.* (eds.). *Podgotovka vtorogo tura imperialisticheskikh voin; sbornik* (Preparation of the second round of imperialistic wars; a collection [of articles]). Moscow, 1934.

———, E. Varga, and P. Lapinsky. *"Razoruzhenie"—podgotovka voiny: doklad L. Ivanova i vystupleniia v Institute Mirovogo Khoziaistva i Mirovoi Politiki* ("Disarmament"—preparation of war; report by L. Ivanov and comments in the Institute of World Economics and World Politics). Moscow, 1932.

Buss, C. A. *Asia in the Modern World: A History of China, Japan, South and Southeast Asia.* New York, [1964].

———. *War and Diplomacy in Eastern Asia.* New York, 1941.

Carr, E. H. *German-Soviet Relations between the Two World Wars, 1919–1939.* Baltimore, 1951.

Castro Delgado, Enrique. *J'ai perdu la foi à Moscou.* Paris, 1950.

Chamberlain, W. H. *Russia's Iron Age.* Boston, 1934.

Clark, R. T. *The Fall of the German Republic: A Political Study.* London, 1935.

Clemens, W. C., Jr. *Soviet Disarmament Policy, 1917–1963: An Annotated Bibliography of Soviet and Western Sources.* Stanford, 1965.

Coates, W. P. (comp.), *USSR and Disarmament: Discussion of Russia's Proposals at Geneva, March 16–24, 1928* . . . Anglo-Russian Parliamentary Committee, London, 1928.

Communist Party of the Soviet Union, Higher Party School, Chair of the International Relations and Foreign Policy of the U.S.S.R. *Mezhdunarodnye otnosheniia i vneshniaia politika SSSR, 1917–1960* (International relations and foreign policy of the U.S.S.R., 1917–1960), Moscow, 1961.

Conference for the Reduction and Limitation of Armaments. *See* League of Nations.

Dashinsky, S. *Britanskii imperializm i anti-sovetskii front* (British imperialism and the anti-Soviet front). Moscow, 1929.

Davis, K. (Wassermann). *The Soviets at Geneva: The U.S.S.R. and the League of Nations, 1919–1933.* Geneva, 1934.

Deborin, G. A. *Leninskaia politika mirnogo sosushchestvovaniia dvukh sistem—general'naia liniia vneshnei politiki SSSR* (Leninist policy of peaceful coexistence of two systems—general line of foreign policy of the U.S.S.R.). Moscow, 1956. Lecture, 31 pp.

———. *Obrazovanie dvukh ochagov voiny i bor'ba za sozdanie kollektivnoi bezopasnosti (1932–1937)* (The formation of the two centers of war and the struggle for collective security, 1932–1937). Moscow, 1947. Lecture delivered June 22, 1947; 29 pp.

Degras, Jane (Tabritsky) (comp. and ed.). *Soviet Documents on Foreign Policy.* 3 vols. London, 1952–53.

Dirksen, Herbert von. *Moskau, Tokio, London; Erinnerungen und Betrachtungen zur 20 Jahren deutscher Aussenpolitik, 1919–1939.* Stuttgart, 1949. English edition: *Moscow, Tokyo, London: Twenty Years of German Foreign Policy.* London, 1951.

Documents on International Affairs, 1928. London, 1929. Supplement to annual *Survey of International Affairs.*

Dorsenne, Jean. *Faudra-t-il évacuer l'Indochine?* Paris, 1932

Dyck, H. L. *Weimar Germany and Soviet Russia 1926–1933: A Study in Diplomatic Instability.* London, 1966.

Enukidze, D. "Imperialisticheskie protivorechiia na Blizhnem Vostoke" (Imperialist differences in the Near East). *Mirovoe Khoziaistvo i Mirovaia Politika,* No. 12, December 1934, pp. 90–107.

Erukhimovich, I. "Obostrenie imperialisticheskikh protivorechii na Tikhom Okeane" (The sharpening of imperialist contradictions in the Pacific Ocean). *Bol'shevik,* No. 24, December 31, 1934, pp. 47–62.

Eudin, X. J., and H. H. Fisher. *Soviet Russia and the West, 1920–1927: A Documentary Survey.* Stanford, 1957.

Eudin, X. J., and R. C. North. *Soviet Russia and the East, 1920–1927: A Documentary Survey.* Stanford, 1957.

Fischer, L. *The Soviets in World Affairs: History of the Relations between the Soviet Union and the Rest of the World, 1917–1929.* 2 vols. Princeton, 1951.

Fischer, R. *Stalin and German Communism: A Study in the Origins of the State Party.* Cambridge, Mass., 1948.

Florinsky, M. T. *World Revolution and the USSR.* New York, 1933.

From the First to the Second Five-Year Plan: A Symposium by J. Stalin, V. Molotov, L. Kaganovich, K. Voroshilov, G. Orjonikidze, N. Kuibyshev, Y. Yakovlev, and G. Grinko. New York, 1934.

Galkovich, M. G. *Soedinennye Shtaty i dal'nevostochnaia problema* (The United States and the Far Eastern problem). Moscow, 1928.

Galperin, A. "Filippiny" (Philippines). *Kolonial'nye Problemy,* Sbornik II, 1934, pp. 176–211.

Gamburg, B. "Mirovoi ekonomicheskii krizis i Kitai" (The world economic crisis and China). *Kolonial'nye Problemy,* Sbornik II, 1934, pp. 3–31.

Gautherot, G. *Le Bolchévisme aux colonies: l'imperialism rouge.* [Paris,] 1930.

Gedar, L. *Anti-sovetskaia politika frantsuzskogo imperialisma* (Anti-Soviet policy of French imperialism). Introduction by Karl Radek. Moscow, 1931.

Genkin, I. I. *Soedinennye Shtaty Ameriki i SSSR: ikh politicheskie i ekonomicheskie vzaimootnosheniia* (The United States of America and the U.S.S.R.: their political and economic relations). Leningrad, 1934.

[Germany, Auswärtiges Amt.] *Documents on German Foreign Policy, 1918–1945*, Series C (1933–1937). Washington, D.C. 1957——.

Ger've, O. "Desiat let politicheskoi deiatel'nosti Ligi Natsii" (Ten years of the political activity of the League of Nations). *Mezhdunarodnaia Zhizn*, No. 1, 1930, pp. 72–85.

——. "Konets Kommissii razoruzheniia" (The end of the Commission on Disarmament). *Mezhdunarodnaia Zhizn*, No. 12, 1930, pp. 54–65.

Ginsburgs, G. "A Calendar of Soviet Treaties, January–December 1961." *Osteuropa-Recht*, Vol. 10, No. 2, 1964, pp. 116–148.

——, and R. M. Slusser. "A Calendar of Soviet Treaties, January–December 1959." *Osteuropa-Recht*, Vol. 8, No. 2, June 1962, pp. 132–164.

Gnedin, E. A. *Razoruzhenie—uzel mezhdunarodnykh protivorechii* (Disarmament—the tangle of international contradictions). Moscow, 1935.

Gomez, X. "Meksika" (Mexico). *Kolonial'nye Problemy*, Sbornik I, 1933, pp. 249–259.

Good, W. T. *Is Intervention in Russia a Myth?* London, 1931.

Goodman, E. R. *The Soviet Design for a World State*. Foreword by P. E. Mosely. New York, 1960.

Great Britain, Foreign Office. *Correspondence Relating to the Arrest of Employees of the Metropolitan-Vickers Company at Moscow* . . . London, 1933. 24 pp.

——, ——. *Correspondence Showing the Course of Certain Diplomatic Discussions Directed Towards Securing an European Settlement, June 1934 to March 1936*. British Blue Book, Miscellaneous No. 3 (1936). Cmd. 4143. London, 1936.

——, ——. *Documents on British Foreign Policy, 1919–1939*. London, 1949——.

——, ——. *Further Correspondence Relating to the Arrest of Employees of the Metropolitan-Vickers Company at Moscow* . . . London, 1933. 20 pp.

Grigor'ev, L., and S. Olenev. *Bor'ba SSSR za mir i bezopasnost v Evrope, 1925–1933 gg.* (The struggle of the U.S.S.R. for peace and security in Europe, 1925–1933). Moscow, 1956.

Gusev, S. I. (Iakov Dralkin). "Na poroge novykh boev" (On the threshold of new battles). *K. I.*, No. 9–10, 1929, pp. 42–62.

——. "Na putiakh k novomu revoliutsionnomu pod"emu" (On the road to the new revolutionary upsurge). *K.I.*, No. 26, July 5, 1929, pp. 12–22.

Halecki, Oskar. *Polish-Russian Relations: Past and Present* . . . Notre Dame, Indiana, 1933.

Hammond, T. T. *Soviet Foreign Relations and World Communism: A Selected Annotated Bibliography*. Princeton, 1965.

Hartlieb, W. W. *Das politische Vertragssystem der Sowjet-Union, 1920–1935*. Leipzig, 1936.

Hayama [Khaiama], U. *Rabochee dvizhenie v koloniakh Vostoka* (Workers' movement in the colonies in the East). Moscow and Leningrad, 1930.

——. *Sovremennyi iaponskii imperializm* (Contemporary Japanese imperialism). Moscow, 1932.

Heller, Otto. "The Recent Events in Manchuria," *I.P.C.*, Vol. 12, No. 35, August 11, 1932, p. 727.

Hilger, G., and A. G. Meyer. *The Incompatible Allies: A Memoir-History of German-Soviet Relations, 1918–1941*. New York, 1953.

Hindus, M. G. *The Great Offensive*. New York, 1933.

——. *Humanity Uprooted*. New York, 1929.

——. *Red Bread*. New York, 1931.

——. *Russia and Japan*. New York, 1942.

Hoetzsch, O. *Le caractère et la situation internationale de l'Union des Soviets*. Geneva, 1932.

[Hitler, A.] *The Speeches of Adolf Hitler, 1922–1939.* 2 vols. London and New York, 1942.

[Indochina.] Gouvernement Général de l'Indochine. *Directions des affaires politiques et de la Sûreté Générale: Documents.* 5 vols. Hanoi, 1933–34.

[Industrial Party (Prompartiia).] "Indictment of the Industrial Party [full text]," *I.P.C.,* Vol. 10, No. 53, November 20, 1930, pp. 1079–1103. "Proceedings of the Trial of the Industrial Party," *I.P.C.,* Vol. 10, No. 54, November 27, 1930, p. 1111–12; No. 55, December 4, 1930, pp. 1136–47; and No. 57, December 11, 1930, pp. 1183–96. Verdict, *I.P.C.,* Vol. 10, No. 57, December 11, 1930, pp. 1171–77.

International Anticommunist Entente, Permanent Bureau. *The Religious Persecutions in Russia: Documents and Facts.* Geneva, 1930. 30 pp.

———, ———. *Bolshevism in China.* Geneva, 1932. 27 pp.

International Colonial Bureau. *Rapport sur la préparation par le gouvernement soviètique des révoltes coloniales.* [The Hague, 193–.]

International Conference on Strike Strategy [Strasbourg, January 1929]. *Problems of Strike Strategy: Decisions of the International Conference on Strike Strategy Held in Strassburg, Germany* [sic]*, January, 1929.* Foreword by A. Lozovsky. New York, 1929. 49 pp.

"Interventsiia protiv Man'chzhurii i podgotovka bol'shoi anti-sovetskoi voiny" (Intervention in Manchuria and preparation of a large-scale anti-Soviet war). *K.I.,* No. 33–34, 1931, pp. 3–9.

Ioelson, M. "Mirovoi ekonomicheskii krizis i kolonial'nyi mir" (The world economic crisis and the colonial world). *Revoliutsionnyi Vostok,* No. 1–2, 1932, pp. 36–42.

Iransky, S. "Pakt Kelloga i Vostok" (The Kellogg Pact and the East). *Novyi Vostok,* No. 23–24, December 1928, pp. xxxi-xlix.

Istoriia mezhdunarodnykh otnoshenii i vneshnei politiki SSSR, 1917–1960 gg. (History of the international relations and foreign policy of the U.S.S.R., 1917–1960). 3 vols. Institute of Foreign Relations, Department of International Relations and Foreign Policy. Moscow, 1961–64.

Iuzhnyi, A. *Iaponiia: politiko-ekonomicheskii ocherk* (Japan; politico-economic sketch). Moscow, 1933.

I-v, L. "Anglo-amerikanskoe morskoe sopernichestvo i strategicheskaia situatsiia na Dal'nem Vostoke" (Anglo-American naval competition and the strategic situation in the Far East). *K.I.,* No. 14, May 20, 1932, pp. 51–61.

L. I. [Ivanov, L.] "Bor'ba Iaponii, SShA i Anglii za Tikhii Okean" (The struggle of Japan, the U.S.A., and England for the Pacific Ocean). *K.I.,* No. 20–21, July 20, 1934, pp. 30–37.

Ivanov, L. N. *Krakh konferentsii po razoruzheniiu, s prilozheniem vazhneishikh dokumentov po razoruzheniiu* (Failure of the conference on disarmament, with the most important documents on disarmament). Kharkov, 1934.

———. *Liga Natsii* (The League of Nations). Moscow, 1929.

———. "Londonskie peregovory i tikhookeanskii uzel protivorechii" (The London negotiations and the Pacific Ocean tangle of contradictions). *Tikhii Okean,* No. 2, October–December 1934, pp. 5–12.

———. "Novyi etap morskogo sopernichestva na Tikhom Okeane" (The new stage of naval competition in the Pacific Ocean). *Tikhii Okean,* No. 4, October–December 1936, pp. 85–95.

———. "Razryv londonskikh peregovorov i morskaia politika ikh uchastnikov" (The breakdown of the London negotiations and the naval policy of the participants). *Tikhii Okean,* No. 1, 1935, pp. 61–71.

———. *SSSR i imperialisticheskoe okruzhenie* (The U.S.S.R. and imperialist encirclement). Moscow, 1954.

———, and P. Primakov. *Morskoe sopernichestvo imperialisticheskikh derzhav* (Naval competition of the imperialist powers). Moscow, 1936.

BIBLIOGRAPHY

————, and P. Smirnov. *Anglo-amerikanskoe morskoe sopernichestvo* (Anglo-American naval rivalry). Moscow, 1933.

Ivanov, V., and V. Lenian. *V interesakh narodov: k voprosu ob ustanovlenii diplomtciheskikh otnoshenii mezhdu SSSR i SShA v 1933 g.* (In the interests of peoples: on the question of the establishment of diplomatic relations between the U.S.S.R. and the U.S.A. in 1933). Moscow, 1957.

Ivashin, I. F. *Ocherki istorii vneshnei politiki SSSR* (Essays on the history of the foreign policy of the U.S.S.R.). Moscow, 1958.

Iz istorii mezhdunarodnoi proletarskoi solidarnosti: dokumenty i materialy (From the history of international proletarian solidarity: documents and materials). 5 vols. Moscow, 1957–61.

Jarman, T. L. *The Rise and Fall of Nazi Germany.* London, 1955.

"K voprosu o zarozhdenii i razvitii Marksizma v Iaponii" (The question of the inception and development of Marxism in Japan). *K.I.,* No. 7–8, March 10, 1933, pp. 76–87.

Kantorovich, A. Ia. *Amerika v bor'be za Kitai* (America in the struggle for China). Moscow, 1935.

————. *Bor'ba za Tikhii Okean* (The struggle for the Pacific Ocean). Moscow, 1932. 93 pp.

————. *Ochag voiny na Dal'nem Vostoke* (A hotbed of war in the Far East). Moscow, 1934.

[Katayama, Sen.] *Sen Katayama: stat'i i memuary* (*K stoletiiu dnia rozhdeniia*) (Sen Katayama: articles and memoirs; on the centenary of his birth). Moscow, 1959.

————. *Vospominaniia* (Recollections). Translated from the Japanese. Moscow, 1964.

Keaton, G. W. *The Problem of the Moscow Trial.* London, 1933.

Kennedy, M. D. *The Problem of Japan.* London, 1935.

Khaitsman, V. M. *SSSR i problema razoruzheniia mezhdu pervoi i vtoroi mirovymi voinami* (The U.S.S.R. and the problem of disarmament between the first and second world wars). Moscow, 1959.

Khorvatsky, V. L. *Pan-Evropa i Dunaiskaia federatsiia* (Pan-Europe and the Danubian federation). Moscow, 1933.

Kleist, P. *Die völkerrechtliche Anerkennung Sowjetrusslands.* Berlin. 1934.

Klenin, F. *Die diplomatischen Beziehungen Deutschlands zur Sowjetunion 1917–1932.* Berlin 1952.

Kniazhinsky, V. B. *Proval planov "ob'edineniia Evropy": ocherk istorii imperialisticheskikh popytok antisovetskogo "ob'edineniia Evropy" mezhdu pervoi i vtoroi mezhdunarodnymi voinami* (Collapse of the plans for "unification of Europe": account of the imperialistic attempts for anti-Soviet "unification of Europe" between the First and Second World Wars). Moscow, 1948.

Knight-Patterson, W. D. (W. W. Kulski). *Germany from Defeat to Conquest, 1913–1933.* London, 1945.

Knorin, V. "Avangardnye boi vtorogo tura revoliutsii" (The vanguard battles in the second round of revolutions). *K.I.,* No. 6, February 20, 1934, pp. 3–10.

————. "Barometr pokazyvaet buriu" (The barometer indicates storm). *K.I.,* No. 7–8, March 10, 1933, pp. 11–18.

Kochan, L. *Russia and the Weimar Republic.* Cambridge, 1954.

Korovin, E. A. *Razoruzhenie: problema razoruzheniia v mezhdunarodnom prave; Liga Natsii v faktakh i dokumentakh, 1920–1929.* (Disarmament: the problem of disarmament in international law; the League of Nations in facts and documents). Moscow, 1931.

————. "The U.S.S.R. and Disarmament," *International Conciliation,* No. 292, September 1933, pp. 293–354.

"Krakh veimarskoi Germanii i podgotovka germanskogo Oktiabria" (The collapse of Weimar Germany and the preparation of the German October). *K.I.,* No. 9, March 20, 1933, pp. 3–13.

Kreitner, G. *Hinter China steht Moskau.* Berlin, 1932.

Krivitsky, W. G. *In Stalin's Secret Service: An Exposé of Russia's Secret Policies* . . . New York and London, 1939.

"Krizis kapitalizma i opasnost voiny" (The crisis of capitalism and the danger of war). *Bol'shevik*, No. 4, February 29, 1932, pp. 1–10. Editorial.

Kublin, Hyman. *Asian Revolutionary: The Life of Sen Katayama.* Princeton, 1964.

Kuchumov, V. "Leninskoe uchenie ob umiraiushchem kapitalizme i konets kapitalisticheskoi stabilizatsii" (Lenin's teaching on dying capitalism and the end of capitalist stabilization). *K.I.*, No. 2, January 20, 1933, pp. 31–40.

———. "Voina i revoliutsiia na Dal'nem Vostoke" (War and revolution in the Far East). *Revoliutsionnyi Vostok*, No. 5, 1933, pp. 5–19.

Kun, Béla. "The Trial is Ended—the Danger of Intervention is Growing." *I.P.C.*, Vol. 10, No. 58, December 18, 1930, pp. 1203–7.

Kutakov, L. N. *Istoriia sovetsko-iaponskikh diplomaticheskikh otnoshenii* (History of Soviet-Japanese diplomatic relations). Moscow, 1962.

League of Nations. *Records of the Tenth Ordinary Session of the Assembly: Plenary Meetings; Text of the Debates [1929].* Geneva, 1929–30.

———. *Treaty Series: Publication of Treaties and International Engagements Registered with the Secretariat of the League, September 1920–July 31, 1946.* 205 vols. London, 1920–46.

———, Commission on Enquiry for European Union. *Minutes of the Commission* . . . , *January–September 1931.* Geneva, 1931. See especially minutes of the Third Session, May 15–21, 1931.

———, Conference for the Reduction and Limitation of Armaments. *Records of the Conference* . . . Series A. *Verbatim Reports of Plenary Sessions.* Series B. *Minutes of the General Commission.* Vols. 1–3. February 9, 1932–June 11, 1934. Geneva, 1932–36.

———, Preparatory Commission for the Disarmament Conference. *Documents of the Preparatory Commission for the Disarmament Conference Entrusted with the Preparation of the Conference for the Reduction and Limitation of Armaments.* Series I-XI, Geneva, 1926–31.

———, ———. *Delegatsiia S.S.S.R. na VI sessii Komissii po razoruzheniiu, 15 aprelia–6 maia 1929 g.* (Delegation of the U.S.S.R. at the Sixth Session of the Commission on Disarmament, April 15–May 6, 1929). Moscow, 1929.

———, ———. *Delegatsiia S.S.S.R. na poslednei sessii Komissii Razoruzheniia* . . . *6 oktiabria–9 dekabria 1930 g.* (Delegation of the U.S.S.R. at the last session of the Commission on Disarmament . . . , November 6–December 9, 1931). Moscow, 1931.

———, ———. *V bor'be za mir: Sovetskaia delegatsiia na V sessii Komissii po razoruzheniiu* (The struggle for peace; Soviet Delegation at the Fifth Session of the Commission on Disarmament). People's Commissariat of Foreign Affairs, Moscow, 1928.

———, Special Assembly, 1932; International Relations Committee. *Report of the League Assembly on the Manchurian Dispute.* Nanking, [1933]. 88 pp. Published in London under the title *Assembly Report on Sino-Japanese Report.*

Lemin, I. M. "Antisovetskaia propaganda v Iaponii" (Anti-Soviet propaganda in Japan), *Tikhii Okean*, No. 1, July–September, 1934, pp. 50–62.

———. *Propaganda voiny v Iaponii i Germanii* (War Propaganda in Japan and Germany). Moscow, 1934.

———. "Voennaia programma iaponskogo imperializma: o pamflete voennogo ministerstva ot 1 oktiabria 1934 g." (War Program of Japanese imperialism; concerning the pamphlet of the War Ministry of October 1, 1934). *Tikhii Okean*, No. 2, October–December 1934, pp. 205–227.

Lenin, V. I. *Sochineniia* (Works). 2d ed. 30 vols. Moscow, 1926–32.

———. *Lenin on War and Peace.* Peking, 1960. 68 pp.

BIBLIOGRAPHY

Liaz, M. A. *Voina pod maskei razoruzheniia* (War under the mask of disarmament). Moscow and Leningrad, 1933.

Lippay, Z. *Behind the Scenes of the "Disarmament" Conference.* Moscow and New York, 1932. 58 pp.

Litvinov, M. M. *Against Aggression: Speeches by Maxim Litvinov, Together with Texts of Treaties and of the Covenant of the League of Nations.* London, [1939].

————. *Foreign Policy of the U.S.S.R.: Speeches and Declarations, 1917–1932.* 2d ed. Moscow, 1937.

————. "Litvinov's Speech at the General Commission of the Disarmament Conference." *I.P.C.,* Vol. 13, No. 7, February 16, 1933, pp. 183–186.

————. *Mirnaia politika sovetov: doklad i preniia na IV sessii TsIK SSSR 4-go sozyva* (Peace policy of the Soviets: report and discussions at the Fourth Session of the Central Executive Committee of the U.S.S.R., Fourth Convocation). Moscow and Leningrad, 1929.

————. *Protiv voin; za vseoobshchee razoruzhenie: Sovetskie predlozheniia o polnom i chastichnom razoruzhenii* (Against wars; for total disarmament: Soviet proposals for total and partial disarmament). Moscow and Leningrad, 1928.

————. *"Soviet dumping" fable: speech of Soviet Commissar of Foreign Affairs, Litvinov, in European Commission [on Enquiry for European Union], May 18, 1931.* New York, 193–.

————. *The Soviet's Fight for Disarmament: Containing Speeches of M. Litvinov at Geneva 1932 and other Documents in Sequel to "The Soviet Union and Peace."* Introduction by A. Lunacharsky. New York, 1932.

————. *S.S.S.R. v bor'be za mir: rech na IV sessii TsIK SSSR 29 dekabria 1933 g.* (The U.S.S.R. in the struggle for peace; speech at the Fourth Session of the Central Executive Committee of the Soviet Union, December 29, 1933). Moscow, 1934.

————. *The USSR and the League of Nations: Speech in the Assembly of the League of Nations, September 18, 1934.* New York, 1934.

————. *Vneshniaia politika SSSR: rechi i zaiavleniia 1927–1935* (Foreign policy of the U.S.S.R.: speeches and declarations, 1927–1935). Moscow, 1935.

Lovestone, J. *Soviet Foreign Policy and the World Revolution.* New York, 1935. 31 pp.

Lukianova, M. I. "Bor'ba iaponskikh rabochikh protiv novoi imperialisticheskoi boini" (The struggle of the Japanese workers against the new imperialist slaughter). *Krasnyi Internatsional Profsoiuzov,* No. 9, 1934, pp. 22–27.

————. "Levo-legalnye profsoiuzy i dvizhenie za edinyi front i edinstvo" (Legal left-wing trade-unions and the movement for a united front and unity). *Materialy po Natsional'no-Kolonial'nym Problemam,* No. 9, 1934, pp. 3–18.

————. "Rabota vnutri reformistskikh soiuzov Iaponii" (Work in the reformist unions of Japan). *Materialy po Natsional'no-Kolonial'nym Problemam,* No. 8–9, 1933, pp. 103–121.

Madariaga, Salvador de. *Disarmament.* New York, 1929.

Mad'iar [Magyar], L. I. "Agrarno-krestianskii vopros v koloniakh" (Agrarian-peasant question in the Colonies). *Revoliutsionnyi Vostok,* No. 2, 1933, pp. 126–142. Lecture delivered on November 21, 1932.

————. "Fashizm i opasnost voiny" (Fascism and the danger of war). *Bol'shevik,* No. 9, May 15, 1933, pp. 20–32, and No. 11, June 15, 1933, pp. 49–68.

————. "Fashizm, voina i mirnaia politika Sovetskogo Soiuza" (Fascism, war, and peace policy of the Soviet Union). *K.I.,* No. 5, February 10, 1934, pp. 22–26.

————. "Lenin i problemy natsional'no-kolonial'noi revoliutsii" (Lenin and the problems of the national-colonial revolution). *Revoliutsionnyi Vostok,* No. 1, 1934, pp. 5–24.

------. "Liga Natsii i voina v Iaponii" (The League of Nations and the war in Japan). *K.I.*, No. 9, March 20, 1933, pp. 20–24.

------. "Marks i natsional'no-kolonial'nyi vopros" (Marx and the national-colonial question). *Revoliutsionnyi Vostok*, No. 3–4, 1933, pp. 5–13.

------. "Mirovoi krizis i konets stabilizatsii kapitalizma" (The world crisis and the end of capitalist stabilization). *K.I.*, No. 23, August 20, 1932, pp. 3–14.

------. "Predely revoliutsionnoi roli kolonial'noi burzhuazii" (Limits of the revolutionary role of the colonial bourgeoisie). *K.I.*, No. 33–34, August 31, 1928, pp. 50–61.

Mahaney, W. L. *The Soviet Union, the League of Nations and Disarmament, 1917–1935* . . . Philadelphia, 1940.

"Man'chzhuriia i kolonial'naia politika Iaponii" (Manchuria and the colonial policy of Japan). *Krasnaia Nov*, No. 1, 1932, pp. 89–95.

[Manuilsky, D. Z.] "K voprosu o revoliutsionnom vykhode iz krizisa v Anglii (Rech tov. Manuilskogo na diskussii po angliiskomu voprosu, 18/XII—1931 g.)" (On the question of the revolutionary way out from the crisis in England—speech of Comrade Manuilsky at the discussion of the English Problem, December 12, 1931). *K.I.*, No. 6, February 29, 1932, pp. 10–19.

------. *Social Democracy—Stepping Stone to Fascism* . . . New York, 1934. Includes the resolution of the Presidium of the ECCI on the situation in Germany, April 1, 1933.

Martynov, A. "Problema pererastaniia mirovogo ekonomicheskogo krizisa v politicheskii" (The problem of the transformation of the world economic crisis into a political one). *K.I.*, No. 34–35, 1930, pp. 8–16.

"Materialy po iaponsko-kitaiskomu konfliktu" (Materials on the Sino-Japanese conflict). *Materialy po Natsional'no-Kolonial'nym Problemam*, No. 3, 1932, pp. 40–84.

Mesina, N. "Bor'ba rabochego klassa Iaponii" (The struggle of the working class of Japan). *Bor'ba Klassov*, No. 8–9, 1931, pp. 48–57.

Mif, P. A. (pseud.). "Bor'ba za gegemoniiu proletariata v kolonial'noi revoliutsii" (The struggle for proletarian hegemony in the colonal revolution). *Bol'shevik*, No. 19–20, November 7, 1934, pp. 84–96.

------. "Krizis reaktsii i novyi revoliutsionnyi pod"ëm" (The crisis of reaction and the new revolutionary upsurge) *Bol'shevik*, No. 10, 1930, pp. 103–114.

------. "Sovremennyi etap revoliutsionnoi bor'by na kolonial'nom Vostoke" (The present stage of the revolutionary struggle in the colonial east). *Revoliutsionnyi Vostok*, No. 7, 1933, pp. 36–48.

------, and G. Voitinsky (comps.). *Okkupatsiia Man'chzhurii i bor'ba imperialistov: sbornik statei* (The occupation of Manchuria and the struggle of the imperialists: a collection of articles). Moscow, 1932.

------, ------ (eds.). *Sovremennaia Iaponiia* (Present-day Japan). 2 vols. Moscow, 1934.

Mikhailov, K., and A. Pronin. "Uglublenie ekonomicheskogo krizisa i revoliutsionnyi pod"ëm v Indii" (The deepening of the economic crisis and the revolutionary upsurge in India). *Revoliutsionnyi Vostok*, No. 1–2, 1932, pp. 55–101.

Miroshevsky, V. "Argentina" (Argentina). *Kolonialnye Problemy.* Sbornik I, 1933, pp. 22–36. See below under "Newspapers and Periodicals."

Molotov, V. M. *Ob uspekhakh i trudnostiakh sotsialisticheskogo stroitel'stva* (Concerning successes and difficulties of socialist construction). Moscow and Leningrad, 1929. Report delivered at the Seventeenth Moscow Province Party Conference, February 23, 1929.

------. *The October Revolution and the Struggle for Socialism.* Moscow, 1931. Address at the meeting of the Moscow Soviet on the occasion of the fourteenth anniversary of the October Revolution, November 6, 1931.

BIBLIOGRAPHY

[Monetary and Economic Conference, London, 1933.] *Mirovaia ekonomicheskaia konferentsiia: problema mezhdunarodnykh dolgov* (The World Economic Conference: the problem of international debts). Moscow, 1934.

Moore, H. L. *Soviet Far Eastern Policy, 1931–1945.* Princeton, 1945.

Myshkin. "Iaponskii sotsial-fashizm na sluzhbe imperializma" (Japanese social-fascism in the service of imperialism). *Revoliutsionnyi Vostok,* No. 1, 1934, pp. 64–82.

N. M. "Aggressiia iaponskogo imperializma na Dal'nem Vostoke" (Aggression of Japanese imperialism in the Far East) *Revoliutsionnyi Vostok,* No. 3–4, 1932, pp. 126–143.

"Nabliudatel" (pseud.). "Itogi Londonskoi konferentsii" (Results of the London Conference [on limitation of naval armaments]). *Mezhdunarodnaia Zhizn,* No. 5, 1930, pp. 3–13.

Nadolny, R. *Mein Beitrag.* Wiesbaden, 1955.

Nasonov, M. "Perspektivy bezrabotitsy v Soedinennykh Shtatakh i lozungi nashei bor'by" (Prospects of unemployment in the United States and the slogans of our struggle). *K.I.,* No. 4, February 10, 1931, pp. 49–55.

Notovich, F. I. *Razoruzhenie imperialistov, Liga Natsii i SSSR* (Disarmament of imperialists, League of Nations, and the U.S.S.R.). Moscow, 1929.

Noveishaia istoriia stran zarubezhnogo Vostoka (Recent history of the countries of the foreign East). Vols. 1–3–. Moscow University, Department of History of the Countries of the East. Moscow, 1954——.

Noveishaia istoriia stran zarubezhnoi Azii i Afriki (Recent history of the countries of foreign Asia and Africa). Leningrad University. Leningrad, 1963.

"Obrashchenie Sovetskogo pravitel'stva raznykh raionov po povodu nasil'stvennogo zakhvata iaponskim imperiazmom trekh vostochnykh provintsii, 25 sentiabria 1931" (Appeal of the [Chinese] soviet government concerning the seizure by Japanese imperialism of three [Chinese] eastern provinces, September 25, 1931). *Programnye Dokumenty Kommunsticheskikh Partii Vostoka,* pp. 229–231. See below under "Communist Parties" "Asia, General."

Okano [Nosaka, Sanzo]. "Iaponskii imperializm i revoliutsionnaia bor'ba trudiashchikhsia mass Iaponii" (Japanese imperialism and the revolutionary struggle of the toiling masses of Japan). *K.I.,* No. 4, February 1, 1934, pp. 28–38.

Pankratova, A., "Obrazovanie vtorogo ochaga voiny v Evrope (1933–1935 gody)" (Formation of the second hotbed of war in Europe, 1933–1935). *Voprosy Istorii,* No. 3–4, 1945, pp. 35–54. Abridged chapter from V. P. Potemkin (ed.). *Istoriia diplomatii,* Vol. III.

Petrovsky, D. A. (Max Goldfarb) (ed.). *Partii Kommunisticheskogo Internatsionala: Spravochnik propagandista; Sbornik statei* (Parties of the Communist International: reference book for the propagandist; a collection of articles). Moscow, 1928.

Piatnitsky, O. A. *The Immediate Tasks of the International Trade Union Movement.* New York, 1931.

——. *Leading the World Proletariat to New Decisive Battles . . .* Moscow-Leningrad, 1934.

——. "O fashistkoi diktature v Germanii" (On the fascist dictatorship in Germany). *K.I.,* No. 25, September 1, 1934, pp. 12–22.

——. "O sovremennom polozhenii v Germanii" (On the present situation in Germany), *Bol'shevik,* No. 10, May 31, 1933, pp. 13–32, and No. 11, June 15, 1933, pp. 30–47; *K.I.,* No. 19–20, July 10, 1933, pp. 40–66.

——. *Les questions vitales du mouvement syndical révolutionnaire internationale.* Paris, 1931.

——. *Urgent Questions of the Day: Unemployment Movement, Factory Organization, Fluctuating Membership.* New York, 1931.

Preparatory Commission for Disarmament Conference. *See* League of Nations.

728

Poland. *Official Documents concerning Polish-German and Polish-Soviet Relations, 1933–1939.* London, [1940].

Poland and the U.S.S.R., 1921–1941. Polish Research Centre. London, [1941].

Polish-Soviet Relations, 1918–1943: Official Documents Issued by the Polish Embassy in Washington by the Authority of the Government of Poland. [Washington, D.C., 1944.]

Popov, K. "Ob istoricheskikh usloviiah pererastaniia burzhuazno-demokraticheskoi revoliutsii v proletarskuiu" (On historic conditions for the transformation of the bourgeois-democratic revolution into the proletarian one), *Bol'shevik*, No. 21–22, November 30, 1928, pp. 35–42; No. 23–24, December 31, 1928, pp. 70–86; No. 1, January 15, 1929, pp. 69–85.

Popov, V. I. *Diplomaticheskie otnosheniia mezhdu SSSR i Angliei (1929–1939 gg.)* (Diplomatic relations between the USSR and England [1929–1939]). Moscow, 1965.

Potemkin, V. P. (comp.). *Istoriia Diplomatii.* Vol. III. *Diplomatiia v period podgotovki vtoroi mirovoi voiny, 1919–1939 gg.* (History of diplomacy. Vol. III, Diplomacy in the period of preparation for the Second World War, 1919–1939). Moscow, 1945.

"Problema gegemonii proletariata v kolonial'noi revoliutsii" (The problem of proletarian hegemony in the colonial revolution). *Kolonial'nye Problemy*, No. 3–4, 1935. Entire number devoted to the discussions and theses adopted at the session of the Institute of World Economy and World Politics on China, Japan, Korea, Turkey, the Middle East, and Africa.

Radek, K. "American Intervention in European Affairs." *I.P.C.*, Vol. 13, No. 24, June 2, 1933, pp. 517–518.

———. "The Arguments of the Polish Press against the Proposed Eastern Pact." *I.P.C.*, Vol. 14, No. 45, August 24, 1934, pp. 1168–70.

———. "British Foreign Policy in the Present World Situation." *I.P.C.*, Vol. 13, No. 20, May 5, 1933, pp. 440–441.

———. "Disarmament or War." *I.P.C.*, Vol. 13, No. 53, December 6, 1933, p. 1243.

———. "Dynamite in the Far East." *I.P.C.*, Vol. 13, No. 45, October 13, 1933, pp. 963–964.

———. "Nachalo krizisa fashizma" (Beginning of the crisis of fascism). *Bol' shevik*, No. 12, June 30, 1934, pp. 37–54.

———. "Novyi etap fashizatsii Germanii" (New stage of fascization of Germany). *Bol'shevik*, No. 3, February 15, 1933, pp. 39–57.

———. "The Political Crisis in Germany." *I.P.C.*, Vol. 12, No. 38, August 25, 1932, pp. 794–796.

———. *Podgotovka bor'by za novyi peredel mira* (Preparing the struggle for the new repartition of the world). Moscow, 1934.

———. *Prezident Goover "spasaet" Evropu: mirovoi ekonomicheskii krizis, protivorechiia imperializma i podgotovka voiny protiv SSSR* (President Hoover is "saving" Europe: the world economic crisis, the contradictions within imperialism, and preparation of war against the U.S.S.R). Moscow, 1931.

Rafail, M. A. "Problemy indiiskoi revoliutsii" (Problems of the Indian revolution). *Novyi Vostok*, No. 23–24, 1928, pp. 1–24.

Razoruzhenie 1933–1936 . . . (Disarmament, 1933–1936 . . .). People's Commissariat of Foreign Affairs. Moscow, 1936.

Rezema, V. "Sobytiia v Gollandskom flote" (Occurrences in the Dutch navy). *Kolonial'nye Problemy*, Sbornik I, 1933, pp. 92–107.

Ross, M. *A History of Soviet Foreign Policy.* New York, 1940. 79 pp.

Sabanin, A. V. *Khronologicheskaia perechen mezhdunarodnykh i mnogostorronnikh dogovor zakliuchennykh s 1919 po 1933 g. s kratkim izlozheniem ikh soderzhaniia* (Chronological enumeration of bilateral and multilateral

treaties signed from 1919 to 1933, with a brief summary of their content).
Moscow, 1933.

———. (comp. and ed.). *Mezhdunarodnaia politika v 1929 godu: dogovory,
deklaratsii i diplomaticheskaia perepiska* (International policy in 1929:
treaties, declarations, and diplomatic correspondence). Moscow, 1931.

———. *Mezhdunarodnaia politika v 1930 godu: dogovory, deklaratsii i diplo-
maticheskaka perepiska* (International policy in 1930: treaties, declarations,
and diplomatic correspondence). Moscow, 1932.

Safarov, G. "The Fight for the Pacific Ocean and the Partition of China."
I.P.C., Vol. 13, No. 55, December 15, 1933, pp. 1253–58.

———. "Imperialisticheskoe gosudarstvo i natsional'no-kolonial'naia revoliutsiia . . ." (The imperialist state and the national-colonial revolution . . .)
Revoliutsionnyi Vostok, No. 3, 1934, pp. 15–34.

———. *Marx and the East.* New York, 1934. 47 pp.

———. "Marks i kolonial'nyi vopros" (Marx and the colonial question).
Kolonial'nye Problemy, Sbornik I, 1934, pp. 3–30.

———. "Mirovoi ekonomicheskii krizis i narastanie revoliutsionnogo pod"ëma v
koloniakh" (The World economic crisis and the growth of the revolutionary
upsurge in the colonies). *K.I.*, No. 3, January 31, 1930, pp. 46–63.

———. *Problemy natsional'no-kolonial'noi revoliutsii* (Problems of the national-
colonial revolution). Moscow and Leningrad, 1931.

———. "Revoliutsionnyi pod"ëm v Indii" (The revolutionary upsurge in India).
Bol'shevik, No. 12, June 30, 1931, pp. 48–60.

Sagalatov, V. "Obostrenie krizisa i revoliutsoinnyi pod"ëm v Brazilii" (The sharpening of the crisis and the revolutionary upsurge in Brazil). *Kolonial'nye
Problemy*, Sbornik I, 1933, pp. 237–248.

Sbornik dokumentov po mezhdunarodnoi politike i mezhdunarodnomu pravu.
Vol. VII, *Mirovaia ekonomicheskaia konferentsiia i problema mezhdusoiuz-
nicheskikh dogovorov* (Collection of documents on international politics and
international law. Vol. VII, The World Economic Conference and the problem of inter-Allied treaties). Moscow, 1934.

Scott, W. E. *Alliance against Hitler: The Origins of the Franco-Soviet Pact.*
Durham, N.C., 1962.

Sevostianov, G. N. (ed.). *Aktivnaia rol SShA v obrazovanii ochaga voiny na
Dalnem Vostoke, 1931–1933* (The active role of the U.S.A. in forming a
hotbed of war in the Far East, 1931–1933). Moscow, 1953.

Shami, A. "Palestinskoe vosstanie i arabskii vopros" (Revolt in Palestine and the
Arab question). *Revoliutsionnyi Vostok*, No. 8, 1929, pp. 25–52.

Shiik, A. "K voprosu o negritianskoi probleme v SShA" (On the question of the
Negro problem in the U.S.A.). *Revoliutsionnyi Vostok*, No. 7, 1929, pp. 138–
167.

Shotwell, J. T. *Poland and Russia, 1919–1945.* New York, 1945.

Shtein, B. "Iz istorii politicheskoi deiatel'nosti Ligi Natsii" (Iapono-kitaiskii
konflikt po voprosu Man'chzhurii) " (From the history of the political activity of the League of Nations—Sino-Japanese conflict over the the problem
of Manchuria). *Istoricheskii Zhurnal*, No. 4, 1945, pp. 71–84.

Shubin, P. "Bor'ba za kolonii i predstoiashchaia voina" (The struggle for colonies and the coming war). *K.I.*, No. 25–26, June 29, 1928, pp. 58–67.

———. "Londondskaia konferentsiia i novaia faza ekonomicheskoi voiny" (The
London Conference and the new phase of the economic war). *K.I.*, No. 19–
20, July 10, 1933, pp. 23–33.

———. "Nadvigaiushchiisia krizis i nastuplenie severo-amerikanskogo imperializma" (The approaching crisis and the attack of North American imperialism). *K.I.*, No. 5, February 3, 1928, pp. 3–42, and No. 8, February 24,
1928, pp. 12–18.

————. "Problemy revoliutsionnogo dvizheniia v Indii" (Problems of the revolutionary movement in India). *K.I.*, No. 14, April 5, 1929, pp. 12–22, and No. 15, April 12, 1929, pp. 15–19.

Sinani, G. "Konets kapitalisticheskoi stabilizatsii v stranakh iuzhnoi i karaibskoi Ameriki" (The end of capitalist stabilization in the countries of South and Caribbean America). *Kolonial'nye Problemy,* Sbornik I, 1933, pp. 174–205.

———— (ed.). *Problemy revoliutsii v Iuzhnoi i Karaibskoi Amerike: sbornik statei* (Problems of the revolution in South and Caribbean America: a collection of articles). Communist Academy. Moscow, 1934.

Singh, Ratan. *A Brief History of the Hindustan Gadar Party, Submitted to the Assembly of the League Against Imperialism . . . on the 27th of July, 1929, at Frankfort on Main.* San Francisco, 1929.

Slovès, C. H. *La France et l'Union soviétique.* Paris, 1935.

Slusser, R. M., and J. F. Triska. *A Calendar of Soviet Treaties, 1917–1957.* Stanford, 1959.

Smith, S. R. *The Manchurian Crisis, 1931–1932: A Tragedy in International Relations.* New York, 1948.

Sovetskii Soiuz v bor'be za mir: sobranie dokumentov i vstupitel'naia stat'ia (The Soviet Union in the struggle for peace; a collection of documents and an introductory article). Moscow and Leningrad, 1929. Abridged English edition: *Soviet Union and Peace: The Most Important Documents Issued by the Government of the USSR Concerning Peace and Disarmament from 1917 to 1929.* London, 1929.

Sovetsko-amerikanskie otnosheniia 1919–1933 (Soviet-American relations, 1919–1933). People's Commissariat of Foreign Affairs. Moscow, 1934. 99 pp.

Soviet Union and the Path of Peace—Stalin-Molotov-Voroshilov-Litvinov-Tukhachevsky: A Collection of Statements and Documents, 1917–1936. London, 1936.

"Soviet Violations of Treaties: Agreements and Promises, 1929–1956." *Soviet Affairs Notes,* No. 216, November 6, 1957, pp. 2–12, and August 10, 1959, pp. 2–15.

Spector, I. *The Soviet Union and the Muslim World, 1917–1958.* Seattle, 1958.

SSSR v bor'ba za mir: rechi i dokumenty. (The U.S.S.R. in the struggle for peace: speeches and documents). Moscow, 1935. English edition: *The Soviet Union and the Path of Peace,* London, 1936.

SSSR v bor'be za razoruzhenie: Sovetskaia delegatsiia v Geneve; fakty i dokumenty (The U.S.S.R. in the struggle for disarmament: the Soviet Delegation at Geneva; facts and documents). Moscow, 1928.

Stalin, I. V. *Ob oppozitsii: stat'i i rechi, 1921–1927 gg.* (On the opposition: articles and speeches, 1921–1927). Moscow and Leningrad, 1928.

————. *Sochineniia* (Works). 13 vols. Moscow, 1946–55. English edition: *Works,* 13 vols. Moscow, 1953–55.

————, *et al. Strategy and Tactics of the Proletarian Revolution.* New York, 1936.

————. *Voprosy Leninizma.* 11th ed. Moscow, 1947. English edition: *Problems of Leninism.* 11th ed. Moscow, 1947.

Stein, G. H. "Russo-German Collaboration: The Last Phase, 1933." *Political Science Quarterly,* No. 1, March 1962, pp. 54–71.

Stoliar, S. "Filippiny i amerikanskii imperializm" (The Philippines and American imperialism). *Kolonial'nye Problemy,* Sbornik I, 1933, pp. 70–95.

Strany Tikhogo Okeana (Countries of the Pacific Ocean). Moscow, 1942.

Strusser, A. (ed.). *Revoliutsionnyi pod"ëm v Indii* (Revolutionary upsurge in India). Communist Academy, Institute of World Economy and World Politics, Moscow, 1933.

Survey of International Affairs. London, 1929–1934.

Sworakowski, W. *The Communist International and Its Front Organizations.* Stanford, 1965.

Sysov, V. "Pod znamenem natsional'no-revoliutsionnoi voiny" (Under the banner of national-revolutionary war). *Revoliutsionnyi Vostok*, No. 3–4, 1933, pp. 232–242. Speech at the December Plenum of the Executive Committee of the Communist Youth International.

Taigin, I. "Iaponiia na Londonskoi konferentsii" (Japan at the London Conference). *Mezhdunarodnaia Zhizn*, No. 1, 1930, pp. 5–16.

[Tanaka, Gi-ichi?] "Memorandum o pozitivnoi politike v Man'chzhurii predstavlennyi 25 iiulia 1927 goda Ministrom Tanaka Imperatoru Iaponii" (Memorandum on a positive policy in Manchuria presented by Minister Tanaka on July 25, 1927, to the Japanese Emperor). *K.I.*, No. 33–34, December 10, 1931, pp. 47–62.

Tanin, D., and E. Yohan. *Voenno-fashistkoe dvizhenie v Iaponii* (Military-fascist movement in Japan). Moscow, 1933. English edition: *Militarism and Fascism in Japan*. Introduction by K. Radek. New York, 1934.

———, ———. *When Japan Goes to War*. New York, 1936.

Taracouzio, T. A. *The Soviet Union and International Law: A Study Based on the Legislation, Treaties, and Foreign Relations of the U.S.S.R.* New York, 1935.

———. *War and Peace in Soviet Diplomacy*. New York, 1940.

Terentiev, N. "Iaponskii imperializm v Man'chzhurii (Japanese imperialism in Manchuria). *Problemy Kitaia*, No. 8–9, 1931, pp. 30–74.

———. "Krizis na Dal'nem Vostoke" (Crisis in the Far East [1932]). *Kolonial'nye Problemy*, Sbornik I, 1933, pp. 31–50.

———. "Mezhduimperialisticheskie protivorechiia i konflikty na poberezhie Tikhogo Okeana" (Inter-imperialist differences and conflicts in the regions of the Pacific Ocean). *K.I.*, No. 8–9, March 30, 1932, pp. 31–40.

Tillet, L. R. "The Soviet Union and the Policy of Collective Security in the League of Nations, 1934–1938." Unpublished Ph.D. dissertation, University of North Carolina, 1955.

Trainin, I. P. *Imperializm na Dal'nem Vostoke i SSSR* (Imperialism in the Far East and the U.S.S.R.). Moscow, 1932.

Triska, J. F., and R. M. Slusser. *The Theory, Law, and Policy of Soviet Treaties*. Stanford, 1952.

Ulianovsky, P. "Uglublenie ekonomicheskogo krizisa v Indii" (The deepening of the economic crisis in India). *Kolonial'nye Problemy*, Sbornik II, 1934, pp. 32–62.

Union of Soviet Socialist Republics, People's Commissariat of Foreign Affairs. *Dogovory o neitralitete, nenapadenii i o soglasitel'noi protsedure, zakliuchennye mezhdu Soiuzom SSR i inostrannymi gosudarstvami* (Treaties on neutrality, nonaggression and conciliation procedure signed between the U.S.S.R. and foreign powers). Moscow, 1934.

United Nations, Secretariat. *Historic Survey of the Activities of the League of Nations Regarding the Question of Disarmament, 1920–1937*. New York, 1951.

United States, Congress, House Committee on Un-American Activities. *Investigation of Un-American Propaganda Activities in the United States as an Agent of a Foreign Power*. Washington, D.C., 1947.

———, Department of State. *Foreign Relations of the United States, Diplomatic Papers: The Soviet Union, 1933–1939*. Washington, D.C., 1952.

———, Library of Congress, Legislative Reference Service. *Disarmament and Security: A Collection of Documents, 1919–1955*. Washington, D.C., 1955.

Valerin, R. *Ot razryva do vosstanovleniia anglo-sovetskikh otnoshenii* (From the rupture to the re-establishment of Anglo-Soviet relations). Moscow, 1930.

Varga, E. "The Failure of the London Economic Conference and the Insoluble Market Problem." *I.P.C.*, Vol. 13, No. 40, September 11, 1933, pp. 863–870.

———. *The Great Crisis and Its Political Consequences: Economics and Politics, 1928–1934*. London, 1935.

———. "The Real Visage of German Fascism." *I.P.C.*, Vol. 13, No. 40, September 11, 1933, pp. 870–874.

———. *et al. Ekonomicheskii pokhod protiv SSSR: sbornik dokladov i vystuplenii v Komakademii* (Economic campaign against the U.S.S.R.: a collection of reports and speeches in the Communist Academy). Moscow, 1934.

———, ——— (comps.). *Lenin i problemy sovremennogo imperializma* (Lenin and the problems of contemporary imperialism). Moscow, 1934.

Vneshniaia politika SSSR: sbornik dokumentov (Foreign policy of the U.S.S.R.: a collection of documents). 5 vols. Moscow, 1944–47. Vol. III, 1925–34. Comp. by A. S. Tisminets.

Voitinsky, G. "K desiatiletiiu martovskikh sobytii v Koree" (The tenth anniversary of the March [1919] events in Korea). *Revoliutsionnyi Vostok*, No. 7, 1929, pp. 31–55.

———. *K.V.Zh.D. i politika imperialistov v Kitae* (The Chinese Eastern Railway and the imperialists' policy in China). Moscow, 1930.

———. "Sobytiia na Dal'nem Vostoke" (Events in the Far East). *Revoliutsionnyi Vostok*, No. 1–2, 1932, pp. 43–54. Report delivered to the students of the Communist University of the Toilers of the East.

———. "Zakhvat Man'chzhurii i politika imperializma" (The seizure of Manchuria and the policy of imperialism). *Mirovoe Khoziaistvo i Mirovaia Politika*, No. 10–11, 1931, pp. 34–56.

———, E. Iolk, and N. N. Nasonov. "Sobytiia na Dal'nem Vostoke i opasnost voiny" (Events in the Far East and the danger of war). *Bol'shevik*, No. 5–6, March 31, 1932, pp. 42–55.

Wang Ming [Ch'en Shao-yü]. "The Conflict over the Sale of the Chinese Eastern Railway." *I.P.C.*, Vol. 13, No. 24, June 2, 1933, pp. 533–534.

———. "O polozhenie v Man'chzhurii i novom nastuplenii Iaponii na Kitai" (On the situation in Manchuria and the new Japanese attack on China). *K.I.*, No. 4–5, February 10, 1933, pp. 8–17.

Weissbuch über die Erschiessungen des juni 1934: autentische Darstellung der deutschen Barthelmaüsnacht. Paris, 1934. French edition: *Le livre blanc austro-allemand sur les assassinats des 30 juin et 25 juillet, 1934.* Paris, [1935].

Wheeler-Bennett, J. W. *Disarmament and Security since Locarno, 1925–1931: Being the Political and Technical Background of the General Disarmament Conference, 1932.* New York, 1932.

———. "Twenty Years of Russo-German Relations: 1919–1939." *Foreign Affairs* (New York), XXV, October 1946, 23–43.

Wollenberg, E. *Der Apparat: Stalins fünfte Kolonne.* Bonn, 1951.

Y-Pi. "Vooruzhennaia okkupatsiia i natsional'no-revoliutsionnoe dvizhenie v Man'chzhurii" (Armed occupation and the national-revolutionary movement in Manchuria). *Tikhii Okean*, No. 1, July-September, 1934, pp. 63–77.

"Za edinyi front bor'by mezhdunarodnogo proletariata" (For a united front of struggle of the international proletariat). *K.I.*, No. 35, December 1934, pp. 3–12.

Zaustashvili. *Chto proiskhodit na Dal'nem Vostoke: sbornik materialov* (What is taking place in the Far East: a collection of materials). Tiflis, 1933.

Zhukov, E. M. (ed.). *Mezhdunarodnye otnosheniia na Dal'nem Vostoke, 1870–1945* (International relations in the Far East, 1870–1945). Academy of Sciences, Institute of Oriental Studies. Moscow, 1951.

———, and A. Rosen (eds). *Iaponiia: sbornik statei* (Japan: a collection of articles). Moscow, 1934.

Zubok, L. I. *Imperialisticheskaia politika SShA v stranakh Karaibskogo basseina, 1900–1939* (Imperialist policy of the U.S.A. in the countries of the Caribbean Basin, 1900-1939). Academy of Sciences. Moscow, 1948.

CHINA, GENERAL

Academy of Sciences, Pacific Institute. *Uchenye Zapiski,* Vol. III: *Kitaiskii Sbornik* (Academic transactions, Vol. III: Collected materials on China). Moscow, 1949.

"Appeal of the Central Executive Committee of the Chinese Soviets [on the imperialists' intervention]." *I.P.C.,* Vol. 13, No. 14, October 6, 1933, pp. 970–971. Signed by Mao Tse-tung.

"Appeal of the Provisional Central Government of the Chinese Soviet Republic [on the Lytton report]." *I.P.C.,* Vol. 12, No. 57, December 22, 1932, p. 1222. Signed by Mao Tse-tung and others.

Ch'êng T'ien-fong. *A History of Sino-Russian Relations.* Washington, D.C., 1957.

Chie [?] Hua. "Second Congress of the Chinese Soviet Republic." *I.P.C.,* Vol. 14, No. 32, June 1, 1934, p. 844.

China, Ministry of Foreign Affairs. *Documents with Reference to the Sino-Russian Dispute, 1929.* Nanking, [1929]. For a Soviet interpretation see: *Sovetsko-kitaiskii konflikt 1929 g.: sbornik dokumentov* (The Soviet-Chinese conflict, 1929: a collection of documents). People's Commissariat of Foreign Affairs. Moscow, 1930.

Chu Ch'i-hua. "The Occupation of Changsha by the Chinese Red Army." *I.P.C.,* Vol. 10, No. 36, August 7, 1930, pp. 697–698.

"Ch'üan-kou ti i tz'u Su-wei-ai ch'ü-yü tai-piao ta-hui hsüan-ch'uan kang-yao" (An outline of the declaration by the All-China Conference of the Delegates from the Soviet Regions). *Hung-ch'i,* No. 112, June 21, 1930.

Clubb, O. E. *Twentieth Century China.* New York, 1964.

"The Constitution of the Chinese [Soviet] Republic Adopted at the First All-China Soviet Congress, November 7, 1931." *I.P.C.,* Vol. 12, No. 2, January 14, 1932, pp. 26–27.

"Dokumenty o polozhenii v Sovetskikh raionakh Kitaia" (Documents on the situation in the Soviet regions of China). *Bor'ba Klassov,* No. 7–8, 1932, pp. 114–127.

Erenburg, C. B. *Grazhdanskaia voina i natsional'no-osvoboditelnoe dvizhenie v Kitae v 1928–1936 godakh . . .* (Civil war and the national liberation movement in China in 1928–1936). Moscow, 1951. 22 pp.

———. *Ocherki natsional'no-osvoboditel'noi bor'by kitaiskogo naroda v noveishee vremia* (Sketches of the national-liberation movement of the Chinese people in modern times). Moscow, 1950.

———. *Sovetskii Kitai* (Soviet China). Moscow, 1933. 96 pp.

Fundamental Laws of the Chinese Republic. Introduction by Béla Kun. New York, 1934. Contains constitution of the Chinese Soviet Republic, agrarian legislation, and laws regulating the Red Army, labor, economics, etc.

Iadynskii, J. A. *The Chinese-Eastern Railway Problem in Contemplation of Law.* Shanghai, 1934.

I-n, N. "O nekotorykh problemakh tekushchego etapa kitaiskoi revoliutsii" (On certain problems of the present stage of the Chinese revolution). *Revoliutsionnyi Vostok,* No. 4–5, 1928, pp. 5–44.

Iolk, E., and O. Tarakhanov. "Sovetskoe dvizhenie v Kitae" (The soviet movement in China). *Problemy Kitaia,* No. 6–7, 1931, pp. 3–52.

Isaacs, H. R. *The Tragedy of the Chinese Revolution.* Stanford, 1951. Rev. ed. 1961.

Ivin, A. A. *Bor'ba za vlast sovetov: ocherki sovetskogo dvizheniia v Kitae* (The struggle for soviet power: outlines of the soviet movement in China). Moscow, 1933.

———. *Ocherki partizanskogo dvizheniia v Kitae, 1927–1930 gg.* (Sketches on the partisan movement in China, 1927–1933). Moscow and Leningrad, 1930.

———. *Sovetskii Kitai* (Soviet China). Moscow, 1931. Deals with the struggle of the Chinese Red Army, 1929–30.

BIBLIOGRAPHY

Kapitsa, M. S. *Sovetsko-kitaiskie otnosheniia* (Soviet-Chinese relations) . Moscow, 1958.
———. *Sovetsko-kitaiskie otnosheniia v 1931–1945 gg.* (Soviet-Chinese relations, 1931–45) . Moscow, 1956.
Kara-Murza, G. S. "Karl Marks i kitaiskaia revoliutsiia" (Karl Marx and the Chinese revolution) . *K.I.,* No. 7–8, March 10, 1933, pp. 88–98.
Kuo, E. [?] *Za Sovetskii Kitai* (For Soviet China). Moscow and Leningrad, 1931.
Kurdiukov, I. F., *et al.* (eds.) . *Sovetsko-kitaiskie otnosheniia 1917–1957: sbornik dokumentov* (Soviet-Chinese relations, 1917–1957: a collection of documents) . Academy of Sciences, Institute for the Study of China. Moscow, 1959.
Li [?] "I s"ezd predstavitelei sovetskikh raionov Kitaia" (First Congress [conference] of the representatives of soviet regions in China) . *K.I.,* No. 9, March 31, 1930, pp. 8–14.
Mad'iar, L. "Dve agrarnye programmy v kitaiskoi revoliutsii" (Two agrarian programs in the Chinese revolution) , *Problemy Kitaia,* No. 3–4, 1930, pp. 60–83.
———. "Sovety v Kitae" (Soviets in China) . *Bol'shevik,* No. 18, September 30, 1930, pp. 71–86.
Mamaeva, R. "Agrarnaia politika Sovetskogo pravitel'stva v Kitae k XV godovshchine Oktiabria" (The agrarian policy of the soviet government in China on the occasion of the fifteenth anniversary of the October [revolution]) . *Agrarnye Problemy,* No. 10–11, 1932, pp. 107–116.
"Manifesto of the Provisional Government of the Soviet Republic of China to the Working Masses and the Governments of the World [by the First Congress of Chinese Soviets, announcing the organization of the soviet government], November 7, 1931." *I.P.C.,* Vol. 11, No. 60, November 26, 1931, p. 1076.
Mao Tse-tung. "Politika kitaiskogo sovetskogo pravitel'stva" (The policy of the Chinese soviet government) . *K.I.,* No. 20–21, July 20, 1934, pp. 24–29, and No. 23, August 10, 1934, pp. 32–51.
———. *Red China: President Mao Tse-tung Reports on the Progress of the Chinese Soviet Republic.* New York, 1934. Speech delivered at the Second Congress of Chinese Soviets, Juichin, Kiangsi, January 22, 1934; 34 pp.
———. "The Situation in the Chinese Soviet Republic: From the Report of the Chairman of the Central Executive Committee of the Chinese Soviet Republic, Mao Tse-tung." *I.P.C.,* Vol. 14, No. 37, June 29, 1934, p. 957, and No. 38, July 6, 1934, pp. 977–978.
———. "The Sixth Campaign of the Kuomintang and the Tasks of the Soviet Districts: A Speech delivered by Mao Tse-tung." *I.P.C.,* Vol. 13, No. 50, November 17, 1933, pp. 1123–24.
"Materialy konferentsii predstavitelei sovetskikh raionov Kitaia" (Materials of the conference of the representatives of the soviet regions of China [1930]) . *Problemy Kitaia,* No. 4–5, 1930, pp. 172–198.
Mif, P. A. (pseud.) , "Chto proiskhodit v Kitae" (What is happening in China) . *Bol'shevik,* No. 12, June 30, 1933, pp. 82–87.
———. "Grazhdanskaia voina i bor'ba za sovety v Kitae" (Civil war and the struggle for soviets in China) . *Bol'shevik,* No. 13, July 15, 1931, pp. 67–79.
———. "Iz opyta bor'by za sovety v Kitae" (From the experience of the struggle for soviets in China) . *Bol'shevik,* No. 4, February 28, 1935, pp. 71–79.
———. *Kitaiskaia revoliutsiia* (The Chinese revolution) . Moscow, 1932.
———. "Kitaiskaia revoliutsiia i nekapitalisticheskii put razvitiia" (The Chinese revolution and the non-capitalist path of development) . *Problemy Kitaia,* No. 8–9, 1931, pp. 3–13.
———. "Krestianskii vopros v Kitae" (The peasant question in China) . *K.I.,* No. 28, July 19, 1929, pp. 40–47.
———. "Narastaiushchii revoliutsionnyi pod"ëm v Kitae" (The Growing Revolutionary Upsurge in China) . *K.I.,* No. 38–39, September 27, 1929, pp. 21–31.

BIBLIOGRAPHY

——. "Novoe v razvitii revoliutsionnogo krizisa v Kitae" (New points in the development of the revolutionary crisis in China). *K.I.*, No. 10, April 1, 1933, pp. 30–37.

——. "Tol'ko sovety mogut spasti Kitai" (Only soviets can save China). *Bol'shevik*, No. 7, April 15,, 1934, pp. 56–69.

M. K. "Bor'ba za sovety v Kitae" (The struggle for soviets in China). *Voprosy Kolonial'noi Revoliutsii*, No. 1, 1931, pp. 14–24.

Nasonov, N. "Dal'nevostochnaia voina i piatiletie kitaiskikh sovetov" (The Far Eastern war and the fifth anniversary of the Chinese soviets). *Revoliutsionnyi Vostok*, No. 3–4, 1932, pp. 160–177.

"New Attack upon the Chinese Eastern Railway, Moscow, September 21, 1933." *I.P.C.*, Vol. 10, No. 44, September 25, 1933, pp. 931–932.

"New Imperialist Intervention against Soviet China: Appeal of the Central Executive Committee of the Chinese Soviet Republic." *I.P.C.*, Vol. 13, No. 44, October 6, 1933, pp. 970–971. Signed by Mao Tse-tung and others.

"Obrashchenie Ts.K. Kitaiskoi Sovetskoi Respubliki k rabochim, krestianam, intelligentsii SShA, Anglii, Frantsii, Iaponii, Germanii . . ." (Appeal of the Central Committee of the Chinese Soviet Republic to the workers, peasants, and intellectuals of the U.S.A., England, France, Japan, Germany . . .) *K.I.*, No. 28, October 1, 1933, pp. 22–24.

"Preparation for Intervention in China by the Capitalist Powers." *I.P.C.*, Vol. 10, No. 37, August 14, 1930, pp. 739–740. From *Pravda*, August 7, 1930, editorial.

"Proekt konstitutsii kitaiskoi sovetskoi respubliki (Priniata I s"ezdom sovetov v Kitae 7 noiabria 1931 g.)" (Draft constitution of the Chinese Soviet Republic; adopted by the First Congress of Soviets in China, November 7, 1931). *Programnye Dokumenty Kommunisticheskikh Partii Vostoka*, pp. 203–221. See below under "Communist Parties" "Asia, General."

"Proekty sovetskikh zakonov k I s"ezdu Sovetov v Kitae" (Drafts of soviet laws [outlined] for the First Congress of Soviets of China). *Problemy Kitaia*, No. 8–9, 1931, pp. 191–205.

Programnye dokumenty kitaiskikh Sovetov: sbornik. (Program documents of the Chinese soviets: a collection). Moscow, 1935.

"Razreshenie agrarnogo voprosa v sovetskikh raionakh Kitaia" (The solution of the agrarian problem in the soviet regions of China). *Na Agrarnom Fronte*, No. 3, 1932, pp. 123–130.

Safarov, G. I. *Ocherki po istorii Kitaia* (Sketches on the history of China). Leningrad, 1933.

——. "Revoliutsiia i kontrrevoliutsiia v Kitae: krakh burzhuaznoi i pomeshchich'ei kontrrevolutsii" (Revolution and counterrevolution in China; failure of the bourgeois and landlords' counterrevolution). *Problemy Kitaia*, No. 4–5, 1930, pp. 3–32.

The Sino-Soviet Crisis: The Actual Facts Brought to Light. International Relations Committee. Nanking, 1929. 10 pp.

Skachkov, P. E., Comp. *Bibliografiia Kitaia* (Bibliography of China). Moscow, 1960.

Sovetsko-kitaiskii konflikt 1929 g.: sbornik dokumentov (Soviet-Chinese conflict, 1929: a collection of documents). People's Commissariat of Foreign Affairs. Moscow, 1930.

Sovety v Kitae: sbornik materialov i dokumentov (Soviets in China: a collection of materials and documents). Communist Academy, Scientific-Research Institute on China. Moscow, 1934. Translated from earlier publication in German.

T. V. "Bor'ba kitaiskogo pravitel'stva v 1930" (The struggle of the Chinese government in 1930). *Problemy Kitaia*, No. 4–5, 1930, pp. 92–98.

Tang, P. S. H. *Russian and Soviet Policy in Manchuria and Outer Mongolia, 1911–1931.* Durham, N.C., 1959.

Targanskii, M. *Vtoroi s"ezd kitaiskikh sovetov* (The Second Congress of the Chinese Soviets). Moscow, 1935.

V. G. "K otsenke politicheskogo polozhenie v Kitae" (Evaluation of the political situation in China). *Revoliutsionnyi Vostok*, No. 8, 1930, pp. 1–24.

Varga, E. "Osnovnye problemy kitaiskoi revoliutsii" (The basic problems of the Chinese revolution). *Bol'shevik*, No. 8, April 30, 1928, pp. 17–40.

Vishniakova, V. "Krestianskoe dvizhenie v Kitae letom 1930" (The peasants' movement in China in the summer of 1930). *Problemy Kitaia*, No. 4–5, 1930, pp. 161–171.

———. "Sovetskaia vlast' v Kitae" (Soviet authority in China). *Problemy Kitaia*, No. 4–5, 1930, pp. 69–79.

Vladimirova, T. *Bor'ba za sovety v Kitae* (The struggle for soviets in China). Moscow and Leningrad, 1931.

"Vozzvanie Tsentralnogo Ispolnitel'onogo Komiteta Kitaiskoi Sovetskoi Respubliki . . ." (Appeal of the Central Executive Committee of the Chinese Soviet Republic [to the workers, peasants, intellectuals of the United States, Great Britain, Japan, France, Germany, and to all enemies of imperialism and friends of the Chinese people regarding Chiang Kai-shek's campaigns against the Chinese Soviets]) , *Programnye Dokumenty Kommunisticheskikh Partii Vostoka*, 231–235.

Vtoroi S"ezd kitaistkikh sovetov (Second Congress of the Chinese Soviets). Moscow, 1935. Introduction by Wang Ming.

Wang Ming. "Sovety v Kitae kak osobaia forma demokraticheskoi diktatury" (Soviets in China as a special form of democratic dictatorship). *K.I.*, No. 31, November 1, 1934, pp. 22–33.

———. "Sovetskii Kitai kak baza razvertyvaiushcheisia agrarnoi revoliutsii i natsional'no-revoliutsionnoi voiny" (Soviet China as the base of the developing agrarian revolution and of the national-revolutionary war). *K.I.*, No. 23, August 20, 1932, pp. 15–24.

Wu, Ai-chen, K. *China and the Soviet Union, a Study of Sino-Soviet Relations.* London, 1950.

Yakhontoff, V. A. *The Chinese Soviets.* New York, 1934.

Young, C. W. *South Manchurian Railway Areas.* Baltimore, 1931.

Zhdanov, M. V. *V boiakh za sovetskii Kitai* (In the battles for soviet China). Moscow, 1932.

COMMUNIST INTERNATIONAL AND PROFINTERN (RED INTERNATIONAL OF LABOR UNIONS)

The Activities of the Comintern (The Third International) for the Sovietization of the World. [N.p., n.d.] 140 pp.

Les Agissements du Comintern pour la Soviétisation du monde (Résumé). N.p. [1936?] 20 pp.

Agitprop. "Agitprop Department of the ECCI on the Fifteenth Anniversary of the October Revolution." *I.P.C.*, Vol. 12, No. 46, October 20, 1932, pp. 994–999.

———. "On the Immediate Tasks in the Agitprop Work of the Mid-European Sections of the Comintern: Resolution of the Conference of the Mid-European Agitprop Department." *I.P.C.*, Vol. 10, No. 54, November 27, 1930, pp. 1118–20, and No. 57, December 11, 1930, pp. 1199–1200.

Borkenau, F. *The Communist International.* London, 1938.

———. *European Communism.* New York, 1953.

BIBLIOGRAPHY

Bukharin, N. I. *Mezhdunarodnoe polozhenie i zadachi Kominterna: otchetnyi doklad Ispolkoma i zakliuchitel'noe slovo na VI Kongresse Kominterna* (The international situation and the tasks of the Comintern: report of the ECCI and concluding remarks at the Sixth Congress of the Comintern). Moscow and Leningrad, 1928.

————. "O nekotorykh voprosakh iz pervoi chasti proekta programmy K.I." (On certain points in the First Part of the Draft Program of the CI), *K.I.*, No. 31–32, August 13, 1928, pp. 32–40.

Carvalto e Souza, D. de. *Komintern,* Rio de Janeiro, 1938

Chamberlin, W. H. *Blueprint for World Conquest, as Outlined by the Communist International.* Washington, D.C., 1946.

Communist International, Sixth Congress. *The Struggle against Imperialist War and the Tasks of the Communists: Resolutions of the VI World Congress of the Communist International.* New York, 1934. 67 pp.

Les Communistes luttent pour la paix. Paris, 1936.

Degras (Tabritsky), Jane (comp. and ed.). *The Communist International 1919–1943: Documents.* 3 vols. London, 1956–65.

Durkee, T. E. "The Communist International and Japan, 1919–1932." Unpublished Ph.D. dissertation, Stanford University, 1954.

15 Years of the Communist International. New York, 1934.

Freymond, Jacques, ed. *Contributions à l'Histoire du Comintern.* Geneva, 1965.

Gortsev, B. (comp.) *Mezhdunarodnoe polozhenie i zadachi Kominterna* (The international situation and the tasks of the Comintern). Saratov and Moscow, 1931.

————. "Tekushchii etap tret'iago perioda i Komintern k XVI S'ezdu VKP (B) " (The present stage of the third period and the Comintern before the Sixteenth Congress of the Communist Party of the Soviet Union). *Bol'shevik,* No. 11–12, June 15, 1930, pp. 85–94.

Jackson, G. D., Jr. *Comintern and Peasant in East Europe, 1919–1930.* New York, 1966.

James, C. L. R. *World Revolution, 1917–1936: The Rise and Fall of the Communist International.* London, 1937.

"Komintern na Vostoke (The Comintern in the East)." *K.I.*, No. 9–10, 1929, pp. 20–42.

Kommunisticheskii Internatsional pered shestym vsemirnym kongressom: obzor deiatel'nosti IKKI i sektsii Kominterna mezhdu V i VI kongressami (The Communist International before the Sixth World Congress: a survey of the activity of the ECCI and the sections of the Comintern between the Fifth and Sixth Congresses). Moscow, 1928.

Kommunisticheskii International v dokumentakh: resheniia, tezisy i vozzvaniia kongressov Kominterna i plenumov IKKI, 1919–1932 (The Communist International in documents: decisions, theses, and appeals of the congresses of the Comintern and the plenums of the ECCI, 1919–1932). Moscow, 1933.

"Kratkii perechen vazhneishikh dat istorii Kominterna" (A short enumeration of the most important dates in the history of the Comintern). *K.I.*, No. 7–8, 1934, March 10, 1934, pp. 140–155.

Kun, Béla. "Bor'ba za edinstvo deistviia" (The struggle for unity of action). *K.I.*, No. 18, June 20, 1934, pp. 3–7.

————. "VKP (B) i Kommunisticheskii International" (The All-Union Communist Party (B) and the Communist International) ." *K.I.*, No. 9–10, 1929, pp. 76–84.

Kuusinen, O. "Imperialisticheskii gnet i problemy revoliutsionnogo dvizheniia v kolonial'nykh stranakh (Na osnove reshenii VI Kongressa Kominterna) " (Imperialist oppression and the problems of the revolutionary movement in the colonial countries—on the basis of decisions by the Sixth Congress of the Comintern) . *Novyi Vostok,* No. 23–24, 1928, pp. vii–xxx.

K. S. "K voprosu o voennoi programme Kominterna" (On the Military Program of the Comintern). *K.I.*, No. 9, March 2, 1928, pp. 34–43.

Lozovsky, A. "Komintern i bor'ba za massy" (The Comintern and the struggle for the masses). *K.I.*, No. 9–10, 1929, pp. 85–97.

McKenzie, K. E. *Comintern and World Revolution, 1928–1943: The Shaping of Doctrine*. London and New York, 1964.

Mif, P. A. (pseud.), "Komintern i kolonial'nyi vopros" (The Comintern and the colonial question). *Bol'shevik*, No. 5, March 15, 1929, pp. 44–59.

————. "15 let Kominterna i kommunisticheskoe dvizhenie kolonial'nykh stran" (Fifteen years of the Comintern and the communist movement of the colonial countries). *Revoliutsionnyi Vostok*, No. 3, 1934, pp. 5–14.

Mingalin, I. "O pererastanii burzhuazno-demokraticheskoi revoliutsii v proletarskuiu v proekte programmy K.I." (On the transformation of the bourgeois-democratic revolution into a proletarian one in the draft program of the CI). *K.I.*, No. 31–32, August 13, 1928, pp. 41–45.

"Mirovaia partiia proletariata novogo tipa (K 15 letiiu Kommunisticheskogo Internatsionala)" (The world party of the proletariat of a new type—on the occasion of the fifteenth anniversary of the Communist International). *K.I.*, No. 7–8, March 10, 1934, pp. 3–14.

Nollau, G. *International Communism and World Revolution: History and Methods*. New York, 1961.

Normann, A. *Bolschewistische Weltmachtpolitik: die Pläne der 3 Internationale zur Revolutionierung der Welt, auf Grund Authentischer Quellen* . . . Berne, 1935.

Piatnitsky, O. A. *Le Monde communiste en action*. Paris, 1930, 69 pp.

————. *The Organization of a World Party*. London, 1928.

————. "15 let Kommunsticheskogo Internatsionala" (Fifteen years of the Communist International). *K.I.*, No. 7–8, March 10, 1934, pp. 22–39.

————. *V bor'be za miroviiu sovetskuiu vlast'; 15 let Kommunisticheskogo Internatsionala* (In the struggle for world soviet power; fifteen years of the Communist International). Moscow, 1934.

"Piatyi Kongress Kommunisticheskogo Internatsionala Molodezhi" (Fifth Congress of the Communist Youth International). *K.I.*, No. 38, September 28, 1928, pp. 9–14.

Pirker, T., comp. *Komintern und Faschismus*. Stuttgart, 1964.

Poslevoennyi kapitalizm v osveshchenii Kominterna: sbornik dokumentov i rezoliutsii Kongressov i Ispolkoma Kominterna (Postwar capitalism in the interpretation of the Comintern: a collection of documents and resolutions of the congresses and the Executive Committee of the Comintern). Moscow, 1932.

Program of the Communist International together with Statutes of the Communist International, adopted at the Forty-Sixth Session of the Sixth World Congress of the Communist International, September 1, 1928. 2d ed. New York, 1933. 96 pp.

Sixth World Congress of the Communist International, July-August 1928. Consists of special numbers, Nos. 39–92 (July 25–December 31, 1928), of Vol. 8 of the English edition of *I.P.C.*, issued with special cover-title and table of contents.

Stenograficheskii otchet VI Kongressa Kominterna (Stenographic report of the Sixth Congress of the Comintern). 5 vols. Moscow, 1929–30.

Varga, E. *Mezhdu VI i VII kongressami Kominterna: ekonomika i politika 1928–1934 g.g.* (Between the Sixth and Seventh Congresses of the Comintern; economics and politics, 1928–1934). Moscow, 1935.

"Voina i blizhaishie zadachi kommunisticheskikh partii" (War and the immediate tasks of the communist parties). *K.I.*, No. 6, February 29, 1932, pp. 3–9.

BIBLIOGRAPHY

Executive Committee of the Communist International

Le Chemin de l'Internationale Communiste: guide pour l'Histoire de L'I.C.; les thèses élaborées par la Section d'agitation et de propagande de l'C.E. de l'Internationale Communiste à l'occasion du XVᵉ anniversaire de l'I.C. Paris, 1934. 53 pp.

"Diskussiia v Professional'noi Kommissii IKKI" (Discussion in the Trade-Union Commission of the ECCI [February 28, 1929]). K.I., No. 23–24, June 20, 1929, pp. 106–127. Speeches by Piatnitsky and Lozovsky.

Piatnitsky, O. A. "Vstupitel'naia rech . . . ob organizatsii neorganizovannykh" (Introductory Speech [at the Trade-Union Commission of the ECCI, February 28, 1929] on the organization of the unorganized [workers]). K.I., No. 23–24, June 10, 1929, pp. 106–109.

"Pis'mo Sekretariata IKKI natsional'nomu administrativnomu Sovetu Nezavisimoi Rabochei Partii" (Letter of the Secretariat of the ECCI to the National Administrative Council of the Independent Labour Party). K.I., No. 19–20, July 10, 1933, pp. 85–87. As printed in the Daily Worker, London, June 26, 1933.

IX Plenum ECCI, February 9–25, 1928

Braun, P. At the Parting of the Ways: The Results of the Ninth Plenum of the Comintern. London, 1928.

"K IX Plenumu Ispolkoma Kominterna" (For the Ninth Plenum of the ECCI). K.I., No. 6–7, February 19, 1928, pp. 3–9.

"O rezoliutsii IX Plenuma IKKI po kitaiskomu voprosu (Postanovlenie Politburo Ts.K. R.K.P.)" (On the resolution of the Ninth Plenum of the ECCI on the Chinese question—decision of the Politburo of the Central Committee of the Russian Communist Party). Materialy po Kitaiskomu Voprosu, No. 15, 1928, pp. 3–5.

Resolutions adoptées à la IXᵉ session plénière de C.E. de l'I.C. (février 1928). Paris, 1928. 56 pp.

Rezoliutsii i postanovleniia IX Plenuma Ispolkoma Kominterna (19–25 fevralia, 1928) (Resolutions and decisions of the Ninth Plenum of the ECCI, February 19–25, 1928). Moscow and Leningrad, 1928.

"Rezoliutsiia po kitaiskomu voprosu, priniata 25 II 1928 g. Plenumom IKKI" (Resolution on the Chinese question adopted by the Plenum of the ECCI, February 25, 1928). Materialy po Kitaiskomu Voprosu, No. 1–12, 1928, pp. 3–6.

X Plenum ECCI, July 3–19, 1929

Molotov, V. M. Komintern i novyi revoliutsionnyi pod"ëm: rech na X plenume IKKI 9 iiulia 1929 g. (The Comintern and the new revolutionary upsurge; speech at the Tenth Plenum of the ECCI, July 9, 1929). Moscow, 1929. 25 pp.

Protokoll des 10. Plenum des Exekutivkomitees der Kommunistischen Internationale, Moskau, 3. Juli 1929 bis 19. Juli 1929. Hamburg and Berlin, 1929.

Thèses, résolutions et decisions adoptées à la Xᵉ session plénière du C.E. de l'I.C. (juillet 1929). Paris, 1929. 67 pp.

Tezisy, rezoliutsii, postanovleniia (iiul 1929) (Theses, resolutions, decisions [of the Tenth Plenum of the ECCI], July 1929). Moscow, 1929. 80 pp.

Theses, Resolutions and Decisions of the Tenth Plenum of the ECCI. New York, 1931.

The World Situation and Economic Struggle: Theses of the Tenth Plenum, ECCI. London, 1929.

XI Plenum ECCI, March 25—April 1, 1931

Browder, E. K. *War against Workers' Russia! Speech Delivered at the Eleventh Plenum of the Executive Committee of the Communist International in April 1931.* New York, 1931. 30 pp.

Cachin, M. *Preparation for War Against the Soviet Union.* Moscow, 1931. Speech at the Eleventh Plenum of the ECCI.

Chemodanov, V. *Unter dem Sturmbanner des leninistischen Komsomol: Bericht und Diskussion über die Lage und Aufgaben der KJI auf dem XI Plenum des EKKI.* Hamburg, 1931.

Itogi XI Plenuma IKKI: sbornik materialov dlia dokladchikov i besedchikov (Results of the Eleventh Plenum of the ECCI: collection of materials for reporters and speakers). Leningrad, 1931.

Manuilsky, D. Z. *Kompartii i krizis kapitalizma: XI Plenum IKKI, stenografiche-skii otchet* (The communist parties and the crisis of capitalism: Eleventh Plenum, ECCI, stenographic report). Moscow, 1932. Also appears in English: *The Communist Parties and the Crisis of Capitalism*. New York, 1931.

———. "Zadachi sektsii Kommunisticheskogo Internatsionala v sviazi s uglu-bleniem ekonomicheskogo krizisa i narastaniem v riade stran predposylok revoliutsionnogo kriziza" (The tasks of the sections of the CI in connection with the deepening of the economic crisis and the growth of the prerequisites of the revolutionary crisis in a number of countries). *K.I.*, No. 12, April 30, 1931, pp. 11–52. Abridged report to the Ninth Plenum, ECCI.

"Materialy XI Plenuma IKKI" (Materials of the Eleventh Plenum of the ECCI). *K.I.*, No. 12, April 30, 1931, and Nos. 13–14 and 15, May 1931.

Stenograficheskii otchet XI Plenuma IKKI (Stenographic Report of the Eleventh Plenum of the ECCI). Moscow, 1931.

Thèses et résolutions de la XI Assemblée plénière du Comité exécutif de l'Internationale communiste, avril 1931. Paris, 1931. 42 pp.

The World Crisis and the International Struggle: An Outline of the Debates and Decisions of the XI Plenum of the E.C.C.I. held in March-April, 1931. New York, 1931.

XII Plenum ECCI, August 27—September 15, 1932

Capitalist Stabilization Has Ended: Thesis and Resolutions of the Twelfth Plenum of the Executive Committee of the Communist International. New York, 1932. Papers presented to the Twelfth Plenum.

Chemodanov, V. *Itogi XII Plenuma IKKI i zadachi KIM . . .* (Results of the Twelfth Plenum of the ECCI and the tasks of the Communist Youth International . . .). Moscow, 1933. 63 pp.

Guide to the XII Plenum: Material for Propagandists, Organizers, Deputies, Training Classes. New York, 1932.

Knorin, V. G. *Fascism, Social-Democracy and the Communist.* New York, 1934. Also: *K.I.*, No. 1–2, January 10, 1934, pp. 60–74. Speech at Twelfth Plenum.

Kuusinen, O. V. "Mezhdunarodnoe polozhenie i zadachi sektsii Kominterna (Doklad na XII Plenume IKKI)" (The international situation and the tasks of the sections of the Comintern—report at the Twelfth Plenum of the ECCI) .*K.I.*, No. 31, November 10, 1932, pp. 12–20; No. 32, November 20, 1932, pp. 13–21; and No. 33, November 30, 1932, pp. 13–32; *Bol'shevik*, No. 20, November 1, 1932, pp. 28–38.

———. *Prepare for Power: The International Situation and Tasks of the Sections of the Comintern.* London, 1932. Speech at the Twelfth Plenum.

BIBLIOGRAPHY

Manuilsky, D. Z. "Konets kapitalisticheskoi stabilizatsii" (The end of capitalist stabilization). *Bol'shevik*, No. 19, October 15, 1932, pp. 13–28. Speech at the Twelfth Plenum.

———. "SSSR i mirovoi proletariat (doklad na XII Plenume IKKI)" (The U.S.S.R. and the world proletariat—report at the Twelfth Plenum of the ECCI). *K.I.*, No. 30, October 30, 1932, pp. 9–20.

———. *Die Sowjetunion und das Weltproletariat*. Moscow, 1932. Speech at the Twelfth Plenum. 40 pp.

The Next Step in Britain, America and Ireland: Speeches and Reports, XII Plenum, ECCI. Moscow, 1932. 81 pp.

[Nosaka, Sanzō.] *The War in the Far East and Tasks of the Communists in the Struggle against Imperialist War and Military Intervention: Report . . . at the XII Plenum ECCI*. New York, 1932. 51 pp.

"O Dal'nevostochnoi voine i zadachakh kommunistov v bor'be protiv imperialisticheskoi voiny i voennoi interventsii protiv SSR" (On the Far Eastern war and the struggle against the imperialist war and intervention against the U.S.S.R.). *Kommunisticheskii Internatsional v dokumentakh*, pp. 990–994. Resolution of the Twelfth Plenum.

Papers Presented to the Twelfth Plenum of the Executive Committee of the Communist International. 7 small vols. New York, 1932.

Piatnitsky, O. A. "Mirovoi ekonomicheskii krizis, revoliutsionnyi pod''ëm i zadachi sektsii Kominterna" (World economic crisis, revolutionary upsurge, and the tasks of the sections of the Comintern). *K.I.*, No. 10, April 1, 1933, pp. 10–22; *Bol'shevik*, No. 4, February 28, 1933, pp. 13–27, and No. 7, April 30, 1933, pp. 32–51. Speech at Twelfth Plenum.

———. *The Work of the Communist Parties of France and Germany and the Tasks of the Communist in the Trade Union Movement*. New York, [1932.] Speech at the Twelfth Plenum. 78 pp.

Theses and Resolutions XII Plenum, ECCI. Moscow, 1933. 36 pp.

XII Plenum IKKI: stenograficheskii otchet (Twelfth Plenum, ECCI: stenographic report). 3 vols. Moscow, 1933.

The USSR and the World Proletariat: Report at the XII Plenum of the Executive Committee of the Communist International, September 14, 1932. New York, 1932. 48 pp.

Uzlovye voprosy revoliutsionnogo dvizheniia Pol'shi na XII Plenume Ispolkoma Kominterna: sbornik rechei . . . (The basic problems of the revolutionary movement in Poland at the Twelfth Plenum of the ECCI: collection of speeches). Moscow, 1933.

XIII Plenum ECCI, December 1933

Heckert, Fritz. *Why Hitler in Germany? The Report of Fritz Heckert, Representative of the Communist Party of Germany to the* [Thirteenth Plenum of the] *Executive* [Committee] *of the Communist International, with Resolution Adopted*. London, 1933.

Kompartii v bor'be sredi molodezhi: XIII plenum IKKI o rabote sredi molodezhi (Communist parties in the struggle among youth; Thirteenth Plenum of the ECCI on work among youth). Moscow, 1934.

Kuchumov, V. "Sozrevanie mirovogo revoliutsionnogo krizisa i kolonial'nyi Vostok" (The maturing of the world revolutionary crisis and the colonial East). *Revoliutsionnyi Vostok*, No. 7, 1933, pp. 25–35. Summary of the Thirteenth Plenum.

Kuusinen, O. V. "Fashizm, opasnost voiny i zadachi kommunisticheskikh partii" (Fascism, the danger of war, and the tasks of the communist parties). *Bol'shevik*, No. 2, January 31, 1934, pp. 42–61, and No. 3–4, February 28,

1934, pp. 81–86. Speech at Thirteenth Plenum, ECCI. English edition: *Fascism, the Danger of War and the Tasks of the Communist Parties* . . . New York, 1934.

———. *et al. Papers Presented to the Thirteenth Plenum of the Executive Committee of the Communist International: Theses and Decisions.* New York, 1934. Articles by O. Kuusinen, O. Piatnitsky, W. Pieck, V. Knorin, Okane Sanzō Nosaka, and Wang Ming.

Manuilsky, D. Z. *Revoliutsionnyi krizis, fashizm i voina: rech na XII plenume IKKI 5 dekabria 1933 g.* (Revolutionary crisis, fascism, and war; speech at the Thirteenth Plenum, ECCI, December 5, 1933). Moscow, 1934. 31 pp. English edition: *Revolutionary Crisis, Fascism, and War.* New York, 1934. 31 pp.

[Nosaka, Sanzō]. *Revolutionary Struggle of the Toiling Masses of Japan.* New York, 1934. Speech at the Thirteenth Plenum.

Piatnitskii [Piatnitsky], O. A. *The Communist Parties in the Fight for the Masses* . . . Moscow, 1934. Speech at the Thirteenth Plenum; 98 pp.

———. *Les Partis communistes en lutte pour la conquête des masses.* Paris, 1934. Discussions at the Thirteenth Plenum.

"Sozrevanie mirovogo revoliutsionnogo krizisa—bor'ba za sovetskuiu vlast vo vsem mire . . ." (The maturing of the world revolutionary crisis—the struggle for soviet power in the entire world . . .). *K.I.,* No. 36, December 20, 1933, pp. 3–18. Summary of the Thirteenth Plenum.

Theses and Decisions, Thirteenth Plenum of the ECCI. Moscow, 1934. 31 pp.

Theses, Reports, Speeches of the Thirteenth Plenum Held in Moscow December 1933. 8 small vols. New York, 1934.

XIII Plenum IKKI: stenograficheskii otchet (Thirteenth Plenum of the ECCI: stenographic report). Moscow, 1934.

"XIII Plenum IKKI" (Thirteenth Plenum of the ECCI). *K.I.,* No. 1–2, January 10, 1934 (entire issue).

Wang Ming [Ch'en Shao-yü] *Revolutionary China Today: Speeches by Wang Ming and K'ang Sheng* [at the XIII Plenum, ECCI]. Moscow, 1934.

Presidium ECCI

"Iz materialov zasedanii Presidiuma IKKI 9–10 iiulia 1934 g. posviashchennago sobytiiam v Germanii i zadacham KPG" (Material of the session of the Presidium, ECCI, July 9–10, 1934, devoted to the events in Germany and the tasks of the Communist Party of Germany). *K.I.,* No. 22, August 1, 1934, pp. 16–48.

Die Kommunistische Internationale über die Lage in Deutschland. Moscow and Leningrad, 1933. Resolution of the Presidium of the ECCI on the Report of F. Heckert, April 1933. 12 pp.

Manuilsky, D. Z. *Ekonomicheskii krizis i revoliutsionnyi pod"ëm: Doklad na Rasshirennom Presidiume Ispolkoma Kommunisticheskogo Internatsionala ot 18 do 29 fevralia 1930 g.* (Econmic crisis and revolutionary upsurge; report at the Enlarged Presidium of the ECCI, February 18–29, 1930). Moscow, 1930.

Thesen und Resolutionen, erweitertes Präsidium des EKKI, February 1930. Hamburg and Berlin, 1930. 61 pp.

Profintern (Red International of Labor Unions)

Every Factory . . . A Fortress! The Tasks of the Revolutionary Trade Union Organizations in the Work at the Factories: Resolution of the VIII Session of the Central Council of the Red International of Labor Unions. London 1931.

Lozovsky, A. "Edinyi front bezrabotynkh i rabotaiushchikh" (United front of the unemployed and the employed). *K.I.,* No. 4, February 10, 1931, pp. 6–10.

———. *Za kontrnastuplenie proletariata: doklad i zakliuchitel'noe slovo na VIII sessii Tsentral'nogo Soveta Profinterna 7–8–17 dekabria 1931 g.* (For the counteroffensive of the proletariat: report and final remarks at the Eighth Session of the Central Council of the Profintern, 7–8–17 December, 1931). Moscow, 1932. 95 pp.

Mirovoe revoliutsionnoe profdvizhenie ot IV do V kongressa Profinterna, 1928–1930: materialy k otchetu Ispolbiuro V kongressu Profinterna. (The world revolutionary trade-union movement from the Fourth to the Fifth Congress of the Profintern: materials for the report of the Executive Committee to the Fifth Congress of the Profintern). Moscow, 1930.

Protokol über 4. Kongress de Roten-Gewerkschafts-Internationale, abegehalten in Moskau von 17 März bis 3. April, 1928. Moscow, 1928.

Report of the Fourth Congress of the R.I.L.U. London, 1928.

Resolutions of the Fifth Congress of the R.I.L.U. Held in Moscow, August 1930. London 1931. 73 pp.

Thèses et Résolutions. Paris, 1928. Of the Fourth Congress, RILU.

The Way Forward: Resolution of the R.I.L.U. Sections and Their Role in the Leadership of the Economic Struggles and Unemployed Movement. London, 1931. Theses adopted at the Eighth Session of the Central Council of the RILU.

COMMUNIST PARTIES

B. V. "O pravil'nom sochetanii nelegal'nykh, polulegal'nykh i legal'nykh metodov partiinoi raboty" (On the correct combination of illegal, semilegal, and legal methods of party work). *K.I.,* No. 15, May 20, 1934, pp. 54–61.

Gusew [Gusev], S. I. (Iakov Drabkin). "At a New Stage: Main Tasks of Anglo-American Sections of the C.I." *I.P.C.,* Vol. 12, No. 49, November 3, 1932, pp. 1059–60.

Piatnitsky, O. A. "Bezrabotitsa v obstanovke nyneshnego ekonomicheskogo krizisa i zadachi kompartii i revoliutsionnogo profdvizheniia" (Unemployment in the conditions of the present world crisis and the tasks of the communist parties and the revolutionary trade-union movement). *K.I.,* No. 22, August 10, 1931, pp. 13–31, and No. 23, August 20, 1933, pp. 20–29.

———. "Bolshevizatsiia kommunisticheskikh partii kapitalisticheskikh stran posredstvom preodolevanii s-d traditsii" (Bolshevization of the communist parties of the capitalist countries by eradicating social-democratic traditions). *K.I.,* No. 11–12, April 30, 1932, pp. 9–21. English edition: *The Bolshevizations of the Communist Parties by Eradicating Social Democratic Traditions.* London, 1932. A report to the CI.

———. "Kompartii kapitalisticheskikh stran i bor'ba za edinyi front" (Communist parties of the capitalist countries and the struggle for a united front). *K.I.,* No. 9, March 20, 1933, pp. 14–19.

———. "Konsolidatsiia kompartii i prichiny nedostatochnogo zakrepleniia politicheskogo vliianiia sektsii Kominterna" (Consolidation of the communist parties and the reasons for the insufficient strengthening of the political influence of the sections of the Comintern). *K.I.,* No. 18, June 30, 1930, pp. 7–26, and No. 19–20, July 20, 1930, pp. 98–101.

———. *Organizatsionnaia rabota v kompartiiakh kapitalistcheskikh stran* (Organizational work in the communist parties of capitalist countries). 2d ed. Moscow, 1929. German edition: *Die Organisationarbeit in den kommunistischen Parteien der kapitalistischen Länder.* Hamburg, 1928. 69 pp.

———. "Problema organizatsionnogo zakrepleniia ideologicheskogo vliianiia kompartii kapitalisticheskikh stran" (The problem of organizational consolidation of the influence of the communist parties of the capitalist countries). *K.I.*, No. 36, September 14, 1928, pp. 18–25.

———. *World Communists in Action: The Consolidation of the Communist Parties* . . . New York, 1932. 64 pp.

———. *The World Economic Crisis: The Revolutionary Upsurge and the Tasks of the Communist Parties.* London, 1934.

Communist Party of the Soviet Union

XV s"ezd Vsesoiuznoi Kommunisticheskoi Partii (B): stenograficheskii otchet (Fifteenth Congress of the Communist Party of the Soviet Union (B) [December 2–19, 1927]: stenographic report). 2d ed. Moscow and Leningrad, 1928.

XVI s"ezd Vsesoiuznoi Kommunisticheskoi Partii (B): stenograficheskii otchet (Sixteenth Congress of the Communist Party of the Soviet Union [June 26–July 14, 1930]; stenographic report). Moscow and Leningrad, 1931.

XVII s"ezd Vsesoiuznoi Kommunisticheskoi Partii (Bol'shevikov) 26 ianvaria–10 fevralia 1934 g.: stenograficheskii otchet (Seventeenth Congress of the Communist Party of the Soviet Union (Bolsheviks), January 26–February 10, 1934: stenographic report). Moscow, 1934.

Istoriia Kommunisticheskoi partii Sovetskogo Soiuza (History of the Communist Party of the Soviet Union), 1959. Second Ed., Moscow, 1962.

KPSS o vooruzhennykh silakh Sovetskogo Soiuza: sbornik dokumentov, 1917–1958 (The CPSU on the armed forces of the Soviet Union: a collection of documents, 1917–1958). Moscow, 1958. Compiled by V. N. Malin and P. P. Moskovsky.

Manuilsky, D. Z. *The Revolutionary Crisis Is Maturing: Report to the Seventeenth Congress of the Communist Party of the Soviet Union on Behalf of the Delegation of the C.P.S.U. in the Communist International.* New York, 1934.

Molotov, V. M. *The Developing Crisis of World Capitalism, the Revolutionary Crisis, and the Tasks of the Comintern: Report of the Delegation of the C.P.S.U. in the Executive Committee of the C.I., and Concluding Speech Delivered at the XVI Congress of the C.P.S.U., Moscow, July 5–7, 1930.* New York, 1930. 55 pp.

Rosenberg, A. *History of Bolshevism, from Marx to the First Five Year Plan.* London, 1932.

Schapiro, L. *The Communist Party of the Soviet Union.* New York, 1959.

Africa and the Middle East

Avigdor, L. "Krizis i revoliutsionnyi pod"ëm v Egipte" (The crisis and the revolutionary upsurge in Egypt). *Revoliutsionnyi Vostok*, No. 1–2, 1932, pp. 102–132.

———. "Uroki revoliutsionnykh boev v Palestine" (Lessons of the revolutionary battles in Palestine). *Revoliutsionnyi Vostok*, No. 3, 1934, pp. 67–85.

"Draft Program of the C.P. of Egypt submitted by a Group of Egyptian Communists to the Parties of the C.I. for Discussion." *I.P.C.*, Vol. 12, No. 23, May 26, 1932, pp. 472–476.

Laqueur, W. Z. *Communism and Nationalism in the Middle East.* New York, 1956.

Nadab. "Pervyi arabskii rabochii s"ezd v Palestine i antimilitaristicheskaia bor'-ba v arabskikh stranakh" (The first Arab Workers' Congress in Palestine and the antimilitarist struggle in the Arab countries). *K.I.*, No. 8, March 20, 1930, pp. 47–52.

Nasonov, N. "Bor'ba iuzhno-afrikanskikh rabochikh i probuzhdenie Afriki" (The struggle of the South African workers and the awakening of Africa). *K.I.*, No. 48, November 29, 1929, pp. 27–33.

"O zadachakh Kompartii Palestiny" (On the tasks of the Communist Party of Palestine). *Revoliutsionnyi Vostok*, No. 1–2, 1932, pp. 297–302.

"O zadachakh kommunistov vo vsearabskom kommunisticheskom dvizhenii: resoliutsiia priniataia na konferentsii Kommunisticheskikh partii Palestiny i Sirii v 1931 g." (On the tasks of communists in the all-Arab communist movement: resolution taken at the conference of the Communist parties of Palestine and Syria in 1931). *Programnye Dokumenty Kommunisticheskikh Partii Vostoka*, pp. 160–169. (See below under "Asia, General.")

"Programma deistvia Kommunisticheskoi Partii Egipta (Program of Action of the Communist Party of Egypt [1931]." *Programnye Dokumenty Kommunisticheskikh Partii Vostoka*, pp. 172–182.

"Programma deistviia Kommunisticheskoi Partii Turtsii" (Program of action of the Communist Party of Turkey [1931?]), *Programnye Dokumenty Kommunisticheskikh Partii Vostoka*, pp. 148–158.

"Rabota sredi krestian i borba s sionizmom" (Work among peasants and the struggle against Zionism). *Revoliutsionnyi Vostok*, No. 1–2, pp. 302–317. Theses approved by the Secretariat of the Central Committee of the Communist Party of Palestine.

"Rezoliutsiia o iuzhno-afrikanskom voprose" (Resolution on the South African problem [by the ECCI]). *K.I.*, No. 44–45, November 9, 1928, pp. 80–84.

"Resolution of the Polit. Secretariat of the ECCI on the Insurgent Movement in Arabistan, Adopted at the Session of October 16, 1929." *I.P.C.*, Vol. 10, No. 6, February 6, 1930, pp. 104–106.

Shiik, A. "Chernaia Afrika na revoliutsionnom puti" (Black Africa on the revolutionary path). *Revoliutsionnyi Vostok*, No. 8, 1930, pp. 235–251. Translated from the *Sunday Worker* (London), October 27, 1929.

"The Tasks of Communists in the All-Arab National Movement, Outlined at the Conference of the Representatives of the C.P. of Syria and the C.P. of Palestine." *I.P.C.*, Vol. 13, No. 1, January 5, 1933, pp. 16–19.

"Zadachi Kommunisticheskoi Partii v derevne: rezoliutsiia VII s"ezda Kommunisticheskoi Partii Palestiny" (The tasks of the communist party in the village: resolution of the Seventh Congress of the Communist Party of Palestine [1931?]. *Programnye Dokumenty Kommunisticheskhikh Partii Vostoka*, pp. 183–200.

Asia, General

Brimmell, J. H. *Communism in Southeast Asia: A Political Analysis.* London and New York, 1959.

Kennedy, M. D. *A History of Communism in East Asia.* New York, 1957.

Programnye dokumenty kommunisticheskikh partii vostoka. (Program documents of the Communist parties of the East). Marx-Engels-Lenin Institute, Moscow, 1934. Edited by L. Mad'iar, P. Mif, and others.

Shen-Yu-Dai [Tai Sheng-yü]. *Peking, Moscow and the Communist Parties of Colonial Asia.* Cambridge, Mass., 1954.

Swarup, R. *Communism and Peasantry: Implications of Collectivist Agriculture for Asian Countries.* Calcutta, 1954.

China

Alekseev, A. *Komsomol Kitaiia* (Chinese Communist Youth League). Moscow, 1935.

Angarov, F. V. *V bor'be za sovetskii Kitai* (In the struggle for soviet China). Tashkent, 1936. Interview with Mao Tse-tung and short biographies of Chinese Communists.

Barandov, G. V. *Kitaiskaia revoliutsiia i bor'ba Kitaiskoi kompartii* (The Chinese revolution and the struggle of the Chinese Communist Party). Moscow and Leningrad, 1934.

"Blizhaishie organizatsionnye zadachi" (The immediate organizational tasks). *Materialy po Kitaiskomu Voprosu*, No. 1, 1928, pp. 4–22. Resolution adopted at the November 1927 plenum of the Central Committee of the Chinese Communist Party.

Brandt, C., B. Schwartz, and J. K. Fairbanks (eds.). *Documentary History of Chinese Communism*. Cambridge, Mass., 1952.

Chung-Kuo Kung ch'an tang Chung-yang Wei-yüan-hui K'uo-ta ti Ti-ssu-tz'u Ch'üän t'i Hui-i I chüh-an (Resolutions of the Fourth Enlarged Plenum of the Sixth Congress of the Communist Party of China). Shanghai, 1931.

Erh chung ch'üan-hui chüeh-i (Resolution adopted at the Second Plenum [of the Sixth Congress of the Communist Party of China, July 1929]. Shanghai, 1929.

Fang [?]. "Revoliutsionnyi krizis i bor'ba kitaiskogo Komsomola s Gomindanom i imperializmom" (The revolutionary crisis and the struggle of Chinese Communist youth against the Kuomintang and imperialism). *Revoliutsionnyi Vostok*, No. 3–4, 1932, pp. 300–307.

Gelder, G. S. (ed.). *The Chinese Communists*. London, 1946. Articles and speeches by Mao Tse-tung, Chu Teh, Pen Teh-huai, and others.

Hatano, Ken'ichi. *Chugoku Kyōsantō 1932–1937 nenshi* (Annual history of the Communist Party of China 1932–1937). 6 vols. Ministry of Foreign Affairs, Information Bureau. Tokyo, 1933–38. Continuation of Hatano's *Shina Kyōsantō-shi* (History of the Communist Party of China), published in Tokyo in 1932.

Hsiao Tso-liang. *Power Relations within the Chinese Communist Movement, 1930–1934: A Study of Documents*. Seattle, 1961.

Hsüeh Chün-tu. *The Chinese Communist Movement, 1921–1937: An Annotated Bibliography of Selected Materials in the Chinese Collection of the Hoover Institution on War, Revolution, and Peace*. Stanford, 1960.

Hu Ch'iao-mu. *Tridtsat' let kommunisticheskoi partii Kitaia* (Thirty years of the Communist Party of China). Moscow, 1952. Translated from the Chinese. English edition: *Thirty Years of the Communist Party of China*. [n.p.,] 1951. 31 pp.

"Iz otcheta Ts.K. Kitaiskoi Kompartii Kominternu: iz doklada tov. Su [?] o polozhenii v partii" (Report of the Central Committee of the Chinese Communist Party to the Comintern: from the report of Comrade Su[?] on the situation in the party). *K.I.*, No. 13–14, May 20, 1930, pp. 89–90.

"Iz rezoliutsii VI s''ezda Kommunisticheskoi Partii Kitaia (iiun 1928 g.)" (From the resolutions of the Sixth Congress of the Communist Party of China, June 1928). *Programnye Dokumenty Kommunisticheskikh Partii Vostoka*, pp. 14–68. (See above under "Asia, General.")

Kara-Murza, G. S., et al. (comps.). *Strategiia i taktika Kominterna v natsional'no-kolonial'noi revoliutsii na primere Kitaia* (Strategy and tactics of the Comintern in the national-colonial revolution on the example of China). Moscow, 1934.

Kuchumov, V. "O nekotorykh osobennostiakh Kitaiskoi revoliutsii i strategicheskikh ustanovok Kitaiskoi kompartii na razlichnykh etapakh revoliutsionnogo dvizheniia" (On certain peculiarities of the Chinese revolution and strategic aims of the Chinese Communist Party during the various stages of the revolutionary movement). *Problemy Kitaia*, No. 12, 1933, pp. 22–45.

McLane, C. B. *Soviet Policy and the Chinese Communists, 1931–1946*. New York, 1958.

Miao Chu-khan [Miao Ch'u-hung]. *Kratkaia istoriia Kommunisticheskoi partii Kitaia* (Short history of the Communist Party of China). Moscow, 1958. Translated from the Chinese.

Mif, P. A. (pseud.) "Agrarnyi vopros na VI s"ezde Kommunisticheskoi Partii Kitaia" (The agrarian question at the Sixth Congress of the Communist Party of China). *K.I.*, No. 43, October 30, 1928, pp. 38–47.

———. "Blizhaishie zadachi Kitaiskoi Kommunisticheskoi Partii" (The immediate tasks of the Chinese Communist Party). *K.I.*, No. 11, March 15, 1929, pp. 11–20.

———. *Heroic China: Fifteen Years of the Communist Party of China*, New York, 1937. 96 pp.

———. "VI s"ezd Kommunisticheskoi Partii Kitaia" (Sixth Congress of the Communist Party of China). *K.I.*, No. 39–40, October 9, 1928, pp. 9–27.

———. "Sovetskoe dvizhenie v Kitae i zadachi Kompartii" (The soviet movement in China and the tasks of the communist party). *Problemy Kitaia*, No. 3, 1930, pp. 3–9.

North, R. C. *Moscow and Chinese Communists*. Rev. ed. Stanford, 1963.

———, and X. J. Eudin. *M. N. Roy's Mission to China: The Communist-Kuomintang Split of 1927*. Documents translated by H. I. Powers. Berkeley and Los Angeles, 1963.

"O krestianskom dvizhenii partizanskoi bor'be i o raionakh sovetskoi vlasti v Kitae (Iz doklada Ts.K.KKP Kominternu)" (On the peasant movement and guerrilla struggle, and the regions of soviet power in China: from the report of the Central Committee of the Communist Party of China to the Comintern). *K.I.*, No. 15, May 31, 1930, pp. 43–48.

"O politicheskom polozhenii i general'nykh zadachakh partii (Rezoliutsiia IV Plenuma Tsentral'nogo Komiteta Kommunisticheskoi Partii Kitaia v ianvare 1931 g.)" (On the political situation and general tasks of the party: resolution of the fourth Plenum of the Central Committee of the Communist Party of China, January 1931). *Programmye Dokumenty Kommunisticheskikh Partii Vostoka*, pp. 69–75.

"Open Letter of the C.C. of the C.P. of China to the Members of the C.P. of Indochina." *I.P.C.*, Vol. 14, No. 43, August 10, 1934, pp. 1116–20.

"Pis'mo Politsekretariata IKKI v Ts.K. Kitaikompartii" (Letter of the Political Secretariat of the ECCI to the Central Committee of the Chinese Communist Party). *K.I.*, No. 51, December 23, 1929, pp. 43–47.

"Proclamation of the C.C. of the C.P. of China to the Workers of the World [on International Solidarity with the Chinese Soviet Revolution, October 12, 1930]."*I.P.C.*, Vol. 10, No. 52, November 20, 1930, pp. 1065–66.

"Revoliutsionnyi krizis v Kitae i zadachi Kitaiskikh kommunistov" (Revolutionary crisis in China and the tasks of Chinese communists). *K.I.*, No. 3, November 10, 1931, pp. 3–12.

"Rezoliutsiia o rabote Kitaiskoi Kompartii v profsoiuzakh" (Resolution on the work of the Communist Party of China in the trade-unions). *K.I.*, No. 38–39, September 27, 1929, pp. 56–58; *I.P.C.*, No. 52, September 20, 1929, pp. 1126–27.

"Resolution on the Present Political Tasks Passed by the Politburo of the Communist Party of China at the Session of June 11, 1930." *Hung-ch'i*, No. 121, July 19, 1930. In Chinese.

Rue, J. E. *Mao Tse-tung in Opposition, 1927–1935*. Stanford, 1966.

Shishkin, P. P. *Bolshevizm v Kitae: obzor deiatel'nosti Severno-Man'chzhurskoi*

Kommunisticheskoi Partii (Bolshevism in China: an outline of the activity of the North Manchurian Communist Party). Shanghai, 1930.

Smedley, A. *The Great Road: The Life and Times of Chu Teh*. New York, 1956.

Tang, P. S. H. *Communist China Today*. 2d ed. Washington, D.C. 1961.

"Vopros o sovetskikh raionakh Kitaia na III Plenume Ts.K.K.P.K., sentiabr 1930" (The question of the soviet regions in China at the Third Plenum of the Central Committee of the Chinese Communist Party, September 1930). *Biulleten Nauchno-Issledovatel'skogo Instituta po Kitaiu pri Komakademii*, No. 5–6, 1931, pp. 16, 22, 48–50, 67–69.

Wales, Nym (H. F. Snow). *Red Dust: Autobiographies of Chinese Communists*. Introduction by R. C. North. Stanford, 1952.

Wang Ming. "Bor'ba s lilisanovshchinoi v kitaitskoi kompartii" (The struggle against Li Li-san's line in the Chinese Communist Party). *Revoliutsionnayi Vostok*, No. 3–4, 1932, pp. 144–159. Abridged text of speech at the Communist University of the Toilers of the Far East, Moscow, April 27, 1932.

———. "Puti bol'shevizatsii kompartii i pobeda Leninizma v Kitae" (The ways of Bolshevization of the Communist Party and the victory of Leninism in China). *K.I.*, No. 3, January 20, 1934, pp. 54–63.

———. "Uglublenie revoliutsionnogo krizisa i zadachi kitaiskoi kompartii" (The deepening of the revolutionary crisis and the tasks of the Chinese Communist Party). *Bol'shevik*, No. 5–6, March 31, 1932, pp. 26–41.

"Zadachi revoliutsionnogo profdvizheniia v Kitae: rezoliutsiia V Kongressa Profinterna" (The tasks of the revolutionary trade-union movement in China: resolution of the Fifth Congress of the Profintern). *Problemy Kitaia*, No. 4–5, 1939, pp. 172–192.

Japan

"Appeal of the C.P. of Japan on the Sino-Japanese Conflict, October 6, 1931." *I.P.C.*, Vol. 11, No. 12, October 8, 1931, p. 947.

Barandov, G. *Revoliutsionnoe dvizhenie v Iaponii i bor'ba iaponskoi Kompartii* (The revolutionary movement in Japan and the struggle of the Japanese Communist Party). Moscow and Leningrad, 1934. 58 pp.

[Eidus, Kh.T.] "Bor'ba za general'nuiu liniiu v Iaponskoi Kompartii" (Struggle for the general line of the Communist Party of Japan). *Sovremennaia Iaponiia*, I, 84–151.

"K deiatel'nosti Iaponskoi kompartii" (On the activity of the Japanese Communist Party). *K.I.*, No. 33, November 30, 1932, pp. 47–60.

Kalinin, I. P. "Kommunisticheskaia Partiia Iaponii" (The Communist Party of Japan). *Bol'shaia Sovetskaia Entsiklopediia*. 2d ed. Vol. 22, pp. 253–255.

Katayama, S., et al. "Declaration of Comrades Katayama, Okano and Yamamoto to the Workers, Peasants, Revolutionary Intellectuals [regarding the desertion of Sano and Nabeyama]." *I.P.C.*, Vol. 13, No. 34, August 4, 1933, pp. 755–756.

Kato. "Blizhaishie politicheskie i organizatsionnye zadachi Iaponskoi Kommunisticheskoi Partii" (The immediate political and organizational tasks of the Japanese Communist Party). *K.I.*, No. 41, October 16, 1928, pp. 18–24.

Kato. "Class Justice against the Communists in Japan." *I.P.C.*, Vol. 8, No. 82, November 23, 1928, p. 1563.

Napier, J. P. *A Survey of the Japanese Communist Party*. Tokyo, 1952. 66 pp.

"Obrashchenie Ts.K. Kommunisticheskoi Partii Iaponii po povodu novykh tezisov Zapadno-Evropeiskogo Biuro Kommunisticheskogo Internatsionala po iaponskomu voprosu" (Declaration of the Central Committee of the Communist Party of Japan in regard to the new Theses of the West European Bureau of the Communist International on the Japanese question). *Pro-*

BIBLIOGRAPHY

gramnye Dokumenty Kommunisticheskikh Partii Vostoka, pp. 79–85.

Okano [Nosaka Sanzō], and Volk. "Iaponskaia Kompartiia" (The Communist Party of Japan). In Zhukov and Rosen, *Iaponiia: sbornik Statei,* pp. 366–372. (See above under "General.")

Okano. "Opastnost voiny i zadachi Kommunisticheskoi partii Iaponii" (The danger of war and the tasks of the Communists Party of Japan). *Bol'shevik,* No. 5, March 15, 1934, pp. 72–87.

"O polozhenii v Iaponii i o zadachakh Kommunisticheskoi Partii Iaponii: tezisy Zapadno-Evropeiskogo Biuro Kommunisticheskogo Internatsionala" (The situation in Japan and the tasks of the Communist Party of Japan: Theses of the West-European Bureau of the Communist International). *Programnye Dokumenty Kommunisticheskikh Partii Vostoka,* pp. 237–254.

"Polozhenie v Iaponii i zadachi K.P. Iaponii" (The situation in Japan and the tasks of the CPJ). *K.I.,* No. 8–9, March 30, 1932, pp. 3–14.

Rodov, B. V. "Bor'ba iaponskikh kommunistov protiv fashizma i aggressivnoi voiny v 30-kh i nachale 40-kh godov" (The struggle of the Japanese communists against fascism and aggressive war in the thirties and early forties). *Sovetskoe Vostokovedenie,* No. 2, 1958, pp. 46–53.

"Resolution of the West European Bureau of the Comintern on the Communist Party of Japan." *I.P.C.,* Vol. 10, No. 4, January 23, 1930, pp. 72–73.

Scalapino, Robert A. *The Japanese Communist Movement, 1920–1966.* Berkeley and Los Angeles, 1967.

Swearingen, R., and P. Langer. *Red Flag in Japan: International Communism in Action, 1919–1951.* Cambridge, Mass., 1952.

Takagi, Katsuo. "Iz opyta raboty K.P. Iaponii v armii" (From the experience of the work of the Communist Party of Japan in the army). *K.I.,* No. 20–21, July 20, 1934, pp. 46–52.

"Tezisy o polozhenii v Iaponii i zadachakh Iaponskoi Kommunisticheskoi Partii" (Theses on the situation in Japan and the tasks of the Japanese Communist Party). *Materialy po Natsional'no-Kolonial'nym Problemam,* No. 3, 1933, pp. 3–24.

"Theses on the Situation in Japan and the Tasks of the Communist Party, Adopted at the Session of the Presidium of the ECCI, July 15, 1927," *I.P.C.,* Vol. 8, No. 2, January 12, 1928, pp. 50–54.

"Vozzvanie Ts.K. k 10-letiiu Kommunisticheskoi Partii Iaponii" (Manifesto of the Central Committee [of the Communist Party of Japan] on the occasion of the tenth anniversary of the Communist Party of Japan [1931]). *Programnye Dokumenty Kommunisticheskikh Partii Vostoka,* pp. 86–93.

India

Communist Activity in India (1925–1950). Bombay, 1951. Originally prepared for the eleventh Conference of the Institute of Pacific Relations. Lucknow, October 1950. 16 pp.

"Draft of the Political Theses of the Central Committee of the Communist Party of India." *I.P.C.,* Vol. 14. No. 40, July 20, 1934, pp. 1024–34.

"Draft of the Provisional Statues of the Communist Party of India." *I.P.C.,* Vol. 14, No. 29, May 11, 1934, pp. 775–778.

Draft Platform of the Communist Party of India. [N.p., 1930.]

Druhe, D. N., *Soviet Russia and Indian Communism, 1917–1947.* N.Y., 1959.

Glading, P. *The Meerut Conspiracy Case.* London, 1933. 19 pp.

Hutchinson, L. *Conspiracy in Meerut.* London, 1935.

Indian Communist Party Documents, 1930–1956. New York, 1957. Institute of Pacific Relations. Compiled by the Research Staff of the Democratic Research Service, Bombay.

Limaye, Madhu. *Communist Party: Facts and Fiction.* Hyderabad (Deccan), 1951.

Masani, M. R. *The Communist Party of India: A Short History.* New York, 1954. Issued under the auspices of the Institute of Pacific Relations.

Mohan Das, S. R. *Communist Activity in India (1925–1950).* Bombay, [1951]. Originally prepared for and presented to the delegates attending the eleventh Institute of Pacific Relations Conference at Lucknow, October, 1950. 16 pp.

"Open Letter to the Indian Communists by the Central Committee of the Communist Party of China, Central Committee of the Communist Party of Great Britain, and Central Committee of the Communist Party of Germany." *I.P.C.,* Vol. 12, No. 22, May 19, 1932, pp. 436–442.

"Otkrytoe pis'mo indiiskim kommunistam" (An Open Letter to the Indian Communists). *Programmnye Dokumenty Kommunisticheskikh Partii Vostoka,* pp. 257–275, Signed by the Central Committees of the Communist Parties of China, England, and Germany, June 16, 1933. Also in English: *I.P.C.,* Vol. 13, No. 51, November 24, 1933, pp. 1153–58.

Overstreet, G. D., and M. Windmiller. *Communism in India.* Berkeley and Los Angeles, 1959.

"Programma deistviia Kommunisticheskoi Partii Indii" (Program of action of the Communist Party of India [1930]). *Programmnye Dokumenty Kommunisticheskikh Partii Vostoka,* pp. 96–112. Also in English: "Draft Platform of Action of the C.P. of India." *I.P.C.,* Vol. 10, No. 8, December 18, 1930, pp. 1218–22.

Spratt, P. *Blowing Up India.* Calcutta, 1955.

Tagore, Saumendranath. *Historical Development of the Communist Movement in India.* Calcutta, 1944.

United States, Office of Strategic Services. *The Communist Party of India.* [Washington, D.C.], 1945. 73 pp.

Other Asian Parties

Aidit, D. *The History of the Communist Party of Indonesia.* [New Delhi,] 1955.

Brackman, A. C. *Indonesian Communism, A History.* New York, 1963.

Kuusinen, O. "O koreiskom kommunisticheskom dvizhenii" (On the Korean Communist Movement). *Revoliutsionnyi Vostok,* No. 11–12, 1931, pp. 99–116.

McVey, R. T. *The Rise of Indonesian Communism.* New York, 1965.

"Manifest I s"ezda Kommunisticheskoi Partii Filippinskikh ostrovov" (Manifesto of the First Congress of the Communist Party of the Philippine Islands [1931?]). *Programnye Dokumenty Kommunisticheskikh Partii Vostoka,* pp. 132–145.

"Platforma deistviia Kompartii Korei" (Platform of action of the Communist Party of Korea). *K.I.,* No. 17, June 10, 1934, pp. 18–26.

"Programma deistviia indokitaiskoi kommunisticheskoi partii" (Program of action of the Communist Party of Indochina). *K.I.,* No. 34, December 10, 1932, pp. 52–64; *Programnye Dokumenty Partii Vostoka,* pp. 114–29.

"Resolution of the First Congress of the Communist Party of Philippines." *I.P.C.,* Vol. 11, *No.* 33, June 25, 1931, pp. 603–604. A summary. The Congress met on May 9–10, 1931 in Manila.

"Resolution of the United Front of the Workers of Holland and Indonesia, Adopted at the Congress of the C.P. of Holland in Amsterdam." *I.P.C.,* Vol. 13, December 23, 1933, pp. 213–216.

Scalapino, Robert A., and Chong-sik Lee. *The Origin of the Korean Communist Movement.* Seoul, 1961. 77 pp.

BIBLIOGRAPHY

United States of America

Browder, E. R. *Communism in the United States*. New York, 1935.

Draper, T. *American Communism and Soviet Russia: The Formative Period*. New York, 1960.

Foster, W. Z. *History of the Communist Party of the United States*. New York, 1952.

———. *Toward Soviet America*. New York, 1932.

Howe, I. *The American Communist Party: A Critical History (1919–1957)*. Boston, 1958.

Stalin, I. V. *O pravykh fraktsionerakh v amerikanskoi Kompartii* (On the right factionaries in the American Communist Party). Moscow, 1930. Speeches at the American Commission of the Presidium of the ECCI and at the Presidium of the ECCI, May 6, and 14, 1929. Also in English: *Stalin's Speeches on the American Communist Party, Delivered in the American Commission of the Presidium of the Executive Committee of the Communist International, May 6, 1929 and in the Presidium of the Executive Committee of the Communist International on the American Question, May 14, 1929*. New York, [1931?]. 39 pp.

The Americas, Other Parties

Alexander, R. J. *Communism in Latin America*. New Brunswick, N.J., 1957.

D. P. D. "Revoliutsionnyi boi na Kube" (A revolutionary battle in Cuba). *K.I.*, No. 5, February 10, 1934, pp. 40–45.

G. S. "Na Kube voznikaiut Sovety" (Soviets are being created in Cuba). *Kolonial'nye Problemy, Sbornik II*, 1934, pp. 137–143.

Gomez, J. "Revolutionary Events in Cuba and the Tasks of the Communist Party." *I.P.C.*, Vol. 13, No. 41, September 15, 1933, pp. 884–888.

Khaskin, M. "Sovety v Chili" (Soviets in Chile). *Kolonial'nye Problemy, Sbornik II*, 1934, pp. 151–175.

"Manifesto of the C.C. of the Communist Party of Cuba and the Youth Communist League of Cuba, August 3, 1933." *I.P.C.*, Vol. 13, No. 39, September 8, 1933, pp. 848–849.

Poppino, R. E. *International Communism in Latin America: A History of the Movement, 1917–1963*. Glencoe, Ill., 1964.

Programnye dokumenty kommunisticheskikh i rabochikh partii stran Ameriki (Program documents of the communist and workers' parties of American countries). Moscow, 1962.

Sinani, G. "Krestianskoe dvizhenie i kompartii Iuzhnoi i Karaibskoi Ameriki" (The peasant movement and the communist parties of South and Caribbean America). *K.I.*, No. 16, June 1, 1933, pp. 47–55.

Villiams. "Ekonomicheskoe i politicheskoe polozhenie v Urugvae i zadachi urugvaiskoi kompartii" (Economic and political situation in Uruguay and the tasks of the Uruguayan Communist Party). *K.I.*, No. 14, April 6, 1928, pp. 30–37.

Europe, General

Lazić, B. M. *Les partis communistes d'Europe, 1919–1955*. Paris, 1956.

Programnye dokumenty kommunisticheskikh i rabochikh partii kapitalisticheskikh stran Europy (Program documents of the communist and workers' parties of the capitalist countries of Europe). Moscow, 1960.

France

Klass protiv klassa: natsional'noe edinenie i Kompartiia Frantsii (Class against class: national unity and the Community Party of France). Moscow, 1928. Discussions at the Ninth Plenum. French edition: *Classe contre classe: la question française au IXᵉ Congrès d l'I.C.*, Paris, 1929. 29 pp.

Fauvet, Jacques. *Histoire du Parti Communiste Francais.* 2 vols., Paris, 1964–65.

Ferrat, A. *Histoire du Parti communiste française.* Paris, 1931.

Le Parti communiste français devant l'Internationale . . . Discours des camarades Manouilski, Thorez, Piatnitski, Barbé, Vassiliev, Lozovski . . . Paris, 1931. Discussions at the Ninth Plenum of the ECCI.

"Problemy frantsuzskoi Kompartii" (Problems of the French Communist Party). *K.I.,* No. 18, June 30, 1930, pp. 37–63

Germany

Collotti, E., ed. *Die Kommunistische Partei Deutschlands, 1918–1933: Ein bibliographischer Beitrag.* Milan, 1961.

Diakin, V. S. *Kommunisticheskaia Partiia Germanii i problema edinogo fronta v gody otnositel'noi stabilizatsii kapitalizma 1924–1928 gg.* (The Communist Party of Germany and the Problem of the United Front in the Years of the Relative Stabilization of Capitalism 1924–1928). Moscow and Leningrad, 1961.

Ehrt, A. *Communism in Germany: The Truth About Communist Conspiracy on the Eve of the National Revolution.* Berlin, 1933.

Fischer, R. *Stalin and German Communism: A Study in the Origins of the State Party.* Cambridge, Mass., 1948.

Flechtheim, O. K. *Die Kommunistische Partei Deutschlands in der Weimar Republik.* Offenbach a.M., 1948.

"Resolution upon the Tenth Plenary [session] of the ECCI and upon the Tasks of the Communist Party of Germany, Adopted by the Central Committee of the Communist Party of Germany." *I.P.C.,* Vol. 9, No. 47, September 4, 1929, pp. 1004–1007.

"Problemy Kompartii Germanii na rasshirennom Prezidiume IKKI" (Problems of the Communist Party of Germany at the Enlarged Presidium of the ECCI). *K.I.,* No. 7, March 10, 1930, pp. 24–45.

Stalin, I. V. "O pravoi opasnosti v germanskoi kompartii (Rech na zasedanii Prezidiuma IKKI, 19-XII 1928 g.) " (On the right [wing] danger in the German Communist Party: speech at the session of the Presidium of the ECCI, December 19, 1928). *K.I.,* No. 52, December 28, 1928, pp. 14–20.

Weber, Hermann (ed.). *Der deutsche Kommunismus: Dokumente.* Cologne, 1963. With bibliography.

Great Britain

Communist Policy in Great Britain: The Report of the British Commission of the Ninth Plenum of the Executive Committee of the Comintern. London, 1928.

"X Plenum IKKI i angliiskaia kompartiia" (The Tenth Plenum of the ECCI and the English Communist Party). *K.I.,* No. 34–35, August 31, 1929, pp. 51–69.

Macfarlane, L. J. *The British Communist Party: Its Origin and Development Until 1929.* London, 1966.

BIBLIOGRAPHY

Novaia taktika angliiskoi kompartii: sbornik (New tactics of the English Communist Party: a collection [of documents]), Moscow, 1928.

Pelling, H. *The British Communist Party: A Historical Profile.* London, 1958.

Poland

Dziewanowskii, M. K. *The Communist Party of Poland: An Outline of History.* Cambridge, Mass., 1959.

Kommunisticheskaia Partiia Pol'shi v bor'be za nezavisimost svoei strany: materialy i dokumenty (The Communist Party of Poland in the struggle for the independence of its country: materials and documents). Translated from the Polish, Moscow, 1955.

"Otkrytoe pis'mo IKKI chlenam Kommunisticheskoi Partii Pol'shi (Open letter of the ECCI to all members of the Communist Party of Poland). *K.I.,* No. 41, October 16, 1928, pp. 38–45.

Spain

"Ko vsem chlenam Kommunisticheskoi Partii Ispanii: pis'mo Zapadnoevropeiskogo Biuro IKKI" (To all members of the Communist Party of Spain: letter of the West European Bureau of the ECCI). *K.I.,* No. 2–3, January 30, 1932, pp. 38–45.

"Platforma sovetskoi vlasti kompartii Ispanii" (Platform of soviet power of the Communist Party of Spain). *K.I.,* No. 31, November 1, 1934, pp. 40–41.

Other

Bellini, F., and G. Galli. *Storia del Partito Communista Italiano.* Milan, 1953.

Rothschild, J. *The Communist Party of Bulgaria: Origins and Development, 1883–1936.* New York, 1959.

NEWSPAPERS AND PERIODICALS

Agrarnye Voprosy (Agrarian problems). Moscow and Berlin. 1927–35. Publication of the International Agrarian Institute, Moscow.

Biulleten'Nauchno-Issledovatel'skogo Instituta po Kitaiu (Bulletin of the Scientific-Research Institute on China). Moscow, 1928–32. Published by Sun Yat-sen University.

Bol'shevik. Moscow. Organ of the Central Committee of the All-Union Communist Party (B). Semimonthly, from April 1924; title changed to *Kommunist* with No. 20, 1954.

Bor'ba Klassov (Class struggle). Moscow. 1931–36. Monthly. Superseded by *Istoricheskii Zhurnal,* August 1937–August 1945, which was superseded September 1945 by *Voprosy Istorii.*

The Communist International. Leningrad, London, New York. May 1919–December 1940. Twice monthly; monthly after January 1936. Organ of the ECCI; appeared in Russian, French, German, Spanish, and Chinese, but the various editions were not identical.

L'Humanité. Paris. Daily. Organ of the Communist Party of France.

Hung-ch'i (Red flag). Shanghai. Frequency varies. Official organ of the Communist Party of China.

International Press Correspondence. Vienna, Berlin, London. 1921–38. Weekly or every ten days. Organ of the ECCI. Superseded by *World News and Views* in 1938, and by *World News,* January 1, 1954. Appears in English, French, German, and Spanish.

Istoricheskii Zhurnal (Historical journal) . Moscow, 1937–45. Monthly. Organ of the Institute of History of the Soviet Academy of Sciences. Preceded by *Bor'ba Klassov;* absorbed *Istorik-Marksist* in 1941; superseded by *Voprosy Istorii,* July 1945.

Izvestiia (News). Petrograd (Leningrad) and Moscow. 1917——. Daily. Organ of the Central Executive Committee of Soviets. Subtitle varies.

Kolonial'nye Problemy, sbornik[i] (Colonial problems, a collection [of materials]) . Moscow. 1933–35. Numbered publications of the Institute of World Economy and World Politics, Colonial Sector, of the Soviet Academy of Sciences.

Kommunisticheskii Internatsional (Communist International). Moscow. 1919–43. Frequency varies. Russian edition of *The Communist International.*

Krasnaia Nov' (Red virgin soil) . Moscow. 1912–42. Irregular. Organ of the Union of Soviet Writers.

Krasnyi Internatsional Profsoiuzov (Red trade-union international). Moscow. 1921–36. Bimonthly. From 1923 appeared also in German, French, English, and Spanish. Organ of the Executive Bureau of the Profintern.

[League of Nations.] *Official Journal.* Geneva. Monthly. 1920–March 1940. Monthly. Published in French and English.

Materialy po Kitaiskomu Voprosu (Materials on the Chinese Question) . Moscow. Irregular. 1927–28. Organ of the Scientific Research Institute for the Study of China, attached to the Communist University of the Toilers of the East. Superseded in 1929 by *Problemy Kitaia.*

Materialy po Natsional'no-Kolonial'nym Problemam (Materials on the national and colonial problems) . See *Natsional'no-kolonial'nye Problemy.*

Mezhdunarodnaia Zhizn' (International life). Moscow. 1920–36. Frequency varies. Organ of the People's Commissariat of Foreign Affairs. Preceded by *Vestnik Narodnogo Kommissariata po Inostrannym Delam,* 1918–22.

Mirovoe Khoziaistvo i Mirovaia Politika (World economy and world politics) . Moscow. 1924–47. Monthly. Organ of the Institute of World Economy and World Politics of the Soviet Academy of Sciences. Absorbed *Tikhii Okean* in 1938. Superseded by *Voprosy Ekonomiki* in 1948.

Natsional'no-Kolonial'nye Problemy: sbornik materialov (National-colonial problems: collection of materials) . Moscow. 1931–37. Frequency varies. Organ of the Scientific Research Institute for the Study of National and Colonial Problems. In 1937 issued under the title *Materialy po Natsional'no-Kolonial'nym Problemam* (Materials on the national-colonial problems) .

New Leader. London. 1922–46. Monthly. Organ of the Independent Labour Party. Preceded by *Socialist Leader* (newspaper) .

Nichi Ronenkan (Japanese-Russian yearbook) . Tokyo. 1928–43. (Sections of these volumes were published in Russian under the title *Ezhegodnik Iapono-Sovetskikh Otnoshenii* (Japanese-Russian relations yearbook) .

Novyi Vostok (New East) . Moscow. 1922–30. Irregular. Organ of the Scientific Association of Orientalists.

Pravda (Truth) . Moscow. 1912——. Daily. Organ of the Soviet Communist Party.

Problemy Kitaia (Problems of China) . Moscow. 1929–35. Irregular. Organ of the Scientific Research Institute for the Study of China; published by the Colonial Department of the Institute of World Economy and World Politics. Preceded by *Materialy po Kitaiskomu Voprosu.*

Proletarskaia Revoliutsiia (Proletarian revolution). Moscow and Leningrad. 1921–41. Irregular. Organ of the Marx-Engels-Lenin Institute of the Soviet Communist Party.

Pu-erh-sai-wei-k'o (Bolshevik) . Shanghai. 1927——. Frequency varies. Organ of the Communist Party of China; often published under camouflaged cover.

BIBLIOGRAPHY

Revoliutsiia i Natsional'nosti (Revolution and nationalities). Moscow. 1930–37. Irregular. Organ of the Council of Nationalities of the Central Executive Committee of the Soviets.

Revoliutsionnyi Vostok (Revolutionary East). Moscow. 1927–37. Frequency varies. Organ of the Scientific Research Association for the Study of the National and Colonial Problems. Connected with the Communist University for the Toilers of the East.

Shih Hua (Honest talk). Shanghai. Frequency varies. Official organ of the Chinese Communist Party.

Sotsialisticheskii Vestnik (Socialist messenger). Berlin, Paris, New York. 1921–63. Monthly. Central organ of the Russian Social-Democratic Labor Party (Menshevik).

Soviet Union Review. Washington, D.C. 1927–34. Irregular, 7 vols. Organ of the Soviet Information Bureau. Vols. 1–4 appeared under the title *Russian Review.*

Tikhii Okean (Pacific Ocean). Moscow. 1934–38. Irregular. Organ of the Pacific Section of the Institute of World Economy and World Politics. In 1938 absorbed by *Mirovoe Khoziaistvo i Mirovaia Politika.*

Voprosy Istorii (Problems of history). Moscow. 1945——. Monthly. Organ of the History Institute of the Academy of Sciences. Superseded *Istoricheskii Zhurnal.*

Vorwärts. Berlin. 1890–1933. Daily. Central organ of the Social Democratic Party of Germany. Suppressed 1933. Reappeared September 11, 1948, as *Neuer Vorwärts.* Hannover. Weekly. Became *Vorwärts: sozialdemokratische Wochenzeitung,* from January 1, 1955——.

World News and Views. See *International Press Correspondence.*

INDEX

Abramovich, R. A., 328
Abyssinia, 109
Acton, H. B., 719
Adler, Friedrich, 414, 708
Adler, Fritz, 117
Afganistan: treaty with, 165
Africa: 109; in world economic crisis, 62; and the revolutionary movement, 62; imperialist rule in, 299
African National Congress, 152
Agitation, 36, 63
Agitprop, 737
Agrarian: program in Arab countries, 216; revolution, 33, 70, 86, 103, 122, 151, 187, 265, 266, 273, 304, 305, 310, 311, 313, 444, 336; slogans of, 337; revolution in China, 71, 307
Agricultural mortgage credit, international, 56
Agriculture: 45; collectivized, xv; mechanized, xv; Soviet, 4
Adit, D., 751
Airapetian, M. E., 719
"Ajax," 18
Aleksandrov (pseud.), 719
Aleksandrov, V., 719
Alekseev, A., 747
Alexander, R. J., 752
Alexandria, 299
Algeria, 29
Ali, M., 719
"Alianza Obrera," 697
All-Arab National Congress, 213
All-Arab Workers' and Peasants' Federation, 215
Alliance system, French, 69
Alliances, military: 37; French system of, 100
"All-Union Bureau," 335
Amende, 239
American Commission of the Presidium of the ECCI, 32–33, 170–80
American Federation of Labor (A.F. of L.), 24, 91, 194, 393, 482, 581, 582
Amsterdam: 57; trade-unions, 127
Amsterdam International, 153, 326, 521, 538, 572

Amtorg, 294
Andreev, Andrei Andreyevich, 286
Angarov, F. V., 747
Anglo-American antagonism, 109
Anglo-Egyptian treaty, 211
Anglo-French imperialism, 37
Anglo-Russian Committee, 14
Anglo-Soviet agreement of 1921, 159
Anglo-Soviet trade agreement (1930), 283
Ankara, 49, 344
Annam Kuomintang of Indochina, 301
Antagonism: 53, 66; between capitalists countries, 24, 380; between imperialists and colonies, 25; between Europe and America, 62; interstate, 108–9; between France and Italy, 110; between America and England, 171, 517; between British and French imperialism, 212; between capitalist world and U.S.S.R., 260; imperialist, 325
Anti-Imperialist League, 219
"Anti-War Day," 38
Arab countries: Soviet policy in, 210–19
Arab East, 288
Arabia: Communist Party in, tasks of, 215–18
Arab-Jewish Conflict, 212
Araki, Sadao, Japanese Minister of War, 552, 571, 600
Arbitration: 81, 126; problems of analyzed, 75–78; British government and international, 77; principle of, 77, 78
Archangelsk, 293
Ardzheno, 719
Argentina: communist workers protest white terror in Mexico, 238
Aristocracy, workers', 81, 90
Armament truce, 54
Armaments: 43, 94, 125; extent of, 54; limitation of, 100; growth of, 171–72, 326, 332
Arnot, R. P., 39n13
Arsenev, E., 719
Asia, crisis in 69–71

INDEX

Associated Press, 14
Austria: 683; Communist Party of, 243–44, 697; revolutions in, 106; proletariat experience in 1927 in, 134
Austrian Social-Democratic Party, 414
Avarin, V. Ia., 519
Avigdor, L., 746

Bailey, Geoffrey, 60n5
Baldwin, Stanley, 201
Baltic bloc, 319–21
Baltic States, 609–18
Barandov, G. V., 747, 749
Barthou, Jean Louis: 405, 407, 620–21, 628, 629, 654; on Soviet entrance into League of Nations, 625, 630
Baruch, Bernard, 336n1
Bauer, Otto, 600
Bavaria: Soviet government in, 106
Beck, Jozef, Polish Minister of Foreign Affairs, 618
Bedacht, Max, 481
Bedouins, 213
Belgian Congo: Negro race in, 288
Belgium: 47, 342; strikes in, 474, 492
Bellini, F., 754
Beloff, Max, 358, 377n1, 720
Beneš, Eduard, 8, 737, 633
Bennet, A. J.: and Bukharin on decolonization, 26; defined decolonization viewpoint, 27
Berlin: 24, 46, 52, 53, 195, 259; and revolutionary upsurge in, 178; Communist Party in, 245; communal elections, 248; recruitment drive in, 249
Berlin treaty of 1926, 403
Bermondt, bands of, 329
Bilateral guarantee agreements on non-aggression, 78
Birkenhead, Lord, 238
Bishop, D. G., 720
"Black Plan," 381
Black Sea, 47
Blockade: 69, 304; economic, 328
Blücher, Vasili Konstantinovich, (General), 363, 401–2; speech on Red Army's preparedness to meet Japanese aggression, 603–8
Bogdanov, P. A., 293
Bogolepov, I., 720
Bol'shevik, 62, 69, 182, 298, 302, 336, 755
Bolshevism: 66, 126, 143, 239, 310, 576; identity of, 127; Chinese detachment of, 315; anti-Marxist conception hostile to, 316; struggle against, 611; path of, 685
Bombay: 203–5; armed clashes in, 289; weavers, 300
Bonch-Osmolinsky, A., 720
Boncour Law, 199. *See* Paul-Boncour, Joseph
Bondage, colonial, 30
Borkenau, F., 738
Börsenzeitung, 660
Bourbons, 333
Bourgeois-democratic revolution: 33, 35, 70, 83, 445; basic problems of, 34
Bourgeoisie: 37, 65, 66, 81, 98, 105, 196; German, xvi, 52; Chinese, 22, 34; attempt to discredit Soviet Union, 23; Indian, 27; petty, 30, 262; international, 41, 52; Japanese, 35; struggle between proletariat and, 80–81; agents of, 95; on disarmament, 216; overthrow of the, 128; British, in South Africa, 148; South African white, 148; American, 198; Zionist, 213
Bourgeois-reformist party, 87
Boycott, economic, 47
Boycott, mass: of workers, 133
Brackman, A. C., 751
Brandler, Heinrich, 154, 156, 383
Brandlerites, 249, 560
Brandt, Conrad, 72n14, 747
Braun, P., 740
Brazil: communist workers protest white terror in Mexico, 238; uprisings in, 474
Breitscheidt, 329
Brest: negotiations, 159; period, 164; peace, 329
Brewer, F. M., 720
Briand, Aristide: 5, 75, 329; plan for European union, 54–55
Briand-Kellogg Pact, 720
Brimmell, J. H., 747
British Communist Party: 26, 50, 82; tasks of, 81–82
British imperialism: 16, 92, 105, 120, 122, 148, 151, 152, 210, 213, 216, 218, 219, 220; decolonization policy of, 121
British Independent Labour Party: 389, 516; Comintern letter to the, 535–40
British India, manganese deposits of, 295
British Industrial Mission, 14

in, 474; revolutionary upsurge in, 492; tasks of CP of, 495–96; Soviet relations with, 633–35

Daily Worker, 238, 247
Dairen: armed uprisings in, 308, 309
Daladier, Édouard, French Premier, 367
Damascus: demonstrations in, 211
Dan, T. I., 46, 328, 335
Danzig, 322
Dashinsky, S., 721
Davis, K. W., 60n15, 721
Dawes Plan, 488, 518
Deborin, G. A., 719, 721
Decolonization: 26–27; in India, 105
Degras, Jane (Tabritsky), 19n3, 20nn, 39nn, 59n1, 60nn, 81, 377, 378, 416, 613n1, 721, 738
Delhi: armed uprisings in, 289
Denikin, Anton Ivanovich, 326
Denmark: municipal policy of, 252
Depression: 84; economic, xvi; world economic, xv
DEROP, 360, 377n3
Diakin, V. S., 753
Dimitrov, Georgi: 415, 559, 652–53; on the United Front, 682–86
Dirksen, Herbert von: 52, 360, 377n8, 721; and Litvinov, 361
Disarmament: 7, 25, 53, 124, 126, 167, 332, 506, 610; Soviet policy on, 7–14; partial and gradual, 10–11; total, 11; partial, 14, 162; problems of, analyzed, 75–78; preliminary condition for, 77; negotiations, 91–94; simultaneous, 92; Soviet proposals for, 140–41; Soviet plan for complete, 141; problem of, 162, 371–77; sabotage of, 317; conferences on, 53, 54, 366, 370, 373, 471–74, 548, 549, 550, 631, 661
Doriot, Jacques, 413, 701
Dorsenne, Jean, 721
Dovgalevsky, Valerian S., 208
D. P. D., 752
Draper, T., 752
Druhe, D. N., 751
Drummond, Sir Eric, 54
Druzhelovsky, 101
Dungan group, 303
Duranty, Walter: 405; questions the Soviet, 624; questions U.S.S.R. on attitude to the League of Nations, 663
Durkee, T. E., 738

Dutt, R. Palme: 27; quoted on Workers' and Peasants' Party, 29
Dyck, H. L., 721
Dzh. G., 659
Dziewanowskii, M. K., 754

Eastern Department of the Comintern, 70–71
Eastern Pact: 410, 659; importance of, 653–56; evaluated, 706–7
Economic crisis: 59, 66, 68, 269, 296; world, 55, 57, 61–64, 65, 241; general, 62; capitalist, 229–32
Economic nonaggression pact: 56, 341–43; Soviet draft of a, 533–34
Egypt: 109, 204, 217, 288, 301; Soviet attitude toward, 81, 82; imperialist rule in, 299; sympathy in, 211
Ehrt, A., 753
[Eidus, Kh. T.], 749
Eighth Congress of Soviets, 160
Eighth Convention of the CP of the United States, 577
Eighth Plenum of the ECCI, 127, 156
Eleventh Plenum of the ECCI, 68–69, 324, 330, 331, 332, 335, 491, 493, 500
Émigrés, Russian, 17, 46
Engels, Friedrich, 676
Entente, 102, 110, 159
Enukidze, D., 721
Erenburg, C. B., 734
Erenburg, G., 70, 351
Erukhimovich, I., 411, 412, 636, 713, 721
Estonia: 7, 402, 660; proletariat experience in 1924 in, 134; and Litvinov Protocol, 166; ratified Moscow Protocol, 169; development of relations with Lithuania, 320; linked by special treaty relations with Poland, 321; Soviet policy toward, 366
Etatisme, 220
Eudin, X. J., 721
Europe: 37, 62, 101; development of, 107; antagonism in, 108; communists of, 194; tasks of communists in, 197; deprived of long-term credits, 229; general political situation in, 320
European Commission, 342
Ewert, 249

Factionalism, 32, 173–76, 179, 181
Fairbanks, John, 72n14, 747
Faiz Mohammed Khan, 49
Fang [?], 747

INDEX

Pan-Islamism, 29
Pankratova, A., 728
Papal "crusade," 324
Papen, Franz von, 359, 391–92, 514, 544, 636–38, 638n
Paris: 5, 89, 345; Communist Party in, 245
Paris Pact, 166, 170
Patek: on nonaggression pact, 50
Paton, John, 394
Paul-Boncour, Joseph, 8, 117, 328, 367, 374
Pavlov, 241
Peking: 17; raid on Soviet embassy in, 193; armed uprisings in, 308
Pelling, H., 754
Pepper, Lovestone, *et al.*, 268
Pepper's theory of "exceptionalism," 198
Peredyshka, xv
Permanent Administrative Commission of the French Socialist Party, 392
Persia: 7, 29–30; guarantee treaties with, 165
Peru: uprisings in, 474
Peshawar: 333; armed uprisings, 289
Petrovsky, A. M., 49
Petrovsky, D. A. (Max Goldfarb, alias A. J. Bennet), 39n16, 385, 728
Philippine Islands: and the revolutionary movement, 62; revolutionary struggle in, 288
Piatakov, Grigori L., 15, 38, 52
Piatnitsky, Osip A.: 72n8, 396, 397, 412, 413, 588, 728, 739, 740, 742, 743, 744–45; on unemployment, 68; on Communist Party of France, 384; on Communist Party of Germany, 385; on united front, 390; on terrorist methods, 390; on the failure of the Nazis to destroy the Communist Party of Germany, 556–57
Pieck, Wilhelm, 412
Pilsudski, Józef: falsifies elections, 323
Pirker, T., 739
Poale Zion, 213, 215, 218
Poincaré, Raymond, 329, 335
Poland: 7, 44, 47, 50, 69, 101, 162; hostility to Soviet Union, 45; armament information exchanged with Soviet, 54; Communist Party of, 63, 243, 562; communists in, 195; troops in, 124; military preparations in, 125, 126; Lenin and, 159; Soviet treaties with, 162; Soviet

signs special protocol with, 163; peace negotiations, 163; attack on U.S.S.R., 165; and Litvinov Protocol, 166; ratified Moscow Protocol, 169; on policy toward Soviet Union, 219–21; *rapprochement* with Germany, 239; and the maturing of a political crisis, 258; attempt to blow up U.S.S.R. embassy in, 261; role of, as anti-Soviet agent, 264; repercussion of U.S.A. crisis in, 268; Soviet embassy in, 270; and armed readiness, 285; development of relations between Baltic states and, 319–20; supports policy of war against Soviet, 320; linked with Estonia, 321; frenzied armament of, 322; falsification of elections in, 323; in alliance with France, 326, 327; Soviet policy toward, 366, 618–20; revolutionary crisis in, 474; revolutionary upsurge in, 491; tasks of communist party of, 495
Polish-Rumanian Convention, 323
Polish triangles, 322
Political Secretariat of the ECCI, 36, 70, 154
Politis, 11
Popov, K., 729
Popov, N.: view on London Naval Conference, 43, 559
Popov, V. I., 729
Poppino, R. E., 753
Le Populaire, 517n1
Port Said, 299
Potemkin, V. P., 729
Pravda: 20n, 43, 58, 229, 241, 264n3, 364, 367, 372, 386, 402, 411, 529: editorial, 42, 47, 67, 69; comments on an apparent increase in Anti-Soviet actions by the capitalist countries, 273–40; on the decisions of the Enlarged Presidium of the ECCI, 256–59; on the Tasks of the Communist Parties, 332–36; evaluation of the Hoover Disarmament Plan, 469–71; on recognition of the Soviet Union by the United States, 550
Preparatory Commission for the Disarmament Conference, 7, 53, 140–41, 162, 370, 431, 432, 663
Presidium of the ECCI, 71, 412, 526, 647
Primakov, P., 723